Swing Shift

Swing

"All-Girl"

Bands of the 1940s

Shift

Sherrie Tucker

Duke University Press   Durham and London   2000

©2000 Duke University Press
All rights reserved
Printed in the United States of America
on acid-free paper ∞
Designed by C. H. Westmoreland
Typeset in Times Roman with Bodoni and Twentieth Century
display type by Keystone Typesetting, Inc.
Library of Congress Cataloging-in-Publication Data appear
on the last printed page of this book.

Contents

Acknowledgments

This project benefits from an embarrassment of riches in the form of incomparable mentors, colleagues, narrators, and friends. I must first thank the women musicians, both those still living and those who, as eighty-nine-year-old former trombonist Velzoe Brown likes to put it, "have modulated to a higher key." This book wouldn't have been possible without their willingness to share their time, memories, photos, recordings, scrapbooks, address books, theoretical frameworks, and narrative strategies. Many women musicians became actively involved in the research process, digging up additional information, confirming memories with friends and associates, even recruiting interviewees. A complete list would be too long, but let me name Martye Awkerman, Clora Bryant, Roz Cron, Laura Daniels, Mary Demond, Peggy Gilbert, Florence Kuhn, Jane Sager, and Vi Wilson for their indispensable assistance in these areas.

Because this book grew in tandem with my dissertation, I owe an unfathomable debt to my dream committee at the University of California, Santa Cruz: Angela Y. Davis, Donna Haraway, and Herman Gray, who never failed to take "all-girl" bands, and me, seriously. Especially, I offer humble gratitude to Angela Davis, who guided me through the research and writing for nearly a decade, generously and tirelessly reading and commenting on literally thousands of pages of drafts from beginning to end, and counseling me on ethical, theoretical, methodological, and political dilemmas as they arose. Donna Haraway and Herman Gray generously read draft after draft, saw what I was trying to do — usually long before I did — and gave me necessary directions, challenges, reading lists, and questions to make it better. Jim Clifford and Steven Feld rounded out my extraordinary qualifying exam committee, which gave me direction at a key crossroads. Other professors, mentors, colleagues, and friends read chapters, collaborated on panels, contributed leads, and discussed issues that helped immensely in complicating my analyses. Thanks to Maylei Blackwell, Darshan Campos, Susan Cook, Teresa De Lauretis, Dana Frank, Sherna Gluck, Lisbeth Haas, Roger Harding, David Heymann, Sarah Jain, Robin D. G. Kelley, Florice Kovan, Mary Letterii, Kim McCord, Bob McMichael, Mark Miller, the late John Miner, Keta Miranda, Ingrid Monson, Kathy Ogren, Naomi Pabst, Kay D. Ray, Chris Russell, Barbara Schottenfeld, Catherine Parsons Smith, Darla Thompson, Marilyn and Roy Tucker, Deb Vargas, Isa Velez, Penny Von Eschen, and the members of Donna Haraway's feminist theory writing seminar (winter 1996), Jim Clifford's race and ethnicity writing seminar (spring 1996), and Teresa De Lauretis's writing seminar (fall 1996). Sheila Peuse helped me in numberless ways, ranging from crisis management, to deadline reminders, to pretending that I hadn't already asked the questions I continued to ask over, and over, and over. At San Francisco State, I owe additional immeasurable thanks to Chinosole, Inderpal Grewal, Whitney Chadwick, and Dee Spencer for their excellent guidance in the women's studies master's thesis that preceded both my dissertation and this book. More special thanks go to the fabulous "No Name" writing group: Kathryn Chetkovich, Lin Colavin, Frances Hatfield, Candida Lawrence, Joan McMillan, Maude Meehan, Claudia Sternbach, Amber Coverdale Sumrall, Dena Taylor, and Ellen Treen. I am thankful to Ken Wissoker at Duke University Press for thinking early on that this project would make a worthwhile book and for struggling with me through the cognitive dissonance that comes from working on a book and a dissertation at the same time. Thanks also to the anonymous readers at Duke for incredibly constructive comments. For invaluable forums that helped me better understand issues of 1940s jazzwomen in relation to those of both earlier and more contemporary women jazz musicians, I am grateful to Haybert Houston, editor of *Jazz Now Magazine;* Matt Watson, director of the Smithsonian Jazz Oral History Project; Janice McNeil, project manager and symposium director for *Sung/Unsung Jazzwomen;* and Tim Hodges and Bob Parlocha at the old KJAZ-FM.

I am deeply grateful to my parents, Marilyn and Roy Tucker, who instilled in me a love for music and a genuine interest in hearing people talk about their lives, and who indulged me in several hundred hours of long-distance conversations about World War II. More humble appreciation and love go out to Roger Harding and his menagerie for unforgettable kindness and friendship.

I also owe many thanks to librarians and archivists at various collections: the patient and knowledgeable curators at the Archives Center at the Smithsonian Museum of American History; the special collections librarians at the New York Public Library of Performing Arts; the media and special collections librarians at the Schomburg Center for Research in Black Culture; Flori Kovan for showing me the ropes at the Library of

Congress; everyone, but especially Esther Smith, at the Institute for Jazz Studies at Rutgers, Newark, New Jersey; Bruce Boyd Raeburn at the Hogan Jazz Archive at Tulane, New Orleans; jazz film archivist Mark Cantor; Matt Watson of the Smithsonian Jazz Oral History Program; Eric Key, Dudley Yates, Rose Sonnier Judd, and especially Phyllis Earles Martin at the John B. Coleman Library at Prairie View A&M University; Bozy White at the International Association of Jazz Record Collectors Library, Oakland, California; Carol A. McCormick, First Sergeant, USA Retired, of the Women's Army Corps Museum, Fort McClellan, Alabama; and trombonist/librarian extraordinaire Pat Mullan at the Berkeley City Library.

I also thank the following journals for permission to reprint previously published material:

An earlier version of chapter 1 appeared as "Working the Swing Shift: Women Musicians during World War II" in *Labor's Heritage,* no. 1 (summer 1996): 46–66.

Chapter 3 appeared as "The Prairie View Co-Eds: Black College Women Musicians in Class and on the Road" in *Black Music Research Journal,* 19, no. 1: 000–000.

Chapter 6 originally appeared as "Nobody's Sweethearts: Gender, Race, Jazz, and the Darlings of Rhythm" in *American Music* 16, no. 2 (1998): 255–88.

Chapter 7 was originally published as "Female Big Bands, Male Mass Audiences: Gendered Performances in a Theater of War" in *Women and Music: A Journal of Gender and Culture* 2 (International Alliance for Women and Music) (fall 1998): 64–89.

An earlier version of chapter 9 appeared as " 'And Fellas, They're American Girls': On the Road with the Sharon Rogers All-Girl Band" in *Frontiers: A Journal of Women Studies* 16, nos. 2–3 (spring 1996): 128–60.

Introduction

"It Don't Mean a Thing

If It Ain't in the History Books"

Only God can make a tree . . .

and only men can play good jazz.

— George T. Simon, *The Big Bands*

When a narrative is constructed, something is left out.

— Gayatri Chakravorty Spivak, *The Post-Colonial Critic*

There were other bands out there, but the men didn't accept us.

So we had to get our own. — Lillian Carter Wilson,

telephone interview with author

There were hundreds of all-woman bands.
A person can get some pretty interesting responses when she goes around making remarks like that.

Hundreds of all-woman bands? I'll bet.

Well, there were a couple of all-girl bands. I remember Ina Ray Hutton, she was a knockout, and Phil Spitalny, were they ever corny, but hundreds? . . .

Oh yeah, I saw something on the International Sweethearts of Rhythm at a women's film festival. . . . All races of women living together and playing music. There were hundreds of bands like that?

All-woman bands *sounds funny. You should say* all-girl. We were all-girl bands *in those days.*

Anyone who thinks that feminist historiography is a piece of cake should try writing about "all-girl" jazz and swing bands. My first attempts at such a history (i.e., my first attempts after I became convinced that there *were* hundreds of all-woman bands) took the shape of heroic epics about skilled women succeeding collectively in a field dominated by men. "I'm researching the sadly neglected history of all-woman bands," I confidently announced to interviewees. I soon learned that most narrators were more comfortable with the term *all-girl bands*. I adjusted my language — although I could not get myself to say "all-girl" without the textual wincing of quotation marks, one set of marks among many that betray generational difference between me and my informants. Despite ongoing adaptations of terminology, the story I looked for continued to be that of women banding together and making it on their own.

Almost immediately, interviews took unexpected twists that did not fit into my plotline. Some narrators announced that they preferred playing with men's bands rather than "all-girl" bands because men's bands had better musicians or because men did not bicker as much. Other narrators baffled me by insisting that "all-girl" bands *really could play* their instruments, unaware, it seemed, that I assumed no less. One narrator expressed her concern over my placing the words "all-girl" in quotation marks. "It makes it look like we were all lesbians," she argued, urging me to let *all-girl bands* stand quote free to show that women musicians were really, truly, *unquestionably* girls. Again, differences between narrators and me were activated. What was the source of her concern? Homophobia? Fear of readers' homophobia? A history of women musicians being automatically perceived as sexually suspect? The narrators' desire to protect the professional reputations of women musicians, both straight and lesbian, reasoned from a pre–gay liberation standpoint?

While I did eventually opt to remove the quotation marks, it was in the interests of economic punctuation rather than from a desire to validate or naturalize girlishness in these bands or in the music that they played. It is my hope that, even quote free, the term *all-girl bands* will resound with historic dissonance — in relation to the women who played in them, the circuits they traveled, and the work they performed. The label summons the complexity of working under an umbrella of both opportunity and devaluation, of the easy dismissal from history of the whole category in later years, and of the disparate repertoire of memories and stakes narrated cross-generationally in the 1990s by women musicians of the 1940s all-girl bands.

The stories I was hearing were far too complex to fit neatly into the heroic pattern I had anticipated. Contradictions abounded — both within and among stories. It was not unusual for a solitary narrator to tell me that most women's bands were terrible but that the one she was in was excellent or that women musicians were a rough lot except for those in her band. The question of what kind of story I might tell became more complicated with each musician I interviewed. My motive shifted from wanting to write all-woman bands into jazz and swing history to wanting to better understand the narrative strategies of women musicians. The ways in which narrators crafted their stories seemed to open up new and unexpected ways of telling jazz and swing history in general, not to mention women's jazz history. I became especially interested in stories that simultaneously countered mainstream notions that women's bands did not exist or were not real and challenged my own second wave feminist hopes for unearthing historical utopian women's communities.[1]

The stories women musicians told me, as well as the stories I tell in this book, are to a great extent shaped by, and in dialogue with, stories that were told about all-girl bands in the circuits of the swing industry. This would include stories told in the press, in publicity, and through the very modes of production and distribution that relegated women musicians to marginalized venues and overlooked them when it came to highly valued products, such as records. The focus of this introduction is how these stories of devaluation and absence are woven into the familiar rhythms of the popular history books about the Swing Era. Often these "other stories" told in the swing histories totally omit all-girl bands. When all-girl bands appear, they are frequently buried under unspoken definitions that take all-man bands to be normal and all-woman bands to be novelties.

Almost immediately on embarking on this project, I encountered notions that all-girl bands lacked an intangible, yet crucial, "authenticity" possessed by men's bands. The man who answered my first telephone call to the American Federation of Musicians (AFM) local in San Francisco responded to my request for information by insisting, "Groups of housewives who got together during the war would not be considered *real bands*. They wouldn't have been professional, and they wouldn't have belonged to the union."

Ah, that explains it. All-girl bands are absent from recorded history because they weren't real!

As the following chapters will demonstrate, this opinion about all-girl bands not being professional union bands is not historically accurate. The vast majority of the women I have interviewed belonged to the union and drew wages when they played in the all-girl bands of the

1940s; some, in fact, were life members of the San Francisco local at the time the exchange reported above took place. But the comment does reveal a great deal about attitudes toward women musicians during the war years. It may also yield clues as to what structures need to be dismantled in order to make new narratives in which women musicians are visible.

For starters, the speaker assumes that the "real" Swing Era ended before World War II and that the women musicians who suddenly became visible during the practical and ideological crises presented by the war had never worked before. His dismissal issues directly from wartime gender and labor discourse; he envisions women musicians as Rosie the Riveters, only instead of acetylene torches or rivet guns they hold trumpets or saxophones as their defining accessories. Also, the comment and the confident belief it expresses allow us to see how thoroughly entrenched is the notion of all-girl bands as not real bands. To insist until the cows come home that they really were real is only to participate in this futile debate. But, before I can begin talking about other ways to talk about this "battle of the bands," it is necessary to address the powerful stories of omission and novelty that pass as common sense in conventional swing histories.[2] It did not matter which way the applause meter swung; women's bands were constructed as inauthentic for a variety of ideological, social, and political reasons.

Dominant Swing Discourse

It might sound odd to speak of a dominant swing discourse, yet a quick trip into the library of nostalgic swing narratives reveals a predictable recurrence of hegemonic riffs. You could almost tap your foot to it. Swing was a music of the 1930s. Benny Goodman was the king of swing. Swing was played by men instrumentalists, although sometimes warbled by women vocalists called *canaries*. All-woman bands seldom appear in dominant swing discourse, and their existence is therefore denied, firsthand reports notwithstanding. Or, in texts where one or two of the hundreds of all-woman bands are permitted a type of existence, they are written about in isolation, as if each was a novelty, a gimmick, a dancing dog in the field of real music. In short, we have no good way of talking about all-*woman* jazz and swing bands until we find new ways of talking about *all* jazz and swing bands.[3]

My own entry into this field of research demonstrates both the pervasiveness and the shortcomings of dominant swing discourse. When I began my research on all-woman bands of the 1940s nine years ago, I simply hoped that I would find sufficient information to write a short paper on the neglected accomplishments of a few women musicians. I did not anticipate that it would be a relatively simple matter to make contact with nearly one hundred original sources who played in the all-woman bands, some of whom were still playing professionally fifty years later. I was astonished when a few inquiries dashed off to newspapers and trade magazines connected me with women musicians eager to give interviews, write letters, fill out questionnaires, and share newspaper clippings, scrapbooks, photos, recordings, and other documents, in hopes that their stories would be entered into the historical record.

Ironically, the reason that I was so surprised when so many women musicians answered my inquiries to such periodicals as *Down Beat,* the *San Francisco Chronicle,* and *Jazz Forum* was not because I had not done my homework but because I had. As a longtime record collector, fan, and disk jockey, I was an avid reader of jazz and swing histories. The fact that I was born a generation too late to participate in what is known as the Swing Era did not prevent me from growing up as a fan of the big bands. Along with fellow musicians from my high school band, I spent the night of my junior prom (1974) ordering Harvey Wallbangers (the only drink we could think of) and dancing at a Count Basie concert at the Elks Club in Eureka, California. We may have been teenagers of the Crosby, Stills, Nash, and Young generation, but we were bona fide fanatics of the big bands, shyly speaking to the Basie musicians (all men, of course) during the break, and making a speechless pilgrimage through the fog-shrouded parking lot to gaze on the band bus. The next year, I defied the rules of my high school radio station's Top 40 format by playing the top hits of the '40s. If I was surprised many years later to discover that there had also been all-woman bands made up of women who were as serious about the music of the big bands as I was, it is because I made it a habit to read the major texts on the swing era, books with such conclusive-sounding titles as *The Big Bands* (by George Simon), *The Wonderful Era of the Great Dance Bands* (by Leo Walker), *The World of Swing* (by Stanley Dance), and dozens more, which repeatedly presented a story in which all-woman bands either did not exist or were barely worthy of comment. In the worst cases, women's bands were ridiculed.[4]

The fact that prominent jazz and swing writers, then and in the years since, did not seek information about all-woman bands, while living sources who played in such groups could be easily located and were eager to be interviewed, suggests that the flaw of the swing narratives is more likely the uncritical reproduction of dominant gender ideology than a case of careless omission. The dominant swing texts are not gender neutral (although they pass themselves off as such); they are histories of musical men. In the gender division of jazz and swing labor, the normal configuration is for men to skillfully operate instruments and for women to perform privatized popular versions of femininity with their voices and bodies. As jokes and cartoons in *Down Beat* indicate, stereotypes about "girl singers" highlighted a shortage of musical knowledge and an entertaining excess of sex appeal.[5] "Girl musicians" often inherited the girl singers' stereotype — that they were unskilled sex objects. But the women instrumentalists were also seen as freaks in ways that girl singers were not, especially girl musicians who played instruments thought of as masculine: drums, trumpets, saxophones, etc. When girl musicians appeared as a feminine spectacle in an all-girl band, they inherited the sexual objectification accorded dancers in chorus lines. Many women musicians with whom I spoke told stories in which they explicitly differentiated themselves from chorines; not surprising when one considers that the chorus line had been traditionally associated with prostitution since the mid-1800s.[6]

Women musicians were consumed as singers who didn't sing, dancers who didn't dance, cross-dressers who performed entertainment understood as masculine in bodies understood as feminine. Dozens of woman trumpet players were dubbed "the female Louis Armstrong," drummers "the female Gene Krupa." A *Down Beat* article in 1937 described the drummer in the all-girl band the Ingenues as "a Gene Krupa in girls' clothes!" Another drummer was described in 1940 as a "skirted Krupa."[7] Robert Allen has described the similarities of spectatorship in freak shows and sex spectacles in his seminal history of burlesque, arguing that it is the "shock of resemblance and similarity in this radical other, and not the freak's total alienness, that is at the heart of the freak's power to enthrall and disgust."[8] Like cootch dancers and female Siamese twins, women who produced big band music were viewed as both "like and unlike ordinary women": freaks, gimmicks, spectacles.[9] If they played well, they earned adjectives like *amazing, incredible,* or the ubiquitous *good for girls.* So, even if they enjoyed enthusiastic and loyal audiences, as many all-girl bands did, their popularity, often based on their ability to look like women and play like men, differed from the popularity accorded men's bands. Men simply did not walk into the same set of expectations when they entered the bandstand. Women did not have to play differently to be consumed differently. Jazz and swing musicianship is gendered before anyone blows a note. These are key elements of dominant swing discourse that we miss when we talk only about men's bands.

Producing a separate history of skilled women instrumentalists will not automatically change the structure of gender built into the histories. Rather than selecting a strategy of setting out to prove that gender is meaningless and that women's bands are as real or as skilled as men's bands, I suggest that we look more closely at gender as the feminist historian Joan Scott defines it: "a field in which power is articulated." Scott advocates producing gendered histories by studying how difference between the sexes is constructed in the following areas: representations, normative concepts, politics, and subject formation.[10] This approach might uncover new ways of understanding the gendered spaces of swing. How was gender difference represented in the spectacles of all-girl band performances? What kinds of masculinities and femininities were represented in men's and women's bands, and how were these effects achieved through sound and image? What versions of femininity were performed, and what versions were not? How were dominant gender constructions affirmed or contested by women musicians? If normative concepts defined women as freaks if they played trumpets, trombones, and drums, what could women musicians do to secure acceptance for themselves on the bandstand? What were the politics of these normative concepts? How were they enforced by labor practices, propaganda, dominant discourses on gender, race, sexuality, and class? What kinds of identities did women develop through their band careers, through producing popular music that women were not thought to be able to play, through their experiences on the road?

In the same way that simply setting out to prove that women played in bands does not dismantle the gender constructions embedded in dominant swing discourse, discussing black women's band participation does not guarantee a departure from the ways in which race discourse operates in jazz and swing histories. The feminized spaces of swing are no more race neutral than the masculinized spaces. The swing gender analyst must diligently pose questions that account for constructions of race difference as well as sex difference. How did race discourse affect which representations were available to black and white women musicians, mixed-race women musicians, and women musicians of color who were not African American? How were concepts of normal womanhood differentiated by race, and how did these affect performance strategies of all-girl bands coded as either black or white? How did the white male subjectivity that shaped dominant jazz and swing histories affect our limited knowledge of all-girl bands?

In asking who is represented in the histories and who is not, I would immediately notice that the African American bands, such as the Prairie View Co-Eds, the Darlings of Rhythm, Eddie Durham's All-Star Girl Orchestra, and the International Sweethearts of Rhythm, have tended to go unmentioned in most major swing texts. They appear prominently in the entertainment pages of the black press of the 1930s and 1940s but somehow do not translate into jazz historiography, generally penned by white men. The all-girl bands that get the occasional (and often trivializing) mention in the histories are the very famous white bands, such as Ina Ray Hutton's Melodears and Phil Spitalny's "Hour of Charm" Orchestra, which offered two extremely different visual representations of idealized white womanhood — the blonde bombshell and the Victorian angel of the hearth, respectively. It is interesting to note that the blonde bombshell image (popularized in the 1930s by Jean Harlow) that Hutton adopted did not shield this most famous of white female bandleaders from rumors in the South that she was a passing "quadroon or mulatto."[11] I point to these rumors not to argue whether Hutton was legally black under the "one-drop rule."[12] Indeed, I have no interest in pursuing her racial history. However, I do think that the speculations around Hutton's whiteness illustrate the power of dominant notions of race and gender to shape how women who played swing were perceived, what versions of race/gender were available to them in the pool of marketable public images, and what versions of race/gender they performed.

One has only to look at cinema representations of black women during the 1930s and 1940s to see that a narrow array of roles could be had in white-owned entertainment venues (what Patricia Hill Collins calls the "controlling images of Black womanhood"):[13] the tragic mulatta, the comic maid or mammy, the hypersexual jezebel. From the tone of pride with which the black press wrote of the International Sweethearts of Rhythm, it would be safe to say that the image of skilled, educated "race women" (meaning black women "who devoted their lives to the advancement of their people"),[14] whose commitment included shopping at black-owned businesses on the road whenever possible, would have been unintelligible to white writers and readers accustomed to the belief that black women were either tragic, funny, or erotic. To undo this pattern of systematic erasure, it is important, when writing about African American all-woman bands, to pay close attention to historical representations of black women. These should not be limited to those depictions popular in the white-owned media but should take into account representations in areas such as the black press. There were 230 black newspapers in the United States during the war years, with 2 million readers. The stories and pictures of black women that circulated in these papers reflected and contributed to significant struggles over meanings of *black womanhood* that challenged dominant depictions. At the same time, such images were sometimes limited by the political agendas of some papers to depictions of black female norms that accorded with biases privileging middle-class upward mobility and that tended to promote a kind of black female beauty that depends on light skin. It is important to study representations of African American women in the black press not just as entertainers but in other roles as well: political figures, college women, defense workers, military women.[15]

As Evelyn Brooks Higginbotham and Darlene Clark Hine have pointed out, black clubwomen's "self-representation as 'super moral' " pushed against a violent history of African American women symbolizing black sexuality for white men. This reworking of Victorian morality was not primarily geared toward black women's claim to a separate sphere, one similar to that occupied by white women — it is important to remember that white women's pedestal served to separate white women not only from white men but from black men and women as well. Rather, the supermorality of the clubwomen aspired toward "the attainment of respect, justice, and opportunity for all black Americans."[16] Thus, the emphasis on chaperons and other forms of behavior modification described by women who played in bands such as the Prairie View Co-Eds and the International Sweethearts of Rhythm may be attributed not just to the repression of black women but also to a kind of "race pride" that involved claiming an aura of "respectability" usually reserved for white middle-class women.

In writing about how black woman novelists "restructured womanhood" through representations of "race women," Hazel Carby has additionally pointed out that, while many black women novelists imbued their black female characters with a desire for "racial uplift," they denied them sexual desire in order to counter a history of "racist constructions of black female sexuality." Carby urges that a consideration of black women blues singers of the same period reveals "a discourse that articulates a cultural and political struggle over sexual relations: a struggle that is directed against the objectifications of female sexuality within a patriarchal order but which also tries to reclaim women's bodies as the sexual and sensual objects of women's song." Black women who played in the all-girl bands of the 1940s inherited the same problematic history of representations of black women as "primitive and exotic creatures" that troubled novelists such as Nella Larsen, but, as musicians, they also inherited the "alternative form[s] of representation" popularized by powerful blueswomen such as Ma Rainey and Bessie Smith.[17]

Both these representational tactics may be seen in black women's musical performances. In fact, African American all-woman bands may have been unique in their ability to link expressions of the political desire of race women with the sensual desire of blueswomen. While black entertainers often lacked access to the middle-class status of the clubwomen or the characters of novels, the influence of these versions of black womanhood can be seen in the publicity generated to advertise African American all-woman bands, particularly those associated with black educational institutions, such as the International Sweethearts of Rhythm (from the Piney Woods Country Life School) and the Prairie View Co-Eds (from Prairie View A&M University). Sally Plackin's interviews with former Sweethearts revealed musicians' beliefs that the band indeed represented "a new image of black women in entertainment." Helen Jones (Woods) felt that black audiences valued the image of "a bunch of black schoolgirls" with chaperons, curfews, and strict behavioral rules. Although praised as race women, the Sweethearts also performed dance music, incorporated blues vocals, and were celebrated for their ability to really swing.[18]

Another representational issue affecting the marketability of black women on the stage is colorism. In the 1920s, 1930s, and 1940s, African American women had a better chance of getting jobs in entertainment, particularly as chorines, if they were light skinned. Several members of the International Sweethearts of Rhythm have suggested that the founder of the band preferred to hire light women. According to vocalist Evelyn McGee (Stone), "Dr. Jones seemed to pride himself on getting very light-skinned girls that looked white in the band. And there were some dark ones, because I'm dark. . . . And I was a little shocked. I thought I was with a lot of whites when I first joined [the Sweethearts] in Anderson, South Carolina."[19] I have mentioned that the International Sweethearts of Rhythm rarely figure in the conventional jazz and swing histories, but it is interesting to note that the Darlings of Rhythm, a band that musicians informed me tended to hire darker women, is even more conspicuously absent.[20]

The bands that have been more often included in dominant jazz and swing histories are those understood as white and glamorous, aspects that jazz and swing historians tend to interpret as inherently visual and unmusical. To acknowledge that mainstream swing histories include certain bands with certain images of white womanhood interpreted as "not jazz" is neither to concede that Ina Ray Hutton's Melodears or Phil Spitalny's "Hour of Charm" musicians were anything other than serious professionals nor to claim that white women never played real jazz. Nonetheless, despite their skill as musicians, their ability to reproduce images of idealized white womanhood (again, regardless of whether these roles were actually available to women who worked as musicians on the road) was a key element assuring their visibility in the entertainment industry and no doubt helped secure them a limited place in history as well.

In the most famous organizations (largely forgotten today but nationally known in their time), bandleaders and musicians took visual precautions through dress and comportment to prove to a dubious public that playing band instruments and upholding contemporary ideals of white, heterosexual all-American femininity were not necessarily mutually exclusive activities. Those groups whose leaders were men reproduced dominant gender norms inasmuch as the women were viewed as obedient to a man. Some of the more commercially successful bands, including the "Hour of Charm," were "feminized" musically, with the inclusion of strings and harps (instruments already associated with dominant notions of femininity and whiteness) to counterbalance the "shocking" (titillating?) appearance of women playing trombones, tubas, trumpets, and drums.

Yet, even when bands compliantly reproduced images of idealized white womanhood, enabling them to achieve a modicum of recognition, the resulting historiography still takes the form of mockery. In his history of the big bands, Arthur Jackson wrote, "Obviously all-girl bands would be a natural visual attraction, and if they got by on looks rather than musicianship, well, that was their prerogative."[21] But was it their prerogative? Bandleader Peggy Gilbert (who still played a mean tenor in 1995 at the age of ninety) wrote of the frustration of trying to explain to club owners — almost always men — that replacing a band member because she "doesn't smile enough, or is too fat, or her hair doesn't look just so," was not the way to "maintain a good sounding band."[22] Gilbert put her finger on precisely the dilemma: there was no place in swing discourse for a "good sounding" all-girl band that got by on musicianship rather than looks. The public imagination was not used to such a concept, and the entertainment industry did not promote the idea. In perfect collusion with this construction of common sense, the swing historian George Simon summed up Ina Ray Hutton's Melodears with the preferred verdict of his profession: "Only God can make a tree . . . and only men can play good jazz."[23] Recognition required an unequivocally drawn separate sphere, yet it was precisely this difference that set women's bands, or *all-girl bands,* as they were known, apart from serious consideration for their music. Erasure is so deeply imbedded in the discourse surrounding all-woman bands that even acknowledgment by big band "authorities," bestowed on a handful of groups, ensures their cancellation.

In thinking about narrative strategies for all-woman bands, we need to pay careful attention to who gets written about in swing histories and who does not and the historically specific versions of gender available to white and black women musicians. When looking at how gender is embedded in representation, normative concepts, politics, and subject formation, it is important to understand that gender constructions affected bands differently on each side of the black/white division across which they operated. Although some mixed-race, Latina, Asian, and Native American women also worked as swing musicians, the racial formation in the social/historical/legal context in which jazz and swing bands moved in the 1930s and 1940s was split along a black/white binary, with regional variations regarding the placement of musicians who were neither black nor white. In some locations, black women passed as Mexican to play in white bands. Black bands occasionally included one or two white members who passed as black on stage. It is also possible that white bands sometimes included light-skinned women who were legally black by the one-drop rule but who passed as white, not only onstage, but offstage as well. In contexts where passing was illegal and dangerous, performers' participation in constructing alternative representations of race and gender was conscious and strategic.

There is no room in dominant swing discourse for women who participated in the complicated processes of crossing race and gender boundaries in the performance and production of this marginalized jazz product known as *all-girl bands*. What other jazz narratives are there, and how might these counternarratives help develop narrative strategies for all-woman bands?

Thirty Years of Counternarratives

African American critics and historians have challenged Eurocentric assumptions of swing historiography; writers of compensatory "women-in-jazz" histories have documented women's participation on every instrument and in every phase of jazz musicianship; and scholars in the emergent field of jazz studies have urged jazz historiographers to move beyond canon formation to the "more historical task of describing jazz activity and its significance in American life."[24] All three of these counternarratives make significant interventions, and all three could benefit from a more persistent analysis of gender. Ethnomusicologists have been ahead of the jazz writers in understanding musical performance as a "means of instilling and perpetuating basic gender values,"[25] and all the counternarratives I now discuss could benefit from such considerations. The important work of feminist musicologists such as Susan McClary could be productively combined with the counternarratives, to explore how notions of gender and race operate within specific musical forms.[26] Incorporation of theories of gender and labor could be productively employed to analyze how women musicians were constructed as inauthentic. Although the counternarratives I am about to describe require the persistent intervention of gender analysis, they are helpful in formulating tactics for traversing the problematic terrain of jazz and swing history.

Although I realize that history books are not the only sites of struggle for women musicians and that jazz and swing histories are in cahoots with such music industry practices as who gets recorded, who works in what venues, and who gets marketed and consumed as real jazz and swing musicians, historical discourse is the ground on which I choose my fray. I hope, however, that deconstructing jazz and swing discourses that omit women will yield insights into what it was like for women instrumentalists to break into frameworks that simultaneously facilitated their careers and denied their presence. This knowledge, in turn, shall inform my narrative tactics. We have looked at some of the discursive maneuvers that make possible women's absence. Now here is a survey of some of the counternarratives that have been busily boring holes through the stubborn principles of conventional swing narration over the years.

Jazz historiography, of which swing discourse is an especially uneasy subcategory, is problematic on many levels, not the least of which is the fact that, although jazz is historically an African American cultural formation, its histories have been penned primarily by white men. Although often fanatically well intentioned, most of these white male journalists, aficionados, and musicologists have mostly not been positioned in ways conducive to challenging origin stories, periodizations, or canons produced by white brokers of black culture. This often-noted observation is repeated here not as an essentialist and reductive argument against white men's ability to write worthwhile jazz histories or to suggest that all jazz writing by white men has been wholly misguided. Nonetheless, the fact that jazz history authorship has been disproportionately white and male has certainly had its race/gender effect on which stories are told the most and how they are told. As Amiri Baraka demonstrated as early as 1963, many narrative structures that dominate jazz historiography (including the Swing Era) transparently reproduce marketing strategies developed by white-owned recording companies to sell black music to white audiences (of which the historians were enthusiastic members). Origin stories tend to mark white production and consumption of black musical forms; periodization reflects episodes of successful commodification of jazz products to white consumers; and canonization continues to reproduce careful and strategic decisions made by white-owned recording companies. Baraka and other African American men writers have challenged this ethnocentric routine and its tenets, sometimes with lasting if limited influence, but have usually failed to provide models that account for women instrumentalists, black or white. Still, the reframing initiated by these critiques provides a useful model for talking about all-woman jazz and swing bands.

The usual beginning given to the Swing Era in the hegemonic narratives is either 1932, the year Duke Ellington wrote "It Don't Mean a Thing If It Ain't Got That Swing," or 1935, August to be exact, when Benny Goodman became an overnight success at the Palomar Ballroom in Hollywood at the end of an otherwise unsuccessful transcontinental tour. In the bold, confident strokes of George Simon: "It began with Benny Goodman."[27] In his seminal social history of African American music, *Blues People,* Baraka countered this proclamation with the observation, "To be a successful (rich) swing musician, one had to be white. Benny Goodman was the 'King of Swing,' not Fletcher Henderson, or Duke Ellington, or Count Basie."[28] Henderson, Ellington, and Basie were all playing big band music characterized by *swing* (back when the word was still a verb) a decade before it was purported to "begin" with Goodman. Interestingly, Goodman himself described the Swing Era of the 1930s as one of "resurgence" rather than origination, but that did not prevent him from becoming the figure whom white fans, journalists, and historians would crown "King" of a "new thing" called "Swing."[29] Commenting on the "arrival" of swing to Fifty-second Street, Billie Holiday observed, "They could get away with calling it new because millions of squares hadn't taken a trip to 131st Street. If they had they could have dug swing for twenty years."[30]

The tenet that swing was born in the 1930s, along with the logic that gave Goodman the title *King of Swing* and Paul Whiteman *King of Jazz,* has been challenged by Baraka and other African American critics, historians, and musicians to such an extent that the implicit racism of the historical boundaries and ranking systems are now at least acknowledged (although by no means abandoned) by writers within the hegemonic frame. The same texts that tell us that the Swing Era began in the 1930s now also casually mention that black bands such as Fletcher Henderson's played swing a decade earlier. The same texts that repeatedly crown Goodman king often simultaneously document that the famous clarinet player's popularity had more than a little to do with the fact that his was a white band that presented black arrangements of black music to white audiences, that, in fact, several of the Henderson arrangements that made Goodman wildly popular were previously performed and recorded by Henderson's own band.[31] Thanks to interventions such as Baraka's, contradictory details now subtly interrupt the dominant narratives.

Time Framed

If tipping the time frame has been successful in rendering African American men musicians historically visible despite years of textual erasure, how might this tactic be usefully employed to reveal African American women, other women of color, and white women? Critiques such as those launched by Baraka and Holiday showed how the accepted mode of talking about the Swing Era as a music of the 1930s leaves out the African Americans who invented, developed, and played swing in the 1920s. Similarly, a frame that cuts off the Swing Era at U.S. involvement in World War II leaves women out of the picture at the other end.

A college textbook on jazz reports, "Because of the military draft and problems of transportation, the Swing Era came to an abrupt end at the beginning of World War II."[32] Indeed, in many histories, the war marks the demise of the Swing Era, with the draft and enlistment given as primary reasons. And the war did affect the men's bands, to be sure. According to the swing historian Ross Firestone, by August 1942, "it was estimated that every name [male] band had lost between one-quarter to one-half its personnel to the armed forces."[33] But the war affected the women's bands quite differently than it did the men's bands, as it affected women quite differently than it did men. All-woman jazz and swing bands, many of which existed in the prewar years or had players who had been working professionally since the 1920s or 1930s, were suddenly visible and in demand. New venues were open to the bands; colleges, such as Prairie View College in Texas, started all-woman bands to make up for the shortage of men; military bands, such as the Marine Corps Women's Reserve Band, were formed; civilian all-woman bands, both amateur and professional, new and already established, provided entertainment to the armed forces; the United Services Organization (USO) featured several all-woman swing bands on its tours. The International Sweethearts of Rhythm played for the black troops in Germany in 1946, the Sharon Rogers All-Girl Band toured the Philippines, Korea, and Japan in 1945–46, and Virgil Whyte's Musical Sweethearts toured bases across the United States in 1945 and 1946.

To end discussion of the Swing Era with U.S. involvement in World War II is to ensure the continued invisibility of all-woman bands. So one of my narrative tactics is to focus on the 1940s, not because there were no all-woman bands in the 1920s and 1930s (there were many), but because the war years form a window of time in which women musicians and women's bands cannot be ignored. If we catch the 1940s in our viewfinder, we will find women.[34]

The Swing Era is an easy deconstructive target once one realizes that, like so many popular music labels, the periodization itself is primarily a commercial construction—it did not have to be historically accurate or inclusive; all it had to do was recruit consumers from the largest affluent demographic group. Swing was an element of music many years before—generally, "to swing" is to emphasize the second and fourth beats (in $\frac{4}{4}$ time)—but the Swing Era was the invention of the white-owned music business, developed as a lucrative way to sell black music as recorded by white artists to white consumers during a particular time period. A common failing of hegemonic American popular music historians (and one that tends to privilege promotion schemes over popular usage and meaning) is to reproduce marketing strategies as historical "epochs" instead of approaching them as advertisements that must be analyzed and problematized. *The Jazz Age, the Swing Era, West Coast Jazz,* all are marketing labels that exemplify what Baraka has called the "cultural lag,"[35] the way that white artists in the United States have been consistently given credit for, and have often actually had the first opportunities to record, music that had been developed and performed earlier by black artists. Tom Reed has recently pointed out how the era known as *West Coast Jazz* was also a time when many black artists who had been playing jazz on the West Coast for decades were forced to go to New York if they wanted to make a living.[36]

I am not suggesting that we discard these labels, for, like the marketing strategies that constructed all-girl bands as inauthentic, rare, or ridiculous, they tell a great deal about power and ideology in the music business and the audiences that music business executives hoped to reach. David Meltzer has described the Swing Era's function as "target[ing] an essentially white middle-class youth market into consuming swing band records, attending dances and concerts, and buying into an identity commensurate with the commercial culture of pop music."[37] I suggest that we reconfigure the Swing Era not only as a youth movement through which a generation of jitterbuggers found expression, identity, and community but also as a splashy ad campaign designed to keep people putting coins in jukeboxes and lining up at dance halls, more akin to Miller Time than to a viable historical time period. Certainly, the idea of a Swing Era was meaningful to people in many other ways as well, but I hope that there is a way of thinking about its cultural, social, and political properties while retaining an awareness of its role as an ad campaign.

Linking Rosie the Riveter to the Bandstand

But, obviously, reframing time is not enough. In fact, by focusing on the 1940s, I risk colluding with the construction of Rosie the Riveter as a substitute for men, which affected women workers during World War II. The figure of Rosie the Riveter is a complicated one, for, although she was depicted as a capable worker, she was also commonly portrayed as performing her patriotic duty — taking a job so that a man could fight. I have explored the effect of this "politics of impermanence" elsewhere[38] and wish to keep these contradictions in mind when I look at the 1940s as a time of visibility and empowerment for women musicians. Just as the Swing Era must be seen, in part, as an ad campaign, so must propaganda surrounding female war workers. The product: a middle-class, white housewife who would fill the labor shortage and then cheerfully return to unpaid housework when the men returned from war. Although most women who worked during the 1940s did not match this profile, the normalization of women in the workforce as a temporary presence greatly affected women's options. As Hazel Carby notes in her discussion of the nineteenth-century cult of true womanhood, a dominant image does not have to describe the majority of women in order to dominate the definition of womanhood that affects the majority of women (in different ways). Proving that most women do not match the ideology does nothing to analyze its effects.[39] The dominant/dominating image of women workers during the war, Rosie the Riveter, epitomized the temporary war worker pitching in for the war effort. Songs and magazine ads reminded the public that Rosie would become a perfect housewife after the war.[40] Even her muscles were temporary.[41] In this sense, while opening new opportunities for working women, discourses on women war workers also served to normalize the notion that gains made by women, including women musicians, would be temporary.

That said, it is important also to acknowledge the ways in which Rosie the Riveter discourse was empowering and transformative for many women workers in the United States. Many of the oral histories in Sherna Gluck's *Rosie the Riveter Revisited* indicate that, even if women were encouraged to go back to their homes after the war (for working-class women, this often translated into being funneled into devalued "women's jobs"), the lived experience of having their labor valued "for the duration" shaped their consciousness. It is no accident that the daughters of that generation of women became the feminists of the second wave of the women's movement. Women musicians I have interviewed, particularly those who came of age during the war, speak with a great deal of excitement when describing the attention bestowed on them by civilian and military audiences. For historians interested in gender as a social construction, the sudden shifts in ideologies regarding womanhood, women's labor, women's patriotism, race relations, class divisions, etc. make the 1940s U.S. home front a fascinating site for study. The ways that women musicians "played these changes" will be further explored in chapter 1.

As Gluck and Susan Hartmann (*The Home Front and Beyond*) demonstrated, it is important to distinguish women in the workforce from Rosie the Riveter propaganda, which advocated a particular kind of patriotic, temporary laborer. What a disaster it would be if we were to read the Rosie the Riveter discourse as an objective history — we would believe that World War II was the first time American women ever took jobs. What I suggest we keep in mind is that, while the war years did offer tremendous gains for many American women, women war workers were seen as substitutes for men who were gone. This discourse is often insufficient or inaccurate for describing the experiences of working-class women, particularly African American women, who did not have the option of being housewives. Many historians agree that African American women, who had been historically confined to the worst jobs and most grievous economic situations, experienced the greatest increase in benefits from wartime labor opportunities. During World War II, over 400,000 black women were able to leave domestic work for higher-paying factory jobs.[42] Yet the popular image of Rosie the Riveter is not a black woman who no longer has to clean houses for white women but a courageous white housewife who has entered the workforce "for the duration" to support fighting men.

While the temporary workforce discourse may have empowered women musicians by providing expanded public acceptance of working women in traditionally men's occupations, it also enabled critics and the public to see them as housewives on a lark instead of as real musicians, even if they had been playing professionally for years. This temporary workforce attitude may help illuminate the tone of disdain that often accompanied references regarding them. George Simon was more typical than outrageous when he wrote that Phil Spitalny's all-woman "Hour of Charm" Orchestra "didn't play very well — and didn't always look so great either."[43]

If we recognize that the ideology that governed wartime propaganda favored a definition of *normal womanhood* in which *woman* meant a white, middle-class housewife who would disappear from the workforce as soon as the war was over, perhaps we can begin to pinpoint exactly where working women have been erased from the dominant jazz and swing narratives. When men returned, women musicians would be "sent home" (or to the typing pool) from studio jobs, orchestras, and major venues at the same time as women welders were "sent home" from the shipyards. The construction of swing as a music of the 1930s complements the construction of all-girl bands in the 1940s as temporary, even if they had been playing long before the war.

Women's History and the All-Girl Bands

On the steam of the second wave of the women's movement and the accompanying interest in documenting and celebrating the nontraditional accomplishments of women in the past, four book-length histories of women in jazz were published in the 1980s. Antoinette Handy documented hidden histories of black women musicians and located her findings in an African American social/historical context in two important works: *Black Women in American Bands and Orchestras* and *The International Sweethearts of Rhythm.* Handy's volumes, along with Sally Placksin's *American Women in Jazz* and Linda Dahl's *Stormy Weather* provide indispensable groundwork for anyone studying women's participation on all instruments and in all eras of jazz (not only as girl singers). The effect of these books is just beginning to appear in recent jazz histories that include a sentence or two about women musicians and direct interested readers to other sources. Yet the fact that "universal" jazz histories (in which women do not exist) have continued to appear subsequent to the publication of these painstaking endeavors tells us something as well.

One of the things this pattern of continuing omission tells us is that the authors and, presumably, the readers of mainstream jazz and swing histories are more invested in particular notions of gender than has been previously acknowledged. The masculinist focus of dominant jazz and swing histories may, in fact, stem from a long-standing white fascination with perceptions of a style of black masculinity associated with jazz and swing performances.[44] If the appeal of mainstream jazz and swing histories is their ability to dispense models of black masculinity to white consumers through information and anecdotes about black men who play jazz and white men who successfully play black music, then it is no wonder that all-woman bands, both black and white, find themselves the subjects of separate histories with limited readerships.

The fact that the continuum of exclusively masculine big band history is largely unbroken indicates that it is not enough to prove that women were there all along, that they played all manner of instruments. I raise this observation, not as a cry of despair, or as a judgment of failure on women's history projects, but as an indication of just how powerful the contours of common sense are, even in such seemingly benign territory as books about jazz and swing. The continued erasure of women from dominant jazz discourse, *despite* a dignified body of published knowledge on women in jazz, points to an ideological morass impervious to pleas for the dignity and heroism of the women who played jazz and swing in the 1940s. Yet the relation between erasure and counternarratives may tell a great deal about power and gender in the popular culture of a particular time and place. Although largely compensatory, these invaluable women-in-jazz texts provide research models, point to new frameworks for looking at jazz histories that include women, and serve as treasure troves of evidence for what is hidden, unspoken, and suppressed in the dominant discourse.

Another effect of second wave feminism is the emergence of a new audience for historical jazzwomen's stories and recordings, an audience provided by the women's music movement in the 1970s and 1980s. Interestingly, the assumptions of women's music discourse sometimes clashed with those of women musicians of the 1940s (as will be further explored in chap. 5). These generation gaps have proved some of the most fascinating and difficult areas in my search for narrative strategies, most particularly in figuring out how to talk about and how to write about sexuality. While the women's music sphere of the second wave was conceived largely as a safe space for celebrating lesbian love, women musicians who played in the 1940s tended to take a more guarded approach to the topic of nontraditional sexuality.

When women musicians addressed sexuality in conversations with me, the dangers associated with the topic were revealed in often indirect ways. Women came out as straight. Women explained why they were single. Women outed other women (and then asked me please not to write about "that"). Sometimes before the interview began, sometimes even before they agreed to an interview, women requested that I focus on music rather than on personal lives. When I asked one woman if the all-girl bands were safe places for nontraditional women to earn a living and live their lives, she responded by explaining how important it was not to be taken for a lesbian, whether one was a lesbian or not, because it could hurt one's own career as well as the careers of other band members. All women musicians, she told me, had to be careful not to be seen in public too often in pairs. Women musicians, straight or lesbian, had to pass as straight.

In my cross-generational and often cross-cultural interviews with women musicians, I was frequently reminded that the very strategy of coming out derives its political power within a particular historical moment that had not yet happened in the 1940s. Certainly, there were "out" nontraditional women who loved women before the gay liberation movement, but did visibility mean the same thing then that it does today? Did women who played in all-girl bands identify with such a strategy? Was the closet considered tragic in the 1940s, or was discretion valued by some sexually nontraditional people in a way that is difficult to appreciate from a post–gay liberation viewpoint? Historical reasons for valuing discretion included being blacklisted by talent agencies, losing bookings for the entire band. Indeed, several narrators expressed admiration for lesbians who protected the commercial viability of the band by being discrete. And does *coming out* mean the same thing for African American women and other women of color as it does for white women, who may have very different cultural understandings of what it means to love someone of the same sex and who are not already discriminated against because of race? African American women may have felt that they needed to protect themselves against additional obstacles to housing, jobs, etc. (and, also, perhaps, particularly excluded from the gay liberation movement of the 1960s and 1970s).

"There are gays and lesbians in all occupations, why pick on all-girl bands?" one narrator challenged. Although I wanted very badly to present all-girl bands as a site where both sexually traditional and sexually nontraditional women worked together and to find out more about how music may have functioned as an occupation where women who loved women could survive, this comment and the experience of being "picked on" that it revealed made me mindful of other perspectives. Women in all-girl bands were sexualized throughout their careers. Those who played nontraditional instruments like horns aroused suspicions that they must be nontraditional in other ways as well. That the women who played in all-girl bands were stigmatized as lesbians inhibited their success in the swing industry, a realm of very clear sex boundaries that women already crossed by appearing on the bandstand instead of the dance floor and by playing in the band rather than standing in front of it in a gown. What a shock to learn that some women musicians felt that they were also being sexualized by feminist historians.

These realizations led me to take a rather different approach to sexuality than strands of women's music discourse might suggest. Rather than explicitly talking about individual women's sexual identities — which I do not have permission to do — I have taken the discretion around sexuality as a kind of privacy that narrators' valued, as an act of agency on narrators' parts in shaping the telling of their histories, and as a diagnostic of how great were the stigmas affecting all women who played in all-girl bands. Regardless of sexual orientation, all women who played in all-girl bands were at times viewed as sexually suspect, either as loose or as lesbian. This was an occupational hazard shared by the many women in other professions who held jobs associated with men or displayed themselves onstage. Again, the second wave of the women's movement provides productive directions that may be retooled for narrative strategies for all-girl bands.[45]

New Work in Jazz Studies

As indicated by the abundance of works emanating from the relatively new academic interdiscipline known as jazz studies, jazz historiography's emphasis on canon formation is giving way to explorations of cultural and political meanings, audience reception, the mediated nature of commodified products, and the social functions of jazz.[46] These developments would appear to bode well for histories of such noncanonical jazz spheres as all-girl bands. While this new work is exciting and potentially transformative of earlier trends in jazz and swing literature, it has been relatively slow to incorporate gender analysis. There is also a troubling tendency in some (thankfully not all) of this scholarship to speak from an academic power base that suppresses earlier critiques. As we have seen, canon formation has been challenged for some time by writers concerned with the marginalization of African American history and women's history from jazz historical narratives, not to mention by jazz musicians who have critiqued the critics all along. Although not the first to make such critiques, jazz studies authors have persuasively argued for the importance of recognizing how record companies determined which jazz practices made it onto records and therefore composed a historical narrative in the studios long before the careful researchers ever donned headphones and sat down to interpret the aural artifacts. While paying close attention to how racial stereotypes were perpetuated through recording practices, however, jazz studies has tended to stop short of speculating how traditional gender constructions were contained and reproduced by the gatekeepers of the recording studios.[47]

Although I read these works with a critical eye, I am excited by the appearance of scholars, critics, historians, and researchers who are interested in transforming jazz-writing practices. With more of an eye toward gender analysis, approaches that take a complex analysis of race and that explore meanings, functions, production, consumption, and representation in jazz sites are instructive for someone attempting to construct a narrative for all-woman bands. How do the various meanings of swing change if the musicians are black women? White women? What did swing mean to the women who earned their livings playing it? How were gender and sexuality differently performed onstage and on the dance floor according to the physical composition of the band members? What kinds of masculinities were performed by Glenn Miller's band, Duke Ellington's, Cab Calloway's? Some interesting work on transformations of jazz and swing masculinity has begun to appear.[48] What models of gendered performance were popularized by girl singers, and how did these affect the performances of all-girl bands?

Oral History

I close with some observations on one aspect of traditional jazz history methodology that I keep. Besides aficionado literature, such as George Simon's collected grand claims, and discography-based works, such as Gunther Schuller's mammoth tomes (which, however scholarly, cannot help but repeat the exclusions of jazz practitioners who were snubbed by recording studios), there is a large body of jazz and swing historiography that relies on the oral histories of artists.

Historians have historically issued warnings to one another about the hazards of oral history practice, but, before I respond to such inevitable cautions, I include one example demonstrating that I am well aware of how oral history can fail to budge a stubborn, ready-made discourse.

As I suggested earlier, by and large, the white men who have written the major swing histories have failed to write about women instrumentalists, especially African American women instrumentalists. I argued that this is due, not to lack of available information, but to the power of hegemony. For instance, the oral histories collected by Stanley Dance in *The World of Swing* (1974) opened many opportunities for research that Dance did not pursue. Granted, his approach improved on many jazz histories. Unlike many other chroniclers of the Swing Era, Dance focused on African American men who were important to the development of the music, although not written about elsewhere, and he constructed his narrative in such a way that it foregrounded the musicians' own words. However, even though many men musicians referred to women musicians in their oral histories, Dance did not provide contextualization for the women so mentioned. In the middle of bandleader Claude Hopkins's narrative we find the following: "And that's how I got my experience, through Caroline Thornton, and also through Marie Lucas, another great pianist, as well as a trombone player and arranger."[49] Thanks to later work by Antoinette Handy, we now know that Lucas was a tremendously influential musician who led an African American all-woman orchestra in the Lafayette Theater in New York as early as 1915,[50] yet Dance gives us no information on her or on Thornton. In Dance's oral history of the trumpet player Jonah Jones we find the following: "We had a chance to come down to New York and try out for a job, but we missed it because a girl called Cora La Redd had a band they liked better."[51] There are multiple references to woman instrumentalists, woman bandleaders, yet Dance does nothing with these revelations. Not in his introduction, not in two panel discussions where he serves as interviewer—nowhere does Dance's authorial voice confirm the existence of women instrumentalists, women bandleaders, or all-woman bands. The two women whose oral histories are included in *The World of Swing* are singers, perfectly in keeping with the hegemonic norm.

An additional conquest of the expected story over the opening of new possibilities appears at the end of *The World of Swing*. In the appendix, Dance provides an interpretation of a roster entitled "Bands in Harlem Theatres." "The increasing use of small bands at the Apollo in the '40s is significant," he writes (keeping well within the narrative that says swing died and bop was born in 1941). But what I see dramatized in this stunning list of who played the Apollo during the war years is that the International Sweethearts of Rhythm appeared there in September 1941,

January and May 1942, January 1943, February and November 1944, and March 1945 — *as often* or *more often* than most men's bands large or small during those years.[52] Yet there is no listing for the Sweethearts in the index of *The World of Swing.* I also see that Eddie Durham's All-Star Girl Orchestra played the famed Apollo in September 1942, February, June, and October 1943, and April 1944. Eddie Durham appears in the index of *The World of Swing,* but his female band does not. These all-woman bands appear only in the appendix, without contextualization of any kind, just the usual directive to notice that small groups replaced the big bands in the 1940s.

Why didn't Dance find someone to interview from the women's bands as his oral histories and appendix would seemingly direct him toward doing? Part of the explanation is found in Gayatri Spivak's theory that, without a place in the narrative, one is silenced. Of course, the discourse that shapes these narratives stems not merely from a lack of imagination on the part of the historians but from powerful ideologies regarding women, race, class, and labor in the United States, structures of thought that continue to stand as obstacles to many woman musicians. This should be obvious by now. But even though Dance did not pursue these clues, their presence in published oral accounts may be carefully read by feminist researchers writing gendered jazz histories. The fact that narratives of both men and women musicians are populated with women, as well as men, musicians is in significant contrast with the world of swing as narrated by historians. Oral histories of men and some women musicians have been collected by a number of jazz oral history projects, including those housed at the Institute of Jazz Studies at Rutgers University; the Smithsonian Jazz Oral History Program; the Central Avenue Sounds Oral History Program at the University of California, Los Angeles; and the Tulane University Oral History of New Orleans Jazz Collection.

There is a temptation to use oral histories as authenticating sound bites. In a sense, this is how they function in Dance's text. The voices of musicians make the history seem "more real," without necessarily challenging the suppositions of historians or readers. If, however, we think of oral histories as events in themselves rather than as clear channels to the "true story," then we can begin to see how they relate to specific contexts.[53] A woman who repeatedly insists, "We were real musicians," is baffling to the feminist historian until she or he understands that the narrator is pushing against powerful structures of discourse, commodification, and practice that greatly affected how she was seen, how she saw herself, and what she had to prove in order to live her life and do her job.

Planning Tactics

In short, my challenge has been to search for ways of talking about women instrumentalists who played in the all-girl bands that do not replicate the conditions of their erasure. My dilemma — and this will be a familiar tune to many feminist historians — is that, if I use the same tools that are used to determine relevance in the dominant swing histories (recordings, record reviews, *Down Beat* polls, existing histories), I, too, will find few women. All-girl bands were marketed as spectacles; they were rarely recorded. If their performances were reviewed, it was often as though their medium was inherently visual rather than auditory, frivolous rather than serious. If, on the other hand, I ignore those tools that ignored women musicians — if I construct a women's swing history in which recuperation of lost women is the sole purpose and, to that end, I deem irrelevant such structures as the recording industry, the press, and the dominant swing discourse — I risk producing a weird supplement to reality in which women musicians appear to have existed autonomously from men in the music business. Not only might this compensatory model fail to locate women musicians within the complicated power relations that shaped their lives, but it might also fail to challenge the structures, textual and otherwise, that omitted women musicians.

I see my tactics as historical narrator as falling into five broad categories. First, I choose to reframe the Swing Era in such a way that women are most apparent. For the purposes of this study, the focus is on what some scholars refer to as *the late Swing Era* rather than on the usual period, the 1930s. Although I focus on the 1940s, I do not imply that women musicians and all-woman bands did not exist prior to World War II. Nor do I imply that the Swing Era is more accurately located in the 1940s than in the 1930s. I choose the 1940s because of the relatively high visibility of women musicians, because of the illuminating ways in which discourses of gender, race, nation, and labor intersect during World War II, and because such a focus underscores the constructedness of Swing Era parameters.

Second, I do not confine myself to band history; I include explorations of gender constructions of the 1940s that affected women musicians and the circuits in which all-girl bands moved. I am interested in comparing the representations and working conditions, as well as public perceptions, of women musicians of the 1940s with figures such as Rosie the Riveter, WACs, USO hostesses, Red Cross nurses, pinups, and movie stars. How did the meanings that women musicians held for their audiences change amid such company? What are the parallels and the divergences between the changes experienced by women musicians of the 1940s and those experienced by other women workers?

Third, I foreground the narratives of women musicians who already imagine themselves, quite correctly, in jazz and swing history. I look to these oral histories, interviews, letters, and conversations, not just for the data that they provide, but in order to learn from narrative strategies developed by jazzwomen. I also try to make relentlessly apparent that I do not take these narratives to be pure nuggets of truth tossed to us from the past. They are portions of narratives that I have selected from pages and pages of transcribed interviews that I conducted with women musicians who based their decisions about what to tell me at least partially on their perceptions of me. My interest in studying the ways in which women jazz instrumentalists tell their stories includes my convictions that (1) the memories of living jazzwomen hold much history that is not to be found elsewhere, (2) there is great value in learning how jazzwomen interpret their own lives and in learning the stories that enable them to craft and maintain identities as musicians, and (3) the shapes that jazz history takes when women musicians tell their stories may prove instructive to anyone interested in expanding our repertoire of this thing we call *jazz history*.[54]

Fourth, I make a point of underscoring travel, acknowledging that a huge part of the job of playing in an all-girl band in the early 1940s was consumed by going on the road during the wartime transportation crisis. "We need to know a great deal more about how women traveled and currently travel, in different traditions and histories," wrote James Clifford, in the context of a discussion of constructions of travel as a masculine endeavor.[55] In response to this call, I have paid careful attention to the enormous role that travel played in the lives of the members of all-woman bands: the incentives, the hardships, the effect on public perceptions, and the unique challenges and experiences that life on the road during World War II presented women musicians. The theme of travel also provides the structure of the book. Part 1 deals broadly with how wartime work and travel conditions affected all-girl bands on theater, ballroom, and military training camp circuits. Part 2 discusses the experiences of African American all-girl bands that traveled in Southern states, often challenging Jim Crow, the system of legal segregation. Part 3 focuses on a unique venue, one that provided many all-woman bands with employment, appreciative audiences, and additional challenges during the war years: USO–Camp Shows.

Finally, I make interventions whenever possible that work toward explicitly gendering jazz and swing history. In other words, recognizing that talking in a nongendered, universal way, as so many dominant swing narratives claim to do, is actually to talk about men's history. To press women into these so-called general frames will reliably render them inauthentic. Instead, I will strive toward presenting a history that looks at ways in which women and men were both present and that recognizes swing culture as a field on which specific gender constructions were affirmed, contested, performed, and consumed.

Tap your foot to this narrative. Swing was an African American musical development in the 1920s, and it is played to the present day. Most of the people who made the most money on swing during the so-called Swing Era were white. Swing was played by both men and women, although usually segregated by gender and race. There were hundreds of all-woman bands.

Playing the Changes of World War II

I

Chapter 1

Working the Swing Shift:

Effects of World War II on All-Girl Bands

> To every musician war is a personal puzzle.
>
> Will I lose my job? Shall I sell my horn? How long will it last?
>
> Will it end my career? — Carl Cons,
>
> "The Effect War Is Having on Music World"

> In these times of national emergency, many of the star
>
> instrumentalists of the big name bands are being drafted. Instead of
>
> replacing them with what may be mediocre talent, why not let some of
>
> the great girl musicians of the country take their places?
>
> — Viola Smith, "Give Girl Musicians a Break!"

World War II did not *invent* all-girl bands, but it certainly gave them a new set of changes to play. It would be preposterous to suggest that the changes on the U.S. home front were anywhere near as drastic as those in any country on whose soil battles were fought. Yet it is also true that, in the early 1940s, Americans did not know that the United States would not be a battle site, or that the country's primary role in the war would be that of megaproducer of goods, or that fewer than 1 percent of the 50 million people (mostly civilians) who would be killed during the war would be U.S. citizens. After the bombing of Pearl Harbor, the threat of the world war abroad loomed large and local. Civilians volunteered as plane spotters and air raid wardens. Blackouts were common in coastal areas. The government relocated and incarcerated 110,000 people of Japanese ancestry (anyone with at least one Japanese great-grandparent) despite a lack of evidence that Japanese Americans were disloyal to the United States. War mobilization on the home front in-

"I haven't seen the new *Beat*—are they his third or fourth wives, or two new members of the brass section?"

Editorials, letters to the editor, and cartoons, such as this one by Lou Schurrer, betrayed *Down Beat*'s ambivalence about women on the bandstand during World War II. *Down Beat,* 15 August 1943, 10. By permission, *Down Beat Magazine.*

cluded radically accelerated patriotism, civilian defense, war bond drives, the government shaping of popular culture and opinion through the Office of War Information, the conscription of soldiers, and the buildup of military training camps and defense industries.

Like other home-front workers and travelers, the women who played in the all-girl bands that barnstormed the nation's ballrooms, theaters, and military installations encountered radically transformed labor and road conditions. Travel on the home front was characterized by extremes of both unprecedented restrictions and unprecedented mobility. At the same time that pleasure driving was banned and gas and tires were rationed, 12 million people left home for military service, and 15 million other Americans moved for other reasons, such as work or opportunities to pursue dreams not possible during the Great Depression of the 1930s. All-girl bands on the road coped with the new travel difficulties and benefited from the spending power, social needs, and restless energy of the millions of dislocated soldiers and workers.

Audience composition changed. Venues changed. Even everyday terms like *woman, worker,* and *musician* took on new meanings, resulting in new opportunities and obstacles for all-girl bands. A sense of this cacophony can be sampled in such swing industry periodicals of the era as *Down Beat.* In a single issue, one can find a cartoon or a joke depicting women musicians as more sexual than musical, editorial debates over whether women could (or should) play jazz, and want ads encouraging women union musicians who could sight-read and improvise to send in a photograph for the consideration of all-girl bandleaders. Articles tracing the travels and praising the skills of women musicians rest uneasily next to updates on their drafted union brothers. Letters from soldiers raving about an all-girl band that visited their camp appear on the same editorial page as impassioned arguments about why men swing musicians should be exempt from the draft.

The war thrust the swing industry (and other industries) into a supply-and-demand crisis that required drastic reconfiguration of workers and consumers. Unlike many industries, however, the swing industry was not impelled to come up with a new product. While automobile plants vied for coveted jeep-manufacturing contracts, dance music took on patriotic meaning without so much as a style conversion. The demand for swing skyrocketed as millions of Americans, isolated from loved ones and far from home, sought diversion, comfort, and social contact through music and dance. Defense workers pursued recreation at "swing shift dances" at strange hours in strange cities. Soldiers yearned for music that reminded them of their private lives and lost leisure and that represented ideas about peacetime America for which they could fight and to which they could dream of returning. At the same time, conscription made it increasingly difficult for men's bands to supply such demands. For men's and women's bands able to accept the plethora of bookings, travel restrictions designed to prioritize transportation for military needs and to conserve such scarce commodities as gas and rubber made it

"At-liberty" and "help-wanted" classified ads illustrate how "girl musicians" in the war years became, among other things, another kind of "draft exemption." *Down Beat,* 1 August 1944, 15. By permission, *Down Beat Magazine.*

difficult for them to keep concert dates. Wartime restrictions on charter buses especially affected African American bands—less likely to be booked in hotels and major ballrooms and theaters, black musicians depended on tours of one-nighters at least partly through the Jim Crow South, where travel was uncomfortable and dangerous for all black travelers and public transportation was segregated.

As the swing industry sought to take advantage of its war boom despite the shortage of men workers and transportation restrictions, American women workers were simultaneously celebrated as never before. Massive recruitment campaigns to make such figures as women welders acceptable to the women who might fill those positions (as well as to their families and the general public) also spilled over into other nontraditional fields. This highly micromanaged transformation in acceptable roles enabled traditional women to step outside their normal experiences without risking exclusion from the category *good women,* but it was a double-edged sword for women who already worked, including those who had played in all-girl bands before the war. While wages went up and opportunities expanded, the sudden increased public awareness of women workers, on bandstands as well as on assembly lines, lent itself to the illusion that all women in the workforce were "Swing Shift Maisies" — 1940s lingo for temporary substitutes for the "real" workers who were off in combat. Entertainment trades that had run features on all-girl bands during the prewar years now captioned photos of such bands with such contemporaneous, if misleading, quips as "The draft is really blowing!"[1]

Certainly, conscription and other radical changes wrought by the war affected women musicians in all kinds of complicated ways, but World War II did not introduce women musicians to the big band business. In fact, many of the women musicians who scrambled from one-nighter to one-nighter during the war years, entertaining the troops, filling the "dance band shortage," playing swing shift dances for defense workers, and traveling on USO–Camp Shows, were the self-same women who had cut their teeth performing in all-girl bands in vaudeville and tent shows, dance halls, ballrooms, carnivals, and theaters a decade earlier. Tenor player Vi Burnside and trumpeter Ernestine "Tiny" Davis, star soloists for the most celebrated African American all-woman band of the 1940s, the International Sweethearts of Rhythm, were both alumnae of the Harlem Play-Girls in the 1930s. Many members of Eddie Durham's All-Star Girl Orchestra, the Darlings of Rhythm, and Jean Park's All-Girl Band had previously played in the Harlem Play-Girls as well as such other black women's bands of the 1930s as the Dixie Rhythm Girls and the Dixie Sweethearts. White women's bands of the 1930s included those led by Rita Rio, Phil Spitalny, and Ina Ray Hutton. Jane Sager, trumpet soloist with Ada Leonard's All-American Girl Orchestra in the 1940s, had played in a host of earlier white all-woman units, including

Rita Rio's band and a group called the Platinum Blonds of America that traveled to Cuba in the mid-1930s. Mary Demond remembered that her professional career started at age seventeen when she discovered a *Down Beat* on a trolley in 1939 and spent her shorthand class answering an ad for a woman trumpet player. Although often remembered as wartime phenomena, many of the most famous all-woman bands, including the organizations led by Ina Ray Hutton and Rita Rio, actually disbanded before U.S. involvement in World War II, and many bands that entertained during the war years, such as the International Sweethearts of Rhythm and Phil Spitalny's "Hour of Charm" Orchestra, had, in fact, been established long before 1941.[2] Thanks to a continuum of earlier bands, the hundreds of all-girl bands that traveled in the wake of Pearl Harbor to fill war-related entertainment demands were not without precedent, nor were they devoid of experienced, professional players.[3]

Even the women who stepped directly out of high school to join all-girl bands during the war were more likely to have previous training than most women welders or riveters. Girls in both black and white high schools had more access to school bands than they did to shop classes. Most of the women I interviewed played in high school bands, and some attained their first professional experiences through their school band connections. Marilyn Merle, Joy Cayler, and Marge Kiewitt all started their own all-girl bands while in high school. Clora Bryant, Helen Cole, and Elizabeth Thomas played with their high school teachers and classmates in a professional dance band in Denison, Texas, before joining the Prairie View Co-Eds. Betty O'Hara played trumpet in a small dance band that included at least two women saxophonists and was led by her high school music teacher. Joan Alfert (Zieger) attended weekly rehearsals of the citywide high school band in St. Louis, after which those so inclined remained to play in a swing band. Trombonist Lois Cronen (Magee) noted that, although improvisation was not taught in high school (or college), the opportunity was there to learn these skills in extracurricular dance bands. Rosalind "Roz" Cron played in junior high, in high school, and subsequently in professional dance bands with her schoolmates Serge Chaloff and Hal McKusick in Boston before going on the road with Ada Leonard and later with the International Sweethearts of Rhythm. While still in high school, bassist Vi Wilson was one of two African Americans in the All-City Orchestra, which consisted of the most promising student musicians in Los Angeles. In addition, she played alongside such talented young musicians as Melba Liston, Clora

Bryant, Doris Jarrett, Minnie Hightower, and Dexter Gordon in a co-ed WPA band led by drummer and music teacher Alma Hightower.

Women long out of high school who joined all-girl bands for the first time during the war were also likely to have transferable musical skills gained as a hobby or from church or other music-industry jobs. Ernestine May's extensive experience as a songwriter, arranger, and copyist made her transition to musical performance even smoother than that from housewife to worker described by the Office of War Information, in which knowledge of how to operate a sewing machine was declared ideal preparation for making liberty ships.[4] Looking for a way to make some extra money to support her three children during the war years, May noticed a magazine ad about a New York agent who was booking black women musicians. "So," she said, "I went and told him that I was a piano player. And he said, 'Well, I need a piano player who sings.' I said, 'Well, I sing, too.' I kind of exaggerated that singing part. . . . He said, 'Play something for me.' Well, the only thing I knew that I could sing was gospel music. So I sang a spiritual, but I put it in, like, swing. That was the only thing I could think to do on the spur of a moment. Would you believe that he hired me?"[5] Like many women musicians, Perri Lee (Poston) had taken piano lessons throughout her childhood. In addition, she had played in her college band. When her mother got a job in a Los Angeles defense plant, Lee landed a job typing and answering the phone for the black AFM local, 767. "One day," she says, "it occurred to me, maybe I'll take one of these jobs!" She won her first audition and was soon making more money in three nights than her mother was making in a forty-hour week.[6] Frances Scher was a staff singer at Tin Pan Alley when Japan bombed Pearl Harbor, and she decided to start an all-girl band to play for civilian defense. Her band not only found itself playing voluntary patriotic jobs but soon experienced commercial demand in Chicago and nearby resort areas, as well as on the road, throughout the war.[7]

This section is not so much an argument about whether the wartime changes were good for women musicians as it is an examination of what those changes were and how they affected the working conditions, public perceptions, and professional strategies of women musicians. What changed for women workers in general and the swing industry in particular during World War II, and how did women musicians in all-girl bands *play those changes*? How did women musicians deal with public perceptions that they were Rosie the Riveter, for example?

Rosie the Riveter is the lasting symbol for women workers during the war, but it is important to remember that, like Swing Shift Maisie, Rosie was carefully designed not just as a capable woman worker but as a *swing shift worker,* a term that, during the war, implied more than the stint between *day* and *graveyard. Swing shift* implied the extra shift, the shift temporarily added for the sole purpose of wartime production. Maisie and Rosie propaganda portrayed women workers as attractive, competent, patriotic, and temporary. Although the Rosie of mainstream advertising images was invariably white, the black press ran images of African American women workers as Rosie the Riveter, celebrating black women's wartime access to better-paying jobs in the defense sectors, drawing from their experiences to expose war plants that broke Franklin D. Roosevelt's Executive Order 8802 forbidding race discrimination in the defense industries, and praising black women workers for their patriotism. Women workers, including those who played in the all-girl bands that crisscrossed the country during the 1940s, reaped both the breaks and the drawbacks of being seen as patriotic Rosies and Maisies working the swing shift.

But Rosie wasn't just a woman worker. She was a particular kind of woman worker, whether she bucked rivets or took hot trumpet solos. The image of an independent Rosie the Riveter, rolling up her sleeves to reveal capable muscles, cheeks glowing with good health and self-esteem, proud of her labor, continues to circulate on feminist T-shirts, coffee mugs, and posters as an icon of women's potential. But even the catchy 1942 novelty tune that provides Rosie's sound track reminds us that our strapping heroine will be riveting only as a conversationalist when "boyfriend Charlie" returns from the marines. So long as her man is away and her country is at war, Rosie will "work for victory" and spend her paycheck on "lots of war bonds."[8] Women who wanted to keep their improved working conditions after the war, who enjoyed their independence, who did not necessarily see their identities as welded to the institutions *wife* and *mother,* and who spent their hard-earned wages on themselves were not good Rosies at all. No, they were Rosie's "bad girl" coworkers — women who were as reviled by society as Rosie was serenaded.

The repugnance the general populace held for "bad Rosies" is part of the story that contemporary feminist posters and coffee cups tend to forget. But this shadow side of Rosie the Riveter was very much apparent in wartime debates about whether women should take the place of men musicians who had been drafted or enlisted. The attitude that women musicians were pitching in for the war effort pervaded the publicity and reviews of the most successful all-girl bands whether the women in them had played professionally before the war or not. "With the war what it is and the draft blowing harder and faster in the male direction, female bands won't be hard to take as time goes into history, especially if they're as good and chockful as beauty as Eddie Durham's crew"[9] — so raved a typical favorable review of an African American all-girl band made up of many musicians who had played in earlier bands. Women musicians might improve their chances for bookings and enhance their popularity by embracing a patriotic Rosie the Riveter identity, or they might risk accusations that they were selfish and unpatriotic by adopting a more enduring image. Reeds player Deloros Conlee (Goodspeed) recalled her irritation at being bombarded by fans inquiring what she planned to do after the war. "We worked before the war, and we would work after the war also," she replied.[10] Although many women workers offered similar rejoinders, to imply that one's labor was disconnected from the war effort was a risky move for women to make during World War II. Publicity for all-girl bands tended to avoid this tack, instead balancing allusions to professionalism with promises of patriotism.

Some women musicians found ways to extract useful dimensions of Rosie the Riveter — her public acceptability as a skilled worker (rather than "daffy housewife"), for instance, and even her patriotism — without necessarily subscribing to the notion that they were temporary substitutes for the real musicians off at war. Most of the women I interviewed, in fact, maintained self-identities as both patriots and professionals. What they had no choice about, however, was their audiences' tendency to think "Rosie the Riveter" when they saw an all-girl band on the stand and to interpret women musicians as substitutes, amateurs, or cheerleaders, no matter how well they performed. Figuring out ways to be taken seriously as musicians without appearing unpatriotic and self-interested was a particular challenge for women musicians during the 1940s.

Oddly enough, being taken seriously as workers was a challenge faced by men musicians as well during World War II. At the same time that women workers were accepted in fields dominated by men, many of those fields, especially those deemed by the federal government to be "nonessential," were feminized as ideas about masculinity became unwaveringly affixed to military service. During the same years that women on the bandstand were asked, "What are you going to do when the war is over?" men musicians and other men civilian workers were scrutinized with the ubiquitous, "Why aren't you in uniform?" While demand for swing bands boomed, the musicians who played in them were likely to be seen as morale boosters, regardless of sex, as chipping in for the war effort, but they were often not recognized as performing real work. Debates between the American Federation of Musicians (AFM), the musicians' union, and various arms of the government over musicians' wartime roles were heated and can be traced in the pages of the trade magazines, including the AFM members' magazine, *International Musician.*[11]

As early as December 1940, Doron K. Antrim editorialized in the pages of *International Musician* that music should be considered an "essential industry," protected and supported by the government because of its value to the war effort. England had found music to be essential, Antrim argued, citing the use of live and piped music in British munitions plants.[12] Debates about the essential or nonessential status of music were carefully monitored in musicians' periodicals, as the outcome of such decisions affected men readers' draft vulnerability. Although music was eventually found to be a luxury and musicians were conscripted along with other nonessential workers, the power of bands to cheer soldiers *was* recognized by the government, and musicians were expected to donate their time to bond drives, armed forces camps, and canteens. "Uncle Sam admits that music is valuable, nay, even indispensable, in the war effort, and Uncle Sam has a way of paying for what he needs, that is, in every case except that of music," argued another *International Musician* editorialist, insisting that music is labor and men's labor at that. "The little house erected for the Bond Drive was the work of architects, carpenters, painters, and plumbers, no doubt paid in good coin of the realm. . . . But the musicians got hearty handshakes to take home to their wives to buy supper with."[13]

Efforts to protect members' jobs during the war frequently brought the union under attack as unpatriotic. James C. Petrillo, the powerful and controversial AFM president from 1940 to 1958 (and perhaps the most caricatured labor leader during World War II), waged widely criticized battles against "canned music," radio broadcasts by student musicians (including the National Music Camp at Interlochen, Mich.), and demanded remuneration, preferably government subsidies, for musicians who entertained the troops. Along with other entertainment guilds and unions, the AFM struggled for and obtained an agreement with the USO (United Services Organization) that only union performers would be hired for Camp Shows. When military bands stepped up their public appearances, the ever-controversial Petrillo declared that they could not do radio broadcasts. A measure of Petrillo's power is that he emerged victorious from his tussle with the War Department, having secured an agreement that military bands could not perform jobs that might be filled by civilian union musicians. Not surprisingly, this triumph further fueled critiques of the AFM's lack of patriotism. Petrillo mitigated such accusations with lavish displays of patriotic fervor, such as his order to the entire AFM "membership of 138,000 musicians to play 'The Star Spangled Banner' at the beginning and at the conclusion of all programs at symphony concerts, park concerts, hotel engagements, dance engagements, theater engagements, Hollywood studios, radio engagements, and so forth."[14] Even during the much-criticized AFM recording ban in 1942 (which forbade members from recording until safeguards could be secured protecting musicians' jobs from the threat posed by "canned music" on jukeboxes and the radio), Petrillo exempted musicians who recorded "V-disks," or "Victory-disks," records made exclusively for the troops and distributed by the War Department. Throughout the war, the union also guaranteed drafted and enlisted musicians dues-free membership.

While the demand for swing and the shortage of men musicians would seem to have placed all-girl bands in a good position to achieve some recognition and upgrade their working conditions, the battles between Petrillo and Uncle Sam left women AFM members in a tough spot. Women's claims to musical expertise did not bode well for their union brothers' struggles to be recognized as indispensable. Public notions of women workers as temporary patriotic substitutes made their holding jobs perceived as morale boosting particularly appealing. Whether band members were paid or not, public perceptions of all-girl bands as amateur were at odds with women AFM members' own ideas about their skills as well as with the AFM's battle to have music recognized as work. Despite popular notions of women workers as patriotic pinch hitters, most women musicians in all-girl bands during the war saw themselves as professionals, and most belonged to the AFM. Union membership was imperative in order to work in hotels, restaurants, ballrooms, or radio.

Trumpet player Laverne Wollerman (whose stage name was Laverne Walters) commented that serious women musicians in the 1940s necessarily joined the AFM: "If we didn't, we stayed home and married the boy next door."[15] One bandleader (who wished to remain anonymous) remembered that the union picketed her band of fellow high school girls (and even placed them on the unfair list in *International Musician*) when they first started to accept professional jobs. When the young women rushed to the union office to join up, they were promptly fined; but, after that punitive initiation, they were accepted by the union throughout the war as viable, professional AFM members. On the one hand, the AFM required loyalty and cooperation from women musicians more than ever before. On the other, if women musicians appeared ready, willing, and able to fill the demand for dance music, they weakened the AFM's case that men musicians were "workers, not shirkers."

Like Petrillo, women musicians had to counteract their demands to be recognized and remunerated as serious professionals with proof of their selfless devotion to Uncle Sam. Used in moderation, Rosie the Riveter was a useful figure in maintaining such a balancing act. In fact, she was made for the job.

"Give Girl Musicians a Break!"

When "famous girl drummer" Viola Smith urged bandleaders to replace drafted men musicians with "hep girls" in her often-quoted *Down Beat* editorial "Give Girl Musicians a Break!" she did not speak as someone who saw women musicians as wartime substitutes. Smith had played with professional all-girl bands since 1925 and had no intention of leaving the music business at the war's end. She had already enjoyed a great deal of recognition and would, in fact, continue to play drums professionally until 1971. Nonetheless, her February 1942 article, published mere weeks after the bombing of Pearl Harbor, shared many campaign strategies with Rosie the Riveter.

Deftly moving between merit arguments about women's equal skills and appeals to popular patriotic notions about women chipping in for the war effort, Smith argued that the present moment "marks the most opportune time we girl musicians have ever had to take our right places in the big dance bands and do our bit to keep up the morale of the country" by keeping "music alive." Her claim that "there are some girl musicians who are as much the masters of their instruments as are male musicians" was wisely tempered with references to fields where women's substitute labor had been more or less accepted. Women work alongside men in factories, her argument continued, a direct invocation of Rosie's acceptance. Why not in bands?

Having implied (with no guarantees!) that replacement would be temporary, Smith used subsequent paragraphs to emphasize women musicians' job qualifications. Because "girls have as much stamina as men," she reasoned, and because they "can stand the grind of long tours and exacting one-night stands," women should be considered for jobs in name bands. Anticipating the usual objections about the limited scope of women's musicianship, she went on to debunk the "idea of girls being able to play only legitimately" — that is, Western classical music — and to declare the existence of " 'hep girls' who can sit in any jam session and hold their own." Smith realized that demonstrating the physical endurance and musical abilities of women musicians would not be enough to expel the inevitable barb that they were "long on looks and short on talent." Rather than completely dismissing the "looks" angle, she argued that looks did not necessarily thrive at the expense of talent. Rosie's public acceptability was owed, after all, not to her equal mastery of tools and tasks perceived as masculine but to her ability to maintain her traditional femininity while helping out with the country's production needs. To a readership already inundated with the notion of women as visual attractions — a notion reinforced by *Down Beat*'s cheesecake covers, girl singer jokes, and sexist cartoons — Smith concluded that the presence of women could provide extra showmanship. "Think it over, boys."

The readers, both men and women, thought it over. Then they fired off their responses in a wave of heated letters to the editor. "I'll tell you right now that I don't like girl musicians," wrote William Peri of Stockton, California. "Girls should leave this kind of business to persons who know what it's all about. And I mean men." Peri's diatribe elicited lively responses both pro and con. Anne Hudee of Fredonia, New York, wrote, "I am a girl musician and I'm sorry but I'll have to say that most men musicians aren't as terrific as you think! I've heard girls play and brothers, some of them give out with the righteous jive!"[16]

The debate continued for months. And it did not always divide neatly into gender camps (if one can take these letters at face value). "Dynamite," a Cincinnati reader, declared, "Through no fault of my own, I happen to be a girl and I definitely agree with William Peri that girls do not make good swing musicians. When it comes to playing good music, girls, how about leaving it to the boys? We ought to be proud to be able to dance to such bands as Tommy Dorsey, Count Basie, Etc. Our place is listening and dancing to music, not sitting in with the band and blowing our brains out." Some men wrote in support of women musicians. Joe Banana of Yuma, Arizona, wrote, "Who is William Peri to state dogmatically that girl musicians are inept? I have run across girl musicians who could blow some men off the stand." Banana then raved over a local tenor player named Doris Everett, whom he described as a combination of Coleman Hawkins, Chu Berry, and Ben Webster.[17]

Certainly, this was not the first debate over the musical abilities of women musicians to appear in the mainstream jazz and swing press. Smith's article and the raft of responses are easily located in an ongoing and seemingly inexhaustible controversy over who the best jazz musicians are and whether they are ever women. These debates and others — which race produced better musicians? should bands be racially integrated? and were bands with vocalists ever as good as bands without vocalists? — raged obsessively in jazz and swing periodicals throughout the 1930s and 1940s. Arguments over whether women could play can also therefore be seen in the broader context in which *Down Beat* and the other trades fashioned themselves as the reigning experts on authentic jazz.

But Smith's plea to "give girl musicians a break" is also historically specific and is crafted with an awareness of AFM concerns in 1942: What will happen to the jobs of drafted men musicians at a time when big band jazz and swing looms as the most popular American music and the biggest morale booster of U.S. citizens and the country enters the war? Will the government declare dance bands essential to national security? Would swing musicians be draft exempt? (The answer would be no, but it would not come for another year.) If not, will 4-F musicians get those jobs? Will the work go to men who have not yet reached or who have passed draft age (eighteen to thirty-five)? Or will women musicians step in to work the swing shift? If so, what will happen to these jobs when the war is over? Could the union remain strong during this crisis?

Ellis Gibson of McAlester, Oklahoma, wrote, "In connection with Viola Smith's article, *Give Girl Musicians a Break,* I have a plan too. Why not take young men or boys into orchestras also. That is, boys from 16 to 18 who are not of draft age."

Robert Toney, of Worcester, Massachusetts, also had a plan: "Who's going to supply the music when the men go? Well, it won't be women! The older generation, Joe Sullivan, George Wettling and their buddies still jive better than fanatical housewives."[18]

Smith's editorial denounced the image of "fanatical housewives," but it did not go so far as to suggest that women should keep their band jobs when the war was over. Her portrayal of skilled, patriotic, attractive women musicians who were willing and able to pitch in during the war crisis identified the parameters of public acceptance. Filling these parameters with ideas of "hep girls" rather than "fanatical housewives" served as a strategic expansion of the limitations, but wartime gender discourse demanded reassurance that femininity would not be lost. Smith's translation of feminine visual appeal, which was usually summoned as proof of women's inability to play, into the positive and masculinized trade term *showmanship* was a stroke of brilliance.

The month following Smith's *Down Beat* editorial, *International Musician* conceded that the "building up of an army of 3,600,000 men is making drastic changes indeed in orchestral line-up" and suggested that "top-flight band membership is going to depend more and more on youngsters eager to show their mettle, on older men who have previously stepped out in favor of youth, and on girls. All-girl orchestras in fact, are notably successful in supplying those necessary build-ups to any swing ensemble: gayety [*sic*], comeliness and ability."[19] By foregrounding gaiety and comeliness, the AFM also found a way to endorse the all-girl bands' ability while reducing the threat to men members worried about the draft. So long as their status as patriotic place markers for men AFM members was intact and their visual appeal as "pretty girls" (not "real" musicians) was emphasized, the presence of all-girl bands in good union jobs could be condoned by the AFM, without signifying self-interested, job-stealing, "bad" Rosie the Riveters.

Women musicians were, after all, among the draft-exempt AFM members who were available to hold union jobs, follow union rules, pay union dues, and maintain the strength of the union while large numbers of drafted men musicians were detained in the armed forces. A month after the bombing of Pearl Harbor, *Down Beat* estimated that 12 percent of the AFM membership was already in the service or subject to call. The lowering of the draft age from twenty-one to eighteen, as well as the classification of music as nonessential, increased those numbers. By July 1944, one-third of the AFM membership was serving in the armed forces.[20] The newly significant status of the "girl musician" as draft exempt is nowhere more apparent than the help-wanted ads in the trades.

The white male norm assumed by mainstream musicians' magazines is reflected in the wording of job ads in *Down Beat* in the 1930s and 1940s. "Drummer available" meant white male drummer and "colored drummer available" black male drummer; "girl drummer" meant white female drummer and "colored girl drummer" black female drummer. Opportunities for black women musicians were the least numerous among such listings in the mainstream trades. Indeed, black women were more likely to find musical employment opportunities in the entertainment sections of black newspapers. During the war, the draft status of white and black men also figured in the want ads. Thus, in the mainstream trades, "4-F drummer" and "girl drummer" were two kinds of white draft-exempt drummer. One *Down Beat* ad of 15 June 1943 demonstrated the primacy of draft exemption when it solicited the services of a "girl or man guitarist with draft deferment." At a time when *4-F* was practically synonymous with cowardice, emasculation, and even treason in the popular imagination, white and black men displayed their 4-F standings prominently in their "at-liberty" ads: "Tenor man—4-F, Experienced, available this month." Help-wanted ads asked for "talented young musicians about 17 or 4F." And opportunities for (white) "girl musicians" appeared with increasing frequency.

So, although the war did not mark the beginning of the all-girl bands, it did signal a period of drastically changed working conditions for both men and women musicians. As the draft and enlistment whittled away at the ranks of men's bands, women's bands profited from the increased range of jobs available to them. Shipping its young men off to war, the nation desperately needed a dose of the dance music that had helped it through the depression. Previously dubious managers of ballrooms and major theaters quickly learned the value of all-girl bands. Women drummers, trumpeters, and trombonists did not look quite so incongruous to a public growing accustomed to the idea that women could build ships, fly planes, and play professional baseball. And, as big band music and representations of idealized American womanhood both became signs for American GIs of "what we're fighting for," all-girl bands became acceptable features on military bases, civilian defense units, and hospitals.[21]

But, along with new attitudes and opportunities, women musicians also encountered new roadblocks. According to tenor saxophonist Peggy Gilbert, at the same time that all-girl bands were able to move into ballrooms and travel "the one-nighters in buses like all of the men's bands did," the vaudeville circuits that provided steady work for women's bands in the 1920s and 1930s were closing down or changing their policies. "When movies with stage shows went out," said Gilbert, "the scene changed completely for all-girl bands."[22] While many women musicians felt optimistic about the hard-won recognition and opportunities they were finally receiving on the road, their audiences tended to see them as just passing through. Trumpet player Jane Sager characterized the difference between playing in the 1930s and playing in the 1940s as a shift from being perceived as professionals to being seen as female companions for soldiers. In the 1930s, "everything was how good we sounded and how the arrangements were and what kind of performance we put on. We had a lot of pride in our work. We didn't want to sound crummy, because there was so much prejudice against women musicians to begin with." In the 1940s, however, musical expertise took a backseat to celebrations of the patriotic "girl next door." "The 'Star Spangled Banner' was flying all over the place," she recalled.[23] While a reputation for supporting "our boys" may have carried positive connotations for a patriotic public, it also carried a promise of impermanence — "good girls" would happily put down their horns when the troops came home.

The 1940s has been called the great era for all-woman bands, but this brief window of public acceptance and expanded opportunity offered a scenario more complicated than "the men were away, so the women could play." It was a time when serious professional musicians were seen as temporary war workers simply because they were women, when the previous vaudeville venues for all-girl bands were disappearing, and when, because of gas and rubber shortages, travel was more difficult than it had been before the war. To top it off, women musicians who took to the road under these conditions were consumed as visual entertainment, primarily as representations of the idealized sweethearts that wartime propaganda and entertainment relentlessly encouraged servicemen to miss or imagine. Bandleader Ada Leonard recalled telling her musicians, "Because you're a girl, people look at you first, then listen to you second."[24] The emphasis on glamour was sometimes a hard pill to swallow, especially for women who thought of themselves as professional musicians and who traveled with all-girl bands solely because other bands would not hire them. "It was my only way to go out on the road and perform," commented alto saxophonist Roz Cron.[25] While the war years saw a few women move into chairs in men's bands—Billie Rogers (trumpet) and Marjorie Hyams (vibes) with Woody Herman, Melba Liston (trombone) with Gerald Wilson, Elsie Smith (saxophone) with Lionel Hampton, Frances Shirley (trumpet) with Charlie Barnet, Edna Williams (trumpet) with Noble Sissle—for the most part jobs for women jazz and swing players remained sequestered in all-girl aggregations.

Although only a few women were hired to play in men's bands, many all-woman groups were organized and led by men, including Virgil Whyte's Musical Sweethearts, Eddie Durham's All-Star Girl Orchestra, and Phil Spitalny's "Hour of Charm" Orchestra. Some men, in fact, were able to avoid being drafted themselves by leading all-girl bands on USO tours. Eddie Durham has spoken frankly about how leading an all-girl band was "the only way" he could "stay out of the Army.... So long as I kept the girls' band, I'd be deferred from the army every six months for the duration." This arrangement involved spending a certain amount of time entertaining for the USO, but its benefits included government-supplied gas coupons and access to a sleeper bus (secured by Mary McLeod Bethune, president of the National Council of Negro Women and a friend of Eleanor Roosevelt's).[26] Durham's band was unique in that it was not strictly all-girl but in 1943 and 1944 had a man drummer, Kid Lips Hackett.[27] Other bands were organized and led by women, including those directed by Joy Cayler and Marilyn Merle. Booking agents had a hand in developing a number of all-girl bands as they sought to fill the market demand. Ada Leonard's All-American Girl Orchestra was started by a woman instrumentalist for an agency; the agent then hooked the band up with the glamorous nonplaying woman leader. The Darlings of Rhythm were acquired by an agency soon after they were organized and fronted by the very agent who booked the band. The International Sweethearts of Rhythm began in the 1930s as a musical fund-raiser for Mississippi's Piney Woods Country Life School for poor and orphaned black children, but by the 1940s it had been transformed into a professional group by a savvy manager—who wooed members away from Piney Woods and hired top arrangers and experienced players—and exploitative agents who profited from both the popularity of the band and the talent and naïveté of its members. All-girl bands fit into the circuits of the wartime swing industry in a variety of ways, some of which will be more fully explored in subsequent chapters on specific bands. The bands I focus on in this book are not selected by means of a ranking system by which I proclaim the "best" or "most important" bands. Rather, I have chosen bands that demonstrate a vast range of strategies by which women musicians "played the changes" during World War II.

Wanted: Women Who Can "Read, Fake, Ride, and Take-Off" (Send Photo)

GIRL MUSICIANS, Brass, rhythm, saxes. Young, attractive, modern readers. Steady engagements. AIRMAIL photo, details. "Take-off"? Dave Schooler's "Swinghearts." — "Help Wanted" (15 June 1941)

GIRL TRUMPET, young, attractive, sing, read and fake, union, for well known combo, location work. Write experience, doubles if any. Send photo immediately. This is THE opportunity for right girl. — "Help Wanted" (1 April 1941)

WANTED GIRL MUSICIANS for location with 5 to 7 piece units. State all in first letter: Experience, reading ability necessary. Ferguson Bros., Agency, Inc. — Ferguson Bros. ad, Pittsburgh Courier, 15 July 1944, 13.

When bandleader Virgil Whyte placed his advertisement in trade magazines such as *Down Beat* and *Variety* for women musicians who could "read, fake, ride, and take-off,"[28] he sought top-notch players with the ability to produce the notes as they appeared on the page as well as the ability to improvise. The women Whyte targeted in his 1943 personnel pitch were serious professionals who read the trades and who would understand the contemporary, vocational language used in the copy. Unlike some recruiting ads for all-girl bands that asked for a photograph, this call did not specify the skill of looking young and gorgeous throughout months of one-nighters, although that was undoubtably another aspect of the job. The advertised criteria included the same kind of jazz and swing musicianship expected of men.

According to trumpet player and teacher Jane Sager, in the professional argot of the day, *fake* meant the ability to play appropriate notes without actually knowing the song. If the piano player knew the song and you did not but you were still able to know in an instant, by ear, which notes to contribute, you possessed the ability to "fake." *Ride* meant to improvise with a strong sense of beat and syncopation (often while other musicians were *riffing,* or playing patterns, behind you). *Take off* meant to improvise a solo jazz chorus, developing your own melodic lines to the chord changes. While riding and riffing are not the same thing, it is possible to ride a riff. It is also possible, although not always necessary, to ride while you take off. Ride is a quality of rhythmic drive. A *ride tenor,* the pride of many bands, men's as well as women's, was a tenor soloist with a strong swing pulse. "A *band* can ride," explained Sager.[29] Along with *playing the spots* (sight-reading), these are the skills that Whyte expected his personnel to bring with them to work in the 1940s. Ads indicate that even bandleaders who requested photos required such skills. Dave Schooler, who urged "young, attractive" applicants to "AIRMAIL photo," also demanded they be "modern readers" who could also "take-off."

While not all the all-girl jazz and swing bands of the 1940s utilized these elements in the same ratios, ads provide an excellent starting point for talking about what the job of playing in such an organization entailed. Theater bands tended to place more emphasis on arrangements and less on improvisation than dance bands. African American bands tended to emphasize improvisation more than white bands. Lillian Carter (Wilson), who played with a number of African American women's bands, including the International Sweethearts of Rhythm, remembered many skilled improvisers among the women with whom she played: "These ladies were musicians! They could take off. They could just take off! That was it. When it was time for a solo, whoom, you got it!"[30] It would be a mistake, however, to make any hard and fast generalizations about race and music in this time period when both black and white bands were incorporating musical elements associated with black and white styles of playing. Ferguson Brothers, one of the largest black booking agencies in the country in the 1940s, consistently listed reading ability and did not specify improvisation in ads for jobs in black all-girl bands. While all the African American women I have interviewed played in bands where musicians took improvised solos, bassist Vi Wilson pointed out that there were financial considerations, as well as cultural ones, determining which bands played arrangements. While the International Sweethearts of Rhythm had some marvelous jazz soloists, they also had arrangements specially written for the band, an extravagance that the management of the lesser-known Darlings of Rhythm could not afford. The Darlings relied more on improvised "head arrangements," according to Wilson, riffs worked out ahead of time by the musicians themselves.

Most of the white women musicians I have interviewed did not take improvised solos, but some did, and most played in bands in which there were two or three good improvisers who were featured. The Virgil Whyte band was, indeed, a white all-girl band whose personnel included several women instrumentalists skilled at executing "hot" or "sweet" improvised solos. These skills were learned from other musicians — in jam sessions, paid lessons, work relationships, and friendships — and sometimes these learning experiences took place in integrated social formations. It is important to note that, as with interracial socializing among men musicians during the 1940s, mixing was often a one-way street, usually taking place in venues of black musicians. Black musicians were not allowed in most venues where white musicians played. White trumpet player Florence Shefte (Kuhn) recalled that several members of Betty McGuire's Sub-Debs went to hear the International Sweethearts of Rhythm in Detroit. After the show, the Sub-Debs went backstage and introduced themselves to the Sweethearts: "They were so gracious and friendly. We felt bad when they tried to catch our band in a club in Flint, Michigan. They were black and even though we tried to tell the manager that they were friends, he would not allow them to enter."[31] White trumpeter Jane Sager, who played in a number of all-woman bands, honed her improvisation techniques by sitting in with African American trumpet giant Roy Eldridge at the Three Deuces in Chicago. Another white trumpet player, Toby Butler, remembered learning her first riff from African American trumpet player Ernestine "Tiny" Davis during her years with the International Sweethearts of Rhythm. Viola Smith, Marjorie Kiewitt, and Roberta "Bobbie" Morrison are three white drummers who studied with the renowned black swing drummer Cozy Cole, who had a drum studio in New York (and who, himself, studied timpani at the Juilliard School of Music). White trumpeter, trombonist, and euphonium player Betty O'Hara recalled that she learned to improvise in a white cultural space: playing at square dances in Indiana. The melodies were too boring for her to repeat them over and over until the dancers were finished, so she found other statements that worked within the chord changes. Later, this skill would serve her in jazz and swing bands. White women who improvised sought membership in bands where they could focus on these skills, which were not always prized in white all-girl bands. Phil Spitalny's "Hour of Charm" Orchestra, for example, emphasized a semiclassical repertoire, instrumentation steeped in strings, harps, and a choir. Trumpet solos would involve difficult double and triple tonguing executions, but the artist would seldom, if ever, be called on to take off. When popular tunes appeared, they arrived draped in elaborate special arrangements rather than swinging extemporaneously from a hot ride tenor supported by riffs worked out by the brass section. Black women with classical training could not get auditions with the "Hour of Charm," nor could they work with other white bands, as a rule, although, as we shall see in part 2, black and white women sometimes played together in black all-girl bands.

Not all African American women I interviewed said they took improvised solos in the 1940s, but a higher percentage did than did the white women. Again, these skills were learned through participation in extracurricular dance bands, through mentorships and friendships, through jam sessions, and, sometimes, through playing along with records. Thelma Lewis's mother, a Louis Armstrong fan, coaxed her daughter to pick up the trumpet at age thirteen. Lewis, who played in numerous big bands and combos where both reading and improvising were necessary, remembered that she always tried to maintain an improvised approach even when reading. "I would read, and then I would memorize that. And I always felt, if you could *play* a song, why *read* it?"[32] In addition to the centrality of improvisation in African American musical traditions, it is important to remember that black musicians were barred from employment in symphonies and needed to know how to improvise in order to make a living as professional musicians. At least two of the African American members of the International Sweethearts of Rhythm in the late 1940s had studied classical music at Juilliard.

The vast majority of women I have interviewed, black and white, received training in school bands, where they played Western classical overtures, primers, and marches. Improvisation was not taught in high school or college music curricula in the 1940s to either black or white students; it had to be learned elsewhere, in a variety of extracurricular settings. Jam sessions where professional men musicians developed and passed along the skills of improvisation often took place in night clubs after hours and were not always safely attended by individual women. But many women did participate in these arenas dominated by men. Some women found opportunities to hone their skills while on the road by attending local jam sessions. Helen Cole and Argie Mae Edwards (Medearis) both remembered jamming in New York City when the Prairie View Co-Eds played the Apollo Theater. Trumpet player Clora Bryant, who studied improvisation by playing along with records and recording her own solos on wire recorder and analyzing them, was also an avid jam session participant on Los Angeles's famed Central Avenue in the 1940s, playing alongside such jazz giants as Hampton Hawes, Teddy Edwards, and Sonny Criss.

The good fortune of having musicians as relatives was another frequent avenue by which women could gain knowledge of jazz and swing techniques. Pianist Martha Young grew up amid an entire family of jazz musicians, including her mother, saxophonist Irma Young, and her two famous uncles, Lester and Lee, who often visited. Pianist Norma Teagarden hailed from a musical family that included a ragtime-piano-playing mother, Helen, and siblings Cub, Charlie, and Jack. She received support and valuable experience from her trombonist brother, Jack, who not only encouraged his sister's musicianship but hired her for his own well-known band on a number of occasions.[33] The good fortune to have a brother or male cousin with similar musical tastes and access to information was often a ticket to the skills and experience that prepared women musicians to hold jazz chairs in all-girl bands.

For many of the 1940s musicians, going on the road with a band provided an escape route from less desirable situations. As early as 1926, white trombonist Velzoe Brown was delivered from a dreaded secretarial career when she added her horn case to those strapped atop the touring car of the Pollyanna Syncopators. For African American women, work options were often far bleaker than the low-paying office jobs that were available to white women. Many black women chose careers as musicians over spending their lives as domestic workers or sharecroppers. Elise Blye (Henderson) found that the wartime demand for musicians made switching from Oklahoma schoolteacher to Hollywood pianist a lucrative option—her salary shot up 300 percent! Band training was often available in school, and, while it was not always recognized as vocational preparation, many women musicians received their first auditions when a bandleader paid a recruitment call to a respected high school band teacher. Clora Bryant recalled that her segregated black high school in Texas prepared boys for jobs in menial labor and girls for careers as maids. But the school band provided important additional job training, which many students, including Bryant, took seriously as a far preferable career alternative.[34]

Women as well as men were fans of the big bands, and it should be no surprise that women with school band training, especially those from musical families, should desire to play the popular music of the day as well as listen and dance to it. It was not at all unusual for narrators to tell me, as did reeds player Betty Kidwell (Meriedeth), "I was born wanting to play in traveling big bands. Dreamed about it and lived my dreams." It is also no surprise that, in a culture where women are seen as domestic rather than professional, their musical skills, acceptable in leisure, should incur substantial devaluation when wages were involved. "It was not an equal opportunity program," quipped Lillian Carter (Wilson). Laverne Walters (Wollerman) recalled, "When male sidemen were making $125–$150/week (big money then), we got $50."[35] While many women made between $75.00 and $85.00 a week, the original members of the International Sweethearts of Rhythm made $45.00 per week *at their peak,* with no extra for recordings.[36]

"We Were *Real* Musicians"

Despite wartime public acceptance of women taking up traditionally male occupations, the pressure for women musicians to look glamorous while playing did not retreat into the background but intensified as glamour became glorified as a patriotic duty. American women could serve fighting men, not only by taking war jobs, or by enlisting themselves, but by posing for alluring pictures patterned after Hollywood pinups and sending them to their sweethearts, volunteering to dance with soldiers at the local USO club, and dating and even sometimes marrying near strangers. Given the emphasis on glamour in 1940s bands, there should be little wonder that women musicians insisting on identities as serious musicians is a recurring theme in my research. Lillian Carter (Wilson) put it bluntly: "We were *real* musicians. I mean, we were not just standing there."[37]

Although all-girl bands usually played the same swing standards with the same instrumentation as men's bands and many women musicians had extensive training and experience, women's burden to prove that they were real musicians constituted a constant, additional part of the job. Bass player Vi Wilson described it like this: "When I walked in on a set, eyes was raised. When I got through playing, I made a believer out of them."[38] "We were *real* musicians" is part of a debate between dubious audiences and serious women musicians that was salient in the 1940s and is alive and well today. No matter that women "made believers" out of skeptical audiences in the 1920s, 1930s, and 1940s — the burden to prove that they are real musicians continues to fall on women jazz players. In June 1995, for example, we find the assertion that "the members of Diva, the all-female big band that kicks off the Playboy Jazz Festival on Saturday, are out to blow a hole in the stereotype that women can't play."[39] One wonders if this is a stereotype through which one can blow a hole.

Public reluctance to accept women as real musicians may be explained by Nancy Fraser's argument that terms such as *worker* and *consumer* are already gendered in capitalist societies and that women who are present in the workplace are subsequently seen as "present differently."[40] Because *worker* is constructed as masculine, women's labor must be made to look like leisure or, at least, like a private drama. American audiences are likely to see women artists as naturally expressing private emotions while accepting their male counterparts as skillfully producing public culture. Witness the widely accepted version of the jazzwoman as a girl singer, who stands in front of the band rather than among its ranks, who dresses in an exquisite gown rather than in a band uniform, and whose musicianship is conveniently masked by lyrics steeped in the emotions of private life. The immediate example that comes to mind is Billie Holiday, who continues to be celebrated for expressing an inordinately tragic private life rather than for her contributions to modern jazz.[41] When touring with Gene Krupa's band in 1941, Anita O'Day attempted to counteract the "different presence" of girl singers by wearing a band uniform instead of a gown. She hoped that the costume change would result in her being "treated like another musician" instead of as a "trinket" to "decorate the bandstand." She soon discovered that a band uniform on a girl singer, even when worn with a skirt instead of pants, did not deflect the constant sexualization and perceptions of difference that came with the job. Rather, it produced additional public interest in her private life. Dressed to match the other musicians, O'Day was perceived as sexually suspect and worthy of rumors.[42] In an era when women musicians could be blacklisted for reputations as lesbians or as sexually loose, when representations of monogamous heterosexual coupling in American popular culture were synonymous with "what we're fighting for," not all careers could afford such maneuvers.

Women's jazz history contains many examples of how women have combined or overshadowed their musical expertise with skilled performances of gender in order to make themselves palatable to the public. While the girl singer is the jazz musician most easily translated into dominant ideals of femininity, the all-girl band, with its spectacle of

Joy Cayler "Queen of the Trumpet" publicity photo, ca. 1940s. "A few glossies are included that make me look like a stripper . . . but that was the mode of the day." *Courtesy Joy Cayler.*

smiling women, dressed in unequivocally feminine attire, who either prove or fail to prove that they can play musical instruments as well as men, is yet another example of how women workers have coped with a public that "looks first and listens second." One has only to look at the publicity photos of all-girl bands to get a sense of how this imperative of difference affected women jazz and swing instrumentalists. Trumpet playing bandleader Joy Cayler enclosed the following note to me when she sent me a package of information on her band: "A few glossies are included that make me look like a stripper . . . but that was the mode of the day."[43] Smiling, made up, wearing glamorous gowns revealing plenty of bosom, holding shining horns aloft as if the tools of the trade struck female musicians as curious, unfamiliar ornaments — a different presence reassured audiences that women who played instruments associated with men retained their femininity.

Glamour as Labor

The ways in which women musicians were seen as "present differently" not only influenced visual representations of musicians in all-girl bands but contributed to numerous practical difficulties as well. Several narrators discussed expectations of some club owners for the musicians to double as B-girls, spending their breaks circulating and encouraging customers to buy drinks. Trumpet player Clora Bryant refused this aspect of the job whenever possible, telling the management, " 'I have a union card and I'm not out here to do that kind of stuff.' The only time I couldn't get away with it was in Chicago at this club. And you either did that or you came up missing. This club was run by some gangsters, you know."[44]

The sexual expectations of ballroom owners, managers, men bandleaders, and military officers proved problematic as well. As will be further explored in part 3, women musicians on USO tours often inherited the stereotype *camp follower,* a misunderstanding that sometimes led military officers to expect more than a musical stage show. This is not to say that women musicians on the road were *always* harassed by the men in the music business, or that they were *never* open to romantic encounters on their own terms, only that constructions of women entertainers and women travelers as loose women provided additional complications for members of all-girl bands.

Bass player Doris Jarrett (Meilleur), who worked with the African American all-woman combo the Queens of Swing raised another aspect of sexualization and feminization of the job when she described costuming difficulties not incurred by male musicians: "If you have on a strapless dress and try to play a bass" — here she paused to let the impossibility sink in — "you would try to pin the dress to your bra, and sometimes it would slip through. I was behind the bass trying to get my chest covered."[45] For Meilleur, glamour was not "just standing there"; it

Strapless dresses and high heels reassured audiences that women musicians were feminine as well as skilled, but they also marked women musicians as visual entertainment rather than real musicians for many audience members, journalists, and historians. Yet many women musicians recalled that it was more work, not less, to perform glamorous femininity and jazz at the same time. Frances Grey's Queens of Swing, ca. 1940s, Los Angeles. *Left to right:* Thelma Lewis (trumpet); unknown; unknown; Frances Grey (drums); Willie Lee Terrell (guitar); Doris Jarrett (bass); Elsie Smith (tenor sax). *Courtesy Clora Bryant.*

was hard work, although it was probably not recognized as such by the audiences who looked at and listened to the Queens of Swing throughout the western states. Playing the bass would have been easier without the additional labor of battling the precarious feminine trappings of the strapless gown. Her bass mentors, Jimmy Blanton and Charles Mingus, certainly did not have to struggle against their clothing on the job. Blanton, famed Ellington bassist and Meilleur's cousin, encouraged her in her bass studies when she was in high school, and the venerable Mingus, a neighbor, taught her hand placement for jazz. Both bassists passed along musical information that would serve her well in the Queens of Swing, but neither could have prepared her for the spectrum of labor required for workers in all-girl bands.

Women musicians frequently mentioned costume challenges, sometimes instrument specific, that made their jobs more difficult. Roz Cron described the pain caused by a saxophone neck strap cutting into skin exposed by low necklines. High heels were uncomfortable for anyone who had to stand for long periods of time, but they were the particular bane of drummers, who had bass drum pedals to contend with. "I always wore heels until I got to the drums and then I'd take them off," explained Bobbie Morrison, who kept a pair of flat shoes hidden behind her drums. Some female drummers kept their heels on, however. "I've seen girls do it," Morrison said. "I don't understand it because it totally changes the leverage."[46]

Other concessions to glamour required some women musicians to lose weight, although a small number of large women found creative ways around this stipulation. African American trumpet player Ernestine Davis built her size into her extroverted stage persona when she took the nickname "Tiny." An extremely popular entertainer, "Tiny" Davis was billed as "245 pounds of solid jive and rhythm" when she toured with the International Sweethearts of Rhythm.[47] White drummer Roberta Ellis (Brower), who weighed 210 pounds during her musical career, came up with the brainstorm of billing herself as "Super Woman." In this way, she took advantage of the wartime popularity of superhero comics, including the 1941 debut of Wonder Woman, who was larger than life, feminine, and an American hero. Brower claimed that becoming "Super Woman" at the drums in Joy Cayler's Orchestra improved the popularity of her act on USO shows.[48] But many other women did struggle to reduce in order to meet the standards required of glamorous female entertainers.

Myopic women musicians were often told that they must shed their glasses in order to work. Florence Shefte (Kuhn) recalled that the two glasses-wearing members of the Sharon Rogers Orchestra were given a choice before going overseas on USO–Camp Shows: memorize all the music, or get contact lenses. Worried about the constantly changing repertoire involved in playing for acts as well as playing the vast band book, Shefte and another trumpet player, Sylvia Roth, opted for contacts — 1940s style. Not the streamlined version of later years, these lenses covered the entire front of the eye, under the lid, and had to be removed with a tiny plunger. "If you wore them more than four or five hours, the liquid would disappear," wrote Kuhn. "I'd see rainbows around lights."[49]

Some bands cultivated youthful images in order to counteract the stigma of female entertainers and women who traveled as sexually excessive. Several groups, both African American and white, were billed as the "youngest all-girl band," and some bands' titles foregrounded youth, such as Betty McGuire's Sub-Debs, or schoolgirl innocence, such as the Prairie View Co-Eds. Although many of the women in these bands were, indeed, very young, it would not be far-fetched to read *youth* as a disclaimer that assured the men in the audience that the women onstage were sufficiently inexperienced in the ways of the world to qualify representing their sweethearts, or potential sweethearts, back home, that they most certainly were not seasoned vaudevillians.

Women musicians who were not as youthful as those in the "youngest all-girl bands" experienced professional pressure to pass as young. When I asked Thelma "Tommie" Dwyer what the postwar period meant to her, she replied, "The end of the war let us be gray haired and let us wear eyeglasses." On a more tragic note, for some women musicians losing their youth was synonymous with losing their livelihoods. Lee Ann Savage, pianist and arranger for the Virgil Whyte band, wrote in 1945, "I'm going on 25 now — and I know I don't have very many more years of playing in public. . . . I know how most people including myself regard 30 & 35 years old women musicians in the jazz field."[50] Whether this fear of aging contributed to her eventual suicide is impossible to say, but the loss of this musician, extremely gifted and dedicated by all accounts, who died believing that women over thirty should not play jazz, is tragic regardless. Savage was not alone in her sour impression of aging women musicians; her understanding was sadly consistent with market demands.

The requirement of performing a particular brand of femininity amounted to additional labor for women musicians. For all-girl bands on the road, the requirement of glamour complicated, and was complicated by, the requirement to travel. Ada Leonard, a white nonplaying bandleader who considered selling glamour to be a key component of her job, complained that the ballroom circuit presented special difficulties to her band because "ballrooms had no dressing rooms for women." My follow-up question was intended to probe the extent of this inequality. "Did ballrooms have dressing rooms for men?" Leonard's reply made mincemeat out of my linear thinking. "No, but you see, what does a man do? He puts on a suit. The face he doesn't bother with."[51]

Baritone sax player Ernest May Crafton (Miller) introduced the topic of glamour as labor at the end of her otherwise upbeat account of the history of the Prairie View Co-Eds. As the interview wound to a close, I asked her what she considered the most important thing for people to know about all-girl bands of the 1940s: "Sometimes we would be in one state one night and have to make it to another state the next night and might get there thirty minutes before time to appear. We had to act like we weren't tired and get all cleaned up, made up, and that was kind of hard. . . . Those one-night stands and things, we'd go up there and have to look like we were fresh as a daisy, and we were just about as dead as a lily on a corpse."[52]

Like Leonard and Meilleur, Miller was well aware of the additional labor requirements for women musicians that did not apply to men. Life on the road was different for women, not because women were inherently weaker, but because the job was different. Alighting from a short sleep in a shabby hotel — or, worse, from a sleepless night aboard a bus or station wagon — resplendent with gowns, heels, makeup, and hairdos, was an act of labor, not leisure, despite the fact that these same trappings would signify to audiences and critics (and, as I have demonstrated in the previous chapter, to an alarming percentage of historians as well) that women's bands were less serious about their music than were men's.

"Any Way You Could Travel, You Did"

Alongside the theme "we were *real* musicians," narrators often spoke of the difficulties of just getting from job to job during World War II. Travel conditions for all-girl bands in the 1940s ranged from seriously hazardous, epitomized by the constant police surveillance and difficulty procuring food and housing encountered by black all-woman bands while touring the Southern states, to the rare comforts enjoyed by the white members of Phil Spitalny's "Hour of Charm" Orchestra. Spitalny's outfit was highly unusual in that musicians slept aboard the bandleader's privately owned train cars, where each member had her own bed and closet. Bands that toured the overseas USO "Fox Hole Circuit" endured the danger of travel presented by proximity to battlegrounds and reliance on war-weary equipment; the Sharon Rogers band survived a plane crash in Japan in 1946. A plane carrying Joy Cayler's group was hit by lightning over the Pacific and forced to make an emergency landing by torchlight on what turned out to be Iwo Jima. The ship transporting D'Artega's all-girl band was attacked by submarines in the Strait of Gibraltar.

Booking agents were not responsible for figuring out how bands would get to jobs; their duty was simply to cook up lucrative schedules. Unless a band was booked on a USO tour — in which case transportation and lodging were arranged — the ball was in the bands' court to arrive at each engagement on time with the right number of pieces, play the job, and get to the next engagement, which might be several hundred miles away. Given the war-related difficulties with public transportation, many bands, men's and women's, found themselves rushing to their gigs in privately owned vehicles, sometimes with exhausted musicians in the drivers' seats. Accidents were not uncommon. Laura Bohle (Sias) remembered a harrowing bus accident in which the driver's back was broken and musicians' injuries included a broken pelvis and several bumps on the head due to a bass violin flying through the air. Because their contract had an "act-of-God" clause, the band was paid despite winding up in the hospital instead of at the gig. Toby Butler related an incident in which the bus transporting the International Sweethearts of Rhythm through southern Florida malfunctioned and was flooded with carbon monoxide: "Passersby removed us from the bus and placed us along the side of the road until we recovered out in the air." "During the war," recalled Ada Leonard, "the musicians put through a rule that a band could not drive over three hundred miles at night for one nighters. Because so many got killed." Yet many bands continued to log extra miles. Doris Meilleur recalled traveling five to six hundred miles per night. Clora Bryant said, "You'd be in Florida one night and they'd expect you to be up in New York the next night or two nights later. You'd have some awful jumps at that time."[53]

Bass player and pianist Betty Knudsen recalled overhearing a conversation in which her future bandleader, Virgil Whyte, and her parents "talked about what things were involved [with traveling in a band] and whether or not Betty would be homesick or is the sickly type."[54] Life on the road could not accommodate homesickness or poor health. Musicians, men and women, needed the stamina to endure constant travel as well as the vitality to play at every engagement. If a twelve-piece band had been promised, any fewer than twelve musicians on the bandstand could constitute a breach of contract. Getting to the job was not easy, however, and musicians who rushed to engagements did so impeded by tire and gas rationing, a thirty-five-mile-per-hour "Victory" speed limit, and low priority for civilians on public transportation.

White bandleader and trumpet soloist Joy Cayler organized her professional all-girl band in 1940 at the age of sixteen. At first, the Joy Cayler Orchestra played locally in the leader's hometown, Denver, Colorado. But Cayler was no casual fan of the big bands; she was fascinated by the world revealed on the radio, where it was commonplace to hear a favorite band broadcast out of Chicago one week and California the next. In 1943, at the age of nineteen, Cayler signed a contract with a professional booking agency and took her band on the road. As bandleader, manager, and trumpet soloist, her responsibilities included the sound of the band, all hiring and firing, and sticking to the promises she had made to all the parents to look out for their daughters, a charge she interpreted as protecting her musicians from unwanted pregnancies — yet another material reality that affected women musicians quite differently than it did their male counterparts. As one man bandleader put it, referring to the relationships between men traveling musicians and women groupies, "May stay all night with 'em — may not. And the next day we're gone. Left a lot of babies like that. Just like the GI's."[55] While most of the women musicians with whom I spoke were protective of their bands' reputations as "good girls" — understandable considering the stigma attached to loose women and traveling women musicians — one narrator remembered the name of a European abortionist that women musicians told each other about, just in case.

Among duties such as proving to audiences that girls could play swing and chaperoning young women who were really her own age, Cayler identified travel as the key challenge: "I think getting the band where we had to be was really a problem. If you had your own bus or something, . . . that would still be a problem for gas."[56] The gas and rubber shortages were palpable effects of the war, the result of sunken oil tankers, Japan's occupation of rubber-producing countries, and the priority given the armed forces' need for these materials.[57] Synthetic rubber, produced domestically in response to the shortage, made for flimsy tires.

In her "Sharps and Flats," Florice Whyte Kovan provides a fascinating view of conditions on the road from her musician mother's diary. The wife of the bandleader as well as a trombonist, Trudy Whyte was more directly involved than the other musicians with negotiating hardships and recording expenses on the road with Virgil Whyte's Musical Sweethearts. Her diary dramatizes what travel was like for the band before the USO took over their travel arrangements. Her entry for 23 August 1944 began, "About 1 AM bought 22 gal gas ($4.00). After that 35 mi before Bloomington, Ill. had burst tire. Removed by trucker ($1.00) and replace by spare (I.R.) 3 mi before Decatur, Ill 2 rear blew out." And, from her entry for the very next day: "Rode 4 mi, another blow out, R, front. Stopped car before blow out. Put on very poor spare. Put name on bus while tire was changed. Rode back to Poplar Bluff, Mo. Contacted ration bd. Made 2 phone calls to Texas ($5.35) Stayed in bus overnight."[58]

Whyte's diary foregrounds travel arrangements, with performance off to the side, a vague activity that appears to have happened between blown tires. Joy Cayler often found herself standing in the middle of the highway flagging down interstate truckers, for help with either gas coupons (the booking agency never gave her enough) or obliterated tires. "The truck drivers were marvelous," she remembered. "They had gas rationing tickets. So we could use them. And then sometimes I just got to some station and they needed a ticket and you pleaded with them to just give us some gas to, hopefully, get to the next town. And tires were a real problem, too. Real problem. But the truck drivers helped there. Any way you could travel, you did."[59]

Train travel was difficult for civilians, and segregated train travel in many states made it especially difficult for African American big bands to travel as a group from one job to another. White bands had a better chance of traveling by train, but the priority system that favored the troops made train travel a tricky proposition for bands that did not own their own train cars. Cayler had been recently reminded by one of her alumnae of a scheme she had used to get the band on a train. "And I wasn't too proud of this," explained the former bandleader, "but you had a job, and you had to do it. And so the GIs would go on first. Officers or GIs. And this is in the States. And then the next one would be anyone that was in a wheelchair, you know, or that needed help. And then it was usually the women, the wives or girlfriends, that were pregnant. And that train would fill up until I could see us not getting on. One time I grabbed a couple of wheelchairs and told a couple of girls to stick their coats in their pants so they'd look pregnant and we could get on! We got on, but you just had to do anything you had to to get there. You couldn't have half the band there and half the band left someplace." Another time, she persuaded a Parcel Post driver to deliver two stranded musicians to the band's next destination.[60]

As will be elaborated in part 2, African American bands, both men's and women's, were more grievously affected by travel restrictions related to the war effort than were white bands. Lacking access to most of the jobs in ballrooms, hotels, and theaters, not to mention broadcasting opportunities, black bands were confined to road trips of one-night stands, mostly in the South, where they bore the difficulties of gas and tire rationing along with the hardship of constant police surveillance and harassment. "You were never sure that you were going to find a decent place to stay or decent food," said Doris Jarrett (Meilleur). "And sometimes you didn't sleep; you just slept as you rode. And that was not very good. In the deep, deep South, it was terrible; it was really terrible." During the war years, the International Sweethearts of Rhythm had a bus equipped with eating and sleeping facilities to temper the risks of traveling through Jim Crow territory. Baritone saxophonist Willie Mae Wong (Scott) attributed the breakup of the Sweethearts, in part, to the eventual irreparable breakdown of their private Pullman-type sleeper bus.[61] Even with the deluxe bus, harassment, arrests, and racism were a constant aspect of their working conditions. Black bands without such transportation available also toured the South, sometimes traveling with white members who passed as black, as did the Sweethearts, under constant police surveillance, both on the road and on the job. Police enforcement of Jim Crow laws included many, often erroneous, attempts to identify and remove white band members from the bandstand.

Despite these difficulties, many narrators counted travel among their most treasured memories. Many women used the opportunity to travel in industrious and creative ways to improve their lives. For Helen Jones (Woods), travel was "equally important" as music, and she credited her band experiences with getting her out of a lonely living situation into a community that could serve as a surrogate family. Laura Bohle (Sias) took the opportunity of her trip with Ada Leonard's band through Rochester to audition for the Eastman School of Music — winning a full scholarship and a recommendation for the Rochester Philharmonic. Many women described the sense of independence they gained from traveling as well as the thrill of visiting sites they had studied in geography and history classes. While the public at large may have taken offense at the notion of women musicians enjoying their mobility while the men were at war, the women themselves spent too much time entertaining troops to see their road activities as unpatriotic. In fact, some women spoke of their travels as expressions of national love and lessons in American history and citizenship. As African American bass player Vi Wilson put it,

> I wouldn't have given anything for that experience I had out on the road. I learned how to be a better person, a better citizen, and if more children were let aloose nowadays and traveled around, the United States today would be a better place. Because you really learn that camaraderie among other human beings and other races. It learns you how to be with one another. And that's what the United States really needs. I truly mean it. 'Cause it really learns you how to live together and be what these United States stand for. Supposed to be land of the free. Freedom for everyone.[62]

"Not Just Standing There"

Lillian Carter (Wilson)'s comment, "We were not just standing there," takes on additional meaning when juxtaposed with descriptions of the labor performed by women in all-girl bands. Women musicians did not just stand there; they played the same types of music as men's bands, jazz and swing standards popularized by Count Basie, Erskine Hawkins, Glenn Miller, and Harry James, often astounding their audiences. The ubiquitous compliment for members of an all-girl band was that they played "like men." Many women I have interviewed disliked this comment, several claiming to have countered with the rejoinder, "You mean, we play like musicians." For the mainstream public, playing well amounted to skill in men and freakish behavior in women, a freakishness that became acceptable and entertaining when blended with reassuring trappings of feminine spectacle, which is also "not just standing there."

As a part of their labor in all-girl bands, women musicians actively negotiated the available pool of acceptable femininity for a public that "looked first, listened second." Sometimes they delivered the sounds and images that their audiences expected, and sometimes they stretched those limits or even defied them. This they did while performing a range of popular musical skills and styles. And, when nobody was looking or listening, they did what they had to do to get to the job. Transportation and labor crises, a swing industry boom, public perceptions of women workers as temporary, a world at war — these are the changes that women musicians played, and, as we shall see, they played them in a variety of ways.

Chapter 2

"Hours of Charm" with Phil Spitalny

Ladies and Gentlemen, tonight the Hour of Charm is celebrating

its tenth anniversary in Cleveland, Ohio. There's a story behind the ten

years of this inimitable all-girl orchestra and choir, a story as interesting

as a modern novel. So tonight, for all our loyal friends, we are going to

bring you the musical autobiography of the Hour of Charm.

"The Hour of Charm" (1 October 1944)

On 1 October 1944, Phil Spitalny marked the tenth anniversary of his "Hour of Charm" Orchestra by presenting a "musical auto-biography" on Armed Forces Radio.[1] The story was dramatized by Spitalny's all-girl orchestra and choir in an aural pageant broadcast exclusively to military personnel. The stagey reenactment of Spitalny's journey state to state in search of talented women was accompanied by the orchestra's trademark effects of quivering strings, dramatic brass fanfares, galloping rhythms, and sweeping flurries from the harp. Whether or not the musically punctuated sketch was as "interesting as a modern novel" to its GI audience, one cannot help but notice that, like many modern novels, the radio narrative failed to account for the lives and experiences of women workers, in this case, those who labored under Spitalny's famous baton. So, today, for "loyal friends" and newcomers alike, I shall re-present the musical autobiography of the "Hour of Charm," only this time the maestro will not have the last word. No, this time Spitalny's version will be placed in dialogue with the memories of the women who auditioned for and played with this most famous, and least jazzy, white all-girl band.

Hold on a minute, I hear some of you grumbling by your Philco radios. If they were the least jazzy and most commercial, why devote a chapter to them? And why kick off a book on all-girl jazz and swing bands with the story of a band that quivered and flurried but didn't generally swing? The quick answer is that Spitalny's "Hour of Charm" was so commercially successful that its sound and character became synonymous with all-girl bands for years to come. The version of musical femininity that fluttered into American living rooms for a half hour every week was the version that introduced thousands upon thousands of listeners to the concept that women were capable of playing band instruments. This was true for many African American as well as white listeners for the radio concert hall was one of the few integrated listening contexts available in the 1930s and 1940s, even though its content was dominated by white performances. African American vocalist Evelyn McGee (Stone) recalled that she had never heard of any all-girl bands before joining the International Sweethearts of Rhythm in December 1939, with one exception: "Baby-sitting one night I did hear Phil Spitalny, that name, and when they were talking about them, it was girls. And I didn't know that girls could blow horns and things."[2] When Eddie Durham hit the road with his African American all-girl band in 1943, he was often billed as "the Sepia Phil Spitalny," to capitalize on the more famous leader's name recognition, even though Durham's band played swing hits of the day rather than the light classical fare, hymns, and patriotic hoopla favored by the "Hour of Charm." Many women musicians, both black and white, were quick to tell me that the bands with which they played were "nothing like Spitalny" or "kind of like Spitalny." It turns out that the word *Spitalny* is not just the name of a bandleader but a useful adjective, with both positive and negative connotations. *Spitalny* means strings and harps and elaborate production numbers. It means an emphasis on a particular brand of femininity. And, for many women who prided themselves on swinging and taking jazz solos, it means the opposite of what they wanted to do. Spitalny disclaimers constituted the opening lines of many an interview.

This chapter is not a Spitalny disclaimer. It is a Spitalny acknowledgment. It is an acknowledgment that the Spitalny creation — the mental image of billowing dresses and cultured white womanhood conjured by the sweeps and flurries of harps and strings and high, "legitimate" soprano voices — shaped audience expectations on a mass level, for better or for worse, for other all-girl bands. It is an acknowledgment that Spitalny and his orchestra achieved the impossible: twenty years of coast-to-coast commercial success for an all-girl band, a feat that included not only concert tours but network radio sponsorships, a reward usually reserved for the most successful and famous (and usually white) men's orchestras. Door receipts from major theaters show that the orchestra was highly competitive, breaking the attendance record at New York's Paramount Theatre in 1938, and coming in second at Chattaqua, New York, only to Franklin D. Roosevelt in 1941.[3] It is an acknowledgment that, because of its reliance on past notions of femininity (notions that were already corny and nostalgic when the band first hit the airwaves in 1934, wildly out of sync during World War II, and frighteningly contemporary in the 1950s), serious women musicians holding down professional jobs were assailed by Spitalny jokes whether they played in the "Hour of Charm" or not. Finally, it is an acknowledgment that the talents and aspirations, the labor, the desires, the experiences of the women who actually worked for Spitalny are buried somewhere underneath all this. To understand something about all-woman bands of the 1940s, one must understand something about the Spitalny phenomenon.

The broadcast continues: "Everywhere he inquired in New York, [Spitalny's] friends and critics urged him to give up the idea. 'You'll never find twenty-two young girls who can play and sing your arrangements,' they said. But he had found Evelyn. And if there weren't twenty-one other talented girl musicians in New York, well then America was big and fruitful. And out of 130 million. . . . Why yes, that was it! He would conduct auditions in every one of these United States if necessary. And so he traveled from state to state." What an inspiring image! One man, who believes in women's abilities, diligently combing the country for talented women. Having found Evelyn Kaye Klein, also known as "Evelyn and Her Magic Violin," Spitalny embarks on a journey to build a band around her. But wait. Where are the other women musicians who would make up his orchestra, who, in fact, play the background to this voice-over about the scarcity of musical women? Are they working? Are they practicing? Are they living lives of musical domesticity with stage careers the furthest thing from their minds? Are they ensconced in family parlors, playing for guests, only to be overheard by the wandering Spitalny, who, beckoned by the sound of their charming accomplishments wafting through an open window, changes their lives forever with an orchestra contract? Or do professional women musicians seek employment even as the maestro scours the nation for women who can play?

It would be fascinating to know the training and work experience of the fifteen hundred women musicians who purportedly auditioned for the initial orchestra in 1934. But our focus is on the 1940s. Even so, because the talent search remained a perpetual feature of "Hour of Charm" publicity for twenty years (auditions were sometimes worked into performances as gimmicks),[4] it is just as pertinent to turn to the musicians who played during the war years and to ask them about their prior experience, training, and decision to audition for Spitalny. Their memories provide a revealing backstage glimpse into the talent side of the talent search.

Drummer Viola Smith, for one, was not sitting at home entertaining guests on her trap set (paradiddles in the parlor?) when Spitalny invited her to join his orchestra in 1942. In fact, Smith had been drumming in professional dance orchestras since 1925. She got her start in a family band known as the Schmitz Sisters (later changed to Smith Sisters), touring on the famed RKO circuit. During the same years that Spitalny debuted his all-woman orchestra, Smith traveled with Jack Fine's Chicago Band Box Revue, engaging in battles of the bands in theaters throughout the Midwest on the Keith-Orpheum Circuit, and sharing the bill with another sister act, the Andrews Sisters, whose hit "Bei Mir Bist Du Schoen" would bring fame to the singing trio in 1937. In the latter 1930s, Smith worked regularly in an eighteen-piece all-woman band on radio's "Major Bowes Show," accompanying the amateur acts in this very popular forerunner of television's "Gong Show." From 1938 to 1941, she flourished in a highly acclaimed band that she organized with her sister Mildred, the Coquettes. Frequently lauded as "Spitalny's only rival," the Coquettes were so successful and their drummer so popular that Smith and her drum set graced the cover of *Billboard* on 24 February 1940. Woody Herman offered Smith a job as a featured act in his Thundering Herd, but she turned him down because the Coquettes were faring so well and because she preferred to work as a regular drummer with a band, as opposed to a special attraction to be brought on and off at some point in the show. But, by 1941, she was ready for a change. She decided to contact Spitalny.

"I was still with the Coquettes," she explained breathlessly, as we snacked on Saltines and scotch in her Manhattan apartment. Out of the corner of my eye, I noticed a trap set shoved under the kitchen table. A four-foot-high cutout of Smith playing her drums was propped against the wall in the hallway. "We were in New York, living at the Claridge Hotel. And there's a ballroom upstairs and we rehearsed up there. And while we were rehearsing up there I told the girls, 'I'm going to audition, but I won't leave the orchestra now, but sometime in the future. I'm getting tired of traveling.' " She had invited Spitalny to come and hear her but did not want to leave her fellow musicians without giving them a lit-

Drummer Viola Smith standing next to a cutout of herself playing drums. New York, 17 October 1996.

tle notice. The diligent discoverer of talented women accepted her invitation. Her big audition, however, was sabotaged by one of the Coquettes, a reeds player who could play two clarinets at once, Rose Gilmartin. "Rose was a terrific musician," said Smith, "and she was a prankster. She had unhooked the legs of the drum. My snare drum. I was playing, and my snare drum went way down, my drum started to turn to the side and it was all chaos! All chaos! And I knew immediately who it was. Rose was the only one in the orchestra who would think of doing that. She was always cutting up." Smith laughed heartily, her admiration for Gilmartin's resourcefulness overwhelming any trace of embarrassment or frustration that may have been there at the time. "That was my audition for Phil Spitalny. But it was so bad, with everything going wrong, that he knew that it couldn't possibly be that I didn't set up right."[5]

In the spring of 1941, the Coquettes disbanded. Afterward, Smith, by then perhaps one of the two most famous woman drummers in the country (sharing the honor with Mary McClanahan of the "Hour of Charm"), worked in various groups. Then, in the spring of 1942, Spitalny needed a drummer, recalled Smith's audition, and — well aware of her skill, fame, and drawing power — invited her to join the band. She stayed for thirteen and a half years, recalling her Spitalny tenure as "a lovely life. Because you worked hard, but we played hard. We had so much free time. We had a few summers off." Many Spitalny musicians, including Smith, spent their free time studying with world-famous music teachers. Smith studied timpani with Sol Goodman of New York's Juilliard School of Music and with Karl Glassman of the NBC Symphony Orchestra. She studied with swing drummer Cozy Cole. Because she played solos, her pay was above union scale. And she was able to keep up her dance band skills in special showstoppers that she described as "a la Gene Krupa." "I used to do 'Sing, Sing, Sing,'" recalled the woman who was often billed as "America's fastest girl drummer." Smith is only one of the musicians on the 1944 radio broadcast whose experience is eclipsed by the drama of Spitalny's quest to prove that women can play.

In 1943, nearly a decade after Spitalny's original talent search, a sixteen-year-old trumpet player from Elgin, Illinois, sat down and wrote a letter to a man about a job. Phyllis Clendening's high school aptitude tests indicated that she could succeed in either music or medicine, and, if it was going to be music, she knew which band she wanted to shoot for. Phil Spitalny's "Hour of Charm" Orchestra was famous, its popular network radio broadcasts having filled the airwaves every week since 1935, the year after the band's debut in New York's Capitol Theatre. Known for their swiftly paced renditions of light classical numbers, Spitalny's group frequently featured the trumpets. Importantly, the personnel, except for the leader, consisted of women — white women, that is, a prerequisite that did not hinder Clendening or Smith but did set the orchestra beyond the reach of African American women musicians. As bassist Lucille Dixon told Antoinette Handy in 1975, "I couldn't even get an audition with Phil Spitalny's all-girl's orchestra, though I knew there were vacancies."[6] Like Dixon, the young Clendening might as well set her sights on the moon as on the Chicago Symphony Orchestra, but, unlike Dixon, who also had extensive training and experience, to dream of eventually playing with Spitalny provided a lofty, but not impossible, goal for the white trumpet student who was already shining in Midwestern band competitions.

Clendening wrote to Spitalny, but she never heard back. So she decided to approach the venerable orchestra leader the next time he came to

Chicago. With a little determination and some luck, perhaps she would be able to speak with the man who had hired so many excellent women musicians and ask his advice on how to prepare for a career in music.

Phil Spitalny's "Hour of Charm" usually played Chicago around Thanksgiving, recalled Clendening during our 1994 interview, and November 1943 turned out to be no exception. The teenager from Elgin attended the next Chicago performance, then ventured backstage. "The doorman called up Spitalny, and I heard him say, 'Send her up.' So I went up. Of course I didn't have my trumpet with me. And I didn't hit it off with him at all. I was wasting his time because I didn't have my trumpet."[7] "Well, go home, and get it," barked the orchestra leader, who was described by another auditionee as an "unpleasant bear."[8] "It was ten-fifteen at night. I said, 'Well, it takes an hour to drive to Elgin and an hour to drive back.' " "Come tomorrow," was the gruff reply. As the dazed Clendening stepped out of the theater, a stranger thrust a microphone in her face, and she found herself participating in an unexpected and surreal interview on national radio.

Man-on-the-street radio announcer: Did you enjoy the show?
Phyllis: Yes, I'm a musician.
Announcer: Well, do you have any aspirations to play with this group?
Phyllis: Oh, yes.
Announcer: That's an awfully big ambition for such a little girl!

Despite the announcer's incredulity (with its implicit caution to "little girls" against setting "awfully big" goals), Clendening made a second trip to Chicago the next day, this time with trumpet case in hand. Marveling at the good fortune of getting feedback on her actual playing in addition to the career advice she had originally sought, she arrived at Spitalny's hotel room and commenced to unpack her horn. Fighting to keep her focus on technique rather than on the curious distractions of the bandleader pacing around the room, entering and exiting, even at one point shaving, Clendening executed her most polished trumpet solo.

To her astonishment, Spitalny offered her a job on the spot. "And I said, 'But I haven't finished high school yet! I just came for criticism.' He said, 'Here I'm giving you a job — any girl in the country would give her right arm to play with my orchestra! And you tell me you want to go back to school!' " Enraged ("beet red," Clendening recalls), Spitalny sent her away. For the second time in two days, she made the long trip back to Elgin, having infuriated the bandleader she wanted so badly to impress.

She didn't think she'd hear from him again, but in March 1944 she received a telephone call ordering her to be in New York in one month to take the place of the trumpet soloist, who was leaving because of poor health. Again, she expressed her wish to finish high school before embarking on her musical career, but Spitalny assured her that she could finish high school between rehearsals. She consulted teachers, family members, even her minister, all of whom told her to go. Solo trumpet with Spitalny! A tremendous break. Not only was the "Hour of Charm" broadcast on Armed Forces Radio; it filled the civilian airwaves every Sunday night on network radio. The NBC broadcast, sponsored by General Electric, meant regular coast-to-coast exposure as well as a steady paycheck. It was one of the top trumpet jobs, possibly the highest-profile brass chair, available to a woman in the United States at that time.

Clendening arrived in New York on her seventeenth birthday, in April 1944, to find Spitalny neither knowledgeable nor interested in how to go about finishing high school long-distance. On her own, she figured out how to enroll in a public school with requirements compatible with those of her school in Elgin. As the youngest member ever hired in the Spitalny organization, "Phyllis and Her Golden Trumpet" finished high school while playing the Capitol, Strand, and Paramount Theaters in New York, rehearsing for and playing the weekly NBC radio broadcasts, and going on the road for two weeks at a time. All this she did while adjusting to an extraordinarily new way of living. Her home base became an apartment in New York, where she was "free to come and go." In contrast, road trips presented strict rules designed to protect the musicians and the reputation of the orchestra: no dating, no friends backstage, no stage door Johnnies, etc. While other bands struggled with gas rationing and the scarcity of civilian public transportation, the "Hour of Charm" traveled comfortably by train in privately owned compartment cars: "The porters were instructed by Spitalny not to allow any people in our cars. And occasionally they would get in. And Spitalny would go out there and say, 'Get out of our cars. We need privacy.' He did kind of look out for us, and I have to say that. He really did look out for me. He'd never had anyone as young as me and he kept telling the other girls, 'You look out for her.' "

On the road, Clendening discovered that the circumstances of her own audition were not at all unusual. Spitalny regularly inspected the local talent. In addition to the practical necessity of keeping the twenty-two orchestra seats filled at all times, Spitalny's reputation as a benefactor of women musicians was an important aspect of his theatrical image — auditions were good publicity. "We played all the large cities. And there were always girls standing in line with their instrument cases, waiting to audition. It was kind of nerve-racking, in a way. Maybe somebody better than you would come along!"

After her roller-coaster start, Clendening ended up staying with the "Hour of Charm" for six years, a steady job for any musician, man or woman, by industry standards. "He took great pride in picking on the new girl," she recalled. "I always said, 'If they can survive a month, they're assured of a job for life.'"

But the job did not last for life. In the late 1940s, the trumpet soloist began to see the writing on the wall. "All the big bands were folding. And I thought, 'What am I going to do if this folds up too?' No one else would hear a woman musician." The first sign of doom was the loss of the General Electric contract. Although GE had been Spitalny's sponsor since what Clendening called "the beginning of time," the arrival of television motivated the company to rethink its advertising strategies. "They auditioned us and Fred Waring for a television spot. And Spitalny would not come down in his price. Fred Waring's group, being a men's group, could wear tuxedos every week and not change their dress. But our group would have to have a different formal every week. You can't have girls in the same formals week after week after week. [Spitalny] wouldn't come down on his price. So Fred Waring got the television [sponsorship]."

The Electric Light and Power Company picked up the sponsorship of the "Hour of Charm" for CBS radio, but only for nine months of the year. The orchestra began to travel more. During the last year of Clendening's tenure, they were not on the radio at all. She began a serious search for alternatives. Despite her six years of featured national exposure both on network radio and in the top concert halls in the country, Clendening was told flat out that the Chicago radio orchestras for ABC, NBC, and CBS would not hire her, nor could she audition for the Chicago Symphony Orchestra. "So I debated long and hard whether I should go to medical school or prepare myself to be a teacher if I couldn't get a playing job. So I went back to school. I think I was twenty-two when I started college. To go to medical school would have taken too many years." Under her breath, she said, "I should have done that instead of going with Spitalny." Although she quickly added that the "Hour of Charm" was "the highlight of my life," she also made it clear how distressing it was to have her hard work and professionalism not taken seriously enough to open doors she was amply qualified to enter. In an episode of "I Love Lucy," Ricky Ricardo summed up popular opinions of the inferiority of all-girl bands when he threatened his men musicians, "The first guy who looks like he's playing in his sleep gets traded to Phil Spitalny" — the ultimate insult.

Clendening did go to college, subsequently entering another field where women were not accepted. She became a high school band director. "The music contests were a big thing. Being the only woman directing a band in each contest, I didn't know if they were going to be prejudiced or what. I always felt that I had to do more than a man would have to do. So I did my own band arrangements for all the music contests. And I really made a name for myself." While directing bands in a small Illinois town, she attended Northwestern University full-time, earning her master's. She was eventually hired at New Trier, an award-winning high school in a North Shore suburb of Chicago, where she not only led the bands but started a jazz program.

Although the "Hour of Charm" did not last forever, it did remain intact for two decades, from 1934 to 1954. During the 1940s, "Hour of Charm" performances adapted to wartime patriotism by incorporating "American Patrol" as a theme song and imparting weekly the "favorite hymns of our men and women in uniform," but the trademark image of the orchestra as a bevy of "charming," "accomplished," genteel young women remained a constant from its depression beginnings. A hint at how all these themes could be collapsed in a World War II context is evident in repertoire that spanned secular and religious, popular and classical, instrumental and choral. "In the Mood," "A Little Old Church in England," "Ave Maria," "Bolero," "I'll Never Smile Again," "Tavern in the Town," and an opera medley appeared — in that order — at one 1941 performance. One reviewer praised a comedy routine, as well, based on a mock Spitalny rehearsal. Affirming stereotypes of "girl musicians" as charming amateurs, the humor stemmed from the "gals doing everything but the right thing. Skit goes over for some nice laughs." Also going over well was the big finish, a deeply serious, if theatrically overstated, flag-waver. "To the patriotic Berlin tune 'God Bless America,' sung by the entire group highlighted by a backdrop of Uncle Sam, show is brought to a smasheroo close."[9]

The "Hour of Charm" demonstrated patriotism by performing for soldiers and sailors in such settings as the USS *North Carolina* and the Boston Stage Door Canteen and for defense industry workers in production plants.[10] When the Women's Army Auxiliary Corps (WAAC) began recruiting for a band at Fort Des Moines, Iowa, *Yank* magazine, a periodical with a GI readership, suggested, "Why not draft Spitalny's girl band into the army?"[11] *Down Beat* knew the answer: WAAC musicians would be paid only $50.00 a month, a fraction of what women musicians could make in Spitalny's orchestra, and "there are more opportunities in private life for girl musicians than ever before."[12] Spitalny's musicians made between $75.00 and $100 a week, the soloists even more. The image of the wage-earning professional woman did not fit the image that Spitalny crafted for his orchestra, however, and he continued to balance the old-fashioned image of domestic angels of the hearth that he had cultivated for his band since 1934 with patriotic musical content and frequent, well-publicized excursions to entertain men and women in the armed forces. A *Down Beat* article in October 1942 teased readers with the headlines "Spitalny Loses Tuba to Navy" but, on a closer reading, revealed that "tuba tooter" Alma Adams had married a Navy ensign and naturally would be leaving the band.[13] In February 1943, the Spitalny audition gimmick was rendered patriotic when tryouts for the women's navy (Waves) drum and bugle corps were held at a Spitalny engagement.[14] In an era when women's roles were radically changing to meet the economic and social needs of the war effort, Spitalny did a remarkable job of retooling a conservative image of femininity for patriotic duty. Although Spitalny did eventually lose some musicians to the women's auxiliaries of the army (WAAC/WAC), navy (Waves), Coast Guard (SPARS), and marines, the orchestra still managed to retain the notion of talented ladies of leisure that the "Hour of Charm" had evoked since its 1934 debut.[15]

Why was this image so successful? How did Phil Spitalny's all-woman orchestra achieve network sponsorship and national renown in the 1930s, a time when gainfully employed women were seen as stealing jobs from men? What did the successful bandleader have in mind when he built his all-woman company in the early 1930s, after leading men's big bands throughout the 1920s? And how did the version of womanhood that proved so popular in the 1930s remain popular throughout World War II when gender roles in other areas of American life were, seemingly, radically transformed?

Cultivating the Cult of True Womanhood

*It was not the novelty of an all-girl orchestra that motivated Phil
Spitalny ten years ago. It was his firm conviction that, properly trained,
women could play popular music as well as men and that they deserved
recognition.* "The Hour of Charm," 1 October 1944

*I always heard that the men wouldn't work for him because he was too
mean. They'd just punch him in the nose.* Robin Vernell Wells,
telephone interview with author

Did Spitalny hire women in the 1930s because he thought they played as
well as men? Or did he hire women because they had fewer options than
men and so were less likely to reject his surly leadership style? Or did he
hire women because he hit on a lucrative entertainment formula that
capitalized on the ideology of true womanhood in which ladies of leisure
played musical instruments in the domestic sphere as charming "accomplishments" (perceived as playing for company rather than as working
for wages). In 1938, Spitalny told *Etude Magazine,*

> Long ago, when I first set out on my experiments with popular taste, it
> was found that light music, to be entirely pleasing, must give the listener
> an impression of sweetness, of charm. And where in the world can you
> find a better exponent of charm than a charming young woman? . . . If I
> were seeking an effect of power, of heavy beats, of sort of military
> precision that commands you against your will, I should certainly not go
> to work with a group of girls. But the effect desired was one of charm, of
> mellowness, of floating, elusive persuasion. And so it seemed the most
> natural logical thing in the world to assemble a band of women and to ask
> them simply to go on being charming women in their playing.[16]

Whether Spitalny actually believed in the inherent sweetness of wom-
en's musicianship, or whether the self-proclaimed experimenter with
popular taste was also a brilliant strategist, his emphasis on charm and
difference in his presentation of women musicians was a winning tactic
for the 1930s. It was, in fact, quite similar to the tactic that had finally
won women the vote in 1920. William Chafe has described the shift in
tactics from the early to the later suffragists as a move from a discourse
of equality to one of difference. According to the later generation of
suffragists, women should vote, not because they are equal to men, but

because they are different from men by virtue of their inherently altruistic feminine natures. Suffragists such as Jane Addams assured nonfeminists that, if women were enfranchised, that difference would produce a moral and caring democracy while continuing dutifully to uphold the domestic sphere.[17]

The "Hour of Charm" musicians were acceptable to the public, not because they were seen as the equals of men musicians, but because they were seen as doing something entirely different, intrinsically feminine, domestic, and amateur, and therefore as posing no threat to the status quo. Filling the airwaves with "hours of charm" rather than with "hours of skill" or even "hours of music," the Spitalny musicians were not perceived as competing with men or as even working. In the words of their conductor, they were simply "being charming women in their playing."

"I think that Spitalny had a picture in his mind of what a girl should look like and act like," said violinist Jeanne Phillips (later Jean Soroka). "He wanted a typical American-type girl. Not forward. Sort of ladylike." Trumpet player Vernell Wells agreed that Spitalny aimed to hire a particular "type of person." The requirements (besides musical ability)? "Nobody was short haired, and everybody looked good in their clothes, well made up." Viola Smith recalled Spitalny's scrutiny of auditionees' dress and appearance, noting that he was "terrified of hiring lesbians."[18]

Like Smith, Jeanne Phillips and Vernell Wells were already playing in the "Hour of Charm" Orchestra when Clendening joined and stayed long after she left. All four musicians' photographs and biographies appear in the full-color programs that were distributed to concert audiences during the 1940s.[19] Under the heading "These Are the Girls," rows of glamorous head shots are captioned with biographical paragraphs. The eight-page program invites the reader to "meet each of them in person, and learn about their homes, honors and hobbies . . . and how they are like 'the girl next door' in your own home town." Just as profiles of female professional baseball players during the war highlighted "domestic skills like sewing and baking,"[20] biographies for the "Hour of Charm" musicians emphasized such feminine activities as "collecting big stuffed dolls" and "Southern cooking." Besides touting her youth as a selling point, Clendening's biography disclosed that she enjoyed horseback riding and has "played trumpet for only five years!" Phillips's biography declared that she "paints Mexican scenes and reads mysteries."

"Of course, I wasn't too pleased with mine," said Wells, referring to the blurb that circulated in concert halls nationwide: "Vernell Wells brings a delightfully fresh beauty and real trumpet talent all the way from Kansas City. She studied at the Kansas City Conservatory and at Kansas University. Vernell won several first prizes in National High School band competitions. Still only a youngster, she has great promise in her field. She takes time off from practice and study for an occasional swim." "I'm really not that interested in swimming," she commented, dryly.[21]

Wells's biography, like others in the program, proudly highlights her music training, awards, and social class (to be inferred from the fact that she had attended college) but ignores her work experience. References to her "fresh beauty" and the "occasional swim" are deemed more pertinent than the fact that the "Hour of Charm" was her fourth job as a professional musician. Before joining Spitalny in 1942, she had played with three other acclaimed all-women bands. She traveled on the road with Count Berni Vici's all-girl theater band from 1939 to 1941, followed by shorter stints with Herb Cook's Swinghearts and Betty McGuire's Sub-Debs. Likewise, even the professional experience of veteran drummer Smith is ignored. Although she is posed in an action shot that depicts her as practically levitating on the steam of her own drumrolls, arms outstretched, sticks in hand, and the caption below hails her as "the outstanding girl drummer in the land," there is no mention of previous milestones of a career that began in the 1920s. The blurb boasts that her "rhythm, timing, and precision" are "of a quality to make men drummers jealous" but concludes with a list of her "relaxation" activities, as if to soften the blow of her threatening skills.

Typical of the narrative line in the "Hour of Charm" program, Soroka's biography emphasizes her education at Texas State for Women and the Juilliard School of Music alongside her recreational preferences but fails to mention her three years on the road with Dave Schooler's all-woman band before joining the "Hour of Charm" in 1943. The program repeatedly constructs an accomplished young woman whose charm has been highly developed in the best schools (read "upper class") and whose femininity (virginity?) remains intact (she retains familiar "girl-next-door" hobbies) while masking any clues that her skills may have been augmented by professional experience. Even articles in the music trades emphasized nonmusical hobbies when Spitalny was interviewed about his orchestra. One *Up Beat* profile was crafted around Spitalny's claim that "girl musicians are superior," tempered by his description of what the "Hour of Charm" musicians do to unwind when they are "tired and unstrung from their work with the band." According to the self-proclaimed champion of women musicians, "they find relaxation" in "preparing their own meals," "beauty treatments," a "home making group," and "gab fests."[22] It is unthinkable that the publicity for a men's band would emphasize education and hobbies rather than prior band experience.

Wells's first audition with Spitalny occurred while she was on tour with Count Berni Vici's elaborate touring theater show. She recalled that Berni Vici's program consisted of "an all-girl orchestra, a line of show girls and a line of dancers." The band sat under a bridge, while the dancers performed above. "And then the band would be pushed forward when we played and then pushed back. There was a lot of movement on the stage." When Berni Vici played New York, Wells set up an audition with Spitalny because the latter orchestra "was more well-known than any other group" and because "the trumpets were featured."

She did not hear back from Spitalny for nearly a year. In the interim, she continued to work steadily with other professional outfits. When she finally received a call to join the "Hour of Charm," it was still not clear whether she had a job or whether she was just being tried out. She took an indefinite leave from her current position in Betty McGuire's band and ended up staying with Spitalny's organization for ten years, from 1942 to 1952.

Wells's description of the arduous labor involved in the "Hour of Charm" belies Spitalny's claim that all he asked of his musicians was to "simply go on being charming women." "He'd get extremely high-strung about how we were playing. He was not real relaxed. And we were under terrific pressure with him. For instance, you know about triple tonguing on a trumpet? Well, what he would do is take it just a little faster than anybody could play it. And this was on NBC! It was frantic, really frantic."[23]

The challenge was welcome, however, on many levels. "It required much work and practice," she explained, "and the trumpet players all kind of stood together as a group because we had so much pressure. . . . What we would do is rehearse all day Saturday and then play our program, or play some more on Sunday, because our program went on at ten o'clock Sunday night in New York. So we played and played and played until we didn't have any lip left. Then we played our program. It was strenuous." During the week, Wells recalled, the various members of the "Hour of Charm" would take private lessons and practice. "I took lessons from the first trumpet in the New York Philharmonic and the NBC

Symphony and that was the time of Toscanini. So I got to see all those wonderful broadcasts of the NBC Symphony." Besides performing the weekly radio broadcast, there were frequent theater bookings in New York, which Wells describes, again, in terms of hard work. "We played the Paramount Theatre six shows a day, and all you could do, really, is eat between shows. If you took a nap, you lost your lip. Your lip would swell. It was tough. Really tough. But we did it."

An additional chore that Spitalny required of his musicians was to play without sheet music when the orchestra went on the road. "We memorized the show every year," explained Wells, "even [pieces] like 'Rhapsody in Blue.' " Clendening also mentioned this detail, explaining that the purpose was so the music stands "wouldn't detract from the beautiful gowns."[24] Spitalny had paid $500 apiece for the hand-beaded gowns worn by the "Hour of Charm" musicians over seven layers of taffeta skirts in concert halls.[25] Again, femininity was emphasized, and additional labor masqueraded as leisure.

"He sounds like a tough task master," I commented. "Yes he was," said Wells. "Svengali, I believe they called him."

Here Come the Co-Eds

In 1945, Phil Spitalny and the "Hour of Charm" musicians were featured in an Abbott and Costello film entitled *Here Come the Co-Eds*. "It was a crazy movie," said violinist Soroka. "It was a story of a girls' dormitory, and we played the girls in the dorm. We are shown singing and playing." She went on to point out that the "singing and playing" bore "absolutely no connection" with the plot of the movie. The goofy comedy revolves around an issue quite salient in the 1940s, the democratization of college education, particularly women's education. A controversy erupts over the scholarship admittance of a dance hostess named Molly to the elite girls' college. Playing the elite but sweet co-eds who welcome the poor but sweet dance hostess into their ranks, the musicians' performance does, in fact, shed some light on the image of the brand of femininity so carefully cultivated in Spitalny's performance strategies and hiring practices. Soroka commented that the "Hour of Charm" musicians could easily be described as "typical college dormitory girls."[26]

The setting for *Here Come the Co-Eds* is the Bixby College for Young

Phil Spitalny's "Hour of Charm" Orchestra. Universal Pictures, 1945.
Courtesy of Phyllis Clendening.

(Opposite)
Vogue Picture Disk R-725.
"Rhapsody in Blue Part I" and "Alice Blue Gown."
Phil Spitalny's "Hour of Charm" Orchestra was one of
the few all-girl bands to record. It is no coincidence
that their carefully cultivated sound and image
conveyed dominant notions of idealized
white womanhood.

Ladies, where a modern (and handsome) dean heroically updates a stodgy curriculum. In one scene, students admiringly sum up the improvements instituted by the new dean: "athletics, makeup, and singing." The students also admire his courageous experiment in awarding a scholarship to a working-class Molly, who, admired by all, ultimately proves that she, too, can cultivate "accomplishments" just as beautifully as the upper-class students played by the Spitalny musicians. Never portrayed as snobs, the young co-eds are depicted as wanting to make their environment inclusive of girls like Molly, who share their values, if not their backgrounds, and who will improve their basketball team besides. They are also never shown studying or engaging in intellectual debate but are depicted instead as coquettishly dropping their handkerchiefs, giggling, and gathering in the evening for impromptu angelic a cappella singing of elaborate choral arrangements. The characterization of women college students in *Here Come the Co-Eds* resembles the well-educated but professionally inexperienced women musicians constructed by the "Hour of Charm" program — an illusion that, as we have already seen, was achieved through careful omission of work experience and the trumping up of wholesome hobbies such as "collecting big stuffed dolls."

Similar to the debates over whether women should vote, nineteenth- and early twentieth-century debates over whether women should receive higher education turned on the question of whether these changes would upset the ideology of separate spheres. As the *Ladies Guide in Health and Disease* warned in 1884, "The young lady who has acquired all the culture and accomplishments which can be secured in the schools, but has no knowledge of the simple arts so necessary to the making of a home and the proper training of a family has neglected the most important part of her education."[27] Yet, by the 1940s, college attendance had become more and more acceptable for women, and women's college education was associated with membership in the middle class. During World War II, the male-to-female ratio of college students shifted radically as men enlisted or were drafted. Women entered such previously male bastions as science and engineering programs. Even as the status *coed* was rapidly becoming acceptable, reports on college women were quick to note that the value of college to (white) women was to enable them to converse intelligently with their husbands, not compete with men for jobs. (Public discourse concerning African American college women was somewhat different, as will be explored in chap. 3.) The

cinematic coeds and the "Hour of Charm" musicians are both represented as young women who have acquired culture and accomplishments without abandoning the domestic sphere. The students at Bixby
revel in learning the skills of leisure. There is no indication that any of
them will become professional athletes, makeup artists, or musicians —
they are simply increasing their value as companions and status symbols
for future husbands. Since their years of training, hard work, and experience had for over a decade been perceived as women's natural charm,
Spitalny's musicians were the perfect actresses to portray the Bixby
student body.

The representation of femininity that Spitalny reproduced in his orchestra has its historical roots in an ideology known as the *cult of true
womanhood,* sometimes referred to as the *cult of white womanhood.*
Although the cult of true womanhood has predominated as an ideology,
Angela Davis has pointed out that this particular version of upper-class,
leisurely femininity was never available to all women. In fact, writes
Davis, the ideology of the housewife as the norm in the United States
was forged during a time when immigrant women were "flooding the
ranks of the working class in the Northeast" and millions of African
American women toiled "as the unwilling producers to the slave econ-
omy in the South. The reality of women's place in nineteenth-century
U.S. society involved white women, whose days were spent operating
factory machines for wages that were a pittance, as surely as it involved
Black women, who labored under the coercion of slavery."[28]

Hazel Carby has pointed out that, even though a life of leisure was not
a reality for most women in the late nineteenth century (or the mid-
twentieth century, for that matter), the cult of true womanhood had a
powerful influence, reaching far beyond its limited membership. Carby
describes the cult of true womanhood not only as a "dominant" image,
practiced by the group in power, but also as a "dominating image, describing the parameters within which women were measured and declared to be, or not to be, women."[29] Spitalny selected musicians who
would function as signs of true womanhood to an audience. Lucille
Dixon did not have to audition unsuccessfully in order to be excluded
from Spitalny's orchestra; as an African American woman, she was
already excluded from the cult of true womanhood, which was the organizing principle and strategy behind Spitalny's success. Additionally, the
white women in the orchestra were required to transmit the image of
idleness emblematic of true womanhood while they were working, a task

partially achieved by Spitalny's investment in the expensive floor-length gowns. Although Robert Allen had the heroines of melodrama in mind in his analysis of the "embodiment of the cult of 'true' womanhood," he could have been referring to the "Hour of Charm" uniforms when he described "dress forms . . . with yards of material billowing down over padded hips" as "giving the impression that the upper body rested on a bell-shaped pedestal."[30]

The idleness that defined appropriate middle- and upper-class white womanhood in the nineteenth century United States (whether or not it was actually lived) was not an idle quality at all but an actively produced sign of the prosperity and, therefore, power of husbands and fathers. A young woman's cultivation of what were called *accomplishments* was, according to Arthur Loesser, a status symbol, bearing witness to her "family's ability to pay for her education and her decorativeness, of its striving for culture and the graces of life, of its pride in the fact that she did not have to work and that she did not 'run after' men." Music was an especially effective accomplishment "because it would be shown off best while actually being accomplished. In this sphere, music reduced itself to singing and playing the pianoforte, though the guitar and the harp were the keyboard's occasional temporary rivals."[31]

Spitalny's "accomplishment" was to extend this status symbol of upper-class white female musicianship to such instruments as tubas, drums, trumpets, and trombones and to superimpose the image of ladies of leisure over a reality of experienced, professional, wage-earning union members. Even the figure of the coed could be said to have functioned as a modernized version of the cult of true womanhood if white college women were not expected to use their educations outside the home. Of course, many white college women did work, but the dominant belief that the coed's goal was to become a worthy conversationalist for her future educated spouse was remarkably similar to nineteenth-century ideas of women's accomplishments as domestic enhancement. Even with the expanded opportunities for education and prosperity available during the war, the typical all-American girl as portrayed in *Here Comes the Co-Eds* or the "Hour of Charm" still precluded most women's realities, even those women who filled these roles on stage, screen, and radio. Although signs of idle genteel femininity were faithfully reproduced in Spitalny's concert and programs, these were not the defining characteristic of his all-white, extravagantly gowned, accomplished, charming orchestra membership. The "Hour of Charm" musicians were also professional, competitive, and highly ambitious, or they would not have been there.

When Soroka applied for work with the "Hour of Charm," she had already traveled for three years with a swing band known as Dave Schooler's Swinghearts. "That's all it [the band] did is travel," she recalled. Life on the road was drastically different than it would be when she joined Spitalny. "In buses you slept sitting up. That's the way it was in Dave Schooler's band. From city to city. You got very little sleep."[32] When Schooler's group played in New York, the violinist enjoyed taking private lessons and decided she wanted to stay. Schooler was, at that time, trying to get his musicians to go overseas on a USO tour, an adventure that Soroka was not anxious to pursue. She arranged to try out for Spitalny.

"I had heard he was the kind of conductor that was impressed with a lot of fast notes," she said. "So I played very fast, and he was quite impressed." She also sang for him in her trained soprano voice and was told, "Violinists don't sing." But he did hire her for the violin section. "There wasn't an opening, actually, when I auditioned. Somebody else had filled it before I auditioned. He put me in in spite of the fact that there was no opening for me. And his wife, Evelyn, didn't like that. She didn't like that at all."

"Evelyn and Her Magic Violin" was the featured act around which Spitalny had built his orchestra. Evelyn Kaye was also Spitalny's lover, a factor that, along with her celebrity status, separated her from the other musicians. "Hour of Charm" musicians variously described Evelyn as "unfriendly," "temperamental," "terrible," and "unhappy." "She had a lot of technical ability," said Soroka, "but I think she was very unhappy." Viola Smith recalled Evelyn as "quite aloof. She was friendly enough, but always in her own little world, very preoccupied. She did a lot of the business, you know, she wrote the checks and she, she did a lot of business for Spitalny. He finally married her, you know. So she was really a very busy girl and we didn't expect her to be hobnobbing with us. The hoi polloi!" Conversely, the "Hours of Charm" program described her life as "a series of musical triumphs," adding that, "Evelyn is strictly feminine in her clothes and mannerisms — and insists her collection of four-leaf clovers is her only hobby."

Despite Evelyn's continued objections, Spitalny changed his mind about singing violinists and began assigning soprano solos to Soroka. Soroka became a featured vocalist while continuing to play the violin.

"That's why I say he was fair," she said. She stayed with the "Hour of Charm" until 1954, for a total of eleven years. "People tended to stay because you couldn't beat Spitalny, the good things. It's true, though, that the orchestra members didn't make [much], well, they made $75–$100 a week. But in those days, that was a livable salary. And I made $350 a week when I started singing."

Soroka married and later went back to school to earn a teacher's certificate. She studied at the Manhattan School of Music, taught for a number of years in the New York City public schools, and later taught privately. When her husband died in the late 1980s, she cut her load down from sixty-five to seventy students a week to ten in order to focus on her violin. In 1994, she belonged to three symphonies and was also giving "a lot of solo concerts."

Smith also stayed until the orchestra disbanded in 1954, after which she continued her professional drumming career until 1971. She worked as a single, "Viola and Her Seventeen Drums," and appeared in the Broadway show *Cabaret* from 1966 to 1970 as the onstage drummer in the all-girl band of the Kit Kat Klub.

"A Man among Women"

Most of the women with whom I spoke from the "Hour of Charm" described Spitalny as brusque, difficult, but, in the final analysis, a fair employer. But there is another side that sometimes emerges in conversations with women musicians about Spitalny. Despite the maestro's belief in the inherent charm of the type of woman he wanted for his orchestra, he apparently sometimes auditioned her in his underwear.

Many women told me the Spitalny underwear story. Some of them asked not to be quoted on this topic. The women who gave me permission to quote them on this aspect of Spitalny's leadership style were usually women who did not wind up working in his orchestra — understandably, they had less at stake than the women who had successfully applied for a position. But some women who auditioned for Spitalny, and won jobs, also related their trials by underwear. Some related perfectly respectable first meetings with the maestro. It is tempting not to air Spitalny's shorts in this chapter, if for no other reason than to protect the women who might be embarrassed. But so many women described the discomfort of such episodes that it would seem irresponsible to leave this aspect out entirely. Although *sexual harassment* is a modern term, not current in the 1940s, many women musicians have come to understand that it describes some of their experiences with men talent agents, club owners, customers, and bandleaders. Spitalny's modus may have been unique, but his operandi was all too common.

Many women (who will remain anonymous) told me audition stories that go something like this: A young woman shows up for her interview at the appointed time, either at Spitalny's hotel room or at his dressing room. She knocks at the door, then is faced with the decision of what to do when he answers it dressed in nothing but his undershorts. Should she forfeit the job by refusing to enter? Or should she go on with the audition, risking further inappropriate behavior?

One auditionee wrote,

> *My* encounter with the old devil was when I was playing Loew's State Theatre in N.Y.C. He called me up and asked me to come to the Central Pk. Hotel. The *only* reason I went was because of the anticipation of a higher salary, for he paid well for those times (1939). He showed up in a pair of shorts (WINTER TIME!) with those spindly legs, and I almost laughed in his face. I said, "If you want to hear me play just go down the street to Loew's State and catch a show." I rushed out of there before he could get fresh with me. Some audition!

This informant found this behavior unconscionable, choosing to spell Phil Spitalny's name as "Phil Spit-All-Over-Me" when she wrote me about this experience. Other informants expressed embarrassment, as if his state of undress reflected badly on their own moral characters. Those who balked at entering the room often felt easier about telling the story than did the women who proceeded with their auditions. Ironically, these reactions are well in keeping with the ideology of true womanhood, according to which refusing to enter the room of a nearly naked man would be the more ladylike option. Oddly enough, this audition practice would appear to risk screening out the version of femininity that Spitalny wished to promote.

In comparison with other kinds of harassment that women experienced in the band business, this scenario may strike today's reader as innocuous, but it is important to note that the shame invoked was monumental for many women musicians who conceived the "Hour of Charm" as the pinnacle of professional opportunity. Some of the women who told me this story did not know that it had happened to anyone else until I told them that I had heard the story before from other auditionees. Others had, between the event and our conversations fifty years later, managed to discover that other women had experienced similar Spitalny auditions. One woman described her audition as beginning normally enough. He answered the door wearing his clothes but "proceeded to undress" in front of her. No one told me that he got fresh with them. Would narrators have told me if he did exploit them further? Even if the Spitalny strip-tease were the only inappropriate behavior in which the famous band-leader indulged, the confusion that Spitalny inflicted on some of his auditionees left a lasting impression on who knows how many young women. Faced with the prospect of trying out for one of the best jobs for a woman musician in the entire country, the decision to enter and play for the nearly naked maestro would be understandable as well as confusing and infuriating. The decision not to enter but to kiss the opportunity good-bye would also be understandable as well as confusing and infu-riating. This behavior complicates any analysis of Spitalny's contribu-tion to the working conditions of women musicians.

When Spitalny died in 1970, Paul Bruun reminisced about his friend-ship with the bandleader: "One day, as our conversation frequently did, it turned to his experiences interviewing girl musicians. It was from this conversation that I learned how Phil determined whether or not his prospects wore falsies. Phil told me, 'Paul, if a girl's breasts move, they are real, if they don't move, she's wearing falsies.' "[33] These words, penned by a self-professed close friend of the Spitalnys, reflect an un-abashed admiration for Spitalny's exploitation of women auditionees. Bruun unself-consciously delights in Spitalny's habit of regaling his friends with the topic of his interviews with "thousands of girls." Even if the exploitation never exceeded the bounds of breast watching and an-swering the door in his Skivvies, these practices bring to mind the flip side of the cult of true womanhood. Women seeking employment were considered fallen no matter what kind of femininity they performed onstage. Without a pedestal to stand on, a tradition of protection is replaced by one of violation.

The narrators featured in this chapter all ultimately presented Spitalny as a fair employer who provided better working conditions than usual for women musicians, protected them on the road, paid them enough and paid them regularly, and provided them with private and comfortable accommodations. Musicians who had worked in other bands appreciated the value of such amenities, the likes of which could hardly be taken for granted in the all-girl band business. In addition, Spitalny treated his employees to extravagant courtesies such as the yearly Christmas party at the Waldorf-Astoria, remembered fondly by Viola Smith.

Yet, while Spitalny may have provided a safe working environment for women musicians once they were "his," the narratives of many women musicians would also indicate that he considered the thousands of unknown young women who arrived for auditions as fair game to shock and ogle. Yet he consistently expressed his mission as setting out to prove "conclusively," as he told his radio audience, "that women have a rightful place in popular music." He told the press that his target audience consisted of housewives who would rather hear "enchantment" than "flash choruses and sock endings," but in the same breath he claimed that housewives loved the all-woman orchestra because it "gave them a feeling that their sex was unshackling the conventional bonds and stepping out in the professional world."[34] However, when women musicians unshackled the conventional bonds and came for an audition, they no longer represented for Spitalny that hallowed domestic sphere of charm and enchantment. Rather, they became the kind of women whose breasts may be stared at by a man in shorts. Once hired, they donned gowns and in performance after performance hailed the domestic sphere, reinforcing past notions of femininity that haunted public attitudes about American women, even as Rosie riveted, Molly the dance hostess went to college, and all-girl bands crisscrossed the nation.

Clearly, Spitalny saw the cult of true womanhood, in part, as a kind of stage effect, or he would not have hired women who tolerated his bare knees. Yet he put enough stock in the abiding significance of the angel of the hearth to maintain this image in his orchestra throughout the war. Perhaps America's attachment to Victorian ideals of womanhood was more obvious to the Russian immigrant than it was to American patriots of the 1940s who were busy celebrating modern versions of American womanhood geared toward winning the war. Perhaps women's place was as confusing a question for Spitalny as it was for audiences to whom he was proving his point.

The orchestra knocks out a rousing version of the "National Emblem March," featuring the brass section and choir. Next comes a high soprano vocal. Finally, the ten-year-anniversary show wraps up, as it did throughout the war, with an instrumental and choral rendition of one of "the favorite hymns of our men and women in uniform." Feminine voices ride the crest of dynamic orchestral accomplishment. God is praised. General Electric is plugged. And another "Hour of Charm" is brought to a close.

Whether the product of chaos, confusion, or strategy, it is precisely Spitalny's convoluted formula — the hiring of hard-working professional women to convey ideas about feminine leisure and domesticity — that spelled his success. Interestingly, this formula is the exact reverse of the Rosie the Riveter campaign, in which a stereotype of domestic, middle-class white womanhood modeled ideas about industrious women defense workers. The "Hour of Charm" reflected and soothed ideological tensions about women's changing roles between 1934 and 1954.

Chapter 3

Extracurricular Activities with

the Prairie View Co-Eds

The absence of millions of men have [*sic*] left vacancies in many fields which are rapidly being filled by the fairer sex. At PV [Prairie View], in order that music may still be kept alive, the co-eds have taken over the horns and strings with tremendous success. — "PV Co-Eds Keep Music Alive While Boys Battle Axis"

I said, "If there's this girl band there and I can play my horn, then that's where I was going to go!" So I turned down Bennett and Oberlin and went on to Prairie View because I wanted to play in the band.

—Clora Bryant, *telephone interview with author*

Oh, we ruled the campus. We were traveling all the time, you know. And we had money! And when we'd go out on weekends, our friends would say, "Bring me something back." And we'd bring them food back and all of that. Oh, we were something else.

— Argie Mae Edwards Medearis, *telephone interview with author*

On the eve of U.S. entrance into World War II, Prairie View College was not just the biggest black institute of higher education in Texas; it was the only four-year public college in the state that African Americans could attend. Founded in 1878, when most white Texans believed that black education was impossible, foolish, and perchance dangerous, Prairie View college (now Prairie View A&M University) shares a proud history with other distinguished black colleges established simultaneously with, and in response to, the rise of the Southern system of mandatory segregation known as *Jim Crow*.[1]

To appreciate the significance of historically black colleges fully, it is important to recall that, before the Civil War, every Southern state except Tennessee legally prohibited the education of black Americans, free or enslaved. After 1865, black education was no longer a crime, but it was still hard to come by as states invented new laws that required black students to attend segregated or Jim Crow facilities. As Angela Davis observed, black people who were able to secure educations under these conditions "inevitably associated their knowledge with their people's collective battle for freedom."[2] From a contemporary vantage point that foresees, among other things, the struggles of the civil rights movement of the 1950s and 1960s, we probably should not be too surprised that the same states that demanded separate education were in no hurry to erect public black schools, especially black colleges. So, while black Americans paid taxes on schools that they could not attend, private black colleges were founded by black churches, Northern missionary and philanthropic groups, and the Freedman's Bureau.[3] Prairie View was one of a small number of public black colleges established by Southern states between 1866 and 1900.

The students who attended Prairie View College in 1940 did so at a time when three-quarters of the 12 million black people in the United States still lived in states where black education was legal only if separate.[4] Despite this formula for unequal social standing of blacks and whites, Prairie View and other historically black colleges prevailed as distinguished centers for higher education, preparing many African Americans to obtain a better and more dignified living. In 1942, Prairie View had an enrollment of 1,420 students. For women particularly — black women constituted half the student body of black colleges even before World War II — a college education provided urgently needed alternatives to menial labor. While white women with high school educations could obtain clerical positions, black women were largely barred from such work but could work as teachers in black schools with some college.[5] In 1940, Prairie View emphasized programs in vocational agriculture, mechanical arts, liberal arts, prenursing, and home economics.[6] In addition, degrees were offered in business and the sciences. Music majors could choose from several degree options in both general music and music education. Prairie View was also the home of a famous extracurricular dance band, the Prairie View Collegians.

Many black colleges in the 1920s, 1930s, and 1940s boasted popular dance bands. These bands were sources of pride as well as entertainment for black audiences both inside and outside the campus walls. Traveling entertainment from black colleges was already a time-honored tradition, dating from nearly as early as the establishment of the colleges themselves. Best remembered today are the Fisk Jubilee Singers, whose many concert tours between 1871 and 1932 raised money to expand Fisk University (founded in 1867); their tours have been credited with creating international awareness of the beauty and power of African American spirituals.[7] They also proclaimed the existence of black colleges wherever they performed. Although different from choral groups in obvious ways, dance bands combined skillful renderings of hits of the day with evidence that black colleges were alive and kicking. The activities of black college bands were widely reported in the college and entertainment sections of national black newspapers, including the *Chicago Defender* and the *Pittsburgh Courier.*

Besides the Prairie View Collegians, other popular dance bands were based at Wiley College in Marshall, Texas; Alabama State College in Montgomery, Alabama; Fisk University in Nashville; Morehouse College in Atlanta; and Wilberforce University in Wilberforce, Ohio. Many musicians from these college ensembles later became famous in the professional music world. Bandleader Erskine Hawkins got his start in the Alabama State Collegians, as did trumpet player Wilber "Dud" Bascomb, who would later star in Hawkins's famous professional dance band. Horace Henderson (bandleader and brother of Fletcher Henderson) led a dance band at Wilberforce during his days as a college student. Drummer Roy Porter and trumpet player Kenny Dorham both played in the Wiley Collegians while studying at Wiley College. Blues singer Charles Brown was a member of the Prairie View Collegians. Like most such bands, the Prairie View Collegians played for both on- and off-campus events. And, like most college dance bands of the day, the Prairie View Collegians was an all-man organization.[8]

However, during the auditions of 1940, bandleader Will Henry Bennett was inspired to make an exception to the men-only status. A gifted alto saxophonist named Bert Etta Davis arrived on the campus that fall. Not only did she possess a serious desire to play in the dance band, but she already had the skills and practical experience that would make her a valuable member. Despite being both a woman and a first-year student, Davis tried out for the famed Prairie View Collegians, the only woman to do so. After waiting for her name to be called — she was twenty-seventh on the roster for saxophonists — she proceeded to dazzle onlookers with her mature jazz playing. There was no doubt that she could read the charts, and she could solo, besides. By the time the dust settled, the woman alto player from San Antonio had walked away with the third saxophone position.

Unfortunately, as Davis explained to Antoinette Handy in 1980, she was prevented from occupying that coveted chair, not by the bandleader, or by disgruntled saxophonists, not by the head of the music department, or by the president of the university — all men — but by the dean of women, who found the concept of a college woman in an all-man dance band entirely inappropriate.[9] Women students played alongside the men in the marching band and the concert orchestra, even in the ROTC band, but the dance band apparently carried less agreeable connotations.

The world was changing rapidly in 1940. The effects of wars in Europe and the Pacific would soon be felt at the Texas college, even filtering down to such entrenched notions as what was considered appropriate regarding college bands and college women. The same semester that Bert Etta Davis tried to join the Prairie View Collegians, the Selective Service Bill was passed by Congress. Men college students were required to register for the draft; military camps were being established in nearby towns. Prairie View was briefly considered as the site for a training school for black pilots, but the Tuskegee Institute in Alabama was chosen instead. Men college students signed up for programs like ROTC with the hope, and sometimes the promise, that they would be allowed to graduate before being called up. The Prairie View Collegians began entertaining the troops, adding military training camps to their performance schedules.

On 2 January 1943, the *Chicago Defender* reported, "Will Henry Bennett and his Prairie View Collegians set something of a record for the number of soldier dates played in one week while on his Christmas tour of army camps, flying fields and USO centers 'deep in the heart of Texas.' They played five engagements for the soldier boys within five days."[10] During the next few months, many of the young men who spent their 1942 Christmas vacation playing for soldiers became soldiers themselves. By the spring of 1943, so many had been drafted that the Prairie View Collegians had become a much smaller band. It still played on- and off-campus events, but there was no guarantee regarding how long the remaining members would be allowed to stay in school. So, in February 1943, Will

Henry Bennett began recruiting women for an all-woman dance band, the Prairie View Co-Eds. Bert Etta Davis, by then a public school music major and secretary of the junior class, would be its star soloist.

The Prairie View Co-Eds of 1943

Margaret Grigsby was a senior biology major with medical school ambitions when Bennett recruited her for his all-woman band. When I interviewed her in October 1997, Grigsby was a retired doctor and emeritus professor of medicine at Howard University, the well-known historically black college in Washington, D.C. According to Grigsby, her college band activities had been recreational only; unlike some other members of the band, she had no professional musical ambitions. Medical school had been her dream since high school, and she was on that path when she played with the Co-Eds. Nonetheless, she spoke fondly about her band experiences, about traveling to places she had never been before, playing opposite celebrities (including Ella Fitzgerald), and performing at the Apollo in New York City in the summer of 1944. She also seemed to get a kick out of the surprised reactions of her fellow doctors as she introduced me as a writer from California who had come to interview her about all-girl bands.

"It was just something extracurricular," she explained. "It wasn't any big deal as far as I was concerned. I just liked doing it."[11] Grigsby grew up in a family where everyone played a musical instrument: "My father played a guitar, my brother cornet. Both my sisters played the piano." Grigsby played trombone at Jack Yates High School in Houston before entering college in 1939. Throughout her college years, she played in the marching band and the concert orchestra (both of which actually were coed). It was from this pool of women musicians in existing bands that Bennett was able to fill the chairs of the Prairie View Co-Eds' sixteen-piece dance orchestra. As a trombonist, Grigsby was instantly recruited for one of the harder-to-fill positions. She enjoyed the new activity but was also deeply affected by the more unpleasant changes taking place on the campus during her senior year: "The Selective Service told the guys that if they'd join some type of group [presumably the Army Reserves or ROTC] they would be exempt from the draft until they graduated." She lowered her eyes and shook her head. "They just suckered them. They swept in on the campus and took every guy they could get their hands on.

Dr. Margaret Grigsby had a distinguished career as a doctor after her experiences as a trombonist in the Prairie View Co-Eds. Howard University Hospital, Washington, D.C., 30 October 1997.

So that didn't leave anybody playing in the [marching] band except mostly girls and a few boys that were too young to be in the draft. In order to have any type of college dances and so forth, the girls in the band were formed into a girls orchestra."

Between the fall of 1941 and the fall of 1943, the number of men enrolled in black colleges was cut in half.[12] Although the draft and enlistment also tipped the gender balance at mainstream (white) colleges, the ratios of men to women were markedly different. White college populations had contained far higher numbers of men than women before the war, but, because black colleges were already composed of equal numbers of men and women students, the disappearance of half the men resulted in a student body where women outnumbered men to an even greater degree than was the case in white colleges.[13] Grigsby recalled that the men musicians had turned down an opportunity to enlist as an intact service band because they believed that they would be allowed to graduate. It is not possible to say whether this promise would have been kept. As in other wars, recruitment offers in World War II did not always materialize according to plan. But many of the men students from Prairie View would regret not having accepted the recruiting offer.

Another musician recruited for Bennett's new band was Bettye Jean Bradley (Kimbrough), a sophomore music education major and alto sax

(Above)
Bert Etta Davis in the foreground
playing the alto sax. The Prairie View Co-Eds
in the background are (*left to right*) Bettye
Bradley (tenor sax), Una White (trumpet), and
Izola Fedford (trumpet). *Courtesy John B.
Coleman Library, Prairie View A&M
University, Prairie View, Tex.*

Bert Etta Davis,
Prairie View College yearbook, 1942–43.
*Courtesy John B. Coleman Library,
Prairie View A&M University,
Prairie View, Tex.*

player from Alto, Texas. A member of both the marching band and the ROTC band, Bradley was a prime candidate for the all-woman dance band. Bennett asked her to join. She accepted, although she had to seek her parents' approval since the band would play off-campus engagements. The bandleader then switched her from alto sax, which she had played in high school, to tenor sax, which was OK with Bradley, who was pleased to discover that it was easier to maintain an acceptable tone on the larger instrument.

Although new to the tenor saxophone, she was no novice when it came to performing music. In Bradley's words, she had played her first instrument, piano, for her church choir "three-fourths of my life from the time I was about nine. I started playing very, very young. And my mother was not a particular fan of boogie-woogie and that was about the right thing at that time." In other words, it might not have been "right" for her mother, but it was the "right thing" for Bradley and for fans thrilled by the enormous comeback the boogie-woogie piano style of the 1920s was making in youth-oriented big band music. Bradley enjoyed popular music styles and spent many hours in the local honky-tonk listening to the jukebox for "anyone who had a good beat." Hoping to steer her toward a career as a concert pianist, her mother sent her to piano lessons, where she learned Beethoven and Chopin. But Bradley's taste in music lay elsewhere and revealed itself in what her mother considered inappropriate ways — such as improvising in church as she accompanied the choir. "Of course I put a lot in it that wasn't in it and my mother gave me the eye!" Bradley laughed at the memory. "And threatened to kill me." She lowered her voice to reproduce the gravity of her mother's disdain for such frivolity. "She did *not* approve." Her mother never came to hear the Prairie View Co-Eds, not even when they traveled throughout Texas, but, as Bradley noted, "I was lucky my mother let me go in the first place. Only after she found out we'd be well chaperoned!" [14]

After filling as many positions as possible with members of the marching band, concert orchestra, and ROTC band, Bennett relied on the flexibility of women music majors to fill the remaining instrumental needs. Argie Mae Edwards (Medearis), a music major from Waco, Texas, was a pianist, but Bennett gave her a vote of confidence as an aspiring band and orchestra teacher when he recruited her for the double bass. "I wasn't playing the bass," said Edwards, "but I had a knowledge of just about all the instruments. They needed a bass player and they didn't have one. So one of the fellas on the campus who did play bass with the male orchestra taught me to play bass. His name was Thomas Cleaver. And so, that's how I made it." Margaret Bradshaw had played saxophone in her high school band in Denison, Texas, but she, too, was asked to learn another instrument as Bennett completed his new dance band. "Those of us in the music department were used to fill in. For example, he only had one trombone, so he gave me a trombone."[15]

Other members of the original Prairie View Co-Eds included saxophonists Charlotte Sims, Bernice Payne (Posey), Melvia Wrenn, and Elizabeth Johnson and trumpet players Marcellus Gauthier and Flores Jean Davis (Webb), assistant secretary of the junior class. As a school band, the Prairie View Co-Eds would suffer steady personnel shake-ups, its ranks raided annually by graduation and at any time by marriage or the patriotic and economic lure of defense jobs. Bennett expected that each year he would need to replace some members — but at least they would not be drafted.

The first version of the Prairie View Co-Eds initially played on campus for dances and events but soon began venturing off campus on weekends, as Bennett arranged for the band to entertain at military bases, theaters, nightclubs, and dance halls in neighboring Texas towns. "He immediately started booking us to play for dances," recalled Bettye Bradley (Kimbrough). "We played in Beaumont, Port Arthur, Houston, just everywhere. There were no men orchestras." Argie Mae Edwards (Medearis) concurred, adding that "during the holidays we would play at the different army camps, Fort Sill, Oklahoma, and all of these air bases here in Texas."[16] Edwards explained that the men's band had been playing off-campus events on weekends but had lost too many of its key players to keep up the pace. So, when the Co-Eds got on their feet, Bennett took the women's band out to fill the local demand for dance bands in both black and white segregated venues. Carl Owens, a talented member of the Prairie View Collegians, took over what was left of the men's band.

At the same time that the Prairie View Co-Eds started to tap the potential of the local dance band shortage and fill the entertainment needs of nearby military camps, a number of African American all-woman bands were enjoying enormous success on a national basis. The International Sweethearts of Rhythm, another band to have originated from a black school, had by 1943 abandoned their affiliation with the Piney Woods Country Life School and were enjoying tremendous popularity on the black theater circuit — the Apollo, Baltimore's Royal, Washington, D.C.'s, Howard Theater. Eddie Durham's All-Star Girl Orchestra — a band built around a nucleus of musicians lured away from the Sweethearts — was formed in January 1942. Durham's All-Stars were already playing major venues such as the Apollo Theater when they were snapped up by Moe Gale's high-powered New York agency in November 1942.[17] The Sweethearts and Eddie Durham's All-Stars also played one-nighters across the South, in dance halls, theaters, and military camps. They were written about (and pictured) regularly in the black press with the same kind of hyperbolic showgirl adjectives that characterized mainstream (white) press reviews of white all-girl bands. "America's great aggregation of gingervating, glamorous gorgeous gals" was the phrase used in a black newspaper story to describe Eddie Durham's All-Star Girl Orchestra. Interestingly, although, like the white press, the black press emphasized beauty, sex appeal, youth, and marital status, when reporting on all-girl bands, it did not routinely obsess over such questions as, "Can girls swing?" as did the white-owned music trades. *Music Dial,* a black-owned trade magazine, often featured articles written by black women musicians, including trumpet player Doli Amenra and bassist Margaret "Trump Margo" Gibson. (Doli Amenra [sometimes Armenra], also known as Dolly Jones and Dolly Hutchinson, was the daughter of Dyer Jones, another black woman trumpet player.) The same *New York Age* reviewer who coined "gingervating" segued easily into the pronouncement that Durham's All-Stars were "femininity possessing musical adroitness."[18]

Within the first four months of the Prairie View Co-Eds' existence, promotional photographs were taken. One presented the brass section in profile: seven young women wearing long floral print skirts, holding their horns to their lips. The trumpet players faced right with the bells of their instruments pointed downward; the trombone players faced left, with their slides angled upward. The overall effect created a theatrical design of diagonal brass tubing. In another shot, the saxophone section, carefully posed in two rows, faced the camera, holding their instruments ready to play. Apparently, someone at Prairie View (Bennett, perhaps?) already understood the commercial potential of the band during World War II. In fact, the costumes worn by the musicians for their publicity photos were nearly identical to those often worn by the International Sweethearts of Rhythm, perhaps in hopes that the association would boost the newer band's popularity.

In the *Chicago Defender* of 17 April 1943, a photograph of eight

Brass section, Prairie View Co-Eds, 1943. *Top, left to right:* Flores Jean Davis
(trumpet), Margaret Grigsby (trombone). *Middle, left to right:* Marian Bridges (trumpet),
Margaret Bradshaw (trombone), Fannie Drisdale (Burt) (trombone).
Seated, left to right: Una White (trumpet), Marcellus Gauthier (trumpet).
Courtesy Ernest Mae Crafton Miller.

members of the International Sweethearts of Rhythm wearing white
peasant blouses, large beaded necklaces, and long skirts that wrapped
around and tied in front illustrated the story "South Likes Them Plenty."
The caption below boasted, "They are booked for return engagements in
the East but are finding trouble getting out of the South because of
increased demands for their services at dances and theaters." On 5 June
1943, accompanying the story "Texas Gals Step out in Music," the paper
published a portrait of the Prairie View Co-Eds' six-woman saxophone
section, wearing the same style of peasant blouse, jewelry, and long skirt.
The accompanying text predicted imminent stardom: "The talk of the
Southwest now is this Prairie View Co-Ed band. . . . So far the aggregation has been heard only in its section of the country but plans a nation-

wide tour this summer and early fall." Although it appears that the summer tour did not materialize for 1943, the women with whom I spoke did recall the band venturing further afield the following academic year, especially during the summer of 1944. Bennett prepared for this expansion by focusing on recruitment.

More professional, experienced players were needed if the Prairie View Co-Eds were going to succeed nationally instead of just locally. Bennett, who had attended Wiley College, home of the famous Wiley Collegians, drew on his collegial connections for leads on women players. Saxophonist-turned-trombonist Margaret Bradshaw has come from a small high school in Denison, Texas, where two Wiley alumni, Walter Duncan and Conrad Johnson, served as band directors and music teachers in addition to teaching other subjects. When Bennett communicated with his colleagues in Denison, he received fortuitous news. Not only were three outstanding women players soon graduating from Terrell High, but all three were regular members of a local coed swing band, playing alongside their teachers for proms and dances in and around Denison. Two trumpet players and a drummer—Bennett had hit the jackpot.

The Terrell High Contingent

When Clora Bryant turned sixteen on 30 May 1943, her prospects were taking a turn for the better. The previous year, her world had nearly collapsed. Her father, who had raised her and her two brothers alone after the death of her mother in 1930, had been falsely accused by some white men of stealing a can of paint. For this, he was assaulted, sent out of Denison, and warned not to come back. Bryant spent many anxious months living with relatives under less than ideal conditions, having already been separated from her brothers because of the war. Her brother Mel had gone to California to join the marines. Her oldest brother, Fred, had been drafted into the army in the summer of 1941. With Fred's departure, Bryant picked up the trumpet he left behind and learned to play it, hoping to join the new marching band that was going to be instituted at Terrell High in September. Not knowing whether she would ever see her father or her brothers again, Bryant poured herself into school activities, especially music. She ran errands and baby-sat for her band teacher, Conrad Johnson, in exchange for private trumpet lessons.

Soon, in addition to playing in the school marching band, she was a member of the municipal band. She also played in a swing band with her teachers and classmates. By the time her father was finally able to secure the protection of an influential politician and return to Denison (after nearly a year of exile), Bryant had become a highly skilled and versatile trumpet player. She was conversant with a variety of genres, including marches, classical, and swing. In the jazz idiom, she invented her own solos and could reproduce famous solos from records (a valuable skill for dance band musicians of the time). As her senior year drew to a close, she received scholarship offers from Bennett College in North Carolina and Oberlin College in Ohio.[19]

And then came a third offer. Bryant easily recalled the details leading up to what was to be a pivotal decision: "My band teacher who had taught me trumpet, Conrad Johnson, he knew the band director at Prairie View College. He told Mr. Bennett about me on account that they had this girl band. And so when it came time for me to make up my mind for where I was going to go, they told me that there was an opening at Prairie View in this band." There were no scholarships available, but Bryant was not easily discouraged. "I said, 'If there's this girl band there and I can play my horn, that's where I was going to go!' So I turned down Bennett and Oberlin and went to Prairie View because I wanted to play in the band. My brother [Fred] was in the service, and he said I could get his allotment money. He would put me through school."[20]

With her brother's financial help and the money she would make working in the band on weekends, Bryant could go to Prairie View and continue playing a range of musical styles that included swing and jazz. Had she gone to Bennett or Oberlin, her musical education would have been in the European classical tradition only. Already engrossed in jazz, Bryant knew that this was the music she wanted to pursue. She also knew that opportunities for African Americans in the classical music field were scarce. A black woman trumpet player would have a difficult enough time carving out a career in jazz; attempting to blaze trails in the field of classical music would have been an additional hurdle, what Jon Michael Spencer calls "crossing the essentialist color line" or performing a genre widely thought to require characteristics that were essentially white and European. These prejudices continue to plague many classically trained African American musicians. One can imagine how difficult this career choice would have been in the pre–civil rights movement years and before symphonies implemented such practices as blind auditions (playing behind a screen so that the judges, in theory, base their rating on skill alone). And it would have been especially difficult for an African American woman who had already crossed the "essentialist gender line" by playing trumpet, an instrument commonly associated with men.[21]

Fortunately, choosing jazz as a performance goal was no sacrifice for Bryant. And, fortunately, at the same moment as she was looking for a college where she could pursue a degree and her musical aspirations at the same time, Prairie View was looking for a woman trumpet player who could improvise. As second trumpet in the Prairie View Co-Eds, Bryant became one of the most vital players, esteemed for her ability to dazzle audiences with her own improvised solos as well as her note-for-note, nuance-perfect renderings of famous solos of Harry James, Dud Bascomb, and other trumpet soloists then popular.

Trumpet player Elizabeth Thomas (Smith) was also a senior at Terrell High in the spring of 1943. She expected to play in the local dance band that summer and then, in September, to enter Wiley College in Marshall, Texas. To her knowledge, there was no band for her to play in at Wiley. But the Music Department had a good reputation, and her impressive band teachers, Wiley alumnae, were living proof of the college's merits. But then, as she recalled, "Will Henry Bennett heard of the three musicians in Denison. After he contacted our parents and we all discussed it, we all decided that we wanted to go to Prairie View." As with Bryant, the deciding factor for Thomas in choosing Prairie View was the chance to play with the all-girl swing band. The opportunity to play professional jobs on weekends was enticing, offering not only practical experience and the chance to travel but also the prospect of earning some money. "It was pretty good for us," Thomas elaborated. "We were able to pay some of our tuition, you see. We had to join the union [the American Federation of Musicians], and each year, the salary would increase. So that was really nice. That really did help our parents out a whole lot with our tuition."[22]

"The band is the *only* way that I had of trying to put myself through school," emphasized Helen Cole, the third Terrell High graduate who chose Prairie View that year in order to play with the Co-Eds. Cole played French horn in her high school band but switched to drums "on a dare." "I was the president of the class," she explained, "and I was putting on a program. The program had to consist of kids in my immediate class, see? And it was a musical. . . . We had everybody in our class but the drummer. So I had to appoint somebody to play the drums." The actual drummer for the school band was in another class, but his brother was in Cole's class, so she decided to appoint him. "I said, 'Well, since you live together, you should be able to learn how to play.' But he said he wasn't going to do it. And so I said, 'Well, let me show you how.' And then I just sat down and started playing. Then the teacher said, 'Helen, you should play.' And I said, 'Oh no, no, no. I can't do that.' And so he said, 'Yes you will. You'll do all right.' I said, 'No, no, no, no.' Well, he made me play anyway. So that's really how I started." With the encouragement of the music teacher, she survived the program and discovered that she enjoyed playing the drums too much to stop. Now, the opportunity to play drums in the Prairie View Co-Eds made it possible for the daughter of a widowed domestic worker to enter college and pursue a business degree.[23]

"Somehow, I was in contact with Mr. Bennett. I don't remember that part. But, evidently, he knew that he was getting a drummer. They didn't have a female drummer when I went down there." Like Bryant and Thomas, Cole had already gained valuable dance band experience by playing in a swing band with her teachers. When she arrived at Prairie View, it was soon clear to Bennett that Cole was a much more experienced dance band drummer than the drummer who was playing with what remained of the Prairie View Collegians: "They had a boy that played *at* them, but I had *experience* with playing because I played all the summer before I went to college. So I played with the boys sometimes."

In three short years, Prairie View College had gone from a place where the dean of women considered it inappropriate for a young woman to play in an all-man dance band to a place where the woman drummer from the all-girl band was often asked to sit in with the men and pick up the beat.

The students who joined the Prairie View Co-Eds in the fall of 1943 had a different relationship to the band than those who had played the previous year. Unlike the earlier musicians who happened to be on campus when the band was formed, many of the new members were drawn to the Texas college, in part, *because* of the all-girl dance band. Some, like the Terrell High contingent, had been recruited especially for the band. In this way, the character of the band was changing from an extracurricular activity to a training ground that attracted professionally inclined musicians.

The May 1944 *Prairie View Bulletin* reflected the new university atti-

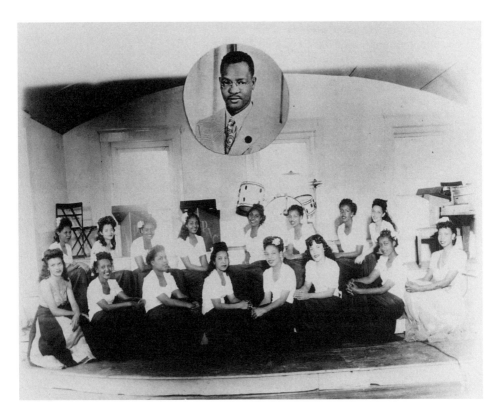

The Prairie View Co-Eds of 1944. *Top, left to right:* Elizabeth Thomas, Bobbye Jean Barton Nunn, Bert Etta Davis, Margaret Grigsby, Doretha Williams, Melvia Wrenn, Jewel Simmons, Flores Jean Davis. *Bottom, left to right:* Marian Bridges, Argie Mae Edwards, Bernice Payne Posey, Marcella Gauthier, Clora Bryant, Ernest Mae Crafton, Helen Cole, Nelda McElroy. *Center:* Will Henry Bennett.
Courtesy Ernest Mae Crafton Miller.

tude toward women musicians: "In an attempt to widen the scope of job opportunities Prairie View takes advantage of even hobbies as a possible means of making an honest living. Thus the famous all girl orchestra— 'The Co-Eds' are encouraged to develop into the best aggregation of its kind in America."[24] "That was just what I always wanted to do," said Ernest Mae Crafton (Miller), a tenor saxophonist from Austin, Texas. "I used to sign autograph books in high school [that] I wanted to be an orchestra leader, but the closest I could get was performing in one." Crafton's inspiration had been sparked, in part, by attending a performance of the International Sweethearts of Rhythm when she was a child.

In fact, her first offer to play in an all-girl band came immediately after that memorable Sweethearts performance — a little too immediately for her to be able to accept since she was only eleven. After the concert, Miller had been invited to play the piano for Dr. Laurence C. Jones, founder of the band as well as of the Mississippi school at which the band was based. "And he talked to my mother and all and he said he'd like to take me to Piney Woods, Mississippi, and he wanted me to play Spanish guitar. You know, they were going to teach me to do this! And I couldn't get any kind of positive reaction from my mama. . . . Oh, I just cried and I really wanted to go with them. I didn't have much sense. And I was just a little kid. And mama didn't know, you know. He seemed like a real nice man, which I'm sure he was, but it was kind of risky to just jump up and leave!" Instead, Miller finished junior high and entered high school, where she learned to play a mean tenor sax in the school band. As graduation approached that spring of 1943, the all-girl dance band at Prairie View College seemed a fine prospect to Miller as well as to her mother and grandmother. "When I went to Prairie View, they were happy for me to play with the band. They didn't have any objections to me being a jazz musician or playing in an orchestra and all. It was nice, then, after I got grown enough."[25] Bennett shifted her from tenor to baritone and she spent two years producing a rich bottom for the Co-Eds' six-person saxophone section.

Not all parents were agreeable to the idea of their collegian daughters spending weekends on bandstands in nightclubs and dance halls. For many African American families, being able to send a daughter to college meant improving her life chances in a social structure that placed black women at the very bottom. Most African American women expected to work, but the relative protection of a college education could afford dignified options, as teachers or nurses, for instance. Opportunities for black women were expanding during World War II, and the hopes that black families invested in collegian daughters grew accordingly. Not only were black college women expected to liberate themselves from menial labor and to achieve or maintain a hard-won place in the black middle class, but they were also often expected to return to their communities after graduation to share their skills and "lift the race." As the author of a 1948 article on women in black colleges put it, "Perhaps it is in the area of community leadership where the responsibilities of the Negro college woman are largest."[26] For a number of reasons, playing in nightclubs and military camps in an all-girl jazz band was not always seen as the appropriate image to accompany these crucial hopes for safer, more dignified lives for black daughters.

Margaret Bradshaw's parents and grandparents were among those who strongly disliked the idea of a college woman in the family playing in a dance band. "We played army bases," said Bradshaw. In contrast, when she lived at home, she was not even allowed to wait at a bus stop if there were soldiers standing there. "I remember we played [at an army base] in San Antonio. And we played a nightclub in Dallas. We did many engagements. We were away from school quite a bit. That was another thing that my folks didn't like."[27]

Prairie View sent chaperons with the band to protect the young women, to regulate their behavior so that it was consistent with college policies, to present a respectable impression of Prairie View campus life to off-campus audiences, and to set the minds of parents at ease. As with most Southern black colleges of the time, the rules on campus were very strict, especially with regard to the separation of men and women. Saxophonist Bettye Bradley (Kimbrough) recalled that she was briefly suspended from the band for hugging a soldier after a concert. She had grown up with the young man in Alto, Texas, and, when she saw him in his uniform in that Dallas audience, a hug seemed appropriate. "I had known him all my life. He was my girlfriend's brother. My best friend's brother. I had been around him all my life. What was I supposed to do? Run up there, and shake his damn hand?" The chaperon's response? "That wasn't behavior becoming to a lady." Bradley was soon allowed back in the band, but the message was clear. Coeds had to adhere to a standard of behavior. In their free time on the road, the musicians could go out only in groups, there was no one-on-one dating, and there was very little fraternizing with the soldiers except from the bandstand. But, for those, like Margaret Bradshaw, accustomed to even stricter rules, the band rules were not hard to accept: "Oh, it was beautiful. You know, I was young, we were all single, and we were so popular. I got loads of letters from soldiers who had heard us play, and it was just that kind of excitement. For a young girl, it was virtually remarkable. I came from a country town where the only time I could leave home to go anywhere was with my cousins who were boys. So that was really something."[28]

Then one night, as the band played a nightclub in Dallas, Bradshaw's father appeared to see for himself what this time-consuming extracurricular activity was all about. By this time the band's repertoire included many blues, jazz, and dance tunes of the day — Count Basie's

"One O'Clock Jump," Erskine Hawkins's "Tuxedo Junction," etc.—not "feminized" à la Spitalny but played as close as possible to the styles of the famous jazz and swing bands that recorded the tunes. The *Chicago Defender* noted that the band played Erskine Hawkins's "Don't Cry Baby" at a USO show in Lawton, Oklahoma, so well "that they had to repeat it several times."[29] Bradshaw's father was not pleased with these accomplishments: "He was really astonished at my playing that kind of music, probably blues or something. And I was learning how to drink, and I had a cup of something set down beside the bandstand, and he didn't like that. So I guess when he came back—my mother and dad were separated—I think they must have gotten together and decided that I would not be in the band anymore." Bradshaw speculated that her father "just didn't think that orchestra life for a girl was what he wanted for his daughter. And neither did my mother."[30]

The heartbreak of having to leave the band intensified when Bradshaw learned that the Prairie View Co-Eds planned to embark on a cross-country tour that summer that would culminate at New York's Apollo Theater. "I didn't go to New York with them," she lamented, but the summer tour of 1944 still worked to her advantage. "I was so upset because they were going to New York to play at the Apollo and I was no longer with them. And I could have been with them. My folks wouldn't let me get back in it. They promised that, if I would be calm, I could go to New York City and work on my master's degree. And they held up their word." After graduation, Bradshaw finally got her trip to New York, where she earned a master's in music and music education at Columbia University.

Coeds on the Road

Margaret Grigsby had already graduated when the band's professional engagements began to pick up, but, because she was still in the vicinity—she taught for a year in nearby Goose Creek, Texas, before going off to medical school—she continued to play with the Co-Eds: "I think it was the year [after my senior year] when they decided that we would go on tour around different places in the country." Newspaper reviews and the memories of other musicians confirm that it was the 1943–44 academic year. "They decided that, in order to get us accustomed to playing before large groups, when they brought a group to Houston to play for a big dance, we would play at the intermission." The long list of big names for whom the Prairie View Co-Eds played intermissions included singer Ella Fitzgerald and former Ellington trumpet player Cootie Williams, who was at that time leading his own popular band. Helen Cole recalled that the band played intermissions for an appearance by prizefighter Joe Louis. At some point, the Co-Eds played a battle of the bands with Eddie Durham's All-Star Girl Orchestra, a date well remembered by Durham trumpeter Thelma Lewis. "They beat us, though!" admitted Lewis. "[The Prairie View Co-Eds] had a better band."[31]

Clora Bryant remembered many celebrity intermissions at Houston's Civic Auditorium during this time period as well as at such other Houston venues as the Down Town Grill and the El Dorado. "At the Civic Auditorium we played intermissions behind a lot of the big bands. We played behind the original Ink Spots," she said. "And, at the time, Joe Louis's wife, Marva Louis, was singing with a band called Mattole's. We played intermission for that group. And we played intermission for King Kolax's big band — he was a trumpet player."[32]

As the musicians began to travel regularly, spending weekends away and rubbing shoulders with celebrities, their status on campus skyrocketed. Argie Mae Edwards (Medearis) laughed as she remembered how the young women professors would beg the musicians to request them as chaperons: "The professors who weren't married, they liked to go with us, too, you know. And they would ask us, 'Girls, where are you going this weekend?' We would say, 'Oh, we're going to San Antonio.' They'd say, 'Oh yeah? I sure would like to go.' " The musicians would then confer and advise Bennett on worthy chaperons. Those who did not "act right," in the judgment of the Co-Eds, were not likely to be asked again. "We'd say, 'Don't take her. Don't take this one.' You know. And so we almost had the run of the dormitories if there was a professor living in there because she would want to go with us on weekends! Oh sure, yes sir. We were important people on the campus."[33]

The Prairie View Co-Eds were quickly becoming important people in the eyes of soldiers at nearby bases as well. December 1943 was the first in a series of Christmas vacations that the all-woman band would spend performing for military audiences. "We would never have a chance to spend Christmas with our parents," recalled Elizabeth Thomas (Smith), "because we would be entertaining the soldiers. Well, we would spend a few days before the holidays with our parents, but on Christmas day we wouldn't spend any time with them. We had fun entertaining the soldiers, and they would look forward to seeing us. There would be quite a few of them that were from Prairie View."[34]

The repertoire of the band grew rapidly, a necessity in the light of such frequent performances. "We did 'Star Dust,' which was popular with the students," said Margaret Grigsby, "and the 'One O'Clock Jump.' Most of the songs that were popular during that time, well, we played them. A couple of blues songs. 'Pistol Packin' Mama.' A couple of Count Basie numbers, I can't remember the names of them right now. But we played just about everything. Just about any of the wartime songs you can think of, we were playing them. Because that's what people wanted to hear. And they wanted to hear things they could dance to as well." Argie Mae Edwards (Medearis) also remembered "Down for Double": "It was a peppy, you know, jazz song. Then we did a lot of other jazz music." She especially recalled Clora Bryant's solos on Count Basie's "One O'Clock Jump" and Harry James's "Two O'Clock Jump." "We had to keep up with all the hit tunes," said Bryant, who remembered a playlist that included many numbers popularized by the big bands: Lucky Millinder's "Sweet Slumber," Jimmie Lunceford's "White Heat," Harry James's "Back Beat Boogie," Count Basie's "Second Balcony Jump," and Woody Herman's "Woodchopper's Ball."[35] In addition, some ballads, such as "I'm Falling for You" and "Don't Get around Much Anymore," featured the band's vocalist, Marian Bridges.

On 4 March 1944, the *Chicago Defender* noted that the "Prairie View college Co-Eds band" was "proving a sensation in the South."[36] Plans to expand beyond the South were disclosed in a feature story in the *Prairie View Bulletin* that spring: "When school closes in June, do you think the girls will relax and go vacationing? Not these super-energetic collegians. They plan to tour the entire country, playing at camps, bases and dance dates."[37] By the time school was out, the black press nationwide was heralding the forthcoming debut of the Prairie View Co-Eds at the famed Apollo Theater in New York.[38]

What had catapulted the "super-energetic collegians" into the big leagues? The band had been signed by Moe Gale's professional booking agency. Gale, a white man and the owner of the Savoy Ballroom in New York, was one of the biggest agents booking black talent in the country; a 1941 *Saturday Evening Post* story called him "the most important single factor in Negro jazz."[39] Other musicians represented by Gale included Cab Calloway, Ella Fitzgerald, Chick Webb, and the Ink Spots. What is less well known about Moe Gale is that he also represented a number of

African American all-girl bands, including Eddie Durham's All-Star Girl Orchestra and Jean Parks' All-Girl Band. In the summer of 1944, Gale launched a unique relationship with the Prairie View Co-Eds.

"I've always heard it said," explained Bettye Bradley (Kimbrough), "and I'm sure it's true, that we were the only band at that time that the Gale agency booked on a part-time basis. We were with the Gale agency out of New York for the summer months."[40] During the school year, the Co-Eds were college students who played gigs on weekends and holidays, often carrying their books with them and studying along the way. But, during the summer, they were full-time professionals, playing several "location" jobs each season, including New York's Apollo and St. Louis's Riviera, with dozens of one-nighters in between. Although the musicians were college students, the Gale agency treated them no differently than any other working dance band as far as work schedules, conditions, and travel were concerned. Traveling in private cars, the Co-Eds covered a great deal of segregated territory on a route that was often physically and emotionally grueling.

"We traveled everywhere," said Bradley, who remembered that the cars traveled caravan style so that, if one station wagon had problems of any kind, they all stopped. "We played for all the army bases, the navy and the marines, air force, whoever, because they gave us coupons for gas. And for tires." Synthetic rubber accounted for numerous blowouts. Margaret Grigsby recalled pulling into a gas station one time with four flat tires. Clora Bryant remembered her embarrassment when the station wagon in which she was riding popped three tires just as it rolled into the tube that would take them *underneath* the Hudson River for their New York debut.[41] All the Prairie View Co-Eds alumnae with whom I spoke mentioned that it was their understanding that playing for the troops is what garnered the band enough gas and rubber coupons to make the cross-country trip. This arrangement — and the fact that all-woman bands were unique in having 100 percent draft-exempt personnel — may have been a significant factor contributing to Gale's interest in booking women's bands during World War II, when travel was especially difficult for civilians.

Among the band ephemera that remains in the John B. Coleman Library at Prairie View A&M University is a tattered press book from Moe Gale's New York offices, instructing promoters on how to rustle up full houses for the Prairie View Co-Eds. On the cover is a picture of the full band in white blouses and long floral print skirts. The women smile sedately, holding their instruments in "at-rest" positions that allow the potential client to check out the instrumentation (four trumpets, three trombones, five saxes, piano, bass, and drums) and glimpse the youthful faces of the players. Inside the booklet, the correct billing of the group is spelled out:

GALE AGENCY, INC.

Presents

PRAIRIE VIEW STATE COLLEGE CO-EDS

ALL GIRL ORCHESTRA

16 GAY, GORGEOUS GLAMOUR GALS 16

The press book continues with catchy slogans and promotional ideas. Under the heading "Punch Lines That Will Help You Sell" are a number of catchphrases typical of all-girl band ad copy of the day, including "Sylphs of Symphony!" "Divine Darlings!" "A Band of Honeys and a Honey of a Band!!" In addition to the usual confectionary sweetheart-darling-honey theme, the academic angle is captured in some slogans, including:

You Don't Have to Go to College

Here's a College You Can Adopt as Your Own.

For These Darlings of Rhythm Will Teach You

All There Is to Know about Swing!![42]

The college theme was important to many audiences of the Prairie View Co-Eds. The band often performed at other black colleges, including the Tuskegee Institute and Howard University, but, even for non-collegiate black audiences, the college connection was crucial, just as it had been for choral groups such as the Fisk Jubilee Singers and men's dance bands such as the Wiley Collegians and the Prairie View Collegians. When the Prairie View Co-Eds traveled from town to town and were advertised and reviewed in the black press, the sixteen black women musicians delivered more than a promise of danceable music. For African American audiences, the talented college women from Prairie View stimulated hopes for social and economic advancement even as they played popular dance tunes of the day. Like the men's college groups, the Prairie View Co-Eds represented the achievements of black education, and, as black college women during World War II, they reminded audiences of the particular gains made by black women at that historical moment. Even those labor historians who are skeptical about the wartime headway achieved by white U.S. home-front women generally agree that the labor crisis of World War II constituted a major watershed for African American women.[43] The Prairie View Co-Eds embodied black women's claims to respectability and upward mobility, qualities historically denied them by the dominant society. But, unlike other images of respectable black womanhood available in the black press at the time — serious, heroic figures such as Mary McLeod Bethune — the image presented by the Co-Eds was youthful and upbeat, a refreshing picture of respectable, educated black women enjoying themselves. They stimulated race pride in black audiences and at the same time posed a challenge to the worldviews of white audiences.

Margaret Grigsby recalled one incident on the summer 1944 tour: "We had to play at Sea Island, Georgia, once. It was the first time they didn't call us Prairie View Co-Eds. They had a poster up there, 'the Prairie View Prancers.' And I got mad right away. I said, 'What do they mean the Prairie View Prancers? They can't call us Co-Eds?' " *Prancers* summoned images of chorus lines, and, although the photograph on the poster made it clear that it was a band being advertised, not a line of dancers, the substitution *Prancers* for *Co-Eds* stung. Grigsby had nothing against dancers. Her cousin Blanche Thompson, also known as the Brown Skin Venus, was a member of Irving C. Miller's Brown Skin Models and would be cheering the Prairie View Co-Eds on from the wings during their Apollo Theater debut. She was upset by the fact that the substitution eclipsed the musicians' college affiliation: "At that time, many Southerners refused to call African Americans anything that reflected progress, so calling us Co-Eds showed we were college educated."[44]

Although the high point of the 1944 tour was the Apollo Theater appearance, the Prairie View Co-Eds spent much of their summer vacation traveling a terrain in which lodging, food, and other facilities were separate, inferior, and scarce, at least as far as African Americans were concerned. A closer exploration of the travel hazards that prevailed in the South for African American entertainers (and African American travelers in general) will be taken up in part 2. The Prairie View Co-Eds navigated the South by sleeping in rooming houses in black neighborhoods and sometimes by sleeping in the cars as they rode to the next job.

Occasionally, black hotels could be found, but Clora Bryant described the conditions as so poor (one discomfort was sharing rooms with bedbugs or "chinches") that the musicians sometimes sat up in the lobbies rather than sleep in their rooms. In terms of food, Argie Mae Edwards (Medearis) said, "I know sometimes we would buy food at the grocery store and then stop at a roadside park, and, other than that, when we'd get to a town, we'd find, you know, black restaurants. Because at that time, you sure couldn't go to another restaurant." Bryant noted that sometimes black eateries would charge traveling entertainers higher prices than they did local black customers. Bettye Bradley (Kimbrough) said that her mother always told her that she looked like she "hadn't eaten" by the end of the summer. When the musicians played for white clubs, they often had to observe such rules as entering through the back and leaving the premises during their breaks. Edwards summed it up: "We didn't have any trouble traveling — because we did what we were supposed to do."[45]

To Bryant's memory, the route took them "from Texas up to Louisiana, on over to Florida, and then up through Virginia, West Virginia, the Carolinas, Tennessee, Alabama, Mississippi. We played all the way up to New York and ended the tour at the Apollo Theater. Which was the highlight of the tour and my life. Playing the Apollo." Playing the famous theater meant meeting celebrities, staying in the Hotel Cecil, and seeing the sights in New York City. After that, the band would travel across the South again. Elizabeth Thomas (Smith) described the return trip to Prairie View: "We would play at the Howard Theater in Washington and also in Baltimore, the Royal Theater. That would be on our way back to the campus. And, of course, we played at Tuskegee."[46]

The Tuskegee Institute is historically important as the black "self-help" industrial arts school founded in 1881 by Booker T. Washington, but, during World War II, it also represented the immediate struggle of African Americans for equality in the military. Tuskegee was the training ground for African American pilots in the Army Air Corps. It took a great deal of pressure from black leaders and the black press for the War Department to agree to train black pilots. Once they were trained, it took additional pressure to convince the War Department to let them fly. In June 1944, the Tuskegee airmen took part in the D day missions over Normandy, proving not only their own abilities and courage, but the ability and courage of African Americans, too often suppressed in a racist system. When the Prairie View Co-Eds played at the institute that summer, the airmen were both war heroes and civil rights heroes.[47]

Many of the Prairie View musicians described the thrill of pulling in to Tuskegee to find the celebrated black pilots enthusiastically awaiting their arrival. Bettye Bradley (Kimbrough) remembered, "Of course, when we'd drive on a base, everyone would come out to help. Oh, we had a marvelous time with that at Tuskegee. The Tuskegee Airmen?" She laughed warmly at the memory. "There were thousands of them emptying out that truck." Clora Bryant's recollection of the "sight of all those handsome young men in their immaculate uniforms" stands in her mind as one of the thrills of the tour. Margaret Grigsby offered a somewhat different take when she mentioned being a little put off by a superior attitude that she felt was exuded by some of the fliers. "Like you're supposed to fall down at their feet or something. But most officers, white and black, had that attitude," she added. Elizabeth Thomas remembered the Tuskegee visit as consisting of "two shows, one for the officers club and one for the noncoms."[48]

Entertaining the troops was an activity that most band alumnae described with enthusiasm. Although the audiences were segregated, the Prairie View Co-Eds played for both black and white troops. Soldiers made for effusive audiences, affirmed Helen Cole. "Oh, yes, boy, I'll tell you, they were very good. They were real appreciative because, I guess, you know how that would be, where you don't see a bunch of girls. They were just thrilled. They made noises and everything." Margaret Grigsby shared one experience that illustrates the intensity of playing for soldiers.

It was Fort Hood or the big fort in Georgia. I don't remember which, but they asked us to play for the soldiers. These were all black soldiers because at that time the army was all segregated. And there were thousands of them. And we were up on the stage playing. They were up in trees! And, when we started playing, they turned loose and fell out of the trees. They yelled, 'That's what I'm fighting for!' Then, when we finished playing, they had all these sergeants lined up, and the army truck, and they passed us hand over hand, the sergeants did, to keep us from getting down on the ground. The way those guys were carrying on, they knew we would have been mobbed! And they just passed us hand over hand and put us on the truck and took us out of there.[49]

Relations between all-woman big bands and their military audiences — mostly men — will be taken up at length in part 3, but Grigsby's description raises issues that call for immediate discussion. In a wartime situation where homefront and battlefield were popularly figured as separated feminine and masculine halves of a country that longed to be reunited after the war, the introduction of women entertainers to men's military environments was heavily freighted with meaning. Popular culture suggested that, even while Rosie the Riveter did a man's job, she dreamed of boyfriend Charlie's return. Similarly, the American GI was depicted dreaming of his sweetheart waiting patiently at home as he huddled in foxhole, barrack, and tank. Ads, magazine covers, and posters overwhelmingly depicted white Rosies and white Charlies, but exclusion from the picture did not mean immunity to the message. GIs were told in subtle and not-so-subtle ways that what they were fighting for were the "girls back home." And women were told that they needed to be worth the fight. When young women who were, not stars, but essentially those "girls back home" were brought on base to play swing music in a dance band, GIs were reminded of their interrupted private lives and the reward that awaited on their return home. The result was a highly emotional and sexualized, intrinsically ideological scenario. Grigsby's story of officers passing the women hand over hand to the truck to protect them from the mob offers an apt metaphor for the many ways in which women's bodies functioned to stimulate the kind of aggressively heterosexual masculinity thought to create effective soldiers.[50]

African American soldiers would also have seen a performance by the Prairie View Co-Eds in an additional political context: that of the struggle to improve the lot of black soldiers in the segregated armed forces. Black soldiers were all too frequently denied the entertainment and other expressions of comfort, respect, and gratitude that were lavished on white soldiers. Pleas for more entertainment for black soldiers, particularly entertainment involving black cultural forms and black women performers, and demands by black leaders for more black officers and more dignified jobs for black soldiers were frequently reported in the black press. When the Prairie View Co-Eds performed for African American soldiers, they represented not only dominant versions of four freedoms patriotism[51] but also African American versions of equal rights patriotism that sought to extend democracy at home as well as abroad (also known as "Double Victory"). The *that* in "*That's* what *I'm* fighting for!" meant something more than the "girls back home" to the black soldiers who cheered the Prairie View Co-Eds. *That* also meant equality for African American soldiers and civilians.

Argie Mae Edwards (Medearis) recalled that, although the band entertained white soldiers at times, this racial configuration was not condoned in the same way as soldiers being entertained by women of the same race: "Well, the white soldiers would be around, especially if they were musicians. They'd come around the bandstand, and sometimes they'd want to play. Well, I never will forget this white woman who owned a club. Boy, she kept those soldiers back like we were poison." Another tension is captured in Clora Bryant's story of black women in the audience at Camp Rucker, Alabama, objecting to black soldiers' flirtatious reception of the black all-woman band because the dynamic left them out in the cold:

> We played this army base, and [drummer] Chico Hamilton was in the band. He was stationed there, and [trombonist] Jimmy Cheatham was stationed there, and somebody else was stationed there. And Chico Hamilton was a good-looking guy. He was fine! He's an egotistical little something anyway. He was a big flirt. It was a small town, and these girls were fighting over who was going to go with him. We were playing this dance, and we were on the stage. We'd had intermission, and Chico had introduced himself. After intermission we're up there playing, and all of a sudden we heard a loud commotion. Then this broad threw a Coke bottle; she was throwing it at the girls. In our front line we had saxophone players, and most of them were light girls with long, pretty hair. This broad had thrown a Coke bottle at the band! It just so happened it hit the jukebox and made a loud noise. We all hit the floor. It was something else![52]

Despite the more harrowing aspects of the road, the Prairie View Co-Eds alumnae generally spoke favorably about their summer travels. As Edwards put it, "I never would have had a chance to travel all around like I did. See different things, and go to different states, and stuff like that." Bradley added her commendation of how well organized the road trips were: "Whoever did it did one heck of a job. We weren't just riding around going nowhere. We knew where we were going whenever we left wherever we left."[53]

The Co-Eds in New York

As the Apollo opening approached, the Texas musicians became electrified. The trip had been successful and thrilling on many levels thus far, but the New York engagement would mean a number of welcome, almost unbelievable, changes. After a month of one-nighters, sleeping in cars and boardinghouses, they would check into a hotel for ten days. Free time could be spent taking in the incredible sights of New York City. Most of the musicians had grown up in segregated sections of small Texas towns; most had never been so far from home when they matriculated at Prairie View. The tour had so far taken them to some pretty rustic venues—they had even played in a few tobacco barns. But playing the legendary Apollo was the big time.

After changing the three synthetic tires that popped in the tunnel, the Prairie View coterie rolled their station wagons into Manhattan. They checked into the Hotel Cecil, which, as Clora Bryant took care to point out, was in the same building as Minton's Playhouse, where bebop was bursting into existence at that very moment. Harlem in 1944 was awe inspiring for the sixteen African American college students from Texas. The Prairie View alumnae with whom I spoke still conveyed a sense of disbelief and awe as they described the Apollo engagement and days and nights spent in New York.

Bettye Bradley (Kimbrough) laughed as she recounted the immensity of the experience: "It was quite exciting to us and I'm sure maybe a little more to me because I'm from a little town, like I say, of fifteen hundred people!" To put things in perspective, the Apollo Theater could have seated the entire population of her hometown! But the tour had prepared the young women for the Apollo crowds: "We very quickly adjusted to it and did our thing that we did everywhere. Because we had played for soldiers. We played for fifteen thousand soldiers at Camp Lee, Virginia, just a sea of faces."[54]

A big difference between location jobs in theaters and one-nighters was that, not only did the band play the usual well-rehearsed repertoire, but it also played for all the acts in the variety show. One of the exciting results of the Apollo booking was that the band was rehearsed by two of the most famous New York bandleaders of the era. As Margaret Grigsby recalled, "Eubie Blake helped us get ready with our music. And also Lucky Millinder."[55] Pianist and composer Blake and bandleader Millinder both enjoyed great popularity in the 1940s. Blake's renown as a songwriter and producer of Broadway musicals since the 1910s and 1920s had landed him the distinguished position as a music director for USO productions in the early 1940s. Millinder, some twenty years younger than Blake, was currently introducing the new musical craze rhythm and blues. Grigsby counted those rehearsals among the most treasured memories of her time with the Co-Eds.

Ernest "Ernie" Mae Crafton (baritone sax, Prairie View Co-Eds), backstage at the Apollo Theatre, 31 July 1945. *Courtesy Ernest Mae Crafton Miller.*

As Argie Mae Edwards remembered it, the band arrived in New York the night before the Apollo opening. Lucky Millinder kept the band up late that night, rehearsing the music for the show. Although she could not recall specific differences between Millinder's and Bennett's techniques, she remembered being struck by the style and expertise of the New York bandleader and the realization that "he really knew what to do! Because he was in all of that, show business, more so than Mr. Bennett. Mr. Bennett was our director, he was good in attending to business, and, of course, he was a good teacher in school. But, when it came to show business, Lucky Millinder, he knew what to do!"[56]

According to Edwards, the band played four shows a day, beginning in the early afternoon and ending late at night: "We'd have a show, and then they'd show a movie, you know. And, after the movie, then the stage deal would come on. They'd show another movie. Show the movie, and then we'd come on. When they'd close at night, we'd be the last [act]. On the show, you would have comedians, and you'd have dancers, exotic dancers and whatever. I remember when the Cats and the Fiddle were singing, they used to play 'Straighten Up and Fly Right,' and then they would have, oh, all these different things to go with the show. Of course, we were the music."[57] Highlights of the band's feature spot included trombonist Jewell Simmons stepping out into the spotlight and driving the crowd wild by singing "Sweet Slumber" in her contralto voice. And Clora Bryant wowed them with her solo on Harry James's "Back Beat Boogie." The Prairie View Co-Eds were a hit at the Apollo, whose audiences were renowned for their frank responses to the acts. Longtime emcee Ralph Cooper once claimed that the Apollo crowd "would boo a dear relative if she was off-key."[58] Not only were the Co-Eds not booed, but they were well enough liked to be invited back the summers of 1945 and 1946.

At the end of the run, the band got a nice plug from Ted Yates, entertainment columnist for the *New York Age,* who hailed their Apollo debut as a notable event and dubbed the band "a swell bunch of gals who are capable musicians."[59] Not bad for a college band that would be hitting the books again in September.

Mrs. Von Charleton

The head chaperon of the Prairie View Co-Eds was Mrs. Von Charleton, who was married to the chair of the Music Department. Most alumnae agreed that she was strict, but some found ways of getting around her, especially in New York. As the youngest member of the Co-Eds, Clora Bryant found herself particularly sheltered by the good intentions of the protective Mrs. Von Charleton: "The chaperon and I would be in bed, and the girls would be sneaking out! I didn't know about that until a couple of years ago!" Bryant learned what she had missed when Edwards spilled the beans forty years later. When I told Edwards that Bryant had clued me in on the secret, she elaborated on how the young Texans (except for Bryant, of course) managed to get away to go hear music in clubs and at jam sessions, adventures that Mrs. Von Charleton would never have condoned: "We'd make sure she was in bed. And she was a sound sleeper. At that time she weighed about four or five hundred. . . . You've seen pictures of these women in history? Those huge women, these queens, and they wore all this jewelry? Well, that's just what she looked like. She was huge, and she would wear all this jewelry all up around her neck and on her fingers, and she weighed about four hundred. Lord, she was a big one. And so, when she'd go to sleep, we knew because we could hear her."[60]

And, as Mrs. Von Charleton reposed, the Co-Eds explored New York's night life. "There was no way she could keep up with us," laughed Margaret Grigsby. "She did well to get in and out of the station wagon! And we weren't doing anything anyway." Grigsby managed to visit Small's Paradise, a Harlem nightclub, with her cousin. Helen Cole was sympathetic to Mrs. Von Charleton's belief in strict rules as well as to the musicians' need to see more of New York than the Apollo, the Cecil, and Coney Island: "We couldn't just be running around, and she kind of kept the band pretty straight until they slipped out." For Cole, slipping out meant the chance to attend jam sessions — and not just as a spectator: "Oh, no, I played. We played. You know, sometimes the guys were a little leery of girls playing drums. But I think they kind of respected me a little bit because they would let me sit in."[61]

The Co-Eds in 1945 and 1946

The first trip to New York was a mighty success. It was also a measure of the opportunities available to the Co-Eds. And in fact the band did subsequently keep up a busy year-round performance schedule that included cross-country trips to the Apollo in the summers of 1945 and 1946. The week at the Apollo in 1945 was distinguished by their appearing on the same bill with Mabel Fairbanks, known as "the world's greatest Colored Ice Skater," in what was advertised in the *New York Age* as "the first attempt that has yet been made to present an ice skater on the stage of a variety theater."[62]

Despite frequent personnel changes, Bennett managed to maintain a full band. A particular blow was Clora Bryant's decision to transfer to the University of California, Los Angeles, in order to join her father, who had obtained a good job in the booming defense industry. Harboring no hard feelings, Bennett penned a letter to the black AFM local (767) in Los Angeles, recommending her for professional trumpet jobs. Margaret Grigsby continued to travel with the band until the week she was scheduled to leave for the University of Michigan Medical School in September 1944: "I got to see places that I had never been before. But it wasn't anything very serious to me. I put the horn down in 1944, and I never picked it up again."[63]

As band members graduated or pursued other opportunities, Bennett advertised for replacements. On 27 January 1945, the *Pittsburgh Courier* announced that "four scholarships are available for girls with sufficient musical ability to play in the Prairie View Co-Eds all-girl band, under the direction of Will Henry Bennett. Applicants accepted by the school may enroll in the second semester which begins February 1st. Mr. Bennett said that a bright future is in store for girls with talent for music."[64] The *Chicago Defender* ran a similar story, urging "girls with some musical ability" to contact Bennett at Prairie View College.[65] That spring semester, the war ended in Europe. On 14 July 1945, in the middle of the second successful trip to the Apollo, another offer appeared for scholarships beginning in September. Applicants "between the ages of 16 and 22" were instructed to contact Bennett, not at Prairie View, but, curiously, in care of the Gale agency.[66]

Japan surrendered on 14 August 1945, bringing an official end to the combat portion of World War II. Yet, although the Prairie View Co-Eds had been formed with the purpose of supplying wartime dance music, a 1946 summer tour was planned. In April 1946, the *Pittsburgh Courier* reported that Bennett had "let out the latch string for new girl musicians." This time, however, applicants were not instructed to contact Bennett at all; instead, they were to send their "good references" directly to booking agent Ralph Cooper at the Gale agency. The story specified that the band needed two trumpet players and two trombonists. There was no mention of scholarships or even of college education. It appears that positions were now being offered to professional musicians who were not necessarily students.[67]

As the 1946 school year ended, a feature in the Prairie View annual, "The World Famous Prairie View Co-Eds," proudly narrated the history of the band:

> When the war took most of the men from the college campus, Will Henry Bennett started thinking. He announced for girls who knew some music.

That was in February 1943. By September they were playing one hour spots on the program with the famous Collegians [the men's band]. By December they were "going it alone." In the summer of 1944 they toured sixteen states playing clubs, theaters and schools. The Gale Booking Agency of New York was so pleased [that] they booked them again the summer of 1945. Another successful summer and now they are booked ahead for the summer of 1946.

This is almost the familiar Rosie the Riveter narrative of defense industry propaganda. Yes, the men went to war, and the women pitched in to keep things running smoothly on the home front. But there is no mention of the war ending or the return of men to campus, no mention of the GI Bill of Rights that would tip the gender balance once again to near parity of men and women at black colleges. According to this version of the Prairie View Co-Eds story, women picked up horns during the war and continued to play afterward.

At the end of the 1946 tour, however, the Co-Eds disbanded. Even so, the musicians did not necessarily hang up their horns and turn into home-makers. Some, like Argie Mae Edwards, returned to school to finish their degrees. Others, like Elizabeth Thomas, decided to pursue other options. For Thomas, this meant returning to Denison to play with a men's dance band. Helen Cole and Bert Etta Davis continued on with a smaller version of the band, although one no longer affiliated with the college. For a short time, the combo would keep the name Prairie View Co-Eds, and, for a time, Bennett would continue to work with them.

Cole reflected on her decision to stay with the combo rather than finish her business degree at Prairie View: "It could have been the wrong decision for some people, but it was the right decision for me. See, it was only my mother and myself. And it's just been like that all my life. She was a widow. So, when I went to school, it helped her. It helped her put me through school. Then, when I chose to leave, I was making pretty good money. And, see, I used to send money home. I've always done that."[68] She worked steadily with the sextet, which consisted of Cole and Bert Etta Davis from Prairie View, pianist Maurine Smith, who had been playing with the Co-Eds but who was not a student at Prairie View, and three women who had no previous association with the band at all: bassist Eileen Chance, tenor sax star Margaret Backstrom from the Dar-lings of Rhythm, and a series of trumpet players that included at one time or another Thelma Lewis, Jean Starr, and Toby Butler. The combo was booked by Ferguson Brothers, the same agency that booked the Darlings of Rhythm. Later, Sweethearts of Rhythm trumpet star Ernestine "Tiny" Davis took over the group, which was booked by Joe Glaser. As Tiny Davis' Hell-Divers, the combo toured fourteen countries. The group even released some singles on the Decca label.[69] In all, Cole spent twenty-five years in combos, winding up as a duo with pianist Maurine Smith. When Smith died in 1971, Cole went to business school to catch up on her accounting studies. She returned to Denison to live with her mother, working as a bookkeeper at a bank until she retired.

After leaving the combo (by then led by Tiny Davis), Bert Etta Davis (no relation to Tiny) worked as a featured soloist in Dinah Washington's road show, earning the name Lady Bird for her affinity with the fleet bebop style of Charlie "Bird" Parker. Clora Bryant spent the next fifty years as a Los Angeles–based jazz musician, taking part in the famous Central Avenue jam sessions that included Dexter Gordon, Wardell Gray, and Hampton Hawes. In 1957, she recorded an album under her own name on the Mode label, *Gal with a Horn.* Ernie Mae Crafton (Miller) put down the baritone and returned to her first instrument, the piano. As of this writing, she is still playing and singing in hotels in Austin, Texas. Several Co-Eds alumnae became professional music educators, including Melvia Wrenn, who was a school band director in Navasota, Texas. Bettye Bradley (Kimbrough), who married a soldier she met at one of the Co-Eds' concerts, taught music in elementary schools for nearly forty years. Margaret Bradshaw taught in New York after earning her master's in music education from Columbia. Argie Mae Edwards (Medearis) taught music in both high school and elementary school for thirty-seven years. When her husband died, she took over his bail bond business. At the time of our interview, she had been the organist for the same church since 1956. Bert Etta Davis also spent a good deal of time later in her career playing in church, only she played her alto sax, not the organ.

In one sense, the formation of an all-woman band at the largest black college in Texas was a direct result of the wartime shortage of men. And it is true that by 1947 the women's band was a thing of Prairie View history. However, as with many real-life Rosie the Riveters, the circumstances fueling the success of the Co-Eds were more complicated than a simple instance of temporary patriotic substitution. Many of the women who played in the Prairie View Co-Eds had extensive musical training and experience before joining the band, and many would pursue careers in music or music education afterward. Some members chose the music program at Prairie View over those at other colleges because its all-girl orchestra afforded them valuable practical experience — playing professional jobs and traveling on the road — that they were not likely to get elsewhere. Some members would not have been able to afford college had it not been for the wages they earned as dance band musicians. Booked by a New York agency and paid union scale, the band was a professional organization as well as an extracurricular activity. And the Prairie View Co-Eds did not passively step aside at the end of the war. For one thing, not only women's bands but also many men's bands folded in 1946, including those led by Benny Goodman, Harry James, and Benny Carter. Like many big bands, both men's and women's, of the late Swing Era, the Prairie View Co-Eds changed with the times — the group became a combo.[70]

Another important way in which the Prairie View Co-Eds differed from the typical Rosie the Riveter of 1940s propaganda is that the women were not white housewives but African American college students. Excluded from the propaganda, but powerfully affected by the economic and ideological changes produced by the war, the Prairie View musicians belonged to a generation of black women for whom the labor crises of World War II would make a lasting difference.

Of course, the Prairie View Co-Eds were also more sheltered than many other African American all-girl bands that traveled. Because they were college students, they hit the road only three months each year. They had the benefit of knowing that, no matter how difficult things were on the road, come September they would be back in their Prairie View dorms, playing local gigs on weekends. In addition, the musicians were accompanied by teachers and chaperons, people genuinely concerned about their safety. They sometimes stayed as guests in the dormitories of black colleges along the way. Other African American all-girl bands faced the hazards of the Jim Crow South without these relative luxuries. And some of them challenged segregation laws while they were at it.

Road Hazards

Chapter 4

Surveillance and Survival

in the Jim Crow South

It was before its time. The International Sweethearts
of Rhythm traveled all over the United States before Dr. King.
—Evelyn McGee Stone, *telephone interview with author*

We all had our escape route, you might say.
When you were told to get out of town in fifteen minutes,
you were out of town in fifteen minutes. The whole bus, the whole
band, everything. — Toby Butler, *telephone interview with author*

We lived dangerously in those days. See, it wasn't
like now. Believe you me, history will find out musicians
were the ones that learned people how to be together.
— Violet Wilson, *telephone interview with author*

A bass player from Eddie Durham's All-Star Girl Orchestra puts her
legs and coat over a trumpet player who hides on the floor while
the police search the bus. The crime? Black women are traveling with a
white woman, breaking Jim Crow laws.

An alto player in the International Sweethearts of Rhythm longs to
wipe a bead of sweat from the side of her nose — but she doesn't dare.
The police are watching, and streaks get people arrested. The crime? If
any of those black women are really white passing for black, it means
that black and white women are working and traveling together and
probably eating together, too — all crimes under Jim Crow.

A member of the California Sweethearts tries to finish her long-
awaited supper but can't help worrying about the two white police offi-

cers who pace between the tables in this "colored" cafeteria. No doubt they'll be at the "colored" dance tonight as well. Segregation is more confusing than she had realized, with these white boys continually crossing the color line. The crime? "Colored" out-of-town women are traveling with too-nice clothes and California plates. Someone is bound to forget her place, forget to step off the sidewalk, or say, "Yes sir, no sir." When any of these crimes occur, the police will be ready.

To understand the conditions under which African American all-girl bands worked and traveled in the Jim Crow South, it is necessary to know something about how African Americans historically have been criminalized in the United States. If the leap from the topic of all-girl bands to that of criminalization seems a disorderly stretch of the imagination, it only goes to show how far we are from being able to see all-girl bands as authentic topics of jazz history. As any enthusiast of books and movies that chronicle the lives of jazz musicians knows, jazz history is crawling with police.

Criminalization — the process by which certain groups of people come to be marked and treated as deviant — is a recurring theme in the narratives of African American jazz musicians, both men and women. In biographies, autobiographies, interviews, and oral histories, African American musicians have documented a history of surveillance and survival. Musicians address criminalization in a variety of ways: through eulogizing gifted colleagues, such as tenor saxophonist Lester Young and blues singer Bessie Smith, whose lives were damaged or destroyed by various kinds of police harassment (by *police* I mean everyone who acts on the social or institutional power to police other people, not just the official police);[1] through humorous anecdotes about outwitting the police; and other kinds of police stories about harassment and attendant strategies for coping and resisting.

The forms of criminalization, often described by African American musicians, include police break-ins (ostensibly looking for drugs); the police planting drugs in hotel rooms, dressing rooms, and hospital beds and then arresting musicians; the forced closing of black nightclubs and dance halls on charges of prostitution or mixed audience policies; and New York's cabaret card policy, which prevented many artists, including Charlie Parker and Billie Holiday, from performing in the venues of their professions. Criminalization on the road in the Jim Crow South included ubiquitous threats of violence, many of them legal or authorized by the law's indifference. For black men's bands, this included the physical and mental brutalizing of black musicians by white vigilantes who saw black men as inevitable rapists of white women.[2] Black men's bands from the North, especially those possessing expensive suits and nice cars, particularly irked Southern white supremacists. Black women's bands that offered an image of talented, successful, mobile black women similarly irritated patriarchal white racists whose worldview was undermined by visions of black women's autonomy. Clora Bryant described the intimidation endured by the Prairie View Co-Eds as including being chased out of public places such as train stations and being quizzed by gas station attendants who did not like the fact that "colored girls" had access to so many gas coupons. Doris Jarrett (Meilleur) recalled that it was not unusual for black women musicians to encounter intimidation by white sheriffs and deputies that would today be classified as sexual harassment. "If you let it bother you, you would wind up slapping somebody, and that wouldn't be too good," she explained. "You just had to be slick and get out of the way."[3] Black women's bands that hired white women were additionally hounded by white police and citizens who saw them as corrupting white womanhood. I say *criminalization,* rather than *harassment,* because the vast array of policing practices (incompletely listed here) not only made life unpleasant for musicians but also served to construct black jazz musicians, and all black people by extension, as delinquent, immoral, drug- and/or sex-crazed criminals in the white public imagination.

Life was especially dangerous for African American musicians on the road in the Jim Crow South, where segregation was forced and legal, where whiteness, defined as pure and superior, was fiercely protected, and where *colored* included anyone with any ascertainable black blood. Recalling his early road trips south of the Mason-Dixon Line in the 1930s, jazz pianist Earl "Fatha" Hines told an interviewer, "I always say we were the first Freedom Riders. . . . oh it was brutal! There were streets we couldn't go down; there were places we could not even look at!"[4] Cab Calloway was not exaggerating when he wrote, "Don't get caught messing with a white woman in the South. It'll be your tail."[5] In fact, black men did not actually have to "mess" with white women to be punished violently. Trombonist Dicky Wells described an incident in Miami in which a black drummer was castrated and killed by a lynch mob after complying with a group of white men who ordered him to teach their dates (white women) how to dance.[6] While black women musicians did not travel under the constant threat of lynching, as did black men musicians, black women were also subject to threats of violence, arrest, and surveillance. They also shared the daily harassment of the Jim Crow system that made it routinely impossible to obtain food and lodging and even access to showers and rest rooms. Blanche Calloway, sister of Cab Calloway and renowned leader of her own all-man band called the Joy Boys, was thrown in jail in Yazoo, Mississippi, in 1937 for using a "ladies'" room at a gas station at six in the morning.[7] Ladies' rooms were for white women, and the separate "colored women's" rooms that the law required black women to use were not always provided.

Because the black theater circuit in the North was small and major white theaters and ballrooms hired black bands infrequently (and then only the famous bands), African American big bands of the 1930s and 1940s, both men's and women's, found it necessary to tour the South.[8] And, during the war, travel — already dangerous and inconvenient — became even more difficult. Wartime restrictions on the use of charter buses, authorized by the Office of Defense Transportation (ODT), made road trips virtually impossible for bands not owning their own buses or cars. The resultant reliance on public transportation meant increased exposure to racist violence, and therefore, as bandleader Cab Calloway and NAACP president Walter White argued to the ODT, the ban on charter buses disproportionately affected black bands. As Calloway and White also pointed out, fewer location jobs (bookings lasting more than a day or two) were available to black bands, and black bands had only limited access to public transportation. Thanks to the persistence of Calloway and White, the ODT eventually lifted the ban "insofar as colored bands were concerned," allocating "five buses for the exclusive use of these bands when their schedules took them through the southern areas."[9] Five buses were scarcely enough to handle all the African American bands traveling the South, but the concession was received as a victory in the black press nonetheless.

A few black bands were fortunate enough to own their own buses at the onset of the charter bus ban, among them the all-woman International Sweethearts of Rhythm. News reports in the black press emphasized the importance of bus ownership for bands that hoped to stay in business. One article predicted that the "most war-proof orchestra in the world at the moment seems to be the International Sweethearts of Rhythm" — not only were the personnel "completely draft-exempt; but just as important is that, unlike the majority of orchestras, they have their own bus." If lodging was unavailable, this deluxe bus could double as a hotel, allowing the musicians to "sleep in it right after the job and wak[e] up three or four hundred miles away in time to get set for another go at syncopation."[10] According to lead trombonist Helen Jones (Woods), the celebrated bus "wasn't the most comfortable place in the world" to get a night's sleep, but "it was better than the places they had to offer traveling black people in those days."[11]

The bus made it possible for the band to meet its grueling schedule of one-nighters, but it certainly did not exempt the Sweethearts from the constant threat of harassment, the scarcity of services and facilities, and the absolute necessity to keep moving, both to get to the next job and for protection. "They were perpetual motion," recalled Sweethearts alto player Roz Cron.[12]

Traveling black musicians, even members of bands that owned their own buses, frequently relied on black families for lodging (as did black travelers in general). "Because we couldn't stay in hotels," explained Sweethearts vocalist Evelyn McGee (Stone), "we had to find black families . . . although it would have been wonderful to have been able to go to a hotel and have some privacy, as opposed to having to impose on black families, who really loved us so much." Sleeping on the bus at times saved musicians and management the trouble of having to find lodging, but it did not help with the problem of finding places to bathe. As saxophonist Willie Mae Wong (Scott) put it, "You should have seen us on a turnpike trying to wash up in a rest room." Of course, the rest room had to be designated *colored* before this feat could even be attempted. Food was another necessity that was hard to come by. "It was not a comfortable thing," said Ernestine May, a songwriter and pianist who played New York nightclubs before traveling with one of Eddie Durham's all-woman combos and, later, a spin-off group from the International Sweethearts of Rhythm. "If you did find a restaurant, mostly you could go to the side and take your food out." In poignant contrast, May described the thrill that the arrival of black entertainers held for black people in small Southern towns. The extra-appreciative reception of these treasured events was palpable from the bandstand and added to the enjoyment of playing: "When you played in a small town, people came. That was something special. They didn't know you were having it rough. When you came out, you were dressed up, you know, and made up. They didn't know, as they say, the gory details."[13]

For black all-woman bands with white members, the problems presented by life on the road intensified — what was already grueling became illegal as well. Traveling together was a crime. Walking down the street together was a crime. Eating together was a crime. Willie Mae Wong (Scott) described trying to get a quick bite to eat in a black restaurant with the International Sweethearts of Rhythm when the whole band suddenly had to flee after police were tipped off that there were two white women in the group. Black families provided lodging for mixed bands just as they did for bands composed entirely of legally black women. Evelyn McGee (Stone) speculated that, while some black families who hosted the Sweethearts may have known that the band was mixed, others may have assumed that the white members were light-skinned black women since there were many black people who were "just as white as any white person." For bands with white and white-looking members, the art of securing the use of other kinds of facilities, such as public rest rooms, became even trickier than usual. Maxine Fields (Knepper), a white member of a spin-off group from the International Sweethearts of Rhythm, recalled the police chasing her and her colleagues out of a bus station rest room in Shreveport, Louisiana, where musicians were taking sponge baths. The band had taken care to locate a facility designated *colored,* but "somebody reported to the police that there were some white girls going in the colored ladies room. No, it wasn't ladies," she corrected herself. "It was 'white ladies' and 'colored women.' "[14]

Commode-on-the-road stories provide excellent examples of how the criminalization of women varied according to race. When Blanche Calloway entered the whites-only ladies room in Yazoo, Mississippi, not only did she break the color line, but she defined herself as a *lady,* staking claim only incidentally to an equal right to public toilets and sinks and, more radically, to the symbolic (and fiercely protected) pedestal that represented the respect, decency, and protection denied her by a system based on separate and unequal treatment. When Maxine Fields used the colored women's facility in the bus station, white police viewed her not only as a white woman walking into the wrong room but as a white woman evacuating that pedestal. On the pedestal, white women were symbols of white racial purity and superiority.[15] Off the pedestal, they became fallen women or female criminals. Angela Davis writes that the criminalization of women has been historically "more complicated" than that of men in that it "has had more to do with the marking of certain women — certain groups of women — as undomesticated and hypersexual, as women who refuse to embrace the nuclear family as paradigm."[16] According to racist ideology, this group of women automatically included both women of color, whose rights to domestic and sexual privacy had never been respected by white America, and white fallen women. Black all-girl bands that defied white police by having black women play alongside one or two white women in the segregated South were seen as hastening the fall of white womanhood and, like Blanche Calloway, as challenging the Jim Crow hierarchies of race and gender.[17]

The term *Jim Crow* derives from a character of blackface minstrelsy in the 1830s that perpetuated one of the most common racist stereotypes of black men of the period: as slow, stupid, and ridiculous (wishful thinking on the part of white supremacists). The system that took its name from this stereotype was the result of the reaffirmation of white supremacy during the decades that followed the demise of the radical Reconstruction government in 1877.[18] With power restored to the hands of former slaveholders, mandatory segregation along a black/white binary ensured the continuation of white privilege in the South. The sexual exploitation of black women by white men that began under slavery (and continued despite miscegenation laws) potentially threatened racial distinction and the success of the Jim Crow system. But, if all mixed-race children were defined as black, then "there was no threat to 'white racial purity,' or to the system of white domination."[19] Implicit in Jim Crow definitions of who was white and who was "colored," was the sexualization, exploitation, and domination of black women as well as the zealous guarding of white women as symbols of racial purity. Black women's bands with white members defied both these sexist and racist routines.

While much has been written about the road hazards experienced by African American men's bands, not enough attention has been paid to how the harassment of black jazz musicians by white police relates to a history of criminalization of nonwhite people in the United States.[20] More needs to be said about how black musicians' continued traversing of this hazardous terrain constituted resistance. And, certainly, while books and documentaries on women in jazz have documented the road hazards faced by African American women's bands, not enough is known about how the policing of black all-girl bands reflected particular modes of criminalization that were both race and gender specific.

I attempt here to respond to what I see as a need to explore how African American all-girl bands were criminalized, how they traveled in the South, the kinds of dangers they encountered, how they dodged, outran, complied with, and resisted the steady policing to which they were subjected, and how their survival strategies challenged the philosophy and institutions of white supremacy. The risks and gains made by members of black all-girl bands compel recognition alongside other wartime civil rights actions of African Americans in the 1940s. Recent scholarship has demonstrated that the war years constitute an important phase of the civil rights movement, as African Americans waged battles for desegregation (in the armed forces, defense industries, and public transportation), for voting rights (the repeal of the poll tax), and for protection from racist violence (the efforts to get Congress to pass an antilynching bill).[21] When in 1963 James Baldwin wrote, "It demands great force and great cunning continually to assault the mighty and indifferent fortress of white supremacy, as Negroes in this country have done so long,"[22] he referred to a long history of daily resistance by black people that prepared the way for the sit-ins, marches, and protests of the 1950s and 1960s. While black all-girl bands were not considered political organizations, their persistence in traveling the South when it was dangerous to do so, in hiring white women when it was against the law, and in bearing nonracist portrayals of black womanhood to Southern black communities is consistent with Baldwin's vision of the "force" and "cunning" that made the civil rights movement possible. In focusing on African American all-girl bands that hired white members, I do not mean to imply that white women's experience is central to understanding the significance of black all-girl bands. Rather, I focus on black women's bands that engaged in these dangerous and illegal integrated hiring practices because of the particular ways that they exposed the contradictions of Jim Crow and wreaked havoc on the logic of the white racist system.

While black and white men's bands also sometimes broke the color line, black women's bands were unique in the particular kinds of challenges they offered to racist ideology. Gender, as well as race, affected how white police responded to racial mixing. African American saxophonist Charlie Rouse recalled an incident on a Southern tour in which a white bass player from Arkansas named Buddy Jones sat in with Dizzy Gillespie's band for one night and "the police came and beat him and clubbed him out of the dance."[23] As a Southern white man, Jones was seen as a race traitor. Had it been a white woman sitting in with the band, however, not only would she have been seen as a race traitor, but she would also have been seen as fallen, and the black men musicians would have been in grave danger for their lives since they would have been seen as her rapists. White trumpet player Jane Sager anticipated this peril to fellow musicians when she turned down an offer to tour with Duke

Ellington after sitting in with his orchestra in New York: "[Ellington] says, 'Janie, you're going South with me, just like Benny Goodman took Lionel [Hampton] and Teddy [Wilson].' I said, 'No, I'm not. I wouldn't do it to you. You know what'll happen. Those guys were men. I'm a woman. You put a woman in there, and you know what they're going to do?' Because they were all saying I was laying everybody in the band. That's how people's minds work."[24]

White "police" (official and vigilante) accepted as a large part of the rationale for the separation of the races the protection of white women from black men (what Angela Davis has called "the myth of the black rapist").[25] The assumption that black men routinely raped white women (despite the violent history of white men raping black women) bolstered much racist activity in the United States during World War II. At Fort Huachuca, Arizona, a military camp where many black soldiers were trained, the barracks of white WACS were shielded by barbed wire, but the barracks of black WACS were not—the assumption being that white women required protection against black rapists but that black women did not warrant protection against assailants of any color.

When white women appeared onstage with black women, it was not only the association with black women coworkers that enraged white police; it was also the spectatorship of black men in the audience. The excuse given many a time for lynching a black man was simply that he had "looked" at a white woman. Black men watching white women on stage alongside "women of their own kind" enraged white supremacists. Black women, however, could, and did, travel with white men's bands. Vocalists Lena Horne and Billie Holiday both experienced insult and inconvenience when they toured the South with Charlie Barnet and Artie Shaw, respectively, but this form of integration apparently did not signal the same challenge to white supremacy. White men were still in power in these arrangements. But, when black women's bands included white women and when they were managed or led by black men (as they frequently were) and played for black audiences (as they usually did), they roundly defied the Jim Crow hierarchy. Yet, for a variety of reasons, black all-girl bands proved particularly difficult for the police, as the official guardians of the color line, to patrol.

The possibilities for covert integration in African American all-girl bands were in themselves tied to specific issues of race and gender. Definitions of black female beauty that favored light-skinned women prevailed in the hiring of black chorines and in traveling entertainment troops such as Irvin C. Miller's Brown Skin Models. Poet, author, and editor Claude McKay had criticized the use of "all-light chorus lines" during the Harlem Renaissance of the 1920s, but the practice continued to be common in the 1930s and 1940s.[26] So, in addition to definitions of *Negro* that included light-skinned people who had any ascertainable "black blood," a "light" bias when hiring black women entertainers made it uniquely possible to slip in white women without detection, at the possible expense of the exclusion of dark-skinned black women. But, while histories of colorism and the one-drop rule might explain why racial mixing was particularly feasible in black women's bands, it does not explain why black women's bands hired white women to begin with. Traveling with a band that straddled the color line meant that, even when the musicians drank only from colored fountains, slept in the homes of black families, and avoided white rest rooms and restaurants, they were still breaking the law. It also meant that the police made frequent attempts to identify and remove white members, a form of harassment that affected not only the white band members but also light-skinned black women who were mistaken for white. And, when bands were run out of town or threatened with violence, or when their jobs were canceled because it was suspected that there were white women in the band, all the musicians were affected.

No aspect of black traveling bands' existence escaped surveillance — behavior was monitored on roads and sidewalks, in restaurants, hotels, and rest rooms, and of course on the bandstand. All band members were affected when police hovered around the bandstand, trying to figure out if Jim Crow laws were being broken. As Helen Jones (Woods) explained,

> When we would play dances, the police would be the security. The white police. Especially when you played larger places, if we played in an auditorium or a ballroom, they always had to get the permission of the police to have the dance. Because a lot of the dance halls were not owned by blacks, they were owned by whites. They would let blacks rent it. So, naturally, they'd have to have police protection. And when they would look on the bandstand and see, you know, someone they knew was white, they'd ask, "What nationality is that gal you got there in the band?" We'd say, "Oh, she's black."[27]

Most of the women with whom I spoke who went on the road with such bands were quick to insist that, at the time, they were not aware of the historical importance of traveling the South with a mixed-race band.

Instead, they often told me that they had merely done what they had to do to survive, that they had needed to fill a vacancy quickly and so-and-so was available, that they were just trying to keep the band together. Yet, despite the many disclaimers that they were too young, too hungry, too naive, or too tired to realize that what they were doing was either dangerous or important, women musicians who played with black bands in the 1940s often told their "police stories" in the 1990s with a sense of post–civil rights movement pride, as did bassist Vi Wilson when she told me that musicians broke the color line for the rest of society.[28] There is more to these stories than just anecdotes from "the bad old days." There is a sense of being on the right and powerless side of a wrong system. Like Earl Hines, the musicians who toured the South in African American women's bands, with or without white members, have come to see themselves as early freedom riders, even if, at the time, their awareness was fully occupied with the daily realities of life on the road.

Vi Wilson, who played with a number of African American all-girl bands that toured the South with white members, dazzled me with numerous stories of harrowing escapes from the police (some of which are related in chap. 6). As I listened to story after story about scrambling onto buses and racing out of town, I was impressed by the courage it took to break Jim Crow laws. Yet the question of why would not go away. Why did black women's bands risk the livelihoods and safety of musicians by adding white members? What was to be gained besides increased risk, harassment, and inconvenience?

I found it somewhat easier to understand why white women, especially those who were interested in learning the styles of playing that were associated with black bands, elected to pass as black to play with the International Sweethearts of Rhythm or the Darlings of Rhythm than why leaders of black all-girl bands hired them. White women musicians who wanted to play jazz sometimes joined black women's bands after becoming dissatisfied with the "corny" or "Mickey Mouse" music that white audiences expected from white women's bands. Bobbie Morrison, who joined a spin-off group from the International Sweethearts of Rhythm after being fired from Ina Ray Hutton's television band (allegedly because her strengths as a drummer leaned more toward "swinging" than "beating"), felt not only that she was more likely to find the music she preferred in black women's bands but that black audiences were more receptive to women players: "I think we were more accepted in the black community than in the white community playing that music."[29]

Wilson's stories, however, did not center around genre preference or audience reception. Rather, they were filled with heroism and danger — risky situations were invariably surmounted by the musicians' solidarity. Usually, the black women in Wilson's stories protected the white women. When I commented on the risks involved in traveling with mixed bands, she responded with the message of musical democracy: "The white musicians and colored musicians, I don't care where we were, we had no prejudice in us. If they'd say gig, the white boys would grab their instruments, the white girls would grab theirs, and we would all get together like a family. And, if they would ever search back in history, you will find that it is because of musicians that we are together today."[30]

Wilson is African American, and I am white. Our conversation about all-girl bands, racial mixing, racism, and police took place in the Burger King at the corner of Washington and Grand in Los Angeles, a little over two years after the police beating of Rodney King, the verdict that cleared the police officers involved, and the resulting rebellion. In 1994, the relation between racism and the police was still salient — the ramifications of the King incident were still being debated, especially in Los Angeles, as we spoke — but we were taking up the topic as it affected all-girl bands fifty years ago. Wilson wanted me to understand the importance of musicians in breaking down prejudice. I wanted to understand why such bands as the International Sweethearts of Rhythm, Eddie Durham's All-Star Girl Orchestra, and the Darlings of Rhythm, all bands with which Wilson herself played at one time or another, toured the South in the 1940s with white members when it would have been infinitely safer (although by no means safe) to do so with an all-black band. "If it was so dangerous to travel with white women," I asked, "then why were they hired?"

The veteran bass player had already answered the question several times, usually by telling me that musicians were not "prejudiced." *Then why didn't white women's bands hire black women?* I wanted to know. "Look," she said, "we played all up here [in the North]. But what we could do is they'd put nut brown powder on. And we made it by. Most of the places we'd make it by, but once in a while we would get. . . ." Her voice trailed off. I knew what they would get. She had already told me. Threats. Searches. Arrests. Insults. Ordered to leave town in fifteen minutes or else. She continued, "Like I told you, musicians weren't prejudiced. We played, and they wanted to play, and we played. And we made it. It was just a few spots we would run into rough territory about it. And we were so mixed up with light girls, we could get by. And, like I told you, the musicians, we changed their minds. You see the races today, we don't have that type of stuff. It took this. These are the ones that paved the way."[31]

Paving the Way

Wilson is not alone in her assertion that jazz and swing musicians of the 1930s and 1940s "paved the way" for integration. Historians may disagree on the extent to which racial mixing in jazz and swing bands inspired a shift toward commitment to racial equality in the wider society, but the fact remains that some jazz and swing bands constituted early integrated social groups in the United States.[32] In the mid- and late 1930s, the entertainment trades and the black press ran many stories celebrating white "name" leaders for hiring black musicians. By the early 1940s, articles also appeared celebrating leaders of "name" black men's bands for hiring white members. On 18 September 1943, the *New York Age* credited Earl "Fatha" Hines with becoming the "first colored leader to add white musicians to his band" as well as "the first leader to include a group of female artists in his permanent organization." In a move that the Apollo Theater ad copy on the same page described as "a great musician's dream come true" and "an achievement of importance to all New York," Hines added two white men musicians and eight black women musicians to his otherwise all-black men's band.[33] Three months later, the *Chicago Defender* reported on Fletcher Henderson's difficulties with southern AFM locals while attempting to travel with three white members.[34]

Then, on 24 March 1945, the *Pittsburgh Courier* reported that "name" black bandleader Lionel Hampton had just hired Herbie Fields, a white tenor saxophonist. "Music has always been a strong wedge in opening the way to better racial understanding," announced the *Courier*, "but for the most part white bandleaders have heretofore taken the initiative in breaking down the color barrier in orchestras. Benny Goodman, Tommy and Jimmy Dorsey, Artie Shaw and Georgie Auld to name a few, broke the ice and signed a number of stellar colored artists. . . . With the possible exception of mixed bands sitting in on recording and jam sessions, colored bands were strictly colored."[35] The article went on to praise Hampton's move as a "noble experiment." It was noble, perhaps, because a trend of black "name" bandleaders hiring white musicians would promote "interracial goodwill" without the benefit of creating new jobs or improving working conditions for black musicians (in fact, a valuable tenor chair for a black musician was sacrificed in this case). It was an experiment, perhaps, because it was unclear whether white America would hear the message of racial tolerance if the test site of integration was a black-owned and -operated band. The benefits of racial mixing in this direction were, indeed, more tenuous than when Hampton himself had been hired by Benny Goodman, signaling the entry, albeit a limited one, of African Americans into the most lucrative and famous sectors of the swing industry. Still, Hampton's gesture could be celebrated for its reappropriation of the moral high ground enjoyed by certain white bandleaders, who tended to receive the credit for breaking the color line (rather than the black musicians, like Hampton, whom they hired). Integration, in other words, became situated as a political commitment of African Americans, not just a paternalistic endowment of white leaders.

Rather than white men selecting one or two "exceptional" black men, the scenario with Hampton as boss is one of an extravagantly moral black man deeming a white man good enough to play in his band and dramatizing interracial goodwill as important enough to justify forfeiting one of the best jobs for a black musician in the country. A black "name" bandleader breaking the color line could be taken as a moral and political challenge to white bandleaders to accelerate the process of integration, as a living example that black people did not necessarily equate integration with token acceptance into the white mainstream, and as a statement that black musicians were even more serious about realizing an egalitarian future than were the successful white bandleaders of the day.

Vi Wilson's version of a history where musicians paved the way resonates with Hampton's hiring of Fields. She speaks from her experiences in black bands that sometimes hired white members. Her version varies in that it does not limit the credit to leaders of any color but praises all musicians. Of course, the most obvious difference in Wilson's interpretation is that her conception foregrounds women as key players. And she has a point. By the time the scoop about Hampton's white sax player circulated as news, the International Sweethearts of Rhythm had been traveling with white members for two years.

By all available accounts, the first African American all-girl band to hire a white member was the International Sweethearts of Rhythm, which added Toby Butler to the trumpet section in 1943. But, long before the Sweethearts hired white women, they included women of color who were not African American as well as light-skinned and mixed-race women who were legally black. In fact, the *International* of the band's title referred to the visible ethnic and racial variety of its membership, which included women who were at least partly Asian, Hispanic, or Native American.

I discuss the "international" theme more fully in the next chapter, but two of its functions were to promote and protect this Mississippi-based black band with light-skinned members as they traveled the segregated South. *International* lent an exotic spin to a racial mix that was sure to arouse the suspicions of the police. Although there would not be white members until 1943, a number of the members of the earlier band could have passed for white. Vocalist Evelyn McGee (Stone), who joined the band in 1939, recalled an occasion when police thought there were white women in the band: "It was in Miami, Florida. I could see officers standing in front of the band so that the people dancing in this dance hall wouldn't get too close. They thought they were all white girls, and they were standing there protecting them."[36] On other occasions, police would "protect" women they thought were white by trying to identify and then arresting them. The "international" theme was, in part, a code announcing that the white-looking women in the band were not North American white women but exotic light-skinned women from other (nonwhite) lands.

The Jim Crow system of segregation divided people into two strictly separate and unequal categories: white and colored. *Colored* meant African Americans (and anyone with any known ancestry thereof), but it also often included, if only by default, people who were neither black nor white. According to baritone saxophonist Willie Mae Wong (Scott), a Chinese American musician such as she herself would have been free to travel with either a black or a white band in the South in the 1930s or 1940s. Having joined when the band was founded in 1936, Scott recalled no problems, personally, traveling with the International Sweethearts of Rhythm and told me, in fact, that she recalled no police harassment of the band as a whole until 1943, when the band started to travel with white members. Lead trombonist Helen Jones (Woods) concurred: "We had a Chinese girl with us in the band, and we had two Puerto Ricans, . . . but we never really got into problems until we started getting white members in the band. Then we had to be careful."[37]

At the same time that the multiethnic but technically "colored" International Sweethearts of Rhythm was making a name for itself and its home base of Piney Woods Country Life School for poor and orphaned black children, a poor and orphaned white child was awaiting the day when she, too, would travel with the band. No stranger to crossing the color line, Toby Butler was legally white but had been raised in Virginia by a black family from the age of seven after the death of her mother. In a letter, she described how she learned about the band:

> I was raised in the black community by a most loving-caring-brilliant lady and her two daughters — the Young family — who were personal friends of Mrs. Rae Lee Jones who managed the Sweethearts. And when the band played in a tiny dance hall in Hampton, Virginia, and in a summer resort — Bayshore, Virginia — they took me to hear this fantastic group — and see all those beautiful instruments played by these lovely young ladies. Whenever the band played, we'd go hear them, year after year. And I knew if I prayed and practiced, one day I'd be a member of the band, too.

When I interviewed Butler, her voice grew warm when she described her annual visits with the Sweethearts when they traveled through Virginia. "Oh, I'd be the first one out there to meet them," she recalled, "and I'd stay with them, listen to them rehearse, and just hang out with them day to day." Although she spoke highly of the family that raised her, she also made it clear that the Young family had very little money and was keeping her out of kindness. She therefore felt an urgency to make her own way. Once she became a Sweetheart of Rhythm, the band became her home and family. "It was my everything," she said. "It was my only thing. My all and all."[38]

But the white police did not see it that way. Butler passed as black as best she could, but, when she was spotted, the band was threatened with violence and arrest. "It was pretty bad," she recalled. "In one place we were warned before we got there not to get off of the bus because they had placed these firebombs, I guess you call them, into the dance hall and they were set to go off. So we never played the gig."[39] Naturally, not playing the gig meant not getting paid.

By the time Butler joined up, the Sweethearts had dramatically separated from the Piney Woods School and the band's founder, Dr. Laurence C. Jones. According to Helen Jones (Woods), who was Dr. Jones's adopted daughter, two bookers from Washington, D.C., convinced the band manager, Rae Lee Jones (no relation to Dr. Jones or Helen Jones), "that we should leave the school and let them manage us and then we would get a good income and things like that. Which they cheated us out of, you know."[40] Some of the more unfortunate aspects of the Sweethearts' management include the fact that the original members were paid far below scale, were told that they owned a house when they did not, and were told that social security had been deducted from their paychecks. Something was deducted, but it did not go to social security.

Leaving the school affected the musicians in a number of ways. Professional arrangers and coaches were hired to help the band become competitive on a professional level. The first person to take on that job was the well-known arranger and bandleader Eddie Durham, formerly a trombonist with Count Basie. Band membership was no longer limited to the Piney Woods student body. When vacancies arose, professional musicians were hired to fill them. This led to the hiring of star soloists from earlier black all-girl bands, notably tenor saxophonist Vi Burnside and trumpet players Jean Starr and Ernestine "Tiny" Davis. It also led to the hiring of the Sweethearts' second white member, alto saxophonist Roz Cron, at the end of 1943.

Unlike Butler, Cron was a Northerner and unacquainted with Southern ways. Hailing from Boston, she was a junior high and high school band section mate of baritone saxophonist Serge Chaloff. In fact, Chaloff, who would later find fame playing baritone in Woody Herman's Thundering Herd, recommended her for her first professional job in the Boston area. By the time the Sweethearts' call for a lead alto reached her ears, Cron had played in numerous local dance bands. She had also already been offered a job with another African American all-girl band, Eddie Durham's All-Star Girl Orchestra, founded by Durham after working with the Sweethearts. Although she sat in with Durham's group, she declined the offer because she was still in high school. After graduating, she worked a season with Ada Leonard's white all-girl band. Although she had considerable big band experience when she joined the Sweethearts and had even toured the South with Leonard's group, she had little knowledge of what it would mean to travel South in a black band. "I never really thought about segregation," she said. "Of course it wasn't taught in the schools. I didn't know it existed, certainly not to the extent that I ran into it. I didn't know that there were real laws out there that said you cannot walk down the street together. Not only can you not work together or marry or socialize, but there were things like sitting on the same park bench. Or if I were to walk down the street, a black person would have to step off the curb. All sorts of things that never occurred to me, and I just hit it all like running into a wall."[41]

Years later, Cron dramatized her first encounter with Jim Crow in a powerful short story written in a musicians' union writing class. In the story, aptly dubbed "Jim Who?" she described a window-shopping excursion with fellow musician Millie Jones, who was African American and Native American and therefore "colored." All went well until, fully unaware of the illegality and danger of her act, Cron sat down at a Woolworths lunch counter and tried to order Cokes for herself and her new friend. The gesture uncannily prefigured the sit-ins of the civil rights movement — except for the fact that Jones squeezed her arm and ran out of the store. Cron followed, thirsty and bewildered — she really wanted that Coke! — and later received a lecture from band manager Rae Lee Jones: "Roz, you did a very dangerous thing today. You put Millie, the whole band, and yourself in jeopardy by sitting down and asking to be served in a downtown facility." Cron's recollection of Jones's warning included sobering rules that she would have to follow if she continued to travel with the band: "If you decide to stay, it is important that you understand that you, or all of us, could be jailed if, at any time, the citizens or sheriffs decide we have white girls working and traveling with us. This isn't an easy thing to do, but if you accept the responsibility and realize the dangers in passing as a colored girl, we can make it work." The story ends with Cron's resolve to "dye my face and hair if I have to because this is where I want to be — with the best damn female big band in America. No law under the name of Jim Crow is going to stop me!"[42]

Cron spent the next three years on the road experimenting with dark makeup, permanents, and making herself inconspicuous. She learned the importance of being "invisible" and of always having ready a good story as to how she came by her "mixed blood." Still, it was not always possible to avoid hazardous situations. She spent a night in jail in El Paso, Texas, for allowing a black soldier in uniform to help her find a taxi one morning when she got separated from the band. The incident occurred well within the war years, when uniformed soldiers were generally held in high regard. Still, the sheriff arrested both Cron and the soldier for the crime of walking down the street together.

By the mid-1940s, Eddie Durham's All-Star Girl Orchestra and the Darlings of Rhythm were also touring the South with an occasional white member. Toby Butler, in fact, played in all three bands at one time or another. The several African American all-girl bands that toured the South during the 1940s were well known to one another. Not only did they share similar schedules and working and traveling conditions, but some bands were built from a nucleus of discontented members from other bands.

Eddie Durham, who had served as Sweethearts arranger and coach after the band broke with Piney Woods, grew unhappy with what he considered the exploitative conditions under which the musicians worked. When he left the Sweethearts, he took some musicians with him and was also able to convince some members of another all-girl band from Piney Woods, the Swinging Rays of Rhythm (who were still with the school), to join his band. In turn, the Darlings of Rhythm core personnel consisted of musicians recruited out of Durham's band. When Durham gave up his band in November 1944, he continued to manage a group made up of remaining members and fronted by Jean Parks. After the disbanding of the International Sweethearts of Rhythm in 1949, the practice of traveling in mostly black groups with a few white members continued in such spin-off groups as Anna Mae Winburn's Sweethearts of Rhythm. The constant movement of musicians between the various black bands in the 1940s provided some mobility for stranded and broke musicians, garnered bargaining power for those in demand, and provided a network for sharing horror stories about and a wealth of survival strategies for traveling the South.

By the time Maxine Fields (Knepper) joined the smaller version of the Sweethearts in 1947, manager Rae Lee Jones was not taking any chances with white women's unfamiliarity with Jim Crow: "When I first joined the band, I wasn't aware that you would really get caught. So the first time that we went down South, Mrs. Jones had a talk with me. She said, 'They'll put you in jail, they'll beat you with hoses so it doesn't show. . . .' I was horrified. It was shocking to me that that kind of thing would happen. So that's what all the learning the talk, putting dark makeup on, all that kind of stuff was about. To survive."[43]

The practice of white people wearing dark makeup, or "browning down," is rooted in blackface minstrelsy, but it took on a different spin in the context of black bands such as the International Sweethearts of Rhythm, Eddie Durham's All-Star Girl Orchestra, and the Darlings of Rhythm. What Frederick Douglass called a theft of "complexion . . . in which to make money" was reappropriated to protect black bands with white members from white racists.[44] Fletcher Henderson's 1943 tour with a mixed band sometimes necessitated the application of burned cork to the faces of his three white members in order to mollify Southern white musicians' union locals.[45] Despite all the publicity that Lionel Hampton sought and received when he hired white tenor player Herbie Fields in 1945, he still found it a necessary precaution to have Fields wear "makeup to darken his face so he didn't stand out so much."[46] As Vi Wilson put it, "The [white] girls would put dark powder on and say they were colored. When the cops would catch us, they wouldn't know whether to arrest us or not."[47]

In nineteenth-century minstrel shows, white actors darkened their faces to put on a show of blackness designed to entertain white audiences. Often, white performers and audiences believed themselves to hold great affection for black culture, but that did not prevent them from delighting in a spectacle of minstrelsy that assured them that "colored" people were comical, mentally inferior, and unequivocally different from white people. Minstrel depictions of "colored" women were conceived as so thoroughly opposed to idealized images of white womanhood that minstrelized characterizations of black women were rarely played by white women in blackface. Instead, these roles were the treasured property of white male actors in blackface and drag, who performed grotesque, comic, hypersexual wench characters.[48] So, oddly enough, one of the ways that browning down was different in black all-girl bands than it was in minstrelsy is that the white performers who darkened their faces to pass for black women were, indeed, women.

Additionally, the application of dark makeup to white women in black all-girl bands challenged Jim Crow in fundamental ways that blackface minstrelsy did not. White women musicians who passed as black sought to blend into the overall image of talented, attractive young black women that had already been achieved by black women and performed for appreciative black audiences. Self-representations of black women as mobile and successful, as beloved "sweethearts" and famous "all-stars," countered white supremacist propaganda about jezebels and mammies. Reviews and articles in the black press often stressed the decidedly antiminstrel portrayals of black womanhood offered by the bands. Of the International Sweethearts of Rhythm, one *Chicago Defender* reviewer gushed, "Not only are the members of the band capable musicians, but they all are attractive and perfectly behaved."[49]

As compliant as this statement may sound today with what we think of as Victorian norms, and as much as we may recoil from the reporter's apparent opinion that beauty and good behavior in black women is news, it is important to recall that black women's claims to womanhood were extremely threatening to the ideology of white supremacy. Images of black women performers as attractive, talented, educated (in the case of the Sweethearts and the Prairie View Co-Eds), respectable, and *swinging,* to boot, offered profound relief, for black audiences and performers alike, from mainstream depictions of black women. This more common degrading pool of representations suffered an enormous gap, what singer/actress Lena Horne described as "the two conventional ideas of Negro womanhood: the 'good,' quiet Negro woman who scrubbed and cooked and was a respectable servant — and the whore."[50] When black women musicians traveled in between these representational ghettos and offered nonracist images of black womanhood to black audiences, they challenged Jim Crow whether they traveled with white women or not.

When white women darkened themselves and blended into a black all-girl band that delivered nonracist visions of black womanhood, the Jim Crow worldview was challenged on a number of levels. How could white police fulfill their destiny as guardians of the color line if common knowledge about differences between black women and white women was so mixed up? How could they perform their duty as defenders of pure white womanhood if the role of protector was usurped by the black women and men band managers and musicians who shielded white women musicians from white police? How could the police embody walking examples of white superiority if they could not tell who was who? How could the one-drop rule be enforced if white-looking black women (who would be arrested if detected in white institutions and social settings) and white-looking white women worked side by side in black performance contexts? When white women's brown makeup made them darker than their light-skinned black section mates, the overall effect was a baffling shell game for the white police—a game that African American all-girl bands often won.

The contradictions of Jim Crow as seen through a makeup jar were not lost on women musicians. White trumpet player Maxine Fields (Knepper) recalled a conversation with her roommate, black drummer Mattie Watson: "One night we were sitting there making up. And she started yelling, 'Isn't this a damn shame?' And I said, 'What's a damn shame?' She said, 'Look at you. You're putting darker makeup on. And I'm sitting her putting lighter makeup on. You're curling your hair, and I'm straightening mine. And we both started cracking up."[51] The scene takes an almost clichéd grass-is-greener beauty commentary and gives it quite a different meaning. This is not simply a case of Madison Avenue selling desire for qualities not already possessed (capitalizing on internalized racism and a fascination with exotic otherness); it appears also as an appreciation for the practical failure of Jim Crow. It is a "damn shame" that the law is racist and does not allow racial mixing—but the joke turns on the fact that race as defined by Jim Crow is so flimsy that the police are fooled by such highly underestimated technologies as hairdos and makeup. The interracial makeup mirror exposes not only contradictions about glamour but also contradictions about how race is defined, detected, and patrolled under Jim Crow. This is a makeup mirror in which success depends not only on musicians' ability to apply cosmetics but also on their accurate knowledge of what police and audiences expect to see when they look at a stage full of black women, in which survival depends on a skillful manipulation of "looks."

One logical outcome of the successful shell game was that the police were so genuinely fooled that they mistook legally black women for white and therefore law-breaking women. In this way, the strategy of "nut brown powder" frequently worked to the disadvantage of light-skinned black band members. Bass player Doris Jarrett (Meilleur), for example, one of the black members of a ten-piece spin-off group called the California Sweethearts of Rhythm, reported: "I traveled with [the California Sweethearts] for about five or six months on what they call the Chitlin' Circuit. We had two white girls that nobody ever said anything to us about. But we had one girl, Ruth, the drummer. She was black, but she had blue eyes, and she was quite fair, and they were going to put us in jail."[52]

Drummer Ruth Raymer, who was born in Kansas and raised in Colorado, described several incidents of surveillance and near arrest from this Southern tour, one instigated by rumors that the band was mixed, the other by police mistaking her for white. "It was a mixed band, and there were white girls, and they wore very dark makeup at that time, very, very dark makeup," she said. "We didn't have any problems with a mixed band until we got to Biloxi, Mississippi. They had had mixed troops march in a Veterans Day parade — this was in the fall of 1949. And it upset some of the local people. So the police heard about this mixed band coming. So, as soon as we got to the place where we were supposed to play, they sent the white girls back to New Orleans. We were recognized. They couldn't play with us. So that left us without key players."[53]

Raymer's account of having to perform without "key players" shows another way in which entire bands were harassed by the police. The self-surveillance necessary to avoid arrest was part and parcel of the difficulties caused by police surveillance. Having to cover for missing players made performances grueling and potentially resulted in docked pay — and Southern tours were grueling enough for black musicians without such added hardships. Raymer recalled other incidents on the road in which the dark makeup that enabled the white women to pass for black resulted in police mistaking her for white and harassing the band: "When we played the Birmingham Theater, the cop on the beat walked in and looked in and said, 'That's some nice gal band you got there, but what are you doing with that white girl on the drums?' Which meant that the three white girls were made up darker than I."

Raymer's experiences as a light-skinned black woman mistaken for white while playing in a black band dramatically illustrate the contradictions of the one-drop rule and the rigid black/white color line of the Jim Crow South. After miraculously completing this embattled tour without winding up in jail, Raymer relocated to Seattle, where she became the only black member of Jack Otto's white all-woman band. Ironically, her presence there failed to provoke guardians of the color line. Perhaps her paradoxical experiences with the California Sweethearts and Otto's band influenced her commitment to the integration of the Seattle locals of the musicians' union (the AFM). During 1952 and 1953, Raymer served on the committee that resulted in the merger of the black Local 493 and the white Local 76.

Although police confusion over who was light and who was white provoked many incidents of harassment, it also underscored the fundamentally preposterous nature of Jim Crow's crusade against the dilution of the white race. It was not news to most African Americans that racial purity, the very fulcrum of Jim Crow, was a myth, but the concept continued to buttress the logic of the laws. The contradiction of laws based on white supremacy and the inability of the white police infallibly to tell black from white could be productively and creatively exploited to protect bands.

"There was a lot of what they call *bedroom integration* in the South. You know, there were a lot of kids that were half black and half white," said Helen Jones (Woods). Many women whom I interviewed, both African American and white, brought up the contradictions of bedroom integration and Jim Crow segregation laws. "That's what really boggles your mind," said Evelyn McGee (Stone). "The prejudice in the South was so strong, and yet these white men were sleeping with all these black women." What the myth of the black rapist covered up was a history of white men's sexual coercion of black women. Laws such as the one-drop rule ensured that offspring of such liaisons would be defined as black, therefore making it possible to retain a population that could be imagined as pure white. Woods, whose own racial heritage included one black parent and one white, went on to explain how the contradictory history of bedroom integration in a segregated society could be used to the band's advantage. When police singled out a legally white musician, band members would reply, " 'She's a mulatto. Her father's white, but her mother's black.' That's one of the things that the girls would say when [the police] said, 'That's no black girl, that's a white girl in the band.' They'd say, 'No, her father's white. She doesn't know who he is.' You know, you'd turn them off like that, you know."[54]

Kinship between blacks and whites was a historical reality that Southern white segregationists preferred to keep tucked away in the colored side of town. "Turning off" the white police by evoking the undeniable presence of black people who did not know who their white fathers were was one way musicians could confront Jim Crow with its own historical contradictions. The resulting police discomfort and confusion could, and often did, serve to defuse potentially explosive situations. Even if the strategy worked, bands might still be ordered to leave town, but at least no one would be arrested. In another evocation of black/white kinship, white band members passed not merely as colored but as "cousins" of light-skinned black women in the band. When the police did not believe Roz Cron's story that her mother was black and her father white, they put her in jail. But, when her two "cousins" showed up at the jail the next morning, she was released: "The manager brought two of the real light-skinned gals, both of whom were half white and half black. They came about five in the morning, before it was light. . . . The sheriff said that he knew that I was passing but he just wanted us to get out of town and never come back to El Paso again."[55] The cousins' strategy was also crucial to one of the Darlings' narrow escapes, as will be described in chapter 6.

By exploiting police confusion about who was black and who was white, traveling bands with mixed personnel exposed the cracks in Jim Crow. While encounters with the law were serious, dangerous, and no doubt frightening at the time, many narrators took great pleasure in relating Keystone Kop–like stories in which black all-girl bands fool the white police. In the late 1940s, Anna Mae Winburn's Sweethearts of Rhythm, a six-piece spin-off group from the Sweethearts' big band, traveled the South. Winburn led the group, her husband, Duke Pilgrim, managed it, and the band traveled with two or three white members at a time. Maxine Fields (Knepper) and Roberta "Bobbie" Morrison, two white players who played with the band at one time or another, both recalled an incident in Fort Lauderdale, Florida.

According to Fields, the band had

> worked a dance, and there were police around, and one of them liked the piano player. He wanted to have a date with her. And she refused, so he was really mad. We went to a place to eat afterward, and the police came and stopped the car. I think there were four blacks and three whites in the car. They stopped the car, and they said, "We know there's some white people. You turn around, and you follow me back to the police station." You know. It was going to be some real trouble. And I had met a Sea-grams 7 salesman at the dance, and I was kind of inebriated. So we're following them back to the police station, you know, my God. And I said, "Hey, Duke, aren't we going right by the hotel where we're staying?" — which was a black hotel. About two blocks down the street. "Aren't we coming to that?" He said, "Yeah." I said, "Well, slow down." He slowed down. All the whites jumped out, closed the door, and [the car] kept following [the police].[56]

"We went back to the hotel!" laughed Morrison. Her version is essentially the same as Fields's, although to her memory the police pulled the car over under the pretext of having caught them speeding. "And, after-ward, Duke told us about what happened at the station. They were furious because, 'Where were the white girls?' 'What white girls? This is a family band!' It was that kind of thing. Duke said that, when he was leaving the station, the sergeant was yelling at the officers who arrested us. 'You've never been to New Orleans? You've never seen a mulatto?' That kind of thing. So it was kind of funny. But there were spots and little incidents like that."[57]

In another story, Fields recalled a close call on the bandstand: "I feel somebody looking at me while I'm playing. And I look down, and here's this policeman with an awful look on his face. There were two of them. And, you know, the looks on their faces. Uh-oh, there's trouble there." But the set ended without incident, and the band packed up to go to the next gig. As it turned out, the band manager, Duke Pilgrim, had once again outwitted the white police at their own game. Pilgrim was a light-skinned black man who was skilled at making his racial ambiguity in the eyes of the white police work to his advantage. As pianist Ernestine May put it, "I'm pretty sure he didn't tell anybody that he was not white." Fields explained the scenario as Pilgrim had related it to her: "There were three whites and three blacks. The police went up to Duke, the manager, and said to him, 'You're not going to tell me there's not any white girls in that band.' Duke said, 'Yeah, there's some white girls. There's two white girls in the band. But, if you're going to cause trouble, you'd better make damn sure you get the right two.' "[58] After being stared at all night by white police trying to decide which two women to arrest, three black women and three white women finished out their gig unmolested. Not wanting to get in trouble for arresting a legally black woman (an ideological as well as professional faux pas), the police went home empty-handed.

According to Ernestine May, one of the black women in this particular version of the band, many potential problems were averted thanks to Pilgrim's ability to manipulate holes in Jim Crow logic as well as police inability to pin him down racially. "He was very light," she recalled. "I think Duke was maybe partially Puerto Rican or Spanish. But he was black. I mean he was not black in color. He looked white. He had straight hair. You would look at him, and you would not know that he was not white. And I think his being that shade and looking white alleviated a lot of problems. Because that would be acceptable for a white manager, which he was. And he drove the car. That would be acceptable."[59] In this case, white women darkening their faces and claiming fellow musicians as cousins were only part of the passing that this group did. May believed that Pilgrim's ability to pass at times as a white man saved the black women's band from many potential troubles on the road. Vi Wilson also recalled that the white man who drove the Darlings of Rhythm's bus sometimes passed as the band manager in order to make travel safer and easier. Even though the laws were supposedly aimed at separating blacks and whites, it appears that gender made a difference. The presence of white men as owners/managers of black all-girl bands did not threaten white supremacy.

While black all-girl bands did not end segregation once and for all, they played an important role, along with countless other African American social, political, and cultural organizations, in paving the way for the civil rights movement to come. Black women's bands traversed the South with white members three years before, in 1946, the Supreme Court found forced segregation in interstate travel unconstitutional. Black and white women musicians in black all-girl bands rode on buses together, ate together, slept together, and worked together four years before the Congress of Racial Equality (CORE) tested the Supreme Court ruling on interstate transportation by sending eight white and eight black people out on an integrated Journey of Reconciliation by bus in 1947 (incurring twelve arrests and one violent attack).[60] Civil rights movement–style integration would later be criticized for focusing on black people's entrance into the white mainstream rather than demanding a radical restructuring of a system built on inequalities. When black-owned and -operated all-girl bands included white members, they practiced a kind of integration that challenged the white mainstream.[61] Even when such bands crossed the color line *covertly,* as they usually did, these crossings and the attendant surveillance shook the foundational notions of white supremacy. Race and gender hierarchies were disrupted when white men were confronted with their inability easily to tell black women from white women, when black women and black men protected white women from white men, when interracial social mixing did not involve sexual coercion. And, on those rare occasions in the late 1940s when the black press reported on the integrated personnel of black women's bands, the purpose of such revelations quite often served to critique the status quo and call for its transformation.

In June 1946, the *Pittsburgh Courier* praised the courage of the International Sweethearts of Rhythm for demanding police protection for their performance at a harvest festival in Rocky Mount, North Carolina, after the Ku Klux Klan had threatened the women with kidnapping and violence.[62] If, amid a history of harassment and criminalization, the demand for police protection seems implausible, it is important to locate this turn of events in an ongoing protest by black musicians and audiences that year. In January 1946, the well-publicized police beating of Cab Calloway in Kansas City had spawned public outrage and protests by prominent black bandleaders, who argued that black traveling musicians deserved police protection, not police brutalization. The Sweethearts' demand for police protection, along with the band's resolve to perform with a mixed band despite the threats of the KKK, bears witness to the contributions of black all-girl bands to the civil rights struggles of the 1940s.

It would be incorrect to insist that black women's bands of the 1940s were consciously oppositional political organizations that toured the South with the purpose of combatting racism. But it is historically illuminating to reflect on what they did do in the context of World War II–era struggles for full citizenship for African Americans. It is no small matter that such bands as the International Sweethearts of Rhythm, Anna Mae Winburn's Sweethearts of Rhythm, Eddie Durham's All-Star Girl Orchestra, and the Darlings of Rhythm proved, well before Freedom Summer, that the holes in Jim Crow were big enough to drive a bus through.

Chapter 5

Internationalism and

the Sweethearts of Rhythm

Leader: Do you want to jump, children?

Band: Yeah!

Leader: Jump, jump, jump, jump!

— Maurice King and

the International Sweethearts of Rhythm,

"Jump Children"

After being virtually ignored by conventional jazz and swing histories, one all-girl band of the 1940s — the International Sweethearts of Rhythm — found itself embraced in the late 1970s and 1980s under the rubric of the women's movement. As we have seen, the International Sweethearts of Rhythm — active from 1937 to 1949 — at any given moment included African American women, mixed-race women, other women of color, and, after 1943, one or two white women. Despite the band's unequivocal position on the "colored" side of Jim Crow's sharp black/white divide, the "international" theme reflected in the band's name referred to the ethnic and racial diversity of its personnel.

The international theme, as I have suggested, offered some protection for these very young women, some of whom did not look black enough to satisfy Southern white police. *International* evoked exotic visitors from other lands, rather than local members of a subordinated group and drew attention away from real or imagined transgressions of the strictly patrolled black/white color line. In this chapter, I consider additional reasons for the appeal of this unique representational tactic. The image of women from many lands, what baritone saxophonist Willie Mae Wong (Scott) termed the band's "international aspect," was useful not solely as a survival strategy against white segregationists; it was also a popular selling point with African American audiences.

Publicity photographs of the International Sweethearts of Rhythm
tended to emphasize the band's ethnically diverse membership. This
sax section photograph was taken in Chicago in 1944. *Clockwise
from lower left:* Grace Bayron (fourth tenor), Helen Saine (third
alto), Rosalind "Roz" Cron (lead alto), Vi Burnside (second/jazz
tenor), Willie Mae Wong (baritone). *Courtesy Rosalind Cron.*

Forty years later, the band's new second wave feminist audience also
derived pleasure, hope, and inspiration from the internationalism of the
Sweethearts of Rhythm. Sisterhood among women was emphasized in
the 1980s, as products commemorating the history and music of the
Sweethearts were stocked alongside contemporary women's recordings
in the inventories of feminist bookstores and distribution outlets, wom-

en's music mail-order catalogs, and women's film festivals as well as gay and lesbian film festivals. Alumnae of the original band were honored at the 1980 Women's Jazz Festival in Kansas City. Marketed as *women's music*,[1] the International Sweethearts of Rhythm became a symbol for such popular concepts of early second wave feminism as *women's creativity, women's community,* and *global sisterhood.* Not surprisingly, these celebrations of the Sweethearts tell more about the desires of second wave feminists than about the musicians who emerged from the Piney Woods Country Life School in Mississippi during the Great Depression.

I do not, however, mean to say either that the later 1980s audience got it wrong or that the band was correctly understood by its earlier 1940s audience. I am simply interested in exploring the ways in which the band's performances were understood by both audiences. Certainly, internationalism was not the *only* meaningful aspect of this band. Both sets of fans celebrated the Sweethearts as the greatest all-girl band of the 1940s. The Sweethearts' origins at Piney Woods Country Life School for poor and orphaned black children was extremely important to 1930s and 1940s black audiences. As with the Prairie View Co-Eds, the proud history of black education traveled with the Sweethearts, even after the band ended its relationship with Piney Woods. The Sweethearts reflected a history of African Americans providing basic education for poor black children, rather than the more middle-class hopes represented by the college-educated women of the Prairie View Co-Eds, but both bands served as reminders of the struggles of African Americans for education as a mode of resistance, freedom, and progress. Yet the international theme of the Sweethearts was unique among all-girl bands in the 1940s and constituted a significant part of the appeal of the band in both the 1940s and the 1980s. I am especially interested in how that theme served to loosen the stubborn mortar between commonly held, problematic assumptions about race, allowing alternative, more democratic ways of thinking about cultural and ethnic variety to be imagined, modeled, and perhaps even realized.

In the 1940s, the International Sweethearts of Rhythm enjoyed an enormous following among the African American audiences who heard them on the black theater circuit, including the Apollo in New York, the Paradise in Detroit, and the Howard in Washington, D.C.; at numberless dance halls and auditoriums throughout the United States; at military camps both stateside and in Europe when the band traveled on USO tours; and over the airwaves courtesy Armed Forces Radio broadcasts of

"Jubilee," a show targeting African American soldiers. Their high profile in the entertainment sections of black newspapers included many
stories praising the band's musicianship as well as its ability to reflect
political strategies more explicitly represented in news and editorial
pages, including "racial uplift," the "international solidarity of the black
and brown races," and the "Double Victory campaign," which called for
victory against racism at home as well as victory against fascism abroad.

Such interpretations of the Sweethearts, however, may tell us more
about the desires of an audience engaged in a multifaceted struggle for
civil rights than they do about the aspirations and experiences of the
musicians. At the same time that the Sweethearts represented "race
pride" in the black press, the musicians themselves, especially the original members, were being exploited, underpaid, and deceived — by African American managers, men and women alike. I therefore also explore
what the international theme of the band meant to the women musicians
who played in it. Despite the exploitation and hardship that they suffered, when interviewed, former Sweethearts frequently told utopian
tales of wonder and possibility. "We were like sisters, really," said vocalist Evelyn McGee (Stone), "I mean, the way the world should have been
long before the Sweethearts of Rhythm." "We knew no color," said
trumpet player Toby Butler, the first white member of the band. "We did
not know white, black, red, or yellow. It didn't matter. We just knew each
other and the love of music."[2]

By examining the musicians' memories, I do not want to imply that
here, at last, in "the women's own words" is the *truth* about internationalism and the Sweethearts of Rhythm. Rather, I wish to explore how
and why this international theme was produced. What rendered this
relentlessly upbeat version of international sisterhood possible? How did
musicians all born and raised in the United States, all living in the single
state of Mississippi (and, after April 1941, Virginia) embody international relations? And how did the women who performed this powerful
symbol of united nations feel about what they were doing? Why did they
do it? And what does it mean to the musicians fifty years later, in the
1990s, to have traveled Jim Crow terrain in a mixed band, to have played
band instruments associated with men, and to have participated in creating an international aspect to what was, in fact, an American band made
up of women who were either legally black or passing for black? I save
the artists' memories for last, however, not because these are the *true*
goods on what the International Sweethearts of Rhythm symbolized, but

because, before discussing how "internationalism" was crafted by the musicians, it two useful first to examine the powerful effects that the band had on two very different audiences that loved them.

Thinking about how audiences in the past felt about particular performances is an imperfect science, reliant on meticulous, historically informed speculation. Yet I do not see it as an idle exercise to wonder what it was about the International Sweethearts of Rhythm that allowed them to appeal to audiences separated by forty years (and, in many cases, by race, class, gender, and sexuality). More important, what enabled the band not only to *entertain* diverse spectators but to stimulate visions of better worlds? Do the Sweethearts have the potential to inspire audiences today? In order to explore the Sweethearts' profound ability to symbolize social harmony in distinct historical contexts, I would like to dim the lights and roll some footage of the band that was seen by audiences in the 1940s and the 1980s.

Establishing Shot

A short film made in 1946 opens with a tightly arranged, but swinging, big band introduction played under these opening credits: "Soundies Presents the International Sweethearts of Rhythm in 'Jump Children' Featuring Anne Mae Winburn."[3] Forty years later, in a 1986 documentary by filmmakers Greta Schiller and Andrea Weiss, *The International Sweethearts of Rhythm,* the same sound track was used to accompany a slightly different title sequence: "Jezebel Productions and Rosetta Records Present the International Sweethearts of Rhythm, America's Hottest All-Girl Band."[4] After the titles fade, the establishing shots from the 1946 film and the 1986 documentary are identical. An artfully angled long shot takes in the whole sixteen-piece band plus its leader, not straight on, but diagonally, over the piano on the right side of the stage. The view is wide enough that all the young women musicians — five on saxophone, four on trumpet, three on trombone, and one each on guitar, piano, bass, and drums — fit in the frame as they play the introduction of the tune "Jump, Children." Seated on a tiered stage behind music stands decorated with valentine hearts, the musicians execute the opening bars of the swing arrangement, remaining at all times attentive to their glamorous leader, who stands in front, facing us, her back to the band, smiles into the camera, and prepares to sing. This shared footage also serves as the establishing shot for this chapter. Viewing it with its distinct reception histories in mind, I sit in the 1990s, wondering what the Sweethearts may have meant to their fans during the Second World War and during the second wave of the women's movement. Some program notes are in order before we continue.

In 1946, the Sweethearts' first fans, African American men and women, viewed the "Jump Children" Soundie on machines called Panorams (jukeboxes with screens) in public places like hotels, drugstores, restaurants, and bars.[5] White viewers of Soundies may have also encountered this film on Panorams in white-designated public places, but, owing to the strict racial segregation of U.S. society in the 1940s, few of them would have known who the Sweethearts were since the band performed live primarily before black audiences and since few white people would have read the black newspapers that regularly reported the activities of this celebrated all-woman band. Many African Americans, on the other hand — whose public entertainment options were restricted to the same venues that the Sweethearts were likely to play and who constituted the readership of black newspapers — would likely be well acquainted with the Sweethearts' performances and publicity. It is also more likely that Panorams in black public places would have been stocked with the Sweethearts' Soundies, just as jukeboxes in black public spaces would be more likely to stock "race records" than would those in whites-only venues.[6]

In 1986, audiences most likely encountered the Sweethearts' cinematic version of "Jump Children" through Schiller and Weiss's documentary at women's film festivals, in women's studies classes, or at gay and lesbian film festivals. The circuits of the second wave of the women's movement that I am going to discuss were much criticized in the 1970s and 1980s by women of color, working-class women, lesbians, and other women excluded from the narrow confines of white middle-class U.S. women's experience, which was frequently held up by movement spokespeople as universal. While it is not surprising that those with the most institutional power would wind up proffering themselves as the model for all liberated women, this effect was the antithesis of what many second wave feminists intended. As Adrienne Rich put it, "Some of us, calling ourselves radical feminists, never meant anything less by women's liberation than the creation of a society without domination. The problem was that we did not know whom we meant when we said 'we.' "[7] Discovering that this "we" left out large numbers of women was disappointing both to the many women who found themselves excluded or found the costs of inclusion too exorbitant and to many of the women who felt relatively comfortable in that restrictive/collective space. Critiques from within the movement that exposed some movement women as reproducing the same kinds of unequal power hierarchies that they claimed to be fighting (supposedly on behalf of all women) offered a painful glimpse of the hypocrisy in a movement that was built, after all, on a foundational image of itself as egalitarian. The anguish of this struggle was felt, and can still be felt, in many women's studies classes, informal study groups, and activist circles.

One of the ways that white middle-class U.S. feminists sought to respond to such criticism was by enthusiastically consuming and celebrating cultural products by women of color. Hazel Carby has remarked on the tendency of women's studies departments to romanticize historical black women "as cultural and political icons," in the process often reducing them "to a single dimension of either suffering or nobility."[8] Carby uses the example of such black women writers as Zora Neale Hurston to illustrate this claim, but the argument could also be readily extended to such musical figures as Ma Rainey, Bessie Smith, and Billie Holiday. It has taken considerably longer for white-dominated second wave circles to engage the theoretical work of women of color. But products by and about cultural figures in the past, especially African American women, were readily incorporated.

Indeed, the second wave of the women's movement is the context for my own introduction to the International Sweethearts of Rhythm. I first saw the "Jump Children" Soundie as a rare collectible (before it was reissued by Rosetta Records on *Jazzwomen on Video, 1932–1952*) at a women-in-jazz film festival and soon afterward saw it again spliced throughout the Schiller and Weiss documentary in a women's studies class. Both films moved me first to tears, then to the library, then to the series of interviews and oral histories that became the crux of this book. Certainly, my attention lingers on the "Jump Children" footage partly because I wish to explore the meanings that this harmonious multicultural band of women held and continues to hold for me as well as for the diverse audiences that continue to view the film through Schiller and Weiss's documentary. And, certainly, I wish to share how my research has significantly transformed how I interpret these meanings. That said, let us return to the opening footage, keeping an eye open for the film's ability to generate salient, if sometimes conflicting, messages about race, gender, nation, coalition, and community across multiple historical contexts.

As the titles disappear, the screen reveals, at some distance, the fifteen young women who make up the band, their music stands, their instruments. The camera then cuts to a medium long shot of Anna Mae Winburn, the glamorous bandleader, who bounces gently on her toes in tempo, front and center, with her back to the musicians. She begins her vocal just as the film cuts to a closer medium shot that places her at the center of the screen: "When you're feeling low and don't know what to do. . . ." The frame is defined by Winburn's face and upper torso. "When you're feeling low and don't know what to do," she repeats. The brass and reeds answer during her pauses with short, musical phrases, known as riffs. "Just stay in the groove, and don't let nothing bother you." The form is AAB blues, so the last line of the stanza answers the first two.

Winburn is wrapped in a black sarong that leaves her shoulders and midriff bare; her abundant, black hair is piled elegantly on her head. She smiles amiably into the camera, conducting the musicians by bouncing gently in time (sometimes in double time) and by waving her hands away from her body, a gesture read by the audience as an attractive visual offering but legible enough to allow the musicians to discern tempo, dynamics, and cues. Occasionally, the camera cuts to medium long or long shots that enable us to glimpse some of the other women in the band—looking like schoolgirls in their decidedly unglamorous white blouses and dark skirts. For that quick moment, we see the women in the band play their instruments and smile (when not blowing into horns). Nobody appears to be "feeling low." Everybody seems to "know what to do." But the camera always returns to close-ups of the leader, who remains the focal point throughout the two-and-a-half-minute Soundie, which also frames the later thirty-minute documentary.

During those brief moments when the camera relaxes its grip on Winburn's head and torso, cutting away to brief takes where we can see a broader picture of the stage, we are reminded that this is a studio, not a live performance. If it had been live, we would see an audience, either seated in theater rows or dancing. It would certainly be a segregated audience, probably a black audience, although there might be white people sitting in the balcony, watching the black people dance on the floor below. But this performance is for the camera. There is no audience within its frame. The audience is the camera and, beyond it, the viewers of the film. And, because there is a camera, this performance is an atypical appearance of the International Sweethearts of Rhythm. Where are the ubiquitous white police, for instance, who normally guarded white-owned Southern dance halls, habitually standing before the band-stand, trying to figure out if any of those light-skinned black women are, in *reality,* fallen white women breaking the color line? The police, after all, were not just protecting *buildings* as property. As we have seen in the previous chapter, they were protecting the very ideology of white purity and supremacy, of whiteness *as* property.[9]

Since the band's beginnings in the mid-1930s, the International Sweethearts of Rhythm had baffled police by presenting a confusing range of skin color while remaining, legally, a black band. Since the founding of the band in 1937, the Sweethearts had included light-skinned, mixed-race women: women who were part African American (and part white, Asian, Latina, or Native American) and therefore legally black by the one-drop rule. After 1943, however, the band traveled with one or two legally white members whose blackness came, not from blood, but from greasepaint. In this Soundie, we do not see the white police studying the musicians, trying to decide which musicians might lack that decisive drop of black blood. We are not aware of surveillance.

Nor does the camera reveal the range of skin colors and racialized physical differences that underwrite the *international* of the band's title. By holding the band at a distance, the camera discourages a reading of the Sweethearts as representing many nations or even as racially mixed. Not even the much-celebrated Chinese heritage of baritone saxophonist Willie Mae Wong (Scott), object of much 1930s and 1940s publicity in the black press, is legible at this distance. Throughout most of the Soundie, Winburn stands directly in front of Wong, although the baritone player can be observed briefly when Vi Burnside rises to take her tenor solo. Quick peeks at white trumpet player Toby Butler are intermittently possible, but she does not stand out, positioned as she is in the back row, in the fourth trumpet chair, popping in and out of the top-right-hand corner of the frame. The director seems to have been unable to decide whether Butler should be in the shot. This footage seems to have been tailored not to offend segregationists yet crafted with enough ambiguity so as not completely to obscure the possibility that the band is mixed, for those to whom this aspect is important.

The International Sweethearts of Rhythm. . . . The logos on the music stands are heart shaped, so the *sweethearts* part makes sense. For wartime audiences, women without men were often perceived as sweethearts waiting at home. The *rhythm* part makes musical sense, especially when drummer Pauline Braddy breaks up the beat during her drum solo. But *international*? . . . The music would certainly not be considered international. Consisting of a swing arrangement of a blues tune, "Jump Children" constituted a common and popular merging of two African American musical forms. The musicians wear skirts and jackets rather than the trademark peasant dresses of indeterminate nationality that appeared in many of their publicity photographs. The one readily visible sign of internationalism is Winburn's dress, a sarong. (Although popularized in the United States by such stars as Dorothy Lamour, the sarong flourished stateside precisely because it was considered exotic and emblematic of Pacific Islanders encountered during the war.) Winburn's sarong winds around her neck, crisscrossing her breasts (where it is secured with a jewel). The camera frames her closely as she takes the next verse.

Winburn's vocal style is not so much a blues delivery as it is slightly torchy but mostly sweet. Still, the next three stanzas are traditional variations on blues lyrics. Do audiences read the next lines as a woman's boast of physical, maybe sexual, stamina or as a more general assertion of ability?

I may be small, but baby have no fear,
I may be small, but baby have no fear,
I can climb a hill without shifting gears.

In the context of an all-girl band playing instruments and musical styles associated with men, both 1940s and 1980s audiences might read this statement as, "OK, we're young and female, but, even though nobody expects us to produce a big, swinging sound, here it is."

The next stanza also comes out of the public domain of blues lyrics. "My mama gave me something" has been interpreted by other singers in other songs as an expression or a promise of female sexual expertise, but Winburn's cheerfully blithe delivery pushes against an eroticized reading:

I ain't good-looking, and I don't have waist-long hair,
I ain't good-looking, and I don't have waist-long hair,
But my mama gave me something that can take me anywhere.

Another set of traditional lyrics, these also receive a nontraditional spin in the context of an all-girl band. The white Euro-American beauty standards suggested by the reference to "waist-long hair" might invite a comparison of the Sweethearts with certain more famous white bands of the day whose renown hinged on meeting dominant white cultural notions of glamour. While the singer/leader is "good-looking" in her role as gorgeous bandleader (one musician recalled Winburn carrying on an unofficial "gown war" with white bandleader Ina Ray Hutton),[10] the other musicians (not engaged in gown warfare) come off more as spunky, talented youngsters than as worldly wise starlets. The "something" that takes them "anywhere" (or at least all over the United States and parts of Europe — farther if you count the geographic and time travels of the documentary) could be read by their fans as their musical ability and their success at delighting audiences with their big band performances and international fame. The "something" comes from their mothers. Is that "something" race? The slave codes that decreed that offspring of white men and black slave women "followed the condition of the mother" would support this interpretation.

Winburn's delivery clearly indicates that that "something" is a beneficial inheritance and one that enables mobility. For 1940s black audiences, that "something" could be read as race pride, with the artists' mothers as valued transmitters of their African American cultural heritage (drawing from the mostly reliable assumption that even the mixed-race band members had black mothers). For 1980s feminist audiences, matrilineal transmission of culture would also resonate, although it would probably not be conceived of as raced. Most likely, it would be embraced as an affirmation of women's culture, which, despite differences among the women who participated in the second wave, was often thought (primarily by white feminists) to cross racial, class, historical, and geographic boundaries.

At this point in the film, the 1946 Soundie and the 1986 documentary diverge. The Soundie will swing on to its musical conclusion. The documentary will cut away to interviews with middle-aged Sweethearts of Rhythm, still photos of the band members and other women of the 1940s, archival footage, and clips from other Soundies made by the band, ultimately returning to the chorus, tenor solo, and final bars of the "Jump Children" Soundie. I stop the films again here to dig more deeply into some of the meanings generated by the International Sweethearts of Rhythm for their audiences.

Other than Winburn's sarong, nothing about the Soundie emphasizes racial or cultural difference. The *international* in the band's title is unintelligible. In order to understand more about what this performance communicated to specific audiences, it is necessary to locate the reception of "Jump Children" alongside the distinct sets of stories that circulated in the 1940s in the black press and in the 1980s in women's music discourse, both of which linked particular ideas about globalness with the Sweethearts of Rhythm.

In both the 1940s and the 1980s, the international aspect of the band was more about ways of conceiving race than it was about alliances between nations, although the "racial project" of the band was interpreted quite differently by the two audiences. For both audiences, the Sweethearts' internationalism contributed to their ability to enact what cultural studies theorist Paul Gilroy has called "utopian promises," in which cultural productions help people envision social alternatives.[11] For black audiences of the 1940s, internationalism was inscribed in the exotic attention paid to the range of skin color, facial features, and origins of band personnel. The black press paid homage to this group of young women imagined to be from around the world (nonetheless identified as "race women") as offering an empowering social alternative to looking at blackness as a monolithic category of second-class status. During the Second World War, complex alliances were drawn between African Americans and colonized and oppressed people in Africa, the West Indies, India, and other locations, who sought to transform the global crisis into a struggle for world freedom. For second wave feminists and women's music audiences of the 1980s, the Sweethearts' internationalism was not so much a new way of looking at blackness as it was a new way of looking at women's community as racially diverse and equally empowered. To a white-dominated women's movement struggling with its own racism, the Sweethearts provided an upbeat vision of multicultural foremothers: women of color and white women, lesbians and straights, all loving each other and working effortlessly together.

Passing for Integrated:
Sweethearts of the Second Wave

I confess that my own attraction to the Sweethearts originates from the very belly of the women's music discourse that I am about to critique. It has become fashionable to expose the shortcomings of the second wave without acknowledging the utopian promises it held for countless women of the 1960s and 1970s. Women-only spaces were developed by those who believed that all women did have something in common as recipients of sexism and that women's organizing could result in havens where women could work together to improve their own lives and the lives of women everywhere. I wept on first viewing the 1986 documentary, taking the film as testimony to the utopian possibilities of women's community. The sight of a multiracial group of women, playing all the instruments in the band, struck me as an example of how women's creativity might transcend racism and sexism. Homophobia seemed vanquished as well. I cheered trumpet player Ernestine "Tiny" Davis as she offered her woman-identified explanation for why she turned down a better-paying job offer from Louis Armstrong. "I loved them gals too much!" declared Davis, imbuing the word *gals* with a meaningful nuance. "I loved them *gals* too much!"[12] And I was delighted to find, in the sound bites of alto saxophonist Roz Cron, a role model for white women's antiracist alliances with women of color.

My introduction to the Sweethearts documentary occurred in my first women's studies class, "History of African American Women," taught by Angela Davis at San Francisco State. Reading Paula Giddings's *When and Where I Enter* and Gerda Lerner's *Black Women in White America,* I was overwhelmed by white liberal guilt and distressed by my first taste of the tension that can erupt when women of diverse races, classes, and sexualities discuss feminism. So it should be no surprise that I experienced great joy and relief when I viewed the Sweethearts documentary. The band appeared to me as a model for how women can live and work together across difference: black women, white women, Asian women, Latinas, Native American women, gay women, straight women. Without universalizing my own reaction, my desire for women to work successfully across difference, so successfully that difference hardly mattered, may provide a clue as to why the International Sweethearts of Rhythm were celebrated by other feminists at that time.

Of course, in order to celebrate the Sweethearts as models of women's ability to cooperate harmoniously, there were certain things the well-intentioned feminist could not know about the band and the times in which it played. It would complicate a celebration of the Sweethearts as a color-blind sisterhood, for example, to know that, while many African American all-woman big bands of the 1940s occasionally hired white members, virtually none of the white all-woman big bands ever hired black members, that, in fact, both black and white men's bands hired women more often than white women's bands hired black women. A celebration of the Sweethearts as an early U.S. women-of-color space —much like the alliances being formed among African American, Latina, Asian American, and Native American women in the 1970s and 1980s —

would be complicated by the knowledge that the band's internationalism had been consciously crafted by the African American man who founded the band as a promotional gimmick and at least partly based on a preference for light-skinned women in black entertainment. A celebration of the band as a space of sexual liberation would be unsettled by the fact that some Sweethearts alumnae were horrified when the documentary was shown at gay and lesbian film festivals and further distressed when Schiller and Weiss followed up their Sweethearts documentary with a film focusing on the forty-two-year relationship between Tiny Davis and Ruby Lucas.[13] All these celebrations would be disrupted if fans knew that the original Sweethearts were grossly exploited by their managers, both men and women (e.g., they were never paid for this Soundies appearance). These complications were not completely ignored, but neither were they emphasized in most material on the band that came out in the 1980s — certainly not in the documentary and not in the liner notes to the Rosetta Records reissues of Sweethearts' recordings and broadcasts. Celebration was encouraged by an emphasis on agency and independence typical of women's histories or "herstories" of the second wave.

D. Antoinette Handy's book on the band diverged considerably in its attempt to locate the Sweethearts' story in an African American historical context rather than celebrate the band as an example of interracial harmony. In her discussion of the relation between the Sweethearts and Piney Woods School, Handy traced the many black history precedents for musical groups as traveling ambassadors and fund-raisers for black educational institutions. Her detailed history of Piney Woods School and its founder, Laurence C. Jones, stands in contrast to other 1980s narratives that present the band's "escape" from the school as an unequivocally heroic feminist moment. She criticized the 1980 Women's Jazz Festival for failing to advertise the tribute to the Sweethearts in the black press (very few black people were present when band members were flown to Kansas City to be interviewed by Leonard Feather, reunite, and participate in a jam session).[14] But these critiques were not echoed in most treatments of the International Sweethearts of Rhythm in the 1980s. It was easy to consume the band as interracial rather than black, as foremothers rather than alive-and-kicking older women who did not necessarily identify with the second wave, and as proof that women's community and women's creativity could transcend racism and homophobia.

It is crucial to consider the resurrection of materials on the Sweethearts in conjunction with the emergent category *women's music* in the United

States in the 1970s. By many accounts, 1972 and 1973 are the pivotal years for women's music as a recorded genre. These were the years that the folklike music with the feminist lyrics expanded beyond the coffee-houses and found its way onto the first women's music albums, including Alix Dobkin's *Lavender Jane Loves Women* (1973), a release that not only featured lesbian subject matter and musicians but was funded, pro-duced, engineered, and distributed by lesbians. In 1973, Olivia Records, the largest producer of women's music recordings, was founded, releas-ing that year a forty-five featuring Meg Christian and Cris Williamson.[15] The first National Women's Music Festival was held in 1974, with the first Michigan Womyn's Music Festival following in 1976.

The first Women's Jazz Festival was held in Kansas City in 1978, the same year that reconsumption of the International Sweethearts of Rhythm began. That year, several women-in-jazz anthologies from Stash Records were released, two of them featuring the Sweethearts.[16] In 1980, the third annual Kansas City Women's Jazz Festival featured a tribute to the International Sweethearts of Rhythm. In the early to mid-1980s, four books on women in jazz focused attention on the Sweet-hearts, Rosetta Reitz reissued International Sweethearts of Rhythm re-cordings on an LP, and two films by Greta Schiller and Andrea Weiss were released and made available on video: *The International Sweet-hearts of Rhythm* (1986) and *Tiny and Ruby* (1988).

But, even as women's music production flourished, a debate raged over what counted as women's music. In a 1988 editorial, Toni L. Arm-strong, editor of *Hot Wire,* responded to accusations that "women's music 'is and always has been' exclusively a 'white-girl-with-a-guitar' circuit." Admitting that it was true that "single acoustic acts have re-ceived the widest recognition and the most attention over the years," Armstrong nevertheless insisted that women's music had always in-cluded a variety of "non-folk-style music" (read "black music") and that the "contributions of women of color" have always been important to women's music. Near the end of the editorial, she conceded that "racism inherent in the white-dominated women's music circuit" may have contributed to the lack of widespread recognition of women of color in women's music, which led to the misconception that it was a white-girls-with-guitars-only space.[17] For Armstrong, the very presence of women of color meant that women's music was not racist, but, be-cause the circuit was racist, women of color, who were always there, were not always recognized.

Armstrong's struggle to acknowledge the marginalization of women of color without giving up the utopian space of women's music points to the ways in which women's music served as a cultural site of struggle in larger conversations about race and racism and who counts as "women" in the second wave of the women's movement. Even when jazz and other forms of black music were taken up in women's music, the debate continued. In 1980, Hattie Gossett wrote, "The current attack on sexism in jazz appears to be a liberating force because women's abilities as instrumentalists are now being recognized. But a deeper look at the 'feminizing' process shows us that the trickbag of cultural ripoff is deeper yet because white women are still being promoted over black women."[18] One could counter by naming African American women who participated in women's music festivals and recordings—jazz pianist Mary Watkins comes to mind. Yet to insist on women's music as an open, democratic space is analogous to, and in cahoots with, a line of thinking that would ignore the ongoing presence and historical interventions of women of color in the second wave of the feminist movement.

It is important to note that, in the 1980s, the time period in which jazz became somewhat more prevalent in women's music (in such venues as the Kansas City Women's Jazz Festivals and through the circulation of products celebrating the Sweethearts and other black women in jazz and blues history, including Billie Holiday and Bessie Smith), the dominant spheres of the women's movement were finally responding to over a decade's worth of critiques by women of color, working-class women, and lesbians, who had long decried the second wave's dominating tendency to limit itself as a narrowly defined project by and for white middle-class women. One such challenge came from the Combahee River Collective in 1977: "As Black feminists we are made constantly and painfully aware of how little effort white women have made to understand and combat their racism, which requires among other things that they have a more than superficial comprehension of race, color, and Black history and culture."[19]

The debate over whether women's music is white girls with guitars must be located within larger debates about the pertinence of the second wave to diverse groups of women. If, as many second wave feminists believed, gender oppression united all women, then how might such feminists respond to the persistence of racism as well as classism, homophobia, and other kinds of oppression within the movement itself? How might antiracist struggles succeed in a movement that clung to a vision of itself as utopian? Enthusiasts fiercely defended women's music festivals against accusations of racism, yet it is no accident that Bernice Johnson Reagon delivered her speech about the challenges of coalition building (now famous in women's studies circles) at a women's music festival in 1981. Admonishing the crowd that a "coalition is not a home," she asserted,

> The women's movement has perpetuated a myth that there is some common experience that comes just cause you're women. And they're throwing all these festivals and this music and these concerts happen. If you're the same kind of women like the folk in that little barred room, it works. But as soon as some other folk check the definition of "women" that's in the dictionary (which you didn't write, right?) they decide that they can come because they are women, but when they do, they don't see or hear nothing that is like them. Then they charge, "This ain't no women's thing!" Then if you try to address that and bring them in, they start to play music that ain't even women's music! And you try to figure out what happened to your wonderful barred room.[20]

The availability of recordings by the International Sweethearts of Rhythm and other historical women-of-color musicians through women's music catalogs (alongside records by Holly Near, Alix Dobkin, and Meg Christian) can be seen as an attempt to expand and open up the "barred room." So can the concurrent musical production of Bernice Johnson Reagon and the African American women's vocal group she founded, Sweet Honey in the Rock. Yet the assumptions of the "barred room" — that women's culture existed, that it in fact tapped into a female essence that transcended differences of race, class, and history — continued to surface in 1980s discussions of the International Sweethearts of Rhythm.[21]

One women-in-jazz historian wrote, "The most famous of the women's bands began in a very humble way, and its story illustrates how female musicianship can flourish when given adequate support and attention."[22] This sentence better fits the "female musicianship" that "flourished" in the 1970s with the "support and attention" lavished on some, although by no means all, women musicians by the women's music branch of the women's movement. The Sweethearts received nowhere near the exposure of the white all-girl bands led by Ina Ray Hutton and Phil Spitalny, so to call them the "most famous" women's band is misleading, as is the suggestion that the "support and attention" that they received from exploitative managers while traveling the Jim Crow South was "adequate." The term *female musicianship* uncomfortably evokes that mysterious quality that essentialists believe is shared by all women; in this case, it obscures the fact that the band was founded by an African American man in the context of a historically black educational institution and that the music the band played was developed by African American men and women both. In all fairness, the author does go on to place the Sweethearts in their specific historical context. Language that situates the Sweethearts as examples of "flourishing" "female musicianship" slides in and out of historical narratives from the 1980s, exemplifying how easily gender could slip into isolation from other aspects of identity in feminist theorizing and "herstory" writing rooted in the white-, middle-class-dominated second wave.

In fact, if we roll the Sweethearts documentary from where we left off, the film crosscuts to Anna Mae Winburn in the 1980s. The interviewer remains unidentified, off-camera and off-mike. We do not know what the question was to which an aging Winburn is responding, but in her brief reply she describes the Sweethearts as "a bunch of women in the world, trying to make their place in the world, among musicians, where prejudice existed because they were women." Again, the way the interview segment is presented implies a thesis about gender oppression, isolated from race and class. The film *does* include information about segregation and racism in the South and contextualizes the band in African American history. However, in its effort to achieve an overall portrayal (in thirty minutes) of the Sweethearts as "courageous and remarkable" rather than as victims, the film skips such key questions as, How was race defined in Mississippi in the 1930s and 1940s? What side of the black/white divide did people of color who were not African American occupy? *Which* white women played with the Sweethearts? It does not make clear, for instance, that the first white member did not join the band until 1943, halfway through the band's existence, nor does it make clear that the first white member had been orphaned at the age of seven and raised by a black family. Trumpet player Toby Butler joined the Sweethearts, not because women had transcended categories like race, but because the black woman who raised her knew the black woman who managed the Sweethearts. When I interviewed Butler in 1996, she continued to play in a band at a black church in Tacoma, Washington, and sing in a gospel choir. Roz Cron, the second white Sweetheart, is featured prominently in the documentary, but, again, we are not informed that Cron is Jewish, which means that she would have had quite a different relationship to white supremacist groups like the Ku Klux Klan while traveling in the South than would a white woman who was not Jewish.

The film also downplays the danger of travel in the South and overlooks the exploitation that occurred once the band went pro. The narrative tracing the Sweethearts from their formation as a poor school band to their move to the big time reads like a Cinderella story without a prince — a meaningful second wave theme. After enthusiastically summarizing the history, hardships, and victories depicted in the film about the "all-girl, interracial band," a *Ms.* magazine reviewer exclaimed, "It's good to be reminded that, before the Women's Movement, there were women brave enough to yearn openly for serious work for themselves — not for God, or family, or country."[23] It is fascinating that, even though the film acknowledges the band as an African American organization operating under the restrictions and hazards of the Jim Crow South, it was still possible for the *Ms.* critic to celebrate the Sweethearts as transcending all social categories except *women.* The reviewer betrays what she thinks the category *women* means when she praises the band for rejecting group identifications such as family and nation (and, implicitly, class and race, although these factors are unspoken) and actually manages to take on the Sweethearts as apt symbols of women's right to fulfilling careers. In stark contrast to the *Ms.* review, Evelyn McGee (Stone) told me the following story when I asked her what was important to her about being an International Sweetheart of Rhythm:

Dinah Washington . . . wanted to know why I didn't leave the Sweethearts of Rhythm. She said, "Evelyn, you could be as big as any of the singers, any of us." But it was like I was glued there. I was eating. There's nothing like being hungry. I was a child of the Depression. My mother was earning five dollars a week and taking care of four children and her mother, and there were many days when I didn't have anything to eat. Nothing could have pried me away from the Sweethearts of Rhythm. I didn't care how famous I could have become. I wasn't leaving those meals.[24]

Despite the white, middle-class, dominant second wave impulse to overlook all categories other than gender, the site of second wave utopia is never the white all-girl bands led by Ina Ray Hutton and Phil Spitalny, just as the iconic jazz singer of the second wave is Billie Holiday and not, say, the white jazz singer Anita O'Day. Even though race was often erased in second wave interpretations, race did matter. Perhaps second wave feminists had an easier time seeing black women musicians of the 1930s and 1940s as oppositional to the mainstream. Perhaps the be-gowned instrumentalists of Hutton and Spitalny, who had access to and therefore frequently represented themselves in the modes of dominant standards of white femininity, just did not look radical enough to 1980s feminists. Perhaps the segregated white space was more difficult to look at than the segregated black space imagined to be international. In any case, it was nonwhite women's spaces that frequently served as utopian visions of nonracist women's community.

It is disarmingly easy to criticize the myopia of the second wave from the vantage point of the 1990s and easy to locate Schiller and Weiss's film and its reception within that frame of thought. Yet I hesitate to stop here because the documentary continues to move me and to move students. The vision of an interracial group of women where white women do not dominate, where blackness has room for all the different black women that there are, where women of color who are not African American and biracial and multiracial women constitute a strong presence, where group identity has room for difference, is still powerful in the 1990s. And another utopian space emerges for me as I continue to show the film in women's studies classes — a space where critical dialogue about the Sweethearts and their documentary illuminates such abstract concepts as the social constructedness of race and gender, the historical and cultural specificity of sexuality, the inextricability of gender, race, class, and sexuality, and the many challenges of writing histories of women of color, gendered labor histories, and other lost histories.

Passing for Segregated: Sweethearts of Double Victory

The International Sweethearts of Rhythm conveyed different meanings for African American men, women, and children in the 1940s than they did for second wave feminists in the 1980s. In her book on the Sweet-hearts, Antoinette Handy includes letters from people who recalled seeing the band in its heyday, live and in person. One of them was written by Thomas Jefferson Anderson, an African American man who heard the band at the Howard Theater in 1940: "Their arrangements were always first rate, the ensembles well executed, and solos always interesting. They played with energy; yet it was their physical beauty that attracted my eye — a group of women the color of the rainbow. Here I sat in a segregated audience and was witnessing a performance by women who looked like they were from all over the world. This was my first visual experience with integration — my glance into what the civil rights movement would be about approximately two decades later."[25]

In some ways, Anderson's memory seems strikingly similar to my own. It is not only the power of their playing but the visibility of cultural difference that attracts him. Yet his joy at seeing "women the color of the rainbow . . . who looked like they were from all over the world" is substantially different from my second wave yearnings for harmony between white women and women of color. Jefferson heard the Sweethearts play three years before the first legally white member was hired, yet the band already symbolized for him an alternative social vision to the historical realities represented by the segregated audience. The band passed as segregated, but it exposed the great diversity within that restricted black space.

Rather than embodying the slogan "Sisterhood is global" coined by Robin Morgan,[26] the Sweethearts demonstrated to audience members such as Jefferson that blackness is global. International as they were, the musicians who made up the Sweethearts of 1940 were not crossing the color line — they would have been legally relegated to the colored side of Jim Crow in Mississippi at that time even if they did not belong to an African American band. This was a system dependent on the fantasy that the white race was "pure," that black was "contaminated," and that anyone with any ascertainable black blood was legally black. People of color who were not African American were often restricted to "colored" social spaces in the Jim Crow South, according to region and time period. It is precisely for these reasons that white women could be mixed into the Sweethearts after 1943 since the band already contained legally black members who looked white. Most of the Sweethearts of 1940, even those purported to represent "many nations," had at least one parent with some African American heritage. By emphasizing the variety of the segregated black sphere and calling it *international,* the Sweethearts were able to produce an entirely legal vision of black diversity that burst beyond definitions of *colored* as second-class status.

Reviews in the black press further indicate that *international* did not necessarily mean black and white cooperation to black audiences who saw the Sweethearts in the 1940s. The *Chicago Defender* praised the "sensational mixed band which is composed of Race, Mexicans, Chinese, and Indian girls," suggesting that their "internationalism" created a new musical genre, combining "the savage rhythms of ancient African tom-toms, the weird beat of the Indian war dance, and the quaintness and charm of the Orient."[27]

Yet the music played by the Sweethearts was neither African, Native American, nor Asian, nor did it pretend to be. The Sweethearts played African American big band music, including standards such as Count Basie's "One O'Clock Jump" and Erskine Hawkins's "Tuxedo Junction" (complete with Vi Burnside's tenor sax rendition of Wilbur "Dud" Bascomb's classic trumpet solo). The style is easily located in the popular big band blues genre as performed by the Count Basie Orchestra and many other groups of the day. In fact, if we roll the footage of the 1946 "Jump Children" Soundie from where we left off, we will hear Winburn sing some more traditional blues lyrics, buoyed by riffs from the band. She sings of how it takes "a rocking chair to rock, a rubber ball to roll," and, finally, "a long, tall daddy to satisfy my soul." These are not lyrics of many nations, unless one is thinking of the many nations that combined to produce African American culture.

While no attempt to internationalize the music is apparent, the visual image produced in the Sweethearts' publicity was consistently that of charming young women, international ambassadors. One 1940s news story described how the Sweethearts spent their two-week vacation, including the statement that "Willie Mae Lee Wong, the Oriental saxophonist, is enroute to China Town in San Francisco to see her people."[28] When I asked Willie Mae Wong (Scott) about that alleged sojourn with "her people," she laughed, responding, "I visited Chinatown, but not on my vacation. On my vacation, I went to Greenville, Mississippi."[29] Wong was born and raised in Mississippi and had attended a black high school. But, for the black press, she frequently symbolized the band's internationalism.

A 1943 *Chicago Defender* article typifies this phenomenon: "The Sweethearts of Rhythm, composed of girls of all races and creeds, features such ace instrumentalists as Margie Pettiford, America's ace girl swing saxophonist, Edna Williams, star trumpet player; Willie Mae Wong, the only Chinese girl in the world to play with a name band, and Vocalist [*sic*] Evelyn McGee."[30] Pettiford, Williams, and McGee were African Americans. Only the mention of Wong, with that curious distinction of being "the only Chinese girl in the world to play with a name band," marks the band as representing plural races and creeds.

The Sweethearts were not the first African American entertainers to employ an international theme. When the band's founder, Laurence C. Jones, chose this particular gimmick for his all-girl band, he acted within a long history of staged representations that liberated U.S. blackness from subordinated social status and made it glamorous, global, exotic. African American men's bands such as the Ali Baba Trio sometimes wore turbans. Vaudeville acts, such as the Six Abdullah Girls, took names or wore costumes that communicated faraway places where black and brown people were the majority and held positions of power. Historically, international identities had also functioned as passports to the white side of Jim Crow. Anna Mae Winburn herself had once adopted a "Spanish" identity. International identities were sometimes taken on to protect black people in the South, where international people of color had a chance of being respected and local people of color were Jim Crowed. A vision of internationalism on the black stage was not immune to fantasies of exotic otherness, but it had the power visually to unite the variety of people subject to discrimination in the United States. Black stagings of internationalism exposed the contradictions of black/white segregation as well as the ambiguities of racial definitions that turned on one drop of blood.

Internationalism in the Sweethearts publicity did not hail generic variety but represented non-European international alliances between people conceived of as black and brown. "The orchestra enjoys the unusual distinction of having seven nationalities in its personnel," wrote a *Chicago Defender* reviewer, three years before the first white member was hired. "There is an Indian [Native American] in the brass section, a Mexican on the saxophone and a Cuban handling a trombone."[31] The one-drop rule enabled the International Sweethearts of Rhythm to be imagined simultaneously as "representing many nations" and as embodying a unified nation, as race women: "Wherever the all-girl orchestra goes, they always bring patronage for Race business enterprises. While here in Dallas they dined at a Race cafe, bought 40 gallons of gas at a Race-owned filling station, and were driven out of town by a Race chauffeur."[32]

Cultural theorist George Lipsitz has commented that "one function of 'black nationalism' has always been to elide national categories — to turn national minorities into global majorities by affirming solidarity with 'people of color' all around the globe."[33] Race pride and internationalism enjoyed a very specific compatibility in the black press during

World War II. In addition to the previously mentioned "Double Victory" campaign, international links were drawn between African Americans and colonized people in Africa, India, and the West Indies.[34]

A perusal of black newspapers of the 1940s makes it clear that African Americans identified with the histories of colonized peoples, that they were more likely, for example, to rally behind Mahatma Gandhi, who sought independence for India as well as for British colonies in Africa and the West Indies, than Winston Churchill, the unapologetic imperialist.[35] International alliances reported in the black press often took the form of messages of solidarity from world leaders, including Gandhi, Madam Chiang Kai-shek, and Ethiopian emperor Haile Selassie, addressed specifically to African Americans. The presence of Chinese and Ethiopian allies was significant to African Americans in that both countries symbolized gallant fights against imperialism and both countries represented "darker races."[36] Powerful expressions of international condemnation of U.S. racism were facilitated by wartime labor and military migration. When Jamaican farmworkers brought to the United States to fill labor shortages were imprisoned for refusing to obey Jim Crow laws, when the Mexican consul protested the Jim Crowing of U.S.-born Mexican servicemen in South Texas, when the Chinese ambassador filed a formal protest against the Jim Crowing of Chinese Americans in Mississippi—these events were as politically useful for African American wartime civil rights struggles as they were politically embarrassing for the U.S. government.[37] Although the Sweethearts did not claim any direct ties to India or Ethiopia or to Jamaican farmworkers or Mexican soldiers, their ability to produce a vision of international black and brown solidarity served as a powerful expression of world freedom—of a world free from racism and imperialism as well as fascism.

In 1944, a young West Indian woman smiled from the pages of the *Pittsburgh Courier* in a British military uniform. The caption below her photo reads, "The international pin-up girl." She is not an International Sweetheart of Rhythm, but she is similarly figured as an international sweetheart in this half-page news story about thirty West Indian women who volunteered for the British Auxiliary Territorial Services (ATS). According to the accompanying article, "The enlistees are colored and white girls and several other racial extractions, including Vivien Huchoy, a Chinese former stenographer." The article continues, "Like their American sisters" in the women's branches of the segregated U.S. armed forces, "these girls exude buoyant pride in their trim uniforms. But diametrically opposite the American pattern, there is no trace of racial discrimination in the A.T.S., and, to this society without a color bar, come colored girls, not to be segregated, but to join the order in a state of equality with white members." In this story, British imperialism is overlooked in favor of antiracism. Presented is an attractive image of an international black female space — one that is not bound by U.S. Jim Crow laws, that has room, in fact, for white women and women of "other racial extractions," including a "Chinese former stenographer."[38] The young "international pin-up girls" of the ATS function in this photojournalistic utopian vision to stimulate the hopes of African American readers for a world without racism, a world much like the one hailed by performances of and publicity about the International Sweethearts of Rhythm.

Sweethearts in Retrospect, Sweethearts of the 1990s

I have mentioned that the utopian visions that the Sweethearts presented to their 1940s and 1980s audiences necessarily suppressed certain information that would have compromised the ability of the Sweethearts to signify better worlds. The exploitation of the band after it left Piney Woods is routinely excluded, as is the band management's conscious construction of internationalism as a gimmick and the role that colorism may have played in the hiring of light-skinned women and calling them *international*. It is understandable that such factors were difficult to reconcile with celebrations of global sisterhood or global blackness. But, interestingly, the former Sweethearts with whom I spoke in the 1990s — older women looking back, remembering, and reconstructing themselves as young women in the 1940s — frankly addressed these mitigating factors yet still described their time with the band as if it was, indeed, a glimpse into a better world.

The strength of Schiller and Weiss's documentary is that it conveys certain aspects of the utopian visions articulated by the musicians. The film's interview segments movingly express the joy the women took in playing well together, in traveling, in the kinds of enthusiastic audience responses they received, and in their pride in breaking Jim Crow laws. These interview sound bites are, indeed, inspiring, even if they stop short of conveying information that I found particularly recurrent and critical in my own conversations with musicians. Certainly, interviews are shaped in part by interviewers, and, admittedly, my interviews with musicians are shaped by the fact that both I and the women I interviewed had seen Schiller and Weiss's documentary. And, certainly, a thirty-minute film cannot cover everything. As Weiss explained, the filmmakers intended to celebrate the band within that short time, and celebrate it they did.

Perhaps the original Sweethearts with whom I spoke (including three of the women interviewed in the documentary) were responding to the upbeat nature of the documentary when they told me repeatedly about how exploited they were by their professional managers after leaving Piney Woods School, or perhaps this part of the story was left on the cutting-room floor because it disturbed the heroic tale of the band running away from school (patriarchy?) to make it on their own, a narrative that would have obvious appeal to the second wave. As Handy has pointed out, the black press was ambivalent about the escape from Piney Woods, celebrating it in some stories, promoting the Swinging Rays of Rhythm that replaced the band at the school in others. Even after the band left Piney Woods, the black press often referred to the musicians as if they were still schoolgirls. The original members I interviewed spoke affectionately about both Laurence C. Jones, president of Piney Woods, and band manager Rae Lee Jones, who encouraged the musicians to run away from the school and go to work for backers Dan Garey and Al Dade, but they also talked critically about how they were taken advantage of in each situation. The Sweethearts' telling of continued exploitation is a key as to where utopias of the second wave and World War II audiences and the utopias articulated by Sweethearts of the 1990s diverge.

"They really cheated us, you know," said Helen Jones (Woods), referring not to Piney Woods but to the post–Piney Woods management. When I commented that the story of the Sweethearts was sad, one exploitative situation after another, she replied, "But, you know, that happened to a lot of musicians. Louis Armstrong's manager stole from him. . . . And Ella Fitzgerald, they stole from her. And the Ink Spots were really the ones that broke up all these managers stealing from the musicians."[39] Jones's approach discourages an interpretation of the Sweethearts as uniquely victimized, managing instead to place the band historically, and accurately, within the web of power relationships where African American musicians were frequently world famous and exploited at the same time and where musicians were not always passive but often fought for their rights.

Willie Mae Wong (Scott)'s account of running away from Piney Woods makes it clear that the musicians had reason to complain about their treatment by the school and that they believed themselves to be standing up for their rights: "The original members were only getting seven dollars a week for food and one dollar extra. Out of that eight dollars a week, we paid for the insurance policy. If something happened to one of us, the money went to the school, not to our beneficiary, like my mother. We felt that if the school is getting the money, the school should be paying the insurance. We should be getting fifteen dollars a week." Rae Lee Jones obtained an agreement from backers Al Dade and Dan Garey that the musicians would be paid the desired fifteen dollars a week, which, unfortunately, was still well under union scale. "We should have been getting more, of course," said Wong, noting that the band was already playing union venues before they left the school.[40] In addition, the band members, many of whom had no home except at the school, were told that they would own a house together. There was a house that they used as a home base during the band's heyday, but they certainly did not own it.

When I asked vocalist Evelyn McGee (Stone) about the Sweethearts' escape from Piney Woods, she replied, "You mean when [Mrs. Jones] stole the band?" "Yes," I said, somewhat surprised at her rephrasing of the question. "Well, not only did she steal the band, but she took most of the money. We were extremely underpaid. But, for me, I was eating three meals a day, and it didn't bother me that much. In retrospect, I should have been very upset, or I should have gone back home. They earned an awful lot of money off the Sweethearts of Rhythm. When we became older and applied for social security, it was deducted from our little salary, but it was never turned in. And that was heartbreaking."[41]

When original Sweethearts alumnae told me about their escape from Piney Woods to the world of professional entertainment managers, they made sure that I understood that they had continued to be exploited. They also made sure that I understood that the band became more famous and a better band than it would have been had it remained at Piney Woods. Perhaps the telling of exploitation becomes a way for these women — many of whom were especially vulnerable owing to their youth, poverty, lack of parental guidance, and professional inexperience — to take a more critical stance toward their working conditions, if only in retrospect. It is also a way, perhaps, of talking back to the audiences who loved them as symbolic interracial protofeminists or internationally connected champions of Double Victory and saying, Yes, we broke boundaries and inspired hope, we fought racism and sexism, and we did this under these conditions! The telling of hardship also provides a context for the kind of utopian vision clung to by many of the original Sweethearts. The topic of hardship often emerged when seeking to explain the unusual bond between members. I say *utopian,* as opposed to *nostalgic,* because the stories the musicians told me take on such themes as human potential, not just this is how the Sweethearts were but this is how the world could be. The Sweethearts with whom I spoke clearly believed their stories to be important enough to share with others. Frequently, women who played in the band told me that their story "ought to be taught in school." Some Sweethearts alumnae expressed the hope that their story would be made into a feature film.

"I think it would make a very interesting story," said Woods, a little sadly since a contract for such a film had recently expired without results. "Anytime you can catch a bunch of women that can live together under the conditions we lived under and have different nationalities that were getting along with each other in times when there was really so much racism, it's a very good story, you know?"

"It is," I agreed, my second wave yearnings stimulated anew. "What do you think made it work?"

"Our desire to see the world," she answered, her voice soft, but her words definite. She'd obviously given this much thought throughout the years. "And, like I say, coming from nothing. And we were afraid. We were all out there in the world by ourselves; we had to stick together, you know. And then to receive the little bit of limelight that we did receive made us feel good and made us proud. You know, we knew it wasn't one person by herself being singled out to get all this praise and things; it was all of us in the group. We were bonded with all of these things."[42]

In addition to hardship and exploitation, another aspect of the band that was absent in the celebrations of both the second wave and the World War II audiences is the conscious construction of the international aspect. Perhaps the most disturbing aspect of the international aspect is its compliance with biases toward light-skinned women in black entertainment. As alto saxophonist and pianist Frann Gaddison put it, "They called them 'international,' . . . but they were all pretty, high yellow girls."[43] The band's founder, Laurence C. Jones, liked to counter the Ziegfeld Follies slogan, "Glorifying the American Girl," with a racially uplifting motto, "to glorify the girls of tan and brown" or of "the brown races."[44] It is instructive to recall that, twenty years earlier, when Irving C. Miller employed a similar slogan, "Glorifying the Brownskin Girl," blues singer Bessie Smith was out of a job for being "too black."[45] Although some dark-skinned women played with the Sweethearts of Rhythm, several narrators described the band as consisting primarily of light-skinned women.

It appears that this "light" aspect of the band's membership originated at Piney Woods. Dr. Jones, who had founded this school for poor and orphaned black and mixed-race children in 1909, prided himself on teaching racial equality.[46] Even so, writes historian Alferdteen Harrison, despite Dr. Jones's ideals and acts promoting racial harmony, light-skinned students were accorded some favoritism at Piney Woods: "Before the mid-1950s and 1960s, generally only very light girls with long curly hair worked in the school offices, learned typing, became members of the rhythm band, or otherwise held positions of prominence as students. The darker students usually worked in the laundry or kitchen and cleaned homes."[47]

While this is not the most noble of all possible explanations for the band's racial mix, it does provide a context for understanding how a Southern black all-woman band famous for its international image could eventually slip in a white woman or two. Also, while internationalism may have been compatible with the colorism of the day under which light-skinned women were preferred, it did hold more room for variety than, say, chorus lines such as Miller's Brown Skin Models, of which uniformity of (light) skin color was part of the draw. *International Sweethearts* implied not one kind of brown woman but an array of physically different women that tempered whatever tastes for colorism or exoticism shaped Jones's hiring preferences with an expansive and inclusive interpretation of colored identity that reflected the internationalism of black U.S. audiences.

According to Willie Mae Wong (Scott), her "Chinese face" was so desired by Laurence C. Jones that she was recruited at the age of fifteen even though she had no musical experience. It was, in fact, Jones who gave her the name *Wong*. Her real surname was Lee, but Jones preferred Wong, perhaps because it sounded more unquestionably Chinese. She was wooed to Piney Woods with the promise of room and board and a scholarship. "When I left Greenville," said Wong, "music was foreign to me. I didn't even have a radio."[48] But she fit Jones's vision of an international band and was destined to become extremely popular during

World War II, when the Chinese allies were held up in the black press as a hopeful sign that the war was not white against colored or necessarily imperialist. And the presence in the band of a young woman who was neither black nor white had a symbolic power for audiences who knew that the black/white binary did not account for everyone, that blackness was bigger than Jim Crow might think.

If the renaming and hiring of Wong for her "Chinese face" seems a deceptive construction of internationalism, it is important to note that Chinese people had been in Mississippi since the end of the Civil War, when whites, worried about black voting power, recruited Chinese and Mexican workers to work as sharecroppers in the Yazoo-Mississippi Delta region. In the 1870s, Chinese workers were relegated to the colored side of Jim Crow. During the 1930s and 1940s, the Delta region instituted a tripartite Jim Crow system, with public schools for black, white, and Chinese. But, because most of the Chinese workers brought in during Reconstruction had been single men, there had been a great deal of intermarrying between Chinese men and black women. The children of such unions were rejected by both Chinese and whites, so they lived in the black community. The Mexican-American workers in the Yazoo Delta were also consistently restricted to the colored side of the racial divide. The inclusion of Chinese and Mexican musicians in a black band reflected the internationalism of black Mississippi communities in the 1930s and 1940s.[49]

Even though Wong hailed from Greenville, Mississippi, rather than San Francisco's Chinatown, as the *Chicago Defender* once suggested, her own family history was profoundly international. Her mother, who was half Native American (Wong was not sure about the other half), was raised by a part-black and part-Chinese family. She married a Chinese man and moved to China. When her husband died, she returned to Mississippi, where she met and married another Chinese man, Willie Mae's father. Her father associated only with Chinese people, and her mother associated mostly with black people, so, when her father died and her mother returned to the black community, Willie Mae entered a black public high school, where she would soon be discovered by Laurence C. Jones.

The internationalism of the Sweethearts of Rhythm also had powerful ramifications for Wong, who credits the band with "taking me away from Greenville." Because the band needed her, she received an unexpected opportunity to travel, to gain new skills, and to make friendships that would last a lifetime: "Music became my life. It wasn't just another school subject. It was a means of being with the orchestra."[50]

The international aspect of the band was not meaningful only to musicians and audience members whose identities blurred the black/white binary. Evelyn McGee, one of the African American members of the band who was not considered mulatto and who described herself as "dark," claimed an interracial and international identity. Making a point that segregation should have been abolished along with slavery, she expounded, "My great-grandfather on my mother's side, his father was the owner of the slaves, who had him by the slave cook. And he came out with blond hair and blue eyes and had eleven children, and some of them came out white, and some of them came out black. And, on my daddy's side, it was the Irish. . . . My grandmother was as white as you are. It should be taught in school."[51]

The documentary is nearly over. The interview sound bites have ended, and we are just in time to see the band of 1946 wind up the Soundie presentation of "Jump Children" with which Schiller and Weiss have framed their documentary. When last we looked, Anna Mae Winburn was singing traditional blues lyrics, and the sixteen-piece band was delivering the catchy phrases of the big swing arrangement.

Suddenly, all instruments sit out except for piano, bass, and drums. Over the driving $\frac{4}{4}$ rhythm accompaniment, Winburn poses the question, "Do you want to jump, children?" to which the band members respond with an enthusiastic "Yeah!" This exchange is repeated three times. The term *children* in black song historically stemmed from spirituals, in which *God's children* referred to those of African descent, to whom in his affection God promised liberation.[52] Perhaps some of this meaning traveled into the 1940s context, but what is also noticeable when the Sweethearts respond with their *Yeah*s is that, as a group, they sound like children. Certainly, this is a different spin than had appeared on earlier recordings of this tune by men's bands.[53] For instance, when Jimmy Rushing sings "Do you want to jump, children?" the musicians in Count Basie's band do not reply one way or the other. But the Sweethearts respond "Yeah," like so many consenting children. In fact, often among the Sweethearts' personnel there were musicians who were literally children. The original group of fifteen Sweethearts (which, by 1946, has been supplemented by older, more experienced players) ranged in age from fourteen to nineteen. As mentioned in chapter 3, saxophonist Ernest Mae Crafton (Miller) was invited to join the band when she was only eleven.

Yet neither the 1946 Soundie nor the 1986 documentary presents a narrative in which teenage girls are recruited by adults who fashion them into a lucrative entertainment unit and then underpay them and expose them to hardships. When Winburn sings "Do you want to jump, children?" and the musicians answer "Yeah!" it appears as a welcome invitation to play an instrumental chorus, which the band then cheerfully performs. Even if the exchange is imagined as an invitation to join a band, the band is imagined, I submit, in both the 1940s and the 1980s context as a better place for all of us.

According to Clarence Major, in the 1930s and 1940s *jump* was defined as "any lively dance done to swing music; music with a bouncing rhythm."[54] When the International Sweethearts of Rhythm respond in the affirmative to "Do you want to jump, children?" they do not follow the dialogue by jumping up and dancing. Instead, they leap from their seats to produce some of that "music with a bouncing rhythm." Winburn concludes, "Jump, jump, jump, jump!" and the camera zooms in for a close-up of tenor soloist Vi Burnside as she rises from the saxophone section to execute a driving, fluid improvisation. It is here that we catch a glimpse of Willie Mae Wong and her baritone sax, to Burnside's left. The entire orchestra stands for the big brass and reeds call-and-response finish as the camera retreats and the screen finally accommodates everyone in the band, from Pauline Braddy on the drums at the top, to Winburn conducting from the bottom, with rows of young women playing saxophones, trumpets, trombones, bass, guitar, and piano spanning the screen from left to right. Fourth trumpeter Toby Butler is revealed, then concealed, then revealed, then concealed, as the camera cuts her in and out of the frame.

The internationalism of the Sweethearts of Rhythm was ambiguous, and it is, in part, that upbeat blur of boundaries that inspires disparate audiences to imagine better worlds — worlds without Jim Crow, worlds without one group dominating others, worlds without racism, sexism, ethnocentrism, and xenophobia.

"Do you wanna jump?" "Yeah."

Chapter 6

The Darlings of Rhythm:

On the Road and Ready to Run

The latest threat to male supremacy in the musical world is a bevy of

beautiful swingsters known as the Darlings of Rhythm.

— "All-Girl Crew Set to Reopen Grand Terrace"

The Darlings of Rhythm was a very fine all-girl black

band, and they never got the recognition that the Sweethearts did.

— Sarah McLawler, *telephone interview with author*

The Darlings . . . were just a bunch of raggedy

women out there playing, you know. Playing hard for the money.

— Frann Gaddison, *telephone interview with author*

Despite the bands' easily confused names, rosters that included many of the same musicians, and similar road schedules during the 1940s, the Darlings of Rhythm and the International Sweethearts of Rhythm were separate entities with significantly different histories. Both were African American all-woman big bands that played the swing hits of the day, both were extremely popular with black audiences in the 1940s, and both traveled the rugged routes of strictly Jim Crow one-nighters with personnel that sometimes straddled the color line. But the origins of the two bands were markedly different, as were some of the survival strategies they employed on Southern road trips. Additional, and perhaps related, differences appear in the ways the two bands were characterized in advertisements, reviews, publicity photos, and the accounts given fifty years later by musicians and fans. Portrayals of the Darlings of Rhythm often offered a distinct contrast to portrayals of the Sweethearts,

"Reed Section, Darlings of Rhythm Orchestra." *Left to right:* Margaret Backstrom (tenor), Margie Lusk (alto), Grace Wilson (baritone), Myrtle Young (alto), Lula Roberts (tenor). *Courtesy Vi Wilson.*

pointing to a divergence in musical styles, costumes, and stage presence and to strikingly different representations of black women musicians.

"The Darlings were just a little opposite of the Sweethearts," insisted Frann Gaddison, who played in the saxophone sections of both bands as well as with Eddie Durham's All-Star Girl Orchestra at various times during the 1940s. When I spoke with her in 1994, she was still a busy professional musician, playing piano in Dallas. In fact, our phone interview took place well after midnight because she was working every evening for the foreseeable future. Energized, rather than exhausted, after a lengthy late-night recording session in 1994, Gaddison elaborated what she saw as a great contrast between the two bands. "The Sweethearts played," she reflected, "but they were pretty girls." Curiously, the "prettiness" of the band seemed to indicate to Gaddison a lack of musical substance. The Darlings, on the other hand, were "raggedy," but they swung. "They'd come in there like they just got through washing dishes or something. Or washing clothes. And people liked them; they were swinging. But the Sweethearts were very lavish, you know, beautiful. They had hairdos and makeup. . . . But they didn't swing."[1]

Whether or not one agrees with the decree that the Sweethearts did not swing (I still think they swung!), the image of the raggedy-but-swinging Darlings of Rhythm suggests an interesting addition to the character of women's participation in all-girl bands. Such descriptions evoke a jazz sphere where women did not necessarily present a glamorous image, where women's "raggedy" appearance is positively equated with a swinging sound, where women command audiences to listen to their music rather than ogle their bodies and produce a "powerhouse" aesthetic described by both musicians and fans as "rougher," "more masculine," and "better" than what audiences expected.

Gaddison's use of the term *raggedy* encompassed both the musical and the physical dimensions of the Darlings. Physically, the term evokes a bedraggled antithesis to glamorous stage norms: "They didn't keep themselves up. They were rough-looking women."[2] That Gaddison compared the Darlings' "look" with that of women tired from washing dishes or washing clothes is a striking reminder that, even though World War II brought with it expanded opportunities, domestic labor was still the largest employer of African American women in the 1940s. Gaddison most certainly referred to women who washed other people's clothes, dishes, and floors for a living — washerwomen — not to women cleaning their own homes, implying a class analysis in her description of the Darlings. Angela Davis notes that blues singer Bessie Smith's tribute to poor and working-class black women (recorded during the same session in which she recorded "Poor Man's Blues") — "Washwoman's Blues" — spoke to the "countless numbers of black women for whom domestic service was the only available option."[3]

Gaddison laughed when she described the look of the Darlings, apparently enjoying her memory of musicians who looked more like tired, everyday women than glamorous stars. Even Hollywood actresses were, if they were black, mostly restricted to roles as domestic workers — and not hardworking, tired, and poor but lazy, doting, and comical. The Darlings' image may well have provided a welcome counter to the usual cinematic portrayal of poor and working-class black women's relation to their labor. That these tired, hardworking women spent their labor energy performing music, traveling, and earning rave reviews in national black newspapers may well have been heartening for working-class black audiences. But why did Gaddison, herself a member of the Darlings, delight in the memory of appearing onstage with a band she describes as "raggedy"? What other social meanings did "raggedy" women "playing hard for the money" hold for fans and musicians? Another key lies, perhaps, in Gaddison's equation of physical appearance and sound. "Pretty" may not swing, but "raggedy" jumps.

In narratives of African American jazz musicians, to call a band *raggedy* is not necessarily a criticism. According to some sources, the late nineteenth-century jazz precursor, ragtime, got its name from its syncopated rhythm or "ragged" approach to musical time. In the context of jazz and swing bands, *raggedy* has often been used to distinguish a relaxed, more individuated, more variably textured approach to ensemble playing from other kinds of methods that value such things as meticulously coordinated sections, strict unison playing, and highly polished executions of elaborate arrangements. As trombonist Dicky Wells put it, sometimes certain bands sounded "almost too perfect. That's the funny thing about jazz. You may rehearse until you're hitting everything on the head, and here come a band like the Savoy Sultans, raggedy, fuzzy sounding, and they upset everything. 'What am I doing here?' you wonder. But that's the way it is. That's jazz. If you get too clean, too precise, you don't swing sometimes, and the fun goes out of the music."[4]

This distinction between bands that are so perfect they don't swing and "fuzzy sounding" bands that "upset everything" was frequently evoked by musicians and listeners when explaining the musical differences between the Sweethearts and the Darlings. Jazz organist Sarah McLawler, for example, preferred the Darlings of Rhythm for their spontaneity. Although McLawler never played with either band, she attended performances by both and wound up hiring three former Darlings—Lula Roberts, Vi Wilson, and Hetty Smith—to round out her successful all-girl combo, the Syncoettes, in the late 1940s. Unlike the Sweethearts, stressed McLawler, the Darlings played music that was "more jazz than it was show. By show," she elaborated, "I mean everything was sort of mechanical. With the Darlings of Rhythm, it was more improvisation; it was more spontaneous. That's what jazz is about. You know, it's like playing off the top of your head, not something that's really set. So that's where the Darlings, to me, were the better group."[5]

Spontaneity and power are two qualities that recur again and again when musicians and fans describe the Darlings' sound. In fact, references to the group as "rough looking" may link visual and musical elements of the Darlings' performances. Certain blueswomen of the 1920s and 1930s inspired the same term — "rough looking" — again with favorable connotations. Trumpet player Doc Cheatham described blues singer Clara Smith, for example, as "rough and mean-looking" and "louder than all of them" and attributed these qualities to her greater popularity than Bessie Smith and Ma Rainey among Southern working-class black audiences.[6] Such an image may have resonated with this blues tradition, which provided a strong cultural precedent for the popularity of black women musicians who delivered performances brimming with spontaneity and power.

Not everyone with whom I spoke agreed that the Darlings was the better band — some, in fact, disagreed. Former Prairie View Co-Ed Clora Bryant, who sat in with the Darlings at the Plantation Club in Watts after she moved to Los Angeles, recalled that the band's personnel changed often and that the sound changed with it: "It was an up-and-down thing. The turnover was so fast. Sometimes they were good, and sometimes they weren't so good. They were being exploited, more than anything."[7] It is possible that the moments memorialized in such spirited descriptions as Gaddison's and McLawler's represent high points in the Darlings' turbulent career.

Unfortunately, those of us who never heard or played with these bands are unable to experience for ourselves the variety of musical and visual representations that might be garnered from a comparison of performances by the Darlings (and other unrecorded African American all-girl big bands) with what little archival film and audio footage exists of the Sweethearts. The Darlings of Rhythm appear to have made neither records nor films. Could this have been because they were considered raggedy — both to look at and to listen to? Were they therefore perceived as less ladylike? Did it matter that they had no upward-mobility myth comparable to what *Jet* magazine called the Sweethearts' "cotton-fields-to-Cadillac success" story?[8] Did it matter that they were not perceived as orphans, or as schoolgirls, or even as youthful, that they were not celebrated as "international"? Were the Darlings considered "too black"? Several women, including Frann Gaddison and bass player Vi Wilson, who played in the Sweethearts briefly before joining the Darlings, mentioned that the Darlings tended to hire darker-skinned women than the Sweethearts. Trumpet player Thelma Lewis remembered that, when she played for the Sweethearts, band manager Rae Lee Jones made her change her appearance. "I had to buy hair," she recalled. "And color, they doctored me up [with light makeup]. You had to be a certain color for her. If I was any darker, she wouldn't have hired me." When Lewis played with the Darlings, however, she noticed no such color bias. As she put it, "The Darlings were all different colored flowers."[9] Was colorism a factor in the unequal documentation of the two bands?

Whatever accounts for the Sweethearts having made three short films (excerpts from which would become Soundies), several Armed Forces Radio broadcasts, and a record produced by Leonard Feather and the Darlings having enjoyed none of these opportunities also in part accounts for the disproportionate attention accorded the two bands in recent years. The 1980s, which brought us two documentaries, a book, several chapters in books, and numerous reissued recordings of the Sweethearts, rendered only sketchy references to the Darlings. Is it reasonable to speculate that the lightness of the Sweethearts contributed to the sense of inclusiveness celebrated by nonblack second wave feminists (a problematic inclusiveness, as we have seen, since it appears that some white women could more readily pass as the light-skinned black women desired by the Sweethearts' management than could some dark-skinned black women)?[10]

It is possible that the Darlings' eschewing of color bias and glamour would have found an appreciative audience among second wave feminists. Ultimately, it is impossible to know. Indeed, it would be difficult to produce a documentary or an entire book about the Darlings given the lack of archival material. It is tempting to assume that we know less about the Darlings because the band was a poor replica of the Sweethearts, an inferior spin-off. But it is also possible that they were less acceptable to the white male–dominated recording and film industries.[11]

While this chapter attempts to explore the Darlings of Rhythm as both distinct from and sharing historical contexts with the International Sweethearts of Rhythm and other African American all-girl bands, the analysis can be only fragmentary, based as it is on woefully few interviews,[12] no recordings, no films, limited scholarly consideration, a smattering of publicity photographs — yet a surprisingly vast amount of news coverage. Taken together, the sources suggest that the Darlings of Rhythm were, at one time, also darlings of the black press, even if (excuse the pun) they are nobody's sweethearts now.

I am by no means suggesting that the Sweethearts have been overdocumented. On the contrary, the International Sweethearts of Rhythm was itself underrecorded, underdocumented, and underacknowledged in jazz history. What I am suggesting is that histories of bands such as the

Darlings may add to our knowledge of sexism and racism (and colorism) in the all-girl band business in significant ways. As I attempted to research how the Darlings were organized and managed, how they played, who they were, and how they traveled the rough roads of the segregated South, many revealing stories about gender, race, class, and jazz emerged in rough-edged, often noninterlocking remnants. I will lay out some pieces, but I will not try to fit them together. It seems important to leave space for what is still missing.

Some Origin Stories

As we have seen, the International Sweethearts of Rhythm were organized in 1937 by a black man at a black school in Mississippi as a means to raise money for and publicize the school. The Darlings of Rhythm, on the other hand, were apparently organized in Harlem in late 1943 by a black woman saxophonist who hoped to improve deplorable working conditions of black women musicians. This part of the story is disputed, depending on whom you talk to.

Saxophonist Lorraine Brown (Guilford) told her story of organizing the Darlings in a questionnaire that she filled out for D. Antoinette Handy's pathbreaking 1980 study of the Sweethearts. Portions of this questionnaire appeared in that indispensable volume, and I am grateful to Handy for sharing the entire questionnaire when I was unable to locate Brown. Brown wrote, "Having been a member of 'the Sweethearts' I observed primarily that the musicians were always BROKE also their health did not seem to be a major concern of management."[13] She went on to describe how, to combat such problems, she invested $5,000 in organizing a band of her own in Harlem in 1943. She claimed to have recruited experienced women musicians from all over the United States, fed them, housed them, supplied costumes, and secured auditions with such well-known talent agents as William Morris and Moe Gale. The agents were interested, she noted, but wanted the band to rehearse more before signing them—an option Brown could not afford.

At this time, the Ferguson Brothers agency in Indianapolis was actively seeking women's bands. Although Ferguson Brothers was a smaller company than those headed by William Morris and Moe Gale, it was one of the largest black-owned talent agencies in the country, handling such popular black bands as the Carolina Cotton Pickers and the

King Kolax Orchestra. Most talent agencies were white owned, even those that specialized in black talent, including Moe Gale and Joe Glaser. Denver Ferguson, president of Ferguson Brothers, was himself African American, as were the agents who worked for him and the performers they represented. Maintaining a high profile in the black press, the agency ran large ads in the entertainment pages — ads that sometimes appeared, by accident or design, directly adjacent to the press reviews of Ferguson Brothers' acts. In addition to the talent agency, Ferguson Brothers owned a ballroom in Indianapolis, where the bands they handled were frequently booked.

Brown decided to give Ferguson a try: "I went out west and we negotiated all day and night until I got what I wanted for the band. One of the *main* features of [the] contract was 'a minimum pay check' whenever *we were not* performing. I don't recall the amount but it was adequate; another was *band outfits* to be responsibility of the *agency* at no cost to the musicians, etc., etc. After fighting all day and night, I returned to New York with a *good* contract."[14]

Just when it appears that Brown's tale will end in feminist victory, the story grows hazy. Brown claims that, just when Clarence Love, an agent for Ferguson Brothers, came to New York to help her get the band together, misunderstandings of some kind arose between her and the musicians, apparently over some of her management decisions. Brown claims that, exhausted, she took a weekend off to rest and that Love took advantage of the rift and hit the road with the band, leaving Brown and her "*good* contract" in the dust: "In the meantime, I was *invited* to join the band as a musician only *not* as owner, organizer. I *refused*. Through the years, I ran into a few of the members of the band who confided to me that they now, too late, realized what I had attempted to do for *girl* musicians. Of course, they *again* were done in by having *no* contract to their advantage."[15]

Curiously, none of the Darlings alumnae with whom I talked were familiar with this story. I was unable to speak with any of the original Darlings, however, although I did speak with members who joined within the first year.

Clarence Love's participation in the Darlings of Rhythm story adds a number of puzzles. A well-known, although unrecorded, African American bandleader in the 1920s and 1930s, Love's style was described as "sweet" and "romantic," never as "raggedy." In contrast to the Blue Devils and other African American bands that played jazz in Kansas City during the jumping years when Tom Pendergast's corrupt behind-the-scenes grip on city management protected gambling and flaunted Prohibition (thus providing venues that employed jazz musicians), Love's bands spent the 1930s producing "sweet" music for white audiences in Kansas City ballrooms. "My hero was Guy Lombardo," Love told an interviewer on the occasion of his induction into the Oklahoma Jazz Hall of Fame in 1990. "Romance with Love" was the slogan of his all-man band, prior to his "discovery" and subsequent leadership of the Darlings of Rhythm.[16] How did this leader of "sweet" men's bands segue into the leadership of a women's band that would be remembered by many as raggedy, rough, and spontaneous? Contrary to reports in the black press, which frequently referred to Love as the Darlings' "musical director and arranger," two former band members could not remember performing any arrangements by Love, claiming instead that the band played stock arrangements, augmented by riffs invented by their section mates.

The chronology available in the black press indicates that Love lost his men's band in 1941 (interestingly enough, it was allegedly stolen from him by another talent agent).[17] The last gig the Clarence Love Orchestra played was at the Sunset Terrace in Indianapolis, a ballroom that happened to be owned by the Ferguson Brothers. Out of a band, Love accepted a position with the talent agency in whose lap he had landed, working as a booking agent, newswriter, and developer of talent. Love's interest in all-girl bands may have been sparked by the success of a vocalist with whom he had once worked who had taken a job directing the International Sweethearts of Rhythm at Piney Woods and then engineered their great escape. Love later claimed that he had planned to manage and book the Sweethearts through Ferguson Brothers when they ran away and went pro, except that his former coworker, Rae Lee Jones, had gotten "obstinate" and decided to manage the band herself.[18] Certainly, visions of lost revenue must have crossed his mind in subsequent years as he read about the Sweethearts' success.

According to a press clipping sent me by Love, "a young girl in New York contacted [him] in Indianapolis, looking for a booking for her all girl band." Love traveled East. "The band had talent, so Clarence Love and the Darlings of Rhythm set out to conquer America."[19] We may well assume that the "young girl" was Lorraine Brown, although this version little resembles her story, in which she figures as owner/organizer of the band; nor does it describe anything like the negotiation process she proudly remembered or explain why she was not among the "talented" musical *conquistadoras* who tackled America with Love in the spring of 1944.

Entertainment columnist Billy Rowe noted Love's trip to New York in January 1944: "Clarence Love, former orchestra leader, now a member of Ferguson Bros. staff," was in New York "making Eastern connections."[20] Less than six weeks later, black newspapers heralded the arrival of the "Darlings of Rhythm, Ferguson Brothers' latest musical finds, who are giving other aggregations a good run for their money."[21] From the onset of Love's tenure as leader of the Darlings, the black press portrayed the new band as a serious event. The musicians were conceived as contenders, bursting full-blown onto a jazz scene replete with formidable women players. "Like thunder out of a blue sky," raved the *Chicago Defender,* "the Darlings of Rhythm, America's all-girl band is on the horizon of fame with Gene Ray Lee, hot trumpeter and Clarence Love, musical director. This all girl orchestra compares with any in the business."[22] The *Pittsburgh Courier* praised Ferguson Brothers for "unearth[ing]" the Darlings and proceeded to describe them as "one of the nation's fastest bands." Although speed was not always a sign of expertise in dance bands and "fast" as applied to an all-girl band could have been taken as meaning "loose," the reporter apparently intended a compliment, for the copy continued with an accolade, clearly emphasizing musical skills: "They do not depend upon their beauty alone to sway their audiences, they really play, all thirteen of them."[23] The story went on to list most of the players by name. Perhaps this evocation of women's names served as a way of hyping the femininity of the group. And, perhaps, individual Darlings were named because they would be remembered by audiences who had heard them in other bands. The *Chicago Defender* went so far as to describe the Darlings' lineup as "celebrity studded."[24]

Trumpet player Jean Ray Lee (sometimes "Gene" in the press) had been a member of the Harlem Play-Girls, a popular African American all-girl band, off and on from 1935 to 1940.[25] Drummer Henrietta Fontaine was a veteran of another 1930s band, having held down the trap set of the Dixie Rhythm Girls in 1937 and 1938. Trumpeter Thelma Lewis, who moved back and forth between Eddie Durham's All-Stars and the Darlings of Rhythm, told me that the Darlings were formed from a nucleus of Eddie Durham's musicians. Indeed, Eddie Durham's All-Star Girl Orchestra was the last band in which Lorraine Brown played before organizing the Darlings. Among the first lineup of the Darlings, Jean Ray Lee, alto saxophonist Josephine Boyd, and trombonist Jessie Turner had all been playing with Durham's band just prior to joining the Darlings. Other Durham All-Stars would also cross over to the new band, including former Harlem Play-Girls tenor star Margaret Backstrom (also known as "Padjo"). Backstrom's defection to the Darlings generated excitement in the black press. *Music Dial,* a jazz magazine produced largely by black musicians, was just one of many publications to proclaim the Darlings' acquisition of Backstrom as news, describing the tenor player as a "nationally famous saxophonist."[26]

The unequivocal stardom accorded certain African American women musicians in the black press was accompanied by debates over which band was the "number one" all-girl band in the nation. The practice of comparing and contrasting the Darlings and the Sweethearts that surfaced in my interviews with women musicians in the 1990s was a continuation of ongoing speculation by musicians, audiences, and reviewers. In 1945, the *Pittsburgh Courier* invited readers to weigh the skills of the star tenor players from the two bands: "Jessie Harper of the Motor City writes that Margaret Backstrom, of the Darlings of Rhythm, is the lick on tenor sax, stating that she is as great or greater than Vi Burnside of the Sweethearts of Rhythm. . . . 'Anyone who can hold an audience under her spell for twenty minutes, execute with excellency any request and demonstrate the complexities of jazz must have something on the ball.' . . . Does anyone challenge the Harper statement?"[27]

Unfortunately, no one seems to have picked up Jessie Harper's challenge as the ensuing debate would perhaps have been useful in teasing out the aesthetic differences that audiences attributed to these representatives of the two bands. In our 1994 interview, Bassist Vi Wilson recalled that it was not unusual for fans to engage in lively speculation over which band possessed the superior soloists. Recalling the rare occasions when the two bands would cross each other's paths on the road, Wilson described the ways the women would entertain fans and enjoy each other's company at jam session showdowns:

Fellas in those days had a competition between the Sweethearts and the Darlings. But the Darlings could play. Boy, we would get in jam sessions with them like, whatever town we were in. The fellas, it was a novelty to them to come see these girls play. They said, "Those girls play like men." We'd have a big jam session. Boy, Vi Burnside would really play. And Padjo she would really play. And, see, the best players, tenor players, were Padjo and Vi Burnside. And Vi Burnside would call Padjo — I think one was Lester Young and the other one called Ben Webster. And they'd come shake hands and get on the bandstand, "Let's blow these fellas down!" Oh, we'd have some good times.[28]

This evocation of the good-spirited "battles" waged between Sweethearts and Darlings in jam sessions is another interesting indication of a special relationship between the two bands. Many of the members knew each other from having played together earlier in other bands. Vi Burnside and Margaret Backstrom may have represented opposing teams and divergent styles to fans in the 1940s, but they had spent two years in the same saxophone section when Burnside joined the Harlem Play-Girls in 1938. One year previously, Burnside had played in the Dixie Rhythm Girls, a group owned by the same man who managed the Harlem Play-Girls, so it is likely that the consumer "sound test" levied on the two tenor players had begun in 1937. The differences between their playing styles continued to provide useful points of reference when in the 1990s musicians attempted to elucidate the lost music of the Darlings. "Vi Burnside was show, but Padjo actually played," explained Thelma Lewis. "Padjo could play fifty choruses, all different." Burnside played "riffs," or patterns, according to Lewis, but Backstrom "played the changes," meaning that she conceived her musical lines as negotiating the chord changes of the tune. The performance styles of the two tenors contrasted in Lewis's memory as well. She recalled that Burnside was a crowd pleaser who moved a lot and got the audience to clap. Backstrom, on the other hand, "stood straight up and played a lot of saxophone." In addition, the Darlings' star tenor "could read a flyspeck too" and doubled on clarinet.[29]

Another musician that former Darlings remembered as one of the band's brightest stars is alto saxophonist Josephine Boyd, who had also played with Eddie Durham's All-Stars. "She was a genius," murmured Sarah McLawler, who heard Boyd play in the Darlings at the Sunset Terrace Ballroom in Indianapolis. "I've seen her blow men off the stage," said Lillian Carter (Wilson), who played with Boyd in Baltimore with the International Sweethearts of Rhythm. Wilson insisted that Boyd helped Dizzy Gillespie invent bebop: "Diz was there, backstage. And Josephine was there. And there was something about what they were doing that they dug it. They dug each other. . . . And Diz was young, and she was young. We were all young!" Gillespie did not remember Boyd when I communicated with him through his road manager, Charlie "The Whale" Lake. However, that news did not deter Wilson's belief that Boyd had helped "set the egg" for bebop: "Sometimes Josephine would just get to herself. Just her and her horn. And run these dumb-sounding changes, you know, like what bebop sounds like. And we'd be saying to ourselves, what in the world is she doing, you know?" Wilson's character sketch of Boyd is consistent with other descriptions of the Darlings as a whole. "She played sax, and I mean she *played* it. She didn't just get up there and stand there and look halfway cute. She wasn't a cute person. She was Josephine."[30]

The network among members of the several African American all-girl bands in the 1940s made it possible for musicians such as Lewis, Gaddison, and Wilson, all three of whom played in a number of bands, to exercise some agency in their careers by moving back and forth between bands. Decisions to move were based not only on aesthetic preferences but also on which bands one's friends had joined or on working conditions, travel conditions, management, and money. Gaddison joined the Darlings after running afoul of the Sweethearts' rules. "The woman that was over the band, Mrs. Jones, she was very strict," explained Gaddison. "She was like having a matron." Gaddison's dismissal, ironically, was due to her desire to see Mary Lou Williams play piano with Andy Kirk's otherwise all-man band. The Sweethearts had a gig in New Jersey that evening, and Andy Kirk's band was playing in New York. Although there was a rule against wearing band uniforms in public when not on a job, Gaddison knew she would not have time to change if she tried to go hear Mary Lou Williams play. So she put a coat on over her band uniform and went out to hear Kirk's band. She missed the band bus to New Jersey but hitched a ride through the tunnel and arrived at the Armory, where the Sweethearts were playing a dance, before the music started. Although Gaddison considered herself punctual and her behavior reasonable, "I got fired from the time I walked in the door."[31] The Darlings did not have such strict rules about what musicians did with their free time.

Thelma Lewis remembered leaving Eddie Durham's All-Star Girl Orchestra on several occasions when "the money got funny" and then returning when the band reorganized. She learned to stay alert to opportunities with other bands during down periods, and she also learned how to be "stingy," as she put it, in order to make what little money she earned last as long as possible. "I could hold a dollar until it cried," she said, laughing.[32] But her laughter had a sad ring to it, conveying a sense of the accumulated experience that taught her to be so protective of her earnings. To this day, she said, she still remembers who owes her money.

The network of bands meant that musicians were not dependent on only the band with which they were playing at any given moment but had several bands that could possibly pick them up if they wanted a change or found themselves stranded. The constant personnel shifts meant that there was a reliable communication system operating among the major African American all-girl bands.

Vi Wilson transferred from the Sweethearts to the Darlings in order to be with her cousin, reeds player Gurthalee Clark, a veteran of the only African American band in the Women's Army Corps. Wilson recalled that Clark and some other members of that WAC band, including trumpet player Constance Hurley, joined the Darlings after returning to civilian life in late 1945. They preferred the Darlings, according to Wilson, because they felt that the "Darlings had the best players. And the Sweethearts were growing more feminine and had all the beautiful uniforms. They had some money behind them. The poor Darlings didn't have too much behind them. We only had two changes, two uniforms."

The difference in financial backing is evinced in the bands' publicity photographs. While the Sweethearts are artistically posed and dressed in trademark flowing peasant dresses or smart traveling suits, the Darlings are lined up in rows, many of the musicians unsmiling and seemingly uncomfortable, and all are dressed in one of the sensible and unromantic uniforms described by Wilson: "We had a red coat with a black skirt and a white blouse. Then we had another one with a checkered jacket with a white blouse. That's all we had. But the Sweethearts had all these beautiful gowns, all kind of gowns, short dresses and all, and they were fabulous with makeup and all, but we just had what we had. But we could play." Unable to afford the elaborate arrangements written especially for the Sweethearts by the likes of Eddie Durham, Jesse Stone, Maurice King, and even Mary Lou Williams, the Darlings relied on the musicians' ability to improvise and to play head arrangements, riffs thought up by the musicians themselves ahead of time and then memorized. "Our music was a little bit more down to earth," said Wilson. "We had more jazz musicians, more rock and roll, and we could ad lib more."[33]

Wilson's differentiation of the Sweethearts as feminine and the Darlings as musicians who "could play" is typical of a kind of division of labor described by Darlings alumnae. The Darlings' music was frequently described as "masculine" by the women I interviewed, espe-

"The Darlings of Rhythm Orchestra." *Top, left to right:* Margaret Backstrom, Helen Taborn, Evelyn Wafer, Lula Roberts, Myrtle Young. *Middle, left to right:* Margie Lusk, Autora Bell, unknown, Grace Wilson. *Front, left to right:* Hetty Smith, Marie Johnson, Bumps Huff, Toby Butler. *Courtesy Vi Wilson.*

cially those who appreciated the band's style. And, perhaps, considering the masculine norm in the jazz scene, it is understandable that even women musicians would consider *feminine* a pejorative description and would term music they enjoyed *more masculine.* "She plays like a man" was a compliment, one freely doled out by the press, men musicians, and audience members, and one about which women sometimes complained during our interviews. But playing "like men" was also seen as a positive thing in that it made it possible to describe women's playing as undifferentiated from — not just equal to — men's. When Backstrom and Burnside took the nicknames of famous men tenor soloists before joining a coed cutting session, they claimed the same musical territory enjoyed by men. To perform jazz without audible gender difference meant women playing instruments and styles that were associated with men. It mean women refusing to restrict themselves to soft or sweet timbres. It meant women improvising. And such women, whose jazz did not produce *feminine difference,* challenged both audiences' definition of *woman* and men's exclusive possession of the most highly valued instruments and styles. Surely, this is another clue as to why the Darlings alumnae with whom I spoke tended to refer proudly to the band's emphasis on musical skills and to downplay such feminine accoutrements as makeup and gowns.

The Darlings were not the only all-girl band to adopt this particular mode of presenting and interpreting their music, but as the interviews make clear, it is integral to the band's identity. Through an emphasis on an aggressive approach to the music, thunderous volume, and authoritative horn and saxophone soloists, the Darlings represent one strategy by means of which women claimed identities as jazz musicians. But the Darlings' conception of jazz is not the way in which all women jazz musicians conceive their art and their gendered musical identities. Billie Holiday, for instance, arguably the most influential woman musician in jazz history, was less than thrilled with the Darlings' approach when the band accompanied her at the Grand Terrace Ballroom in Chicago in June 1944.

Unladylike Sounds

The Darlings had not been on the road a month when newspaper reports began to point excitedly toward their forthcoming appearance at Chicago's Grand Terrace. The famous ballroom ("world-renowned," according to the *Chicago Defender*) had been closed for three years but still retained its eminence as the site where Earl Hines "rode to music's peak" during his long reign (1928–38) as the ballroom's resident bandleader. Other bands that had held forth on the celebrated bandstand included those led by Fletcher Henderson and Count Basie. To play for the reopening of the Grand Terrace was a coup for any band. The Darlings were fortunate to have landed such a high-profile booking so soon in the band's history — one with a nationwide radio hookup no less.[34] As soon as Love secured this prestigious booking, he managed to work some mention of it into most Darlings press releases, many of which made it into print.

"Prior to their opening at the Grand Terrace, the Darlings of Rhythm are scheduled to do a string of one-nighters in Florida as well as dates at the Roller Rink, Louisville, KY and the Colosseum, Evansville, Ind.," announced the *Pittsburgh Courier* in early March 1944. "The Darlings of Rhythm, America's dream band are headed eastward playing Norfolk and Newport News and several engagements later this month," reported the *Chicago Defender* in April. "These famous girls have broken attendance records in more than a dozen cities and are receiving requests for return engagements galore. After closing Tidewater area, they trek southwestward, playing engagements in Georgia and Louisiana enroute to Chicago where they open the Grand Terrace sometime early in June."[35] All that spring, items reporting where the Darlings were playing — Tennessee, Ohio, Michigan, Georgia, Virginia, Texas, Oklahoma, Kansas — also reminded readers of the band's June destination.

As the anticipated booking approached, the *Chicago Defender* announced that the Darlings' vocalist, Helen Taborn, had begun sharing the "honors as canary with Joan Lunceford."[36] According to jazz historian Frank Driggs, Joan Lunceford was one and the same as Baby Briscoe, who had led the Harlem Play-Girls in the late 1930s. D. Antoinette Handy notes that Briscoe also led a men's band known as the Dukes of Rhythm in New Orleans in the early 1940s.[37] In addition to Briscoe/Lunceford, who handled some of the vocal numbers and eventually wielded the baton, the band now consisted of Lula Roberts, Grace Wilson, and Josephine Boyd in the sax section, Marie Johnson on first and Jean Ray Lee on second and "hot" (jazz) trumpet, trombonists Jessie Turner and Autora Bell, Ozzie "Bumps" Huff (who would later marry Clarence Love) on piano (some reports say her specialty was boogie-woogie), bassist Lillian Jones, drummer Henrietta Fontaine, and vocalist Helen Taborn.

Curiously, although the grand reopening was repeatedly hyped in both the *Pittsburgh Courier* and the *Chicago Defender,* neither of these national weekly African American newspapers indicated that Billie Holiday would appear on the same bill, or that the Darlings would be accompanying her, until the reviews of the show appeared. Holiday herself had vowed never to sing at the Grand Terrace again after being fired in 1936 by ballroom proprietor Ed Fox for singing too slowly.[38] Less than two weeks before the anticipated booking, *Variety* announced that the Grand Terrace reopening bill would consist of the "Darlings of Rhythm 14 piece girl orchestra, a line of 14 girls, Two Bits of Rhythm, Mayberry and Johnson, Joe Stack, Jessie Davis and others, still to be booked."[39] Apparently, Holiday's starring role had yet to be confirmed.

By the time the Darlings arrived in Chicago, the news had reached them that they would be appearing with Billie Holiday. The instrumentalists, at least, were thrilled. It is difficult to imagine how the two vocalists would have felt about performing in the same show as the great jazz singer. Several members of the International Sweethearts of Rhythm told D. Antoinette Handy that, when Holiday appeared with the Sweethearts in August 1941 — three years before her date with the Darlings — she had resented sharing the bill with the band's vocalist, Evelyn McGee.[40] McGee (Stone) fondly remembered the incident: "Billie Holiday was the featured attraction that week, and I sang first and broke up the house. And she went to Mrs. Jones and told her, 'Put that little McGee girl on after the band plays the opening number.' I intimidated her, but she was paying me a great compliment."[41] In the spring of 1944, reviewers in the black press were in the habit of comparing Darlings' vocalist Helen Taborn with Billie Holiday, a practice that did not bode well for smooth relations between the band and the famous singer. Despite such comparisons, Holiday's popularity among jazz fans and critics, if not the general public, was unsurpassed in 1944. In January of that year, she was easily elected best jazz vocalist by jazz critics in the first ever *Esquire* poll. As part of that honor, Holiday had recently appeared at New York's Metropolitan Opera House in an all-star band made up of the other poll winners — becoming the first African American to sing at the Met.[42] It was also the first time Holiday had ever been invited to sing in a concert hall.

By June 1944, the Darlings had also enjoyed their share of honors, which were considerable for a band so recently formed. Beginning in April, the *Chicago Defender* occasionally let slip its usual allegiance to the International Sweethearts of Rhythm, dubbing the Darlings "America's No. 1 all-girl orchestra" (along with raving about Darlings' vocalist Helen Taborn being "in the same class with Billie Holiday and Ella Fitzgerald").[43] All reviews since the band's formation, in fact, had been wildly favorable, and the Darlings were riding high on the attention. So, while the Darlings had heard about Holiday's occasional foul temper through the musicians' grapevine and may have even anticipated possible resentment of Taborn's vocal numbers, they did not foresee the magnitude of her unfavorable reaction to the instrumentalists' handling of her charts.

"She screamed at us!" exclaimed Frann Gaddison, who vividly remembered the scene. "She called us a bunch of names. . . . She just cussed us out in rehearsal. Called us a bunch of bitches, you know. She had a bad mouth, anyway." The cussing out did not surprise the musicians so much as the content of Holiday's critique: "She was saying, 'Haven't you heard of Paul Whiteman?' " Whiteman, a famous white band leader of the 1920s whose all-man band specialized in "sweet" numbers and elaborate arrangements, often stated that his mission was to "make a lady out of jazz," a goal that was, oddly enough, antithetical to that of the Darlings of Rhythm. The Darlings did not want to make a lady out of jazz—for them, that would have meant crafting some kind of feminine imitation of jazz, and they considered themselves real jazz musicians. The Darlings emphasized the very qualities—power, spontaneity, drive—that Whiteman hoped to eradicate by making jazz "symphonic," the musical equivalent to the pedestal. Whiteman's project was to elevate jazz, to make it respectable, to bring it into the concert hall. By the 1940s, Whiteman's band was considered "square," "corny," and "watered down" by many white and black jazz listeners alike. As the Darlings played Holiday's charts with characteristic punch, the musicians felt themselves in fine form—that is, until Holiday rebuked the very attributes that were prized by the band members. "She wanted us to soften down, " mused Gaddison. "And we were busting those notes! We had a drummer that was, you know, *bad* as any guy out there."[44]

Clearly, Gaddison meant *bad* in the African American vernacular sense of "extremely good," but her description of the drummer's skills gives a clue as to the grounds for Holiday's objection. Holiday's own approach to crafting an identity as a female jazz artist did not consist of "busting notes," nor did it entail straining to be heard over instrumentalists who "busted notes" behind her. Holiday's intervention into the usual gender division of jazz labor included her insistence that instrumentalists, usually men, listen to her as she listened to them and interact with her in the same spirit of collaboration and with the same respect they would accord any other soloist in the band. In this way, she transformed not only the role of the jazz singer but the role of the jazz instrumentalist as well. Her preference for tenor saxophonist Lester Young's softer-toned, behind-the-beat style to Herschel Evans's bigger, harder-swinging, Coleman Hawkins–inspired sound explains, in part, why she might try to "soften down" the Darlings.[45]

The musical collaboration of Billie Holiday and Lester Young and other members of Count Basie's band in the mid- and late 1930s heralded not only a new approach to modern jazz but also a new approach to the traditional gender organization of the music. In a conversation with jazz writer Max Jones, Holiday praised Lester Young's playing in part because he "didn't try to drown the singer."[46] The usual convention had the girl singer stand in front of the band—a kind of audiovisual decoration. Holiday and Young charted new territory, where a woman vocalist and a man horn player might meet as equals, inspire each other, create new approaches to both voice and saxophone, and expand the possibilities of jazz itself. Young once told an interviewer that, when he played the records that he and Holiday had made in the 1930s, it sounded to him like "two of the same voices . . . or the same mind."[47] References to this musical relationship abound in the jazz literature, often accompanied by speculations regarding the nature of their personal relationship, described by one critic not just as platonic but as "amazingly" platonic.[48] Interestingly, Young's voicelike approach to his horn, a radical departure from Coleman Hawkins's aggressive tenor style, also frequently inspired ridicule and speculation that he might be homosexual — the very reactions that met women instrumentalists "who played like men."[49] Holiday's critique of the Darlings strangely echoes a well-documented incident in Young's career. During the unhappy months he spent in Fletcher Henderson's band as Hawkins's replacement, Henderson's wife, trumpet player Leora Meoux, spun Coleman Hawkins's records, coaxing, "Lester, can't you play like this?"[50]

Interestingly, when Billie Holiday cussed out the Darlings, she did not say, "Can't you play like Lester Young?" Instead, she invoked the name of a white bandleader who came to prominence by "sweetening" jazz and making it appeal to a mass white audience, who described his contribution as that of a musical missionary who set out to tame jazz of its "demonaic energy, and fantastic riot of accents."[51] *Metronome* editor Doron Antrim congratulated Whiteman for "rescu[ing] jazz from the jungles" and "civiliz[ing] it."[52] When Whiteman claimed to have made "a lady out of jazz," he most certainly meant "white lady," since no African American woman was accorded the status of "lady" by the dominant culture at that time. Yet Billie Holiday called herself "Lady" ("Lady Day" was Lester Young's coinage). As Susan Cook has pointed out, Holiday's embrace of the nickname "Lady" represents a significant challenge to the racial and gender stratification then prevailing in the United States.[53] Even as Holiday re-defined the role of the jazz singer as equal to the jazz instrumentalist, she claimed the social respectability and feminine difference represented by the word *lady*. She made the term *lady* cross the color line and transformed it to include a range of women traditionally excluded from the pedestal: women of color, women from poor families, women who cussed people out, women who were jazz singers. Holiday's reworking of the term resembles what Angela Davis has called her ability to "relocate" the "sentimental love songs" of the white popular song idiom into "a specifically African American cultural tradition and simultaneously challenge the boundaries of that tradition."[54] Yet it appears that Holiday's expansion of the boundaries of *lady* and *jazz* did not extend far enough to include black women musicians who played horns, reeds, and rhythm, who owned only two costume changes, and were proud of their powerful big band sound.

Was Holiday trying to make ladies out of the Darlings? If so, why was it necessary to evoke Whiteman's white men's "symphonic jazz" band? More troubling, is the possibility that Holiday objected to the Darlings' music as too black, that somehow an element of musical whiteness, or crossover at least, was necessary to make black women musicians into ladies. Was the evocation of Whiteman's white band meant to discourage qualities in the Darlings' playing style associated with African American working-class culture — "jump" tunes, boogie-woogie, blues, head arrangements, and riffs? Or perhaps the Darlings delivered their aesthetic with such determination that Holiday felt that an extremist tack was necessary just to cut the decibels enough to get her songs across. Perhaps the Darlings' own embattled sense of themselves as big band jazz players who happened to be women could not afford the reworking of the roles of vocalist and instrumentalist that Holiday demanded; perhaps their ability to drown out the vocalist was an important element of their proof to audiences that they were real jazz musicians, not feminine imitations.

Had Holiday launched her critique during a rehearsal of "Trav'lin' Light," the one tune (and a hit) she recorded with Whiteman's orchestra, the reproach would make a more literal kind of sense — she may have wanted the live performance to sound more like the record. (This would have been a good trick, however, since Whiteman used strings under Holiday's vocal and, other than the bass in the rhythm section, the Darlings had no strings.)[55] But Gaddison did not remember the repertoire covered in this otherwise unforgettable rehearsal. Her explanation — that Holiday wanted the band to "soften down" — makes musical sense in terms of the singer's well-documented preference for a sensitive collaboration among instrumentalists and vocalists. Still, there was something else going on — an insult, perhaps, a rejection, a pulling of rank — although we may never know what exactly was intended. The Darlings were proud of their mighty brass and driving rhythm. Surely the great jazz singer recognized that the band had no intention of sounding like Whiteman. The sting of her remark could be detected in Gaddison's telling of the story; she returned several times to the comment: "She kept saying, 'You all ever heard of Paul Whiteman?' Because she recorded with Paul Whiteman. It was strange, you know, and la-di-da."[56]

The story of Billie Holiday and the Darlings of Rhythm represents for me not the superiority of one method by which black women crafted identities as jazz artists over another but rather a fascinating instance of a clash between two entirely different strategies in a single historical moment, both of which were sometimes successful in carving out spaces in which black women musicians could work. Although it is Holiday who is known today as the quintessential woman jazz artist and the Darlings who are virtually unknown, some reporters in the black press actually seemed more excited by the Darlings' performance at the Grand Terrace. A reviewer from the *Chicago Defender* devoted accolades to the "musical gyrations" of the "14 collaborators of Swing" and to Joan Lunceford as "petite and vivacious songstress and Lady of the Baton," before praising Holiday's "magnificent chirping" and "fashionable gowns."[57] Columnist Al Monroe got personal (might he have heard about the rehearsal?) when he pronounced that Holiday's behavior at the Grand Terrace "didn't help her popularity here. . . . She responded to none of the few encores received and co-workers say she 'sat' on everyone who sought her friendship."[58] It appears that the Grand Terrace represented an unhappy booking for Holiday, one damaging to her sense of herself as both an artist and a lady; she did not like to sing in variety acts, she did not like singing with loud bands, and she could have seen her booking with an all-girl band as an insult. For the Darlings, however, the Grand Terrace represented a milestone. It offered perks not usually available to black women who were not singers or dancers. Three shows nightly (11:00 P.M., 1:00 A.M., and 3:00 A.M.), playing behind the acts of forty artists ranging from comedians to chorus lines, may sound grueling, but, for musicians accustomed to one-nighters, the gig meant four weeks of steady work in one place. It also meant rare access to one of swing's primary technologies for success — live radio broadcasts, the opportunity to work with the greatest jazz singer in the world, and a source of fame that would linger in press mentions of the band throughout its lifetime.

Darlings on the Road

On 22 July 1944, the *Chicago Defender* announced, "Clarence Love, leader and director of America's Class A all-girl orchestra will close his

Grand Terrace engagement to take to the highways latter part of July" on a tour of "Indiana, Illinois, Ohio and Pennsylvania."[59] The band was so popular between the summer of 1944 and the early months of 1946 that it is possible to track their road schedule from newspaper stories and band listings in the black press as well as in the "Top-Flight Bands" column of the *International Musician.* They never were included in *Down Beat's* "Where the Bands Are," however, although the International Sweethearts of Rhythm were frequently listed there.

News items appearing during July and August indicated that the Darlings had acquired two additional experienced trumpet players, Ann Cooper and Estelle Handy, and that, after barnstorming the dance halls of the Midwest, the band had worked its way east, hitting Delaware, Virginia, New Jersey, Maryland, Pennsylvania, New York, Connecticut, and Massachusetts. The *Courier* greeted their upcoming arrival in New York City, Newark, Albany, Boston, and New Haven with the exclamation, "This will be their first Eastern appearance after a long stay at the Grand Terrace Cafe in Chicago."[60] September and October found them traveling and playing their way through Arizona, California, Oregon, and Washington, delighting entertainment-starved black soldiers at Fort Huachuca, Arizona, and making other notable appearances at the Silver Slipper in San Diego and Seattle's Turf Room. While on the West Coast, Love brokered more talent, signing on tenor star Margaret Backstrom and vocalist Pat LaMar. Regarding his selection of LaMar ("delineator of sweet numbers"), the *Courier* praised Love for his "keen eye for talent and eye for the beautiful," and Love was paraphrased as saying something to the effect that "Pat adds just the touch needed to make the Darlings the perfect picturesque and musically superior orchestra."[61] November found the Darlings headlining in such venues as the Village Barn in Tulsa, Oklahoma; the Cotton Club in Longview, Texas; the East Texas Cotton Club in Lufkin, Texas; and the Harvest Club in Beaumont, Texas.

The new year, 1945, brought more onslaughts of one-nighters, moments of glory, and personnel changes, all glowingly reported in the press. The year started off with a bang as the Darlings were selected from among twenty-five nominees to play the annual private dance known as the Twelve Mo Ball held annually at the Walker Casino in Indianapolis. *Music Dial* reported Clarence Love as declaring, with a publicist's flair for overstatement, that "this affair will be the crowning point of his life."[62] A Southern tour followed, with standing-room-only appearances in Mississippi and Tennessee. At some point in the spring or summer of

"Darlings of Rhythm in Hollywood." In front of Metro Goldwyn Mayer Studios in Hollywood, 1945. *Courtesy Vi Wilson.*

1945, drummer Hetty Smith replaced Henrietta Fontaine. In April, the *Chicago Defender* noted that "Little Toby of the SWEETHEARTS OF RHYTHM band is out of the organization."[63] By June, Toby Butler was showing up in photographs and stories as a member of the Darlings of Rhythm. The acquisition of a white member was not publicized — that the band was integrated would remain covert until Butler's arrest in 1946.

In June 1945, the Darlings finally outdid their Grand Terrace publicity by traveling to Los Angeles in what the *Pittsburgh Courier* referred to as "real style": "The Army has provided them transportation in a B-29 bomber from Amarillo Texas where they entertained GIs."[64] After their spectacular airborne entrance, the band opened at the Plantation Club in Watts on 21 June. Newspaper reports hinted at exciting opportunities awaiting them on the West Coast: "A recording session and a probable movie is in the making if the deal jells. After the Coast bash a series of Eastern dates is being lined up."[65] A publicity photo shows the Darlings lined up in front of their eighteen-passenger sleeper coach at the Metro Goldwyn Mayer studios, smiling, perhaps at their good fortune in the City of Angels. Yet, despite the hoopla and rumors of MGM contracts, recordings, and overseas tours, it appears that what greeted the Darlings after their four weeks in Los Angeles was yet another string of stateside one-nighters, this time hitting such swinging towns as Yakima, Everett, and Walla Walla, Washington, and adding to their list of venues such places as the Pelican Theatre in Klamath, Oregon, the Civic Auditorium in Oakland, and the Brown Bomber ballroom in San Francisco.[66] A month later, they were still doing one-nighters, only now in the Midwest, where in a single September week they played Norfolk, Nebraska; Worthington, Minnesota; Des Moines, Iowa; Waterloo, Iowa; Omaha, Nebraska; Sioux Falls, South Dakota; and Battle Lake, Minnesota—in that order. By Christmas, they were still on one-nighters, this time in Florida.

What is missing from these breezy newsprint itineraries is, of course, the working and traveling conditions of the musicians, who were, after all, African American women and one white woman, racing from gig to gig across terrain that was often inhospitable, even dangerous, and where integration was against the law. These missing "road hazards" were remembered and vividly described by bassist Vi Wilson. By matching events from Wilson's memory with stories from the press, it appears that she joined the Darlings in either late 1945 or early 1946. What she found was a band that had less money behind it, fewer resources, and a more poorly equipped bus than the Sweethearts, but the same problems. Among her memories of traveling with the Darlings were many stories of the particular challenges faced by the band and their strategies for meeting them—including the hiring of a white bus driver.

"Bob was our bus driver," said Wilson. "He would tell the white sharecroppers down there, 'These are my girls, and they work for me.' And that's how we could get by."[67] Interestingly, the famous African American radio choir Wings over Jordan also used a white bus driver for Southern tours. It seems that the hiring of white men to drive the buses and communicate with the white men in charge of gas stations and dance halls was, ironically, one kind of integration that actually eased the rigors of Jim Crow travel for some black entertainers.[68] According to Wilson, Bob had other qualities useful for the task of safely conveying African American travelers in the South—he was a former race-car driver from Indianapolis: "We had a word that we'd say: *West.* That was our password. When any trouble would happen, he would just shoot down one street and up another, and we'd holler, 'West, west,' that was the danger word, and we would run. Wherever we were, we would drop everything and run. . . . Bob would gun his motor three times, . . . and we knew something was wrong. And the person would hold the door, and, as he'd drive past, we'd run for the bus, and he'd reach down and grab hands and swing 'em in. And he'd turn the corner until the last one was in, and, when the last one was in, we'd say 'West,' and we'd pull the cord three times, and we'd slam the door and make it out of town."[69]

Not long after Wilson joined the Darlings, Clarence Love rushed home to Tulsa to care for his dying father. He would remain in Tulsa, eventually opening a nightclub. And, in his place, Ferguson Brothers installed a one-armed trumpet player named Leroy McCoy. Wilson remembered that the band accidentally left McCoy on the road somewhere during a bathroom break in the middle of the night. A typical latrine stop, she recalled, involved the women going around on one side of the bus and the men (Bob and McCoy) on the other: "Now, the last person in is supposed to check to see that everybody's on the bus," she explained. "Somehow or another down there, we were in Louisiana or Mississippi or somewhere, [McCoy] went out to the rest room. He went out over here, and we were on this side. . . . So Bob hit the cord, and he says, 'All clear?' and somebody said, 'Aw, go ahead. We're OK.' Hit the cord three times, and they closed the door. They left McCoy out there on the road with nothing but his stocking cap on his head, his robe, his pants, and his undershirt. And drove off. We had this gig, we had to be there the next night. Pretty soon, somebody said, 'Where's McCoy?' And we had gone about fifteen or twenty miles down the road. And we had to be at that gig because, you know, whenever you missed a gig, they could dock you if you didn't have the number [of musicians] to fulfill the contract. We said, 'Oh my God. He's not in the bus!' We must have left him on the road."[70]

The band went ahead to the gig, and trombonist Jessie Turner, who had studied music at Wayne State University, led the band, while McCoy trudged the miles of Southern highway by foot in his nightclothes. Wilson confided that she often wondered if the band had left McCoy on the road on purpose, acknowledging that most of the musicians preferred Jessie Turner as a leader: "But they said they really didn't know he wasn't on the bus."[71] McCoy arrived safely at the dance hall by the break, and he took over the baton without recriminations. In June, he was still listed in the press as leader of the Darlings. By July, however, Jessie Turner would appear in newspaper reports as the band's leader, the William G. Powell agency would be advertised as the booking agent, and the band would be referred to as the "newly reorganized" Darlings of Rhythm.

Women from Mars

One of the things that made travel in the South dangerous for the Darlings also plagued the Sweethearts: police suspicion that they were breaking Jim Crow laws. It was not safe for the band to advertise itself as integrated, nor did its membership lend itself to the construction *international,* even including as it did some light-skinned members and one white member. So the knowledge that the band was interracial remained covert. Still, the highest profile the Darlings would ever achieve was the result of running afoul of the police in Milledgeville, Georgia. "I have a clipping that I'll have to show you one time where they caught us in the Darlings," informed Wilson, by way of introducing her telling of the incident. "They had arrested Toby."[72]

The story of Butler's arrest would move the Darlings of Rhythm out of the entertainment section of the *Pittsburgh Courier* and onto the front page, complete with a photo of the white trumpet player captioned "Georgia Law Got Her." The headlines read, "Out of Tune! White Girl in Mixed Orchestra Arrested by Georgia Police."[73] Other black newspapers ran the story, and the incident even rated the Darlings a first-page story in *Down Beat,* which had, up to that moment, not been much interested in the band.[74] The *Courier* news copy stated the facts: "Charging that Toby Butler, trumpet player with the 'Darlings of Rhythm' all-girl orchestra, is white, and therefore breaks a law when she travels with Negro members of the unit in Georgia, police officers here halted the band's itinerary last week by arresting her."[75]

According to Wilson, the police threw Butler into a squad car and were preparing to drive her down to the station: "Toby had to sit in the back seat, and she whispered to us, 'I will never let them take me to jail because you know what they do to white girls that are with [black bands. They misuse them] just like they misuse colored girls.' She said, 'They'll never do that to me.' She had a little thirty-two pistol in her purse. And she said, 'When he puts his foot on that starter, I'm going to blow him away.' And we would just cringe; we said, 'We're not going to let them take you.' "[76]

Now, this is Wilson's memory of the event, her version of what she believed was happening. Butler's own account made no mention of a pistol in her purse, a sensible omission from any number of perspectives. Butler simply informed me that she was indeed detained in Georgia and that the newspaper clippings were accurate. If, however, a Southern white woman in 1946 believed that rape was a possible consequence of being jailed for breaking Jim Crow laws, it would hardly have been an irrational fear. Nor would it have been irrational for such a woman to carry a weapon to protect herself. Not only would a white woman have been seen as a criminal for associating with black people, she would be perceived as a fallen woman, a traitor to race and Southern chivalry, and therefore deserving of social as well as legal punishment.

Wilson reached into an envelope of memorabilia and retrieved a photograph of a young white woman with long brown hair: "Now this is Toby, the one I told you about, who was going to blow the cops away. . . . But you know what happened? Jessie went and leaned up on that car with her cigarettes and started talking. . . . 'Now wouldn't you feel real stupid going to your supervisor, telling them that you've got a white girl in the car, and this girl is my cousin? Now look at me.' Jessie was very fair, same color as Toby. . . . Well, in our band, we had light girls and darker girls mixed up. . . . So she said, 'Now this girl is my first cousin, now you can take her if you want to, but you're going to probably get fired.' Oh, she just kept talking, and they kept looking, country hicks, they kept looking at one another. And, you know, she talked Toby out that car!"[77]

Before the police officers could change their minds, the musicians calmly but swiftly escorted Toby to the bus, all boarded it, and they were out of town in a matter of minutes. The police watched them disappear, perhaps kicking themselves for letting that white-looking light-skinned black woman plant the doubt in their mind that that white-looking white woman wasn't really white. In Wilson's telling, the story ended with this twist: "They don't know that today they should be thanking Jessie for saving their lives."[78]

Another of Jessie Turner's tactics is recorded in her press statement, which appealed to so many reporters in both the black press and mainstream trades that the trombonist was quoted in nearly every report of the incident. Identified as the leader of the Darlings by this point, Turner explained the integration of the band in matter-of-fact, merit-based, colorblind terms: "Since the reorganization of the Darlings of Rhythm, my sole interest is in building the best musical unit possible and as long as my girls conduct themselves properly and display ability, I do not see that it would matter even if there were a few women from Mars mixed in."[79]

Turner's color-blind rhetoric is fascinating in this Jim Crow context. By invoking the mainstream integrationism brandished by postwar white liberals, Turner made it seem as though only the police believed that race was important and that black women musicians gave it little thought, even as they risked their lives touring the South with a white woman in the band. The irony, of course, is that all African Americans in the South were forced by circumstances to think a great deal about race and to know the rules in order to survive. Turner's awareness of the life-and-death stakes, and her expertise in manipulating the loopholes of the Jim Crow laws, is evident in her rescuing Butler from the police car, getting the entire band safely out of Milledgeville, and shaping a statement to the press that would circulate widely. Even in the North and West, entrance into previously segregated spheres was achieved, not by color-blind gatekeeping or merit-based hiring decisions, but by active protest, mostly by the people who had been historically discriminated against.

Turner's press statement exploited the following logic: Toby Butler displayed ability and conducted herself properly; therefore, she could be in the band. In this way, Turner turned on its head the notion of integration usually imagined in discussions of merit-based hiring. Because the black woman leader of the Darlings was color-blind, she could see that the white woman employee was able and properly behaved enough to remain in the organization. Is there an implicit social critique here? Turner, was, after all, modeling integrationist values that were still preached more often than practiced. Even though the music magazines frequently praised certain bands as paragons of color-blind virtue, other news items and editorials betrayed mixed feelings about mixed bands. One 1937 *Down Beat* editorial actually held up music's color-blind quality as an argument against integration in bands. Praising music for having "no racial lines," the editorialist captured the ambivalence of many mainstream swing liberals by arguing that "mixed groups" are unfair to musicians because such a band "arouses racial prejudice and focuses the public's attention on its social aspects — NOT ITS MUSICAL VALUES!"[80] In other words, *because* music was color-blind, bands should not arouse race consciousness. Certainly, leaders and bookers of white all-girl bands were not yet prepared to say, "I don't care if you're black or white or green and from Mars; if you can play, you can be in my band." Nor was mainstream U.S. gender and race ideology accustomed to black womanhood being held up as the proper category to which a gifted white woman might aspire.

In casting the one white member as the "woman from Mars," Turner turned the tables on who is normal and who is Other. While *Down Beat* may have been entranced with Turner's color-blind language, which appeared to fit so neatly with the magazine's own claim to rise above race, African American readers of the story in both the trades and the black press surely caught the irony of Turner's reframing of the situation. For once, black women were depicted as normal, and the sole white woman was Other, so exotic that she was not only of another color but from another planet. She wanted to play with the Darlings, and they accepted her. The Sweethearts may have been international, but the Darlings were intergalactic.

Yet, as we have seen, the Darlings of Rhythm were so alien to the paradigm of even that forgotten category *all-girl band* that no recordings or films document their performances and their history is all but lost. Turner's commonsense remark about musical ability mattering more than race, color, or gender was not the way the industry worked, a fact certainly known by the Darlings of Rhythm.

Indeed, all all-girl bands were vulnerable to being perceived as "women from Mars," in varying degrees and not all employers were as tolerant of inter- and intraplanetary differences as Jessie Turner. Women who broke too many rules wound up on the cutting-room floor of earthly history. As the Darlings' case suggests, some exclusions were more complete than others.

USO—Camp Shows

Chapter 7

Female Big Bands, Male Mass Audiences: Gendered Performances in a Theater of War

When I used to sit on that stage and play, I used to pick out one or two in the front rows and, like, play to them and make them feel like — not that I wanted anything to do with them — but make them feel like they were special. . . . It's hard to put into words what I felt. It's just that I felt wonderful helping people fighting for our country. — Doris Kahl Nilo,
interview with Florice Whyte Kovan

We could have spit on the floor, and they would have applauded.

— Jane Sager, *telephone interview with author*

In her history of the United Service Organization (USO), Julia Carson described USO–Camp Shows as a "far-flung program" to bring entertainment and therefore respite from "terrible uncertainties" to American soldiers in worldwide theaters of war. This "nostalgic hour" designed to cheer and comfort soldiers involved "listening to music — American style" and "looking at pretty girls, like no other pretty girls in the world — American girls."[1] If American-style music and pretty girls were thought to build soldiers' morale, then it should be no surprise that that combination embodied in all-girl bands found a welcome niche in USO–Camp Shows. Women musicians were "girls from home," not "women from Mars," when they traveled on USO tours.

During the war, most entertainers, both women and men, added visits to military posts and hospitals and special canteens and recreation clubs for soldiers to their regular schedules. All-girl bands proved popular

USO–Camp Shows sticker.

Soldiers waiting in line to hear Joy Cayler and Her All-Girl Orchestra,
Camp Polk, La., ca. 1943–44. *Courtesy Joy Cayler.*

with military audiences in all these venues, but they were popular to the point of pandemonium when they traveled to the actual theaters of war with the newly formed, vaudeville-style USO–Camp Shows. The USO–Camp Shows literally transformed battlegrounds into theaters, and battlefield settings also transformed the kinds of social meanings that all-girl bands could generate for the musicians and their GI audiences alike.

Although the most commonly revived image of the USO–Camp Shows is that of soldiers cheering such well-known stars as Bob Hope, GIS also thronged to see lesser-known or unknown actors, comedians, singers, dancers, acrobats, and musicians, among them a number of all-girl bands. Stateside military audiences lined up to hear Ada Leonard's All-American Girl Orchestra, Eddie Durham's All-Star Girl Orchestra, Freddie Shaffer's band, the Marion Gange Trio, and Virgil Whyte's Musical Sweethearts. On the overseas Foxhole Circuit," soldiers in the Philippines, Korea, and Japan cheered the Joy Cayler Orchestra and the Sharon Rogers All-Girl Band, while those in Europe packed makeshift theaters to see the International Sweethearts of Rhythm, D'Artega's All-Girl Orchestra, and an all-girl band led by drummer Rae Scott.

For women musicians, traveling with the USO made it possible to be patriots and adventurers as well as professionals. It also meant not having to deal with some of the problems of wartime travel (e.g., gas rationing or transportation). The salary of $84.00 per week was a sacrifice for some and a windfall for others, but it was steady, and, for those who traveled abroad and who were lodged at the USO's and the army's expense, most of it went directly into the bank—the only time many of the women were ever able to save money. Many women got a chance to see parts of the world they would never otherwise have seen, to experience unprecedented popularity both as entertainers and as women, and to gather extraordinary adventures and memories beyond everyday home-front life. As one informant put it, laughing, traveling with the USO was a chance to "scare our folks half to death!"[2]

The GIS in the USO audiences, however, tended to see these women in a different light—as reminders of and even substitutes for their girls back home, as a reward for fighting the war, as embodiments of what they were fighting for. Indeed, this interpretation was encouraged by army brass and USO policies. For soldiers, all-girl bands functioned as powerful symbols of sex and romance, home and family, the private lives they had left behind. But visions of home and nation varied greatly according to the factors shaping an individual's point of view (among them race, class, gender, and sexuality). Not surprisingly, patriotism was interpreted in a variety of ways when all-girl bands played in military settings, interpretations that often clashed in the USO theaters.

It is 1945, early postwar Germany. The staging areas are swarming with GIS impatient to be shipped home. Even though the war continues in the Pacific, the U.S. Army has requested that one hundred USO entertainment units be immediately deployed to the ETO (the European Theater of Operations). Idleness is not the bane of busy soldiers, but is a serious army concern now that the battles are over. Since V-E Day (Victory in Europe), GI idleness has resulted in shootings, fights, joyrides, accidents, and the increased patronage of local brothels.

The USO obeys. The eyes of the soldiers are fixed on sixteen young white women who occupy the stage with trumpets, saxophones, trombones, violins, piano, bass, and drums. The members of D'Artega's All-Girl Orchestra smile fetchingly at the crowd, looking as glamorous as possible after yet another long, dusty ride in two open-air trucks. The leader, Al D'Artega, raises his baton and leads the orchestra in his own hit composition "In the Blue of Evening." The D'Artega theme song is a romantic, yearning ballad, and the sixteen women musicians not only play it expertly, with all its dramatic sweeps and inflections, but perform double duty by smiling at "our boys" when they aren't blowing, a chore that sax player Zoe Rutherford has described as decidedly unromantic in her original poem (enthusiastically circulated among her fellow band members):

> So get with this deal — make with the allure,
> And remember one thing, this is no Cook's Tour.[3]

Allure is a USO command. Although women overseas USO entertainers wear WAC (Women's Army Corps) officers' uniforms offstage, the *Guide to the Foxhole Circuit* has instructed them to dress onstage like "girls back home on an important Saturday night date."[4] For D'Artega's crew, this means "making with the allure" in the same light blue washable jersey dresses they have worn (and tried not to wear out) in every field, flatbed truck, and bombed-out theater between here and Italy.

"And now," D'Artega's voice reverberates over the PA system, "we have Laura, from the 'Windy City' of Chicago. . . ." Years later, Laura Bohle (Sias) will chuckle while relating this story during our interview,

Laura Bohle playing bass for men in veteran's hospital. USO–Camp Shows publicity photograph. *By permission, Billy Rose Theatre Collection, The New York Public Library for the Performing Arts, Astor, Lenox and Tilden Foundations.*

remembering the "ohhhhhs" and the "yeahs" that reached her from the sea of men. Cheering for her? For the band? For the name *Laura*? The word *Chicago*?[5]

She lifts her bow and pours her classical training into the opening phrase of a ponderous and difficult bass solo. Majestic musical lines sweep out into the audience. Suddenly, there's a crack from the drums, followed by a baroque-sounding brass fanfare. The drums answer back, only this time kicking in with a syncopated swing feel, punctuated with cymbal crashes for excitement. This draws a rousing hot riff from the brass and reeds. D'Artega, who has wandered to the rear of the bandstand during the hoopla, swipes Laura's bow with a dramatic flourish, and the bass player plucks the strings furiously with her fingers; it's the pizzicato jazz theme from "Trigger Fantasy" by Glenn Miller bassist Trigger Alpert. The crowd goes nuts, hooting, dancing, laughing, yelling. It's popular music from home and more than that. It's the reminder of girls back home, girls with names like Laura from places like Chicago. Only these American girls start out performing highbrow classical music only to shift midstream to blow honest-to-God big band swing. The combination is just the ticket for the hundreds of impatient, bored GIS, desperately in need of a fresh vision of America.

While white soldiers roar with delight as Laura from Chicago wows them with her exuberant jazz plucking, black soldiers in the vicinity are also waiting to be shipped home. But, as at other USO performances for white GIS, black GIS are not welcome. Either a separate show will be staged for them later (with, in some cases, the best seats reserved for Nazi prisoners of war), or they will have to wait until a Negro unit of the USO–Camp Shows arrives.[6] While swing music was widely touted as democratic, praised by both black and white newspapers and music magazines for an appeal that crossed race, class, and regional lines, the USO, like the U.S. armed forces (and most AFM locals), was racially segregated during World War II.

USO–Camp Shows for white audiences began before the bombing of Pearl Harbor, but it was two years before Harlem-based producer Dick Campbell was hired to create black USO shows for African American as well as white troops.[7] Even then, black soldiers complained that the major black bands of the day, such as those led by Duke Ellington, Lionel Hampton, and Cab Calloway, were not sent on the Negro Overseas Circuit and that many acts that were sent were outdated. From 1942 to 1946, Campbell, the only African American of the fourteen Camp Shows producers (and the only one not offered a job in television when the war was over, even though his theatrical career had also included acting, directing, and founding an off-Broadway theater), put together over sixty-five shows that worked "almost simultaneously in military installations throughout the world." Although his position with the Camp Shows enabled him to employ African American artists and to provide entertainment for black military personnel, it also put him in the uncomfortable position of what he later described as selling "performers like cattle" in a market where black entertainers often were paid less than their white counterparts.[8] To add insult to injury, posters for "all-Negro" shows frequently depicted degrading minstrel images.[9]

Editorials and letters printed in the black press throughout the war document a mass organizing effort meant to pressure the USO–Camp Shows to provide the same quality of entertainment for black as for

white troops. If it seems odd to wage such a struggle on the USO stage —
at a time when black soldiers were relegated to the most menial jobs,
routinely denied advancement, and sometimes treated worse than Nazi
prisoners of war — it may be helpful to think of popular culture as important in shaping national identity. Civil rights battles were waged over the
USO–Camp Shows just as they were over such more obviously serious
issues as equality in labor, defense, transportation, and education.[10] Approximately 1 million African American men and women served in the
armed forces during World War II, and black artists made up over two
hundred different acts in the Negro units of the USO. However, as might
be expected, racist practices abounded in USO–Camp Show settings.
The black press reported on insufficient facilities and food for black
entertainers, inferior conditions and outdated shows for black GI audiences, and the failure of the USO to send enough women entertainers to
areas where black GIs were stationed. "Once again," wrote columnist
Billy Rowe of the *Pittsburgh Courier,* "GIs in the Pacific Theater of
Operations will have to fall back on their memories of lines of pretty
girls, since reports of the two most recent and most densely populated
with girls sent out by the USO have proved mirages."[11] Throughout the
war, the black press treated the issue of entertainment for soldiers as an
integral part of the "Double Victory" campaign.

Conceived by such African American organizations as the NAACP, the
March on Washington movement, and the Urban League, the Double
Victory campaign was an attempt to take advantage of the wartime
economic and ideological crises and push not only for victory against
fascism abroad but also for victory against racism at home.[12] Even before
the United States entered the war in Europe, whether African Americans
should support the conscription of black men was an issue that was hotly
debated in the black press. As Congress tackled the issue during the
summer of 1940, the *Chicago Defender* polled black women on the
streets of Chicago, finding that most "were opposed to the president's
plan to draft their men into military service."[13] Alongside such optimistic articles as "Discrimination Crumbles as War Hysteria Mounts" appeared counterarguments, often written by women, opposing the conscription of black men. One report told the story of a woman whose
husband had fought in World War I only to return to the United States
after the Armistice and suffer the humiliation of life under racism.[14] And
a full-page editorial urged, "Instead of wasting our men and money on
imperialist war mongers who cry for Democracy, why shouldn't we

utilize our men, our money and our cultural heritage by making Democracy work in our own country? A Negro mother would not hesitate one second in sacrificing her sons for such a cause!"[15]

Yet, when the black press announced in its 21 September 1940 headlines that Roosevelt's new draft bill would call up thirty-six thousand African American men, the mood was celebratory, owing to language in the bill that promised to "wipe out discrimination." Perhaps African Americans would enter flight and officers training, and perhaps this would lead to improved working conditions in defense industries and beyond. By the spring of 1942, the notion of Double Victory had permeated African American communities as major black newspapers ran stories, not just on the front page, but on the society page, and in the editorial, sports, and entertainment sections, all united by the common theme, "Victory at home, and victory abroad."[16]

At the same time that news reports described African American organizations' campaigns to integrate the armed forces, entertainment news focused on musicians' efforts to integrate bands, theaters, and musicians' union locals.[17] The goal of such integrationist tactics was not pluralism, in the sense of many different peoples coexisting without rocking the status quo, so much as the lasting improvement of the living and working conditions of African Americans.[18] When victories on the entertainment front occurred, they were heralded as momentous events: "At last it has happened! After insistent clamoring from the boys on the fighting fronts, a colored orchestra will go overseas under the auspices of the USO–Camp Shows. And the band selected was none other than Snub Moseley's."[19] The same tone of collective victory — not just for entertainment-starved soldiers but, symbolically, for all African Americans — was employed in stories reporting on the Persian Gulf tour of Chauncey Lee's USO troupe, notable for providing "the first American Negro woman that the boys had seen in almost two years."[20] "Servicemen throughout the nation are trying to educate the USO in the matters of entertainment," wrote *New York Age* columnist Alfred A. Duckett, elaborating that "the bulk of recent mail" from black soldiers to the USO "has deplored the nice, easy musical outfits to which the men in uniform have been treated. The soldier-lads want bands which can riff and go to town so their letters state. Understand USO–Camp Shows are considering International Sweethearts of Rhythm for tour of service camps. They ought to do well because they combine feminine charm (which soldiers don't ignore) and talent a-plenty."[21]

Letter-writing campaigns and columns such as Duckett's must be located amid a flurry of related Double Victory struggles — it was in this context that the International Sweethearts of Rhythm finally embarked on their six-month European USO tour in 1945. Not only were they the first black women to tour the ETO with the USO — they were the first "negro USO troop" to be sent to Europe.[22]

After being excluded from some shows and given later, separate, seatings at others, black soldiers give a rousing welcome to the seventeen young women who are billed as the "hottest band on the ETO."[23] Many of these soldiers have heard the Sweethearts before, possibly on the Armed Forces Radio program "Jubilee," which had featured the band with Lena Horne in 1944, or perhaps back in the States, either on the USO tour that baritone sax player Willie Mae Wong (Scott) recalled as stretching between Michigan and New Orleans[24] or at any number of venues on the black theater circuit. Some soldiers had even written the State Department requesting the Sweethearts' tour. "We broke it up over there," recalled vocalist Evelyn McGee (Stone). "The GIs just went wild. And it wasn't just because we were women."[25] The audience roars as leader Anna Mae Winburn taps off a frenetic tempo and the Sweethearts launch into a tightly arranged version of "Lady Be Good."

The entire band in unison plays a rapid descending five-note sequence, which is answered by Pauline Braddy's cut-time drums, as if to signal just how fast this rendition is going to be. Again, the sequence, and, again, the drums. The reeds take the first chorus in swift, close harmonies, full of swirling figures and elaborations around the melody. In the short spaces between phrases, the brass respond with a flurry of notes at the same breakneck tempo. As the excitement builds to a seeming peak, tenor soloist Vi Burnside rises from the sax section to push it even higher with a hard-swinging solo. While the crowd whistles and cheers, the entire band punches out a few lines, then halts suddenly. It's time for a show-stopping drum solo by Braddy. Chorus after chorus, Braddy's drums draw shouts of applause at every new configuration of paradiddles. As the crowd rises, clapping and yelling, the ensemble rejoins the drums to start guiding this piece to a close. But, before the big finish, the band sits out again, this time revealing a tinkly Basie-like piano solo at the high end of the keyboard. The pianist's name is Johnnie Mae Rice, and her uncluttered musical statement culminates in the syncopated one-octave riff that has appeared in black bands for many years and that will later be transformed by Dizzy Gillespie into the bebop anthem "Salt Peanuts." The band hits the finale. The soldiers respond with wave after wave of thunderous applause.

What thoughts, feelings, and pictures flashed through the minds of the soldiers and sailors who heard "home" when they sat in foreign fields and listened to all-girl bands in USO shows during World War II? Did they imagine themselves in the company of potential sweethearts? Did they think of their sisters, school friends, cousins, neighbors, aunts, teachers, mothers? Did they pick out which girl they would try to talk to or dance with if a party materialized later? Did they perceive themselves as basking in the artistry of one of the great big bands from home? How did girls and swing combine in the minds of military audiences? And why were these performances attractive to the USO, whose job it was to manage the leisure of U.S. servicemen? A brief USO history is in order, before meditating on the kinds of patriotism inspired by Laura Bohle's quick switch from classical to jazz, by Johnnie Mae Rice's placement of the "Salt Peanuts" riff.

The USO: A Solution to the Problem of on-Leave Recreation

Even before the United States officially entered World War II, concerns about military leisure struck terror in the minds of pre-Pearl Harbor (pre-mobilization) U.S. citizens. Townspeople from coast to coast feared the imminent invasion of "our communities" by "outsiders" who would populate the already proliferating military camps and defense plants.[26] The brainchild of President Franklin D. Roosevelt, who also served as the organization's first honorary chairman, the USO was incorporated on 4 February 1941 from six private, already existing, well-respected civilian agencies with scrupulous public reputations: The Salvation Army, the National Catholic Community Services, Young Men's Christian Association, Young Women's Christian Association, National Traveler's Aid Association, and the National Jewish Welfare Board.

USO centers sprouted up all over the United States, luring service personnel with promises of doughnuts, dancing, and friendly hostesses. Because the agencies that made up the USO tended toward the prudish when it came to entertainment,[27] an outside committee was set up to handle in-camp activities. Camp Shows became a USO affiliate on 22 October 1941. The USO would provide the funds, and Camp Shows would produce live entertainment for soldiers. The task called for diverting audiences that consisted overwhelmingly of men under the age of twenty-five, 50 percent of whom had never seen a so-called legitimate play.[28] Two traveling circuits were set in motion stateside, patterned after the vaudeville circuits that were then in their death throes. The Fox Hole Circuit soon followed on the heels of overseas-bound American troops.[29]

Women musicians who traveled with USO shows were part of a larger project designed to prevent servicemen from generating vice and corruption (such as drunkenness, gambling, and consorting with prostitutes) in towns reluctantly hosting military camps. In this way, their job included protecting the property, and thus securing the patriotism of American citizens. In order to qualify as "good, clean entertainment," women employed by the USO–Camp Shows had to evoke a kind of femininity opposite to that of the dreaded "camp followers" (prostitutes, promiscuous women, and lovers), who, like USO entertainers, followed the troops. When the Camp Shows moved overseas, USO entertainers protected national interests by inspiring soldiers' willingness to risk their lives in battle (also known as *morale*). And, at the war's end, their performances were meant to kindle the obedience of the young men who were about to return home and contribute to the production of postwar prosperity. Women Camp Shows entertainers had to be perceived as "good girls," they had to be desirable, and they had to stimulate fantasies of a homeland that soldiers still cared about after fighting a war. As Benedict Anderson has observed, nothing inspires love of nation quite so well as culture.[30]

American popular culture in the 1940s was full of women and music, though not necessarily in the shape of all-girl bands. Still, as women from home who played the music of home, all-girl bands were well positioned to drum up patriotic love. In fact, they were able to combine effects of swing and pinup girls, two cultural products favored by the Office of War Information.

Producing Private Obligation

As publicity shots of women musicians from the 1940s make painfully clear, all-girl bands could simultaneously deploy the ideologies invoked by posters of sexy Hollywood pinup girls and swing music. According to

Robert Westbrook, pinups were promoted by the Office of War Information to remind American men of the women who could arouse their sense of private obligation: their mothers, their sisters, their wives, their sweethearts.[31] Pinups were also intended to divert soldiers' desires from local women (a postwar concern). Although not all soldiers and musicians were heterosexual, the pairing up of women entertainers and vast audiences of men reflected another army anxiety that pinups were intended to alleviate: how to maintain an atmosphere of compulsory heterosexuality in a homosocial environment. Laura Bohle (Sias) recalls one lesbian musician who refused to join D'Artega's band on its USO tour because she thought "there'd be too much competition."[32] While the story was told as a joke, one wonders whether the aggressive heterosexism of the U.S. military stage deterred the musician from participating in the spectacle of the USO–Camp Shows. As John D'Emilio and Estelle Freedman have demonstrated, pinups were thought to "encourage heterosexual fantasy in the sex-segregated military."[33]

Army anxieties about homosexuality, venereal disease, camp followers, and foreign war brides were particularly acute near the end of the war, when soldiers would soon be reentering civilian life. Fraternization between black U.S. soldiers and white German women was a singular source of army consternation. In 1945, official army policy banned mixed marriages between black GIs and white European women, even if both parties and their parents approved the union, and *even if* the couple was expecting a baby — a stunning contradiction of national morality codes for same-race couples.[34] After being treated better by the white Germans than by white people in the United States, some black GIs were not eager to return home.[35] Robert Robinson reported the results of his survey of musicians' explanations of this phenomenon as early as July 1944 in *Music Dial,* an African American music magazine: "Whereas Hitler and his immediate followers were busy sprouting race hate, the rank and file of German people treated them all swell. . . . [According] to 70 percent of those whom I questioned, more prejudices were shown in England than any other European country; still they all agreed, England's prejudices were nothing compared to our brand in America."[36]

Army opposition to social mixing between African American men and white German women may explain why Camp Shows would deploy a black all-woman band on a six-month tour of Germany at the end of the war. If all-girl bands were meant to instill love of country in alienated and battle scarred men through fantasies of girls from home, it makes sense that, given the segregated system, care would be taken to stimulate desire for *same-race* girls.[37] In chapter 9, this strategy of interesting men in same-race, opposite-sex compatriots will be explored as it operated in the deployment of white American women to entertain white American soldiers in the Pacific.

Pinup Politics

Pinups permeated U.S. culture during World War II. Betty Grable's legs graced footlockers, airplane noses, and tank innards, with the full approval of commanding officers. Not only did photographs of Hollywood stars circulate widely, but the pinup formula was copied in magazine and newspaper features to present the girl back home as both sexy and patriotic. Both the black press and the mainstream press engaged in this practice. The *Pittsburgh Courier* and the *Chicago Defender* both ran weekly amateur pinup photographs, often including the young woman's mailing address for soldiers who wished to write. The *Pittsburgh Courier*'s pinups or " 'Double V' Girls of the Week," often doubled as WACs, defense workers, or Red Cross nurses. The 27 June 1942 "Double V" Girl posed in full Rosie the Riveter garb in a machine shop. The caption read, "Attractive Edmonia Jackson . . . Lincoln University graduate, is doing her bit on the home front by preparing herself for skilled industry in the present huge war-time all-out to beat the Axis."[38]

Letters to the editors of trade magazines such as *Downbeat* and *Music Dial* launched urgent appeals for pinup photographs to be shipped off to faraway places. Usually, soldiers wrote requesting photographs of vocalists or movie stars, although at least one photograph of the International Sweethearts of Rhythm was requested in *Music Dial*.[39] *Downbeat* offered a unique boon for "the men in service, here and abroad," in a regular feature entitled "Your Kiss Autograph." This unusual pinup was not a photograph at all but a lip print of popular dance band singers such as Kay Starr.[40] Black soldiers' pleas for same-race pinups were crafted along Double V lines. One private's request to the readers of the *Pittsburgh Courier* for "colored pin-up girls" included the lament, "We have enough of the Grables, Lamours, etc."[41]

Pinup politics diverged along racial lines. The most popular white pinup, Betty Grable (whose popularity went up, not down, when she married bandleader Harry James during the war and had his baby), shared her domestic skills in fan magazines, anticipating hegemonic postwar June Cleaver gender roles.[42] Lena Horne, on the other hand, the most popular African American pinup, was celebrated in the black press during the war, not for sharing her recipes, but for refusing to appear in segregated theaters, turning down movie roles that degraded African Americans, and making highly publicized critiques of Jim Crow policies in the armed forces and the USO.[43] Horne quit the USO on political grounds in 1945, objecting to the organization's policies of segregating audiences and giving preferential treatment to Nazi prisoners of war over black soldiers. She continued entertaining at military camps, however, financing the tours herself.[44] Another favored pinup of black GIs was jazz pianist Hazel Scott, also a champion of desegregation and public antiracist protests (and one of the few black artists of the era to integrate the jazz and classical genres without being accused of "inauthenticity" by the white critics).[45] Public images of both Grable and Horne articulated salient patriotisms of the time. Grable as pinup hailed the dominant culture's celebration of an imagined prosperous and private status quo. Horne exemplified the "Double V," in which victory over racism was conceived as a necessary component of victory over fascism.

Swing Nation

According to David Stowe, the official deployment of swing through Armed Forces Radio, V-disks (unbreakable long-playing records available only to service personnel), Glenn Miller's forty-two-piece Army Air Force Band, and USO–Camp Shows occurred in a historical context in which "morale was best protected," not by stimulating "national pride" through "patriotic songs, but by appealing to an exclusive and privatized notion of aesthetic experience."[46] Bandleader Joy Cayler recalls that, while civilian audiences wanted to hear patriotic numbers, the servicemen wanted to hear swing.[47] The U.S. government's delivery of swing to the troops, as well as Hitler's banning of jazz and swing, helped define this popular music as a powerful sign of nation. Stowe also claims that swing was attractive for its perceived ability to unite diverse segments of U.S. society: black and white, North and South, urban and rural. While white soldiers in 1945 might still have been able to believe in swing's ability to unite the nation, black soldiers who served in the segregated armed forces — at a time when even blood plasma was segregated by the

American Red Cross — could hardly be expected to retain much stock in swing's "utopian promise."[48]

If soldiers and civilians of the dominant group, however, could still swallow the notion that swing reflected patriotic pluralism, then swing was ideally suited as a platform from which white America could counter African American, as well as Axis, accusations of American racism (the weak spot in the national image). German and Japanese propaganda capitalized on the reality of U.S. racism, easily visible in the segregation of African Americans in the armed forces and the internment of Japanese Americans as well as in the national histories of the genocide of Native Americans, the enslavement of Africans, and imperialist policies.[49] But, given swing's status as an early integrated social formation (most bands were not racially mixed, but those that were made social history) and as a popular African American form that white Americans admired and played and to which they danced, it is easy to see how swing could represent ethnic inclusion for many white Americans, even though its most popular forms often represented exclusion for many nonwhite Americans. The autobiographies of bandleaders Benny Goodman and Artie Shaw, who, like many swing musicians, were the children of immigrants, indicate that participation in black music provided a route to inclusion in all-American whiteness for some ethnic Americans.[50]

While swing may have represented America's transcendence over racism for some, for many African Americans it represented another instance of the white music industry making money on black cultural innovation. The fact that black musicians were far more likely to be assigned to combat than white musicians (who had a better chance of being admitted to segregated service bands) did little to promote a fantasy that swing articulated a pluralistic and fair society.[51] During the Battle of the Bulge, German loudspeakers played blues and jazz records (usually banned by Hitler) to appeal to African American troops to change sides, arguing, "You're treated much better in Europe."[52] Swing as a lucrative, white dance music simply could not carry the same meanings for most black and white listeners, which is why it is important to note that, while the white dance music variant of swing was commercially dominant, it was only one competing form of cultural struggle within American popular music during World War II.

Gunther Schuller describes a three-way wartime split between white dance music, rhythm and blues, and bebop (all of which made appearances under the rubric *swing*). "Black audiences could no longer tolerate increasingly insipid and tame dance music of white bands," he wrote, adding, "they weren't particularly invited into that world anyway."[53] African Americans on the home front were experiencing the war as offering new possibilities. As workers migrated from the rural South to defense industry opportunities in Northern cities, regional black musical styles combined to produce new forms. Blues and big band music developed into rhythm and blues in bands such as Lucky Millinder's, and an entirely new musical form, bebop, was being developed by African American musicians "as a reaction against the sterility and conformity of swing."[54] While white America, in need of comfort and reassurance, was drawn to "bland sing-along ballads," writes Neil Wynn, black America needed music that reflected "more change rather than stability."[55]

In the 1940s, the musical variety described by Schuller was often found within bands and even within arrangements, suggesting that the music itself, rather than band personnel, constituted the most significant sphere in which swing was integrated. In the all-girl bands, Ada Leonard's All-American Girl Orchestra (the first version) and D'Artega's All-Girl Orchestra both incorporated strings with their swing (taking advantage of the availability of the many classically trained white women violinists and harpists), infusing associations of whiteness, femininity, and "class" into their sound. White bands led by Sharon Rogers, Joy Cayler, and Virgil Whyte did not use strings (except for the standard standing bass) and played hits of the day popularized by both white and black swing bands. The International Sweethearts of Rhythm played swing standards popularized by black and white bands as well as special arrangements that had been made for them by top black arrangers of the day. Yet it was also not unusual for Ada Leonard's white band to play Count Basie's version of "One O'Clock Jump," or for the African American Prairie View Co-Eds to play Harry James's version of Basie's hit, or for the Virgil Whyte band to add variety (and to express solidarity with Poland) by swinging Chopin's Polonaise in A Major, or for traces of bebop and generous helpings of rhythm and blues "honking" to inflect Vi Burnside's swinging tenor solos with the International Sweethearts of Rhythm.

Popular music of the late swing era was so commonly understood in racial terms that black and white musicians, as well as many fans, understood certain elements of swing as connoting blackness and others as connoting whiteness. These understandings reflected not necessarily an essentialist belief in genetically determined musical style but rather a knowledge of the many traditions that made up swing. In fact, some black bands were said to play in a white style, and vice versa.[56] The women I interviewed often referred to musical elements as *white* or *black*. When I asked Ruth Raymer, a black drummer, to elaborate after describing one band as leaning "more toward the tastes of the white people," she explained, "Rhythm and blues was black oriented, plus there were people doing beautiful standards, like Nat King Cole singing those lovely pieces. There were straight black jazz bands." Raymer's explanation indicates a great variety in styles within the divisions of taste, her definition of *black taste* in music including rhythm and blues, standards, and jazz. When I asked her to describe white taste in music, she replied, "There were fewer improvised solos, more arrangements, I don't know how to say it, more white oriented for a white listening audience."[57]

White alto saxophonist Roz Cron referred to a quality she called "uptight white rhythm" when describing the difference between playing in a white all-girl band and the black International Sweethearts of Rhythm.[58] For musicians and fans, emphasis on the second and fourth beats in a $\frac{4}{4}$ piece denoted blackness, or at least knowledge of black music, as did emphasis on improvisation. Execution of four even beats and sticking to the melody suggested whiteness. Musical narratives offer a glimpse into how racial politics were communicated, how they clashed and competed in the swing arena. And, when all-woman bands played for the troops, musical narratives may also tell a great deal about race-differentiated ideas about gender, class, nation, and home.

Reading the Move from Classical to Swing in "Trigger Fantasy"

When Laura Bohle (Sias) finds herself without a bow in the middle of her lugubrious classical bass solo, she doesn't miss a beat. She digs right in, plucking the strings in a vigorous jazz-style walking-bass line. The crowd goes berserk. What does this moment in the all-woman enactment of "Trigger Fantasy" trigger? Possibly, it dramatizes a preference for American popular culture over European high art. (The classical canon was, after all, overwhelmingly German.)[59] But, for the D'Artega musicians, as opposed to Glenn Miller's band, to evoke a stirring national symbol, not only must they perform music that signifies America, but they must also perform gender in such a way that the space of *respectable white American womanhood* accommodates working, women swing musicians. How did they avoid being stigmatized as loose women? What kinds of patriotism were stimulated by this temporary wartime alliance between an all-woman big band and the men in military mass audiences?

If the symbols of the modern nation do not stand still but slide from position to position, then there is no reason why yesterday's novelty act cannot become today's patriotic gesture, and vice versa.[60] Historical reasons for why all-girl bands enjoyed new patriotic currency during the war include such material factors as the normalization of homosocial working environments (including the sex-segregated armed forces). As portrayed by Claudette Colbert in the film *Since You Went Away* (1944), the idealized middle-class white woman could work with women across class (and sometimes race) lines and be seen as pitching in for the war effort rather than as embarrassingly poor, spinsterly, or fallen. Public opinion had pragmatically swayed to view women's labor in traditionally masculine occupations as patriotic. Even Rosie the Riveters were not celebrated merely as women working (until they were rediscovered by the second wave of the feminist movement); they were admired by the public as women freeing working men to fight. These are just two changes in daily life that may explain why all-girl bands were more easily translated into national coherence in the 1940s than they were in the 1930s.

Also, the symbols that add up to a love of nation may hold different meanings for different consumers at any given moment. The D'Artega performance teems with messages about gender, class, race, and nation, all of which could be interpreted and pieced together differently depending on how its audience members were positioned. On the one hand, the D'Artega musicians are dressed to resemble girls back home on an important Saturday night date; therefore, they represent good girls. On the other hand, they are performing on the stage, in front of thousands of men, on the road. Therefore, they are not angels of the hearth or sweethearts waiting faithfully at home. They are young, attractive women who are intentionally transmitting allure. Are they patriotic sex symbols, like pinups? Then there is the music they play, everything from romantic ballads to swing standards, all of which might be associated with a sweetheart back home — except that, in the fantasy that the Office of War Information wanted to encourage, the sweetheart would be held tenderly in her soldier-sweetheart's arms on a dance floor back home, not slapping the bass fiddle like Slam Stewart. What did it mean to white male military audiences when white girls played swing?

My guess is that the classical reference provides a bridge to this potentially disruptive but ultimately enthusiastic received space. In delivering "Trigger Fantasy," the musicians, particularly the bass soloist, demonstrate classical music training, valued as a becoming attribute in upper-class, white European and American women since the Victorian era. To those audience members positioned by race and/or class to look to Europe for cultural validation, Sias's arco (bowed) technique alleviates anxiety about white women playing music classed *low* or raced *Negro*. The classical introduction establishes the performers' respectability, whiteness, and parlor-culture womanliness, enabling them to let down their hair, so to speak, without falling from their pedestals.

Even though many of the most famous and most lucrative bands of the Swing Era were white, the music's appeal for white audiences cannot be separated from the danger and titillation that white consumers had historically attached to black music since the 1920s. Jazz historian Kathy Ogren points out that, in the debates about the merits of jazz in the 1920s, white critics and fans alike believed that jazz exerted power over human behavior — that it encouraged "sexual permissiveness, interracial mixing, lewd and lascivious behavior, and a state of mind similar to alcoholic intoxication."[61] The Swing Era is, in a certain sense, the highly commodified continuation of the Jazz Age, in which young white musicians and listeners produced a subculture from African American culture, "modernizing" themselves through the consumption of black music, language, and style and white fantasies of exotic otherness.[62] White women playing swing edged ever so near to one of the most inflammatory social taboos of the white U.S. imagination: racial mixing involving white women. The classical false beginning of "Trigger Fantasy" was well suited to establishing a white, middle-class foundation to the aura of these "modern" young women who would titillate, but not topple, the status quo.

During the very same years that some white women's bands used strings and classical references to establish their acceptability as women swing musicians, African American bandleader/composer Duke Ellington suffered relentless berating by the critics for his insistence on writing symphonic works and suites that roamed too far afield from what white jazz aficionados believed to constitute authentic jazz.[63] I have mentioned that Hazel Scott was one of the few African American artists to survive damaging criticism while swinging the classics. The fact that Benny Goodman, Paul Whiteman, Stan Kenton, and other white male bandleaders made their early Third Stream (classical/jazz fusion) border crossings with far less hassle than Ellington indicates that the surveillance of the genres depended a great deal on the race and gender of the performers. As men, these white bandleaders could incorporate jazz without risking "loose" reputations. As white men, they could incorporate classical elements without being considered inauthentic by the critics. As white male citizens of a nation quickly becoming a world power, they could simultaneously set foot on "home turf" and "other shores" without being seen as exceeding their bounds.

Yet not everyone in the mass military audience was positioned to feel welcome in a musical environment standardized by European notions of high art. In these cases, the spurning of the classical in favor of the popular may account for the appeal of Sias's performance of "Trigger Fantasy." This interpretation suggests quite another affirmation of nation, with the projection of the image of girls from home being celebrated as an act affirming class solidarity. That class solidarity did not necessarily extend, however, to officers, who often expected women entertainers' patriotic duty to extend to after-show parties, dates, and sexual favors. But "the enlisted men were great."[64] A performance in which popular culture wins out over high culture could be read as a class-based expression of support for GIs.

The discourse of sexual patriotism affected many young women during the war. Not only were photographs of titillatingly posed movie stars sanctioned by the U.S. government because of their ability to "boost morale," but young women, under the obligation of making themselves worth fighting for, came to believe that "entertaining young servicemen on leave" was their "patriotic duty."[65] The message that "women married soldiers and sent them overseas happy was hammered at [American women]," many of whom wed servicemen they barely knew.[66] And, with the long shadow of camp followers looming over military mythology, sexy visual standards sometimes created problems by leading to the expectation that the musicians would also service the troops. Women entertainers therefore often found themselves judged by seemingly contradictory standards: Like pinups, they were supposed to be sexy. Unlike camp followers, they were supposed to be "good girls." If either link in this complicated chain was disturbed, the USO didn't want them.

As we shall see in chapter 9, members of the Sharon Rogers band waged an arduous battle against the USO and the army to earn the right not to fraternize with the officers, but they had nothing negative to say about the enlisted men.[67] Tenor saxophonist Peggy Gilbert told of how high-ranking officers in Alaska canceled a hospital ship show so that the women in the all-girl band could mingle at a party instead. The band did, however, escape from the party and make it to the ship in time to perform for the injured GIS.[68] In her history of the USO, Maxene Andrews confirms that many women USO entertainers did indeed run afoul of officers' sexual expectations and that they were often punished for not cooperating by being given unpleasant assignments. Such battles with officers, according to Andrews, left many entertainers with "renewed love and respect for the enlisted men."[69]

Class solidarity between women musicians and GIS (along with prevalent perceptions of women performers as loose) may also have made it difficult for patriotic women USO entertainers to hold enlisted men responsible for actions thought to be inappropriate. Doris Kahl (Nilo) of Virgil Whyte's stateside band related a story of two paratroopers who were court-martialed for trying to break into her hotel room. Although she identified the culprits and wanted them arrested, she attributed the soldiers' behavior to "a couple of wild girls" in a unit traveling just ahead of the Virgil Whyte band who had given the "good girls" in the USO a bad reputation.[70]

Certainly, some young women who traveled on USO tours were available for romantic encounters on their own terms. "We went steady with someone every place we went," laughed alto sax player Dotty Cygan (Wilmeth).[71] Adventurous young women who enjoyed the relative freedom of the road may not have seen themselves as wild girls, available to everyone, but the reputation of camp followers was always lurking in the public and military imagination. It could be easily applied at the least provocation and could prove damaging to the reputation of a USO band.

Bandleader Joy Cayler explained that a band's reputation often preceded it through the military grapevine. And a reputation for not fooling around made life much easier for an all-girl band. Cayler attributed her band's longevity in the USO to the fact that she strictly protected the women's reputations. Interestingly enough, Cayler's ironclad rule for fraternizing contained a clause regarding class solidarity. After performances, she allowed only half an hour for a party with the officers and half an hour for a party with the enlisted men, and, if there was not enough time for both, the officers got the rain check. As she put it, "The officers had it good, in a way, compared to the poor GIS."[72]

Although the musicians from the International Sweethearts of Rhythm whom I interviewed insisted adamantly that they never experienced sexual pressure from officers (who were white), the patriotism articulated in the Sweethearts' performances for black GIS could also be described as one of both class and race solidarity. Evelyn McGee (Stone) recalled her dismay at learning that the "officers mess hall was always better than the enlisted men's. I didn't understand that. I thought they all ate the same thing, but they didn't." The Sweethearts preferred to eat with the enlisted men, said Stone, because, despite the inferior mess hall, the GIS "would cook something special for the band."[73] Baritone saxophonist Willie Mae Wong (Scott) confirmed this, recalling that the black GIS would cook "corn bread and soul food" for the musicians.[74]

All the Sweethearts with whom I spoke insisted that there had been no incidents on the USO tour that could be considered sexual harassment in today's terms. It may be that the solidarity between black USO entertainers and black GIS was so great that it would not be broken fifty years later in an interview with a white woman of another generation (of course, I do not expect anyone I interview to tell me *everything*). And it may be that the Sweethearts were not sexually harassed because the black soldiers had lobbied so long and so hard for their appearance, because their tour occurred in the context of the Double Victory campaign, and because their reputations as musicians, rather than as just a gimmick, preceded them when they played for black audiences. That they were virtually unknown by white audiences, most of whom had heard only the more famous "feminized" white bands, such as Spitalny's "Hour of Charm," may have been the reason that the Sweethearts were received as an "authentic" black jazz band rather than as an inauthentic all-girl band and therefore spared harassment. Roz Cron recalled that the Sweethearts especially "bowled over" the white GIS.[75] Other Sweethearts alumnae with whom I spoke agreed that they were well treated by white soldiers. The Army and USO troops were both, for the most part, racially segregated, but a kind of mixing was allowed that sometimes matched audiences of one race with entertainers of another. The arena of international warfare that was the "Fox Hole Circuit" seems to have created a fleeting context about which a Chinese American woman baritone saxophonist from Mississippi who played in an African American all-girl band could say, "White soldiers were glad to see us because we were home folk. We were Americans."[76]

Unlike D'Artega's band, the Sweethearts did not need to prove that they were classically trained before switching into a swing mode. Indeed, such a move would have made their lives even more difficult, as the field of classical music was fiercely protected as a white cultural domain.

In the later 1940s, in fact, at least two black members of the Sweethearts had studied at such prestigious music conservatories as Juilliard but were effectively banned from professional symphony orchestras. The Sweethearts, as black women, were not expected to adhere to, or even have access to, a private sphere in which amateur musicianship was a sign of a woman's gentility. Most black women expected to work, and music had historically provided a preferable alternative to domestic labor or sharecropping. A black all-girl swing band was unusual, but it did not suggest the same fall from the pedestal to black audiences as a white all-girl swing band might to white audiences.

Reading the Riff in "Lady Be Good"

When Johnnie Mae Rice plays the riff that will later reappear as Dizzy Gillespie's "Salt Peanuts" theme, she demonstrates her knowledge of the black public domain of historical riffs. Gayl Jones has contrasted African American and European American improvisation aesthetics, describing the former as one informed by a continuum of black music history and the latter as " 'thrown together' or 'tossed off.' "[77] Rice's solo is not a series of casually selected notes that fit the chord changes but a musical reference to a jazz history that extends beyond the period of mainstream popularity known as the Swing Era. The "Salt Peanuts" riff was played by Louis Armstrong much earlier and would soon be played by the beboppers.[78]

While their sound was African American, their publicity proclaimed the Sweethearts to be international, an identification that, as discussed in chapter 5, was not inconsistent with African American patriotism. In the article " 'Double V' Band a Hit," the *Pittsburgh Courier* announced that the Sweethearts had attended a performance of Lionel Hampton's " 'Double V' orchestra," where they "pledg[ed] their support to the [Double V] campaign." The domestic and international links of the Double V resonated with the black international yet still American image hailed by the Sweethearts. A special services reporter urged Seventh Army "hepcats" stationed in Germany to "make a date with a 'Sweetheart' of an orchestra," which he praised for being "made up of girls who are proud to be either Negro, American Indian, Chinese, or Mexican and prouder still to be All-American."[79] Of particular importance to Double V solidarity, black GI audiences could see that there were women

International Sweethearts of Rhythm, publicity shot in USO uniforms for 1945 USO–Camp Shows tour. *Courtesy Rosalind Cron.*

in the band who could pass as white but chose not to. And, whether these segregated military audiences knew it or not, the Sweethearts of 1945 also included two white members, both passing as black. In fact, when Paul Robeson finally convinced the USO to send a mixed concert troop overseas, the *Chicago Defender* pointed out that the Sweethearts served as a precedent for this victory.[80] While not vocally critical of the segregationist policies of the armed forces, the International Sweethearts of Rhythm quite literally embodied a challenge to those policies when they toured with the USO, just as when they toured the Southern United States. They only passed as a segregated band.

Musicians in WAC Clothing

Perhaps differentiating their reception from that of white all-girl bands, the Sweethearts were apparently not required to perform in costumes that made them look like the soldiers' Saturday night dates. According to Roz Cron, Willie Mae Wong (Scott), and Helen Jones (Woods), the

Sweethearts performed, not in gowns, but in their official USO WAC officers' uniforms.[81] Musicologist Catherine Parsons Smith suggests that, if this was the case, perhaps the different dress code reflects army anxiety to contain black women's sexuality.[82] There is much evidence to support such a theory, including Alberta Hunter's recollection that black women were not allowed to wear "smart clothes" when performing for white audiences.[83] The Sweethearts, like Hunter, did perform for white soldiers as well as black soldiers in segregated USO audiences. However, photographs indicate that other African American women who entertained overseas did indeed wear gowns onstage and WAC uniforms offstage, just as the white women entertainers did. Hunter's own photographs depict her wearing gowns during her World War II USO performances. And in her oral history she describes the contraction of arthritis that resulted from wearing "slinky gowns" in freezing weather as an expression of her patriotic duty. Sweethearts vocalist Evelyn McGee (Stone) recalled that she and Winburn definitely wore gowns onstage. Scott remembered wearing the skirt rather than the pants of the WAC uniform and ditching the combat boots. However, no photographs could be found documenting what the Sweethearts wore during their European performances. Whether or not they performed in WAC uniforms, a few words on the relation between entertainers in WAC clothing and actual WACs is in order.

The women's branches of the armed forces did provide a patriotic alternative to the pinup, although one far less appealing to the general public. The much-maligned WACs and other military women inherited stereotypes of " 'camp followers' or 'mannish women.' "[84] Hollywood representations of WACs exploited these notions of servicewomen as either too sexual or not sexual enough. Much of the comedy of Joseph M. Newman's *Love Nest* (1951) stems from the jealous reaction of a returning GI's ideal stay-at-home wife (June Haver) when her husband's army buddy, "Bobbie," turns out to be a sexually excessive, party-girl WAC (Marilyn Monroe), supporting public suspicion that WACs served their country by servicing the troops. While this stereotype may have amused the general public, it infuriated servicewomen, who had been targets of a nationwide slander campaign in 1943 designed to portray them as members of the comfort industry.[85] Conversely, the humor of Cary Grant's ability to pass as a WAC in Howard Hawks's *I Was a Male War Bride* (1949) relies on the popular acceptance of the stereotype of WACs as masculine women. As these comic portrayals would suggest, WACs and other servicewomen were routinely denied the fervent respect enjoyed by most men in the service during the war. In fact, servicewomen were so plagued by reputations as either prostitutes or lesbians that they were sometimes barred entry to USO clubs and stage door canteens set up by theater people to entertain servicemen. Even at the Hollywood Canteen, famed for its liberal policies allowing, for example, racially integrated dancing, servicewomen were sometimes restricted to the mezzanine and not allowed on the main (dance) floor.[86] Ironically, while WACS saw themselves as serving their country, they were widely perceived as the antithesis of the all-American girl that servicemen were supposed to be fighting to protect.

Perhaps the stigmatization endured by military women explains why WACS were often hostile to women USO entertainers. Another reason for their resentment could have stemmed from the fact that the War Department prohibited "the use of WACS in theatrical productions . . . [although] male military personnel were frequently used in traveling productions such as *This is the Army*."[87] Women musicians on the USO Fox Hole Circuit were outfitted with WAC officers' uniforms, to the consternation of many actual WACS. I have heard stories of unfriendly encounters between WACS and women USO entertainers, even of incidents in which WACS sabotaged USO performances. Laura Bohle (Sias) recounted a story in which a USO musician in a WAC uniform refused to obey marching orders from a WAC officer as they were shipping out together, taunting rank-and-file servicewomen as well as officers by "walking her own sweet way."[88] The USO entertainers enjoyed the benefits of the uniform — they could go to officers' clubs, and they could date officers — but, like pinups, they did not have to march.

Although African American WACS suffered from the malign treatment meted out to WACS in general, their roles as active fighters in the Double Victory campaign earned them a relatively heroic stature in the black press. White WACS fighting for better opportunities in the army were hardly likely to be respected as patriots by white servicemen. However, when black WACS fought for better jobs and treatment, they were likely to be perceived as being on the same side as black servicemen, sharing, as they did, the experience of inferior conditions and limited opportunities of the Jim Crow army. Struggles of black WACS were frequently interpreted by the black press as rallying cries for Double Victory. Examples of such causes célèbres include the push to have black WACS sent overseas (finally realized in the deployment of the 6888th Postal Battalion to the ETO in 1944), the 1945 case of four black WACs who were sentenced to a year of hard labor for refusing to perform menial labor not required of white WACs, and numerous cases of WACs in the South who were beaten for refusing to adhere to Jim Crow policies.[89]

A particularly interesting campaign in support of black WACs, and one especially pertinent to this discussion, arose when the army decided to discontinue the only black WAC band. It was a classic Double V scenario: The black WACs at Fort Des Moines, Iowa, were barred from membership in the official (white) WAC band, so they formed their own. Although not officially authorized, the band patterned itself after the established WAC band in instrumentation and repertoire. Its members took music classes at Drake University, rehearsed, and began performing at bond drives and recruiting rallies. In June 1944, the army granted them a band rating. However, a month later, after they played well-received concerts and a parade for the thirty-fourth annual NAACP conference in Chicago, the army stripped their band rating, and members of the black WAC band were demoted and reassigned to other duties. "I had received three stripes that I was very proud of," said clarinetist Gurthalee Clark, "and they took them all back." Speculating as to why the band was deactivated, Clark commented, "We were getting too many assignments, I guess."[90]

Trumpet player Clementine McConico Skinner described the massive letter-writing campaign launched by the musicians: "We sent letters to important and influential persons we knew soliciting their support in our effort to keep the band from being deactivated. Personal letters were sent to: A. Philip Randolph, . . . Walter White, Mary McLeod Bethune, . . . and approximately 90 others. We spent the evening writing these personal letters and then took the trolley into Des Moines to mail them to avoid any action by the Army against us."[91] Mary McLeod Bethune and other high-profile leaders responded almost immediately with their support. Pressured by black leaders, the black press, and the black public, the army reversed its decision, and the black WAC band was celebrated as one of the "victories at home" of the Double V.[92] If the Sweethearts did indeed perform in WAC officers' uniforms, the resonance with images of the black WAC band or any number of Double V causes centered on black WACs might have given them a patriotic appeal that white USO musicians in WAC uniforms would not have had.

"WAC Band Number 2" at Fort Des Moines, Iowa, was the only African American WAC band during World War II. Efforts to reinstate the band after the Army disbanded it resulted in the largest WAC letter-writing campaign during World War II. The campaign was successful, and the band was reactivated as the 404th Army Service Forces Band. *Courtesy Vi Wilson.*

The question remains, How did the women musicians who performed in all-girl bands on USO tours conceive of their patriotism? How did they answer my question, fifty years later, about what traveling with the USO–Camp Shows meant to them?

Knowing that she will be on the road for a long time, Sias herself has purchased the score to Trigger Alpert's "Trigger's Fantasy" and has persuaded her boss to include it in the band's repertory so that she can keep up with her bow work. She is classically trained, but her aspirations exceed delighting guests in the parlor. Her chair in the Rochester Philharmonic and her scholarship to the Eastman School of Music are being held for her "for the duration." When she returns, she will again take them up and, in addition, will befuddle her Eastman teachers by leading a series of all-girl swing bands and combos in the Rochester area. For now, she considers herself to be serving her country with her considerable professional skills, skills that are available to her, in part, because of the privileges that her race affords her; in part, because men musicians have been drafted; and, in part, of course, because she has strived toward a career as a serious musician since early childhood. Yet the notion of the professional woman is probably not what is striking a chord with her cheering audience; indeed, this possibility is preempted by assumptions about traditional, domestic white womanhood.

While Vi Burnside takes her tenor solo, Pauline Braddy wows them on the drums, and Johnnie Mae Rice lays down her neat Count Basie "Salt Peanuts" riff, Helen Jones (Woods) counts off the measures on her lead trombone part and thinks how lucky she is to see the world. One of the orphaned children raised at Piney Woods Country Life School, she joined the band to "get out of Mississippi" but never expected this six-month tour of Europe. She also never expected to make the $84.00 a week she is being paid to entertain the black troops. Later, she will tell me, "We were just a bunch of country girls. It was the most exciting thing in the world to see another part of the world. The only sad part was Germany was mostly in ruins. . . . We got a chance to see Paris. I think that, as a whole, the Sweethearts felt that they were very, very privileged, with our background, to have been able to see most of the United States and another country, too. That was quite an honor."[93]

Unfortunately, the $84.00 a week that she earned during those six months, far more than the usual salary of the original Sweethearts, never got to her. The band's manager, Rae Lee Jones, offered to put the money in the bank since Woods did not know how to open an account. When she came back and asked for it, Jones said that she was sorry but that she'd spent the money. With nowhere else to go, Woods would wind up living with Jones in Omaha after the last spin-off group of the Sweethearts broke up in the early 1950s. Having no other job skills and an education that ended when she was fourteen, she would study hard to become a licensed practical nurse. When she became old enough, she would try to collect the social security that the band management had skimmed from her paychecks, only to learn that social security didn't know that the Sweethearts had ever existed. Had the soldiers realized that the celebrated International Sweethearts of Rhythm were being exploited by their black manager, it would have been a cruel blow to Double Victory. They might also have been surprised to know that, for at least one girl from home, during the twenty years she was with the band, stateside and abroad, the band was her home.

Willie Mae Wong (*left*) and Anna Mae Winburn (*right*). Snapshot taken during International Sweethearts of Rhythm USO–Camp Shows tour, Germany, 1945. Women USO entertainers overseas were required to wear WAC officers' uniforms when out in public. *Courtesy Helen Jones Woods.*

Ina Byrd, posing with jeep. International Sweethearts of Rhythm USO–Camp Shows tour, 1945. *Courtesy Helen Jones Woods.*

Seventh Army soldiers, Ina Byrd (*left*), Helen Saine (*right*). International Sweethearts of Rhythm USO–Camp Shows tour, 1945. *Courtesy Helen Jones Woods.*

Some of the women with whom I spoke saw the hardship and danger that they endured as an expression of their patriotism. The International Sweethearts of Rhythm, for example, were sent to Germany in the winter without the necessary warm clothes. They traveled in small open trucks and were regularly pelted with rain and snow. And they were often housed in unheated quarters. Both Joy Cayler's and Sharon Rogers's bands survived forced water landings when the airplanes in which they were traveling had to be ditched. The ship that brought D'Artega's band to Italy survived a submarine attack in the Strait of Gibralter. In the weeks leading up to V-E Day, the band played near the front lines as it followed the troops north. D'Artega drummer Marjorie Kiewitt recalled playing a show extra carefully after being warned, "Don't hit those drums too hard . . ." — an unexploded bomb rested under the stage. Another time, a German Piper Cub spotter plane appeared circling overhead while the band played. Troops and entertainers dispersed quickly, and the concert site was bombed fifteen minutes later.[94]

Such experiences created a feeling of solidarity with the GIs. And that solidarity was only strengthened by the fact that most of the musicians had family and friends in the service and many had lost a loved one. For instance, one of bandleader Anna Mae Winburn's brothers had already been killed in Normandy when she traveled overseas with the Sweethearts, and another brother remained stationed in Europe.

As these women told me about the dangers that they had faced or about the day-to-day trials of sleeping in bombed-out barracks, washing up in their helmets, and defrosting their trumpet valves over hot coals, they often conveyed a strong sense of pride. They had not simply boosted the soldiers' morale but taken an active part in military service themselves. They risked their lives, saw the world, and performed patriotic work, but, unlike WACs, they did not risk losing their membership in the category "all-American girls." Like Rosie the Riveter, they performed valued work for decent wages and received some recognition for their abilities. Many were able to save money and travel for the first time in their lives. "Yes, it was patriotic," agreed Kiewitt, "but it was not *just* because I was being patriotic. I *wanted* to go. I *wanted* to see the rest of the world."[95]

At least some of these women's patriotism was expressed as pride in what American women had been able to accomplish amid the ideological chaos brought on by the war. Some women who played in all-girl bands on overseas USO tours would continue their careers as professional musicians when the war was over, but they would never again represent for their audiences patriotic American womanhood in quite the same way. As the men returned from the trenches, all-girl bands would find themselves excluded from the national vision and erased from the national memory.

Chapter 8

Battles of a "Sophisticated Lady":

Ada Leonard and the USO

Ada Leonard and her all-girl ork has been signed

to play at army camps throughout the country for the next 16 weeks.

A morale builder? — "Ada Leonard Ork Will Tour Camps"

I was interviewed on television a few years ago about girl bands.

The interviewer said, "You got a lot of work during the war because

the men were gone, didn't you?" And I said, "We got a lot of work

during the war because we were good."

— Ada Leonard Bernstein, *telephone interview with author*

The first all-girl band officially signed by the USO was Ada Leonard's All-American Girl Orchestra. This band of white women musicians underwent many changes in personnel, repertoire, and style over its fifteen years of existence but was largely renowned for its ability to play both "sweet" and "jump." Leonard herself was distinguished by her classy brand of glamour. Gliding about the stage in a tight-fitting evening gown, her dark hair in a bun, she brandished her baton with the sophistication and grace of a prima ballerina. Not harming her popularity was the common knowledge that Ada Leonard had once been a famous Chicago stripper.

While it might seem unusual that a former stripper would be allowed to lead a group of "all-American girls" on a USO tour, it is important to note that Gypsy Rose Lee, perhaps the most famous stripper in U.S. history, was also a popular USO entertainer. Lee, who, like Leonard, was famous for making her audiences think she was taking off more than she actually was, took off even less when entertaining the troops. A sample of her "pretend" striptease can be seen in the film *Stage Door Canteen*

Ada Leonard, photograph by Bruno of Hollywood, New York City. *Courtesy Betty Kidwell Meriedeth.*

(1943). After removing a few accessories — a stocking here, a hair ribbon there, a garter, a hat, a glove — the notorious Gypsy Rose Lee ends her act as she began, wearing a floor length skirt with a prim white blouse. To the servicemen begging for more (or, rather, for less), she teases, "Oh, boys, I couldn't. I'd catch cold." Ada Leonard, however, did not even pretend to strip, nor did she allude to her previous occupation (although sometimes the press reminded audiences of her colorful past). When audiences shouted, "Take it off!" as Ada Leonard's all-American girls "took off" on their instruments, the aloof leader kept her cool, which added to her mystique. "She had an instinct for male psychology," affirms Patrick Devaney, a fan who attended performances in Minneapolis.[1]

The ability to convey sex and propriety in the same breath was a hot commodity during World War II. Hollywood movies, pinup posters, and USO shows produced images of all-American girls that attempted to merge two fantasies previously polarized by a lingering Victorian sensibility: the sexy starlet and the girl next door. Hollywood managed this wartime schizophrenia in creative, if predictable, ways. In *Two Girls and a Sailor* (1944), the two qualities are literally divided into two girls, who are, incidentally, performers in their own private stage door canteen.[2] Gloria DeHaven embodies the sexy, boy-crazy little sister; her traditional girl-next-door big sister is played by the queen of the girls next door, June Allyson. In the end, both types of all-American girls are rewarded with marriage proposals from their favorite servicemen. In *Pin Up Girl* (1944), Betty Grable plays both poles at once in her role as a Missouri-bred girl who pretends to be a glamorous USO star in order to catch her man. In the end, it is her ability to pull off the combination that spells her success. Not an easy stunt for real-life women, the move between sensible, marriageable girl and glamorous, sexy starlet is for Grable's character as simple as putting on and taking off her glasses.

For Ada Leonard's All-American Girls, the balancing act was more complex.

Ada Leonard Meets the All-American Girls

The story of Ada Leonard and her All-American Girls begins before the band had either a name or a leader and before the leader knew how to lead a band. But, as Leonard related it, the desire to conduct came long before the opportunity.

"I was in a big show, and Rita Rio had a girl band with it. And I thought to myself, I do all those things she does. I dance, I sing, I *talk*." In 1994, retired from show business for nearly forty years, Ada Leonard still had a flair for performance. Her low voice and expert comic timing enlivened the delivery of such understatements as, "I *talk*." But, then, her notices from "A Night at the Moulin Rouge" indicate that she did not have much of a chance to talk in that 1939 extravaganza. A San Francisco reviewer raved about Rita Rio's band-leading skills, her dancing, her singing, her "pert, petite and vivacious" personality, and then described Leonard's part in the show as a "striptease . . . done with artistic finesse as she unfolds, in a series of evening wraps."[3] In Denver, Colorado, the theater reviewer praised Rio's expert band leading and "big personality" for calming an audience made impatient by a delayed curtain. Only after much ado about Rio's versatility did the reviewer mention "Ada Leonard, whose graceful near-nude dances are startling bits of artistry."[4] This show apparently marked a point in Leonard's career when she insisted on work that would show off her other skills. The daughter of showpeople, she had grown up accruing theatrical expertise. Her mother played piano, saxophone, and violin, danced ballet, and designed costumes. Her father was a dramatic actor. Leonard began performing in stage shows at the age of three, singing (in harmony, according to her mother), dancing, and acting. Along with her three siblings, each born on the road in a different state, her knowledge of show business was more multifaceted than her notices would indicate.

"So, I thought, well, I'll get an all-male band. The man that I worked for was going to get one for me, and it never came through. He just sort of let the ball drop."[5]

But the desire for a band remained. After "Moulin Rouge" closed and Leonard was back working in Chicago, an agent told her about an all-girl band that had been rehearsing for months but had not yet made its debut. The group already had talented, experienced players, original charts, and a booker anxious to send them out on jobs. All they needed was a glamorous leader. Leonard, who had studied piano and cello but "played both lousy," boned up on her conducting.

The Musicians Meet Ada Leonard

The members of that busily rehearsing Chicago band were not pleased to learn that Leonard would lead them. Organized months earlier by saxophonist Bernice Little, the band consisted of experienced players, or, as *Down Beat* put it, "some of the best fem cats in the trade"[6] — musicians who were serious about their music and serious about being taken seriously.

Among these musicians was trumpet player Jane Sager. "I helped organize this band; in fact, I wrote two charts," she recalled. In 1940, Sager, who had worked with both men's and women's bands since the mid-1930s, was working with the Chicago Women's Symphony and playing casuals around town with a number of groups, scrambling to make a buck. As she put it, there were "Italian and Polish dances — Greek dances in $\frac{5}{4}$ rhythm. *Ouch!* And tons of bar mitzvahs." She had big hopes for the band that would become the All-American Girls: "We had four violins. We thought we were going to be real jazzy and classy." The band's agent, Al Borde, was scouting for an appropriate big-name bandleader before sending them on the road. "So they told us, we've got your leader. And her name is Ada Leonard. I said, 'Oh my God, that's the

Jane Sager, ca. 1946. *Courtesy Jane Sager.*

burlesque queen. She's working down at the Rialto Theater in Chicago, the big burlesque house.' "[7]

"Were we upset!" recalled Sager. Still, she convinced two other trumpet players to go with her to take a look at their new leader in action. Sager knew from her earlier experiences of working with Rita Rio's band in the mid-1930s (she had left before Leonard's stint in "A Night at the Moulin Rouge") that a glamorous leader was essential in the all-girl band business. In a letter, she described her first glimpse of Leonard. "We went (sneaked in) to the Rialto Theater, where she was headlining, and hid up in the balcony so no one would see us. Ada had *absolute class* — never 'took off' a thing, and glided with beautiful grace across the stage. We *knew* she would make a great leader if *only she had a beat.* Well, she had one."

The three trumpet players may have been ready to forget that Leonard was a burlesque queen and give her a chance, but the other musicians remained skeptical. The stakes were high. The band was slated to open Christmas week, in only two weeks, at the State and Lake Theater, a big-time Chicago venue. New shows, Sager recalled, "usually played little theater dates (we called them toilets) before an opening!" In this case, the band would have to debut at a major theater without the benefit of break-in dates out of town. And the bandleader had yet to go over with the musicians, most of whom had not caught her act at the Rialto.

"I got myself a book that showed you the different beats with illustrations," recalled Leonard. "I faced these girls" — most of whom were older than she was. "And they looked at me like, '*She's* going to lead *us*?' Because I'm not a playing musician. And they knew my name. But Jane Sager was smart enough to know why I was there. So I took the score of 'St. Louis Blues,' a sort of concert arrangement — I took it home, and I stayed up all night until I had that thing down pat. And I came to rehearsal the next day, and I conducted the whole thing straight through. And the girls applauded. But, if it wasn't for Jane, I would have quit." She shuddered at the memory. "All those people staring at you like, '*You're* going to lead *us*?' "

Sager went to bat for Leonard because she knew that, with a glamorous leader, the band could hit it big. The Rialto performance had proved to her that Leonard knew her way around a stage. But Sager also knew that Leonard would need coaching: "I remember spending up until 3 A.M. in Ada's apartment going over numbers and getting the various tempos in Ada's head. It was a killer time! I will never forget the opening show. I would give each tempo off the end of my horn. She *stared so hard* at me that I was almost hypnotized, but we made it, and she was a smash hit."

Advertisements for the show at the State and Lake began running the day before the 20 December 1940 opening and appeared daily in the *Chicago Tribune* throughout the week-long engagement: "Roadshow stage smash! 'All American Girls' Band. 16 Swing Coeds 16. Led by Ada Leonard. Plus Big Vaudeville."[8] The band shared the bill with assorted vaudeville acts and the opening of Columbia Pictures's *Blondie Plays Cupid.* While the band itself was not pictured in the ads, the likeness of their new leader was prominently displayed to the right of the ad copy. Her high heels poked into the bottommost lettering announcing the movie feature, the curves of her legs framed the vaudeville credits, and her upper torso virtually nudged the words *"All American Girls" Band.* Her lower body was shown in profile, but her upper body and head twisted outward so that her demure smile was aimed directly at the reader. On opening day, the ad was larger, the copy elaborated on its description of the leader ("Beautiful, Glamorous Ada Leonard, Sultry Siren of Swing"), and the musicians were hailed as "16 Lovely Loreleis of Rhythm."[9]

While no explicit reference to burlesque appeared in these ads, phrases such as *sultry siren* and *lovely Loreleis* and the persistent emphasis on Leonard's body suggest that little attempt was made to create a clear distinction between the bandleader's new and old careers. A more circumspect entertainment columnist wrote, "Ada Leonard makes her debut as an orchestra leader this week,"[10] tastefully shifting the famous name to its new context without sensationalizing. While it is impossible to determine whether the audience came to see a famous stripper or a new all-girl band, Ada Leonard's All-American Girls were well enough received to be invited back to the State and Lake that spring with the "Oomph Revue of 1941."[11] One *Variety* reporter described the band as "a good looking outfit that plays some excellent arrangements" and praised Leonard's "bang-up appearance" as a "lesson in showmanship."[12] "I couldn't have done it without Janie," said Leonard. "I put the baton in her hand," agreed Sager.

The band's second engagement was a New Year's Eve show at the Orpheum Theater in Minneapolis, about which Sager recalled two near disasters. First, singer Gertrude Niesen, who was appearing on the same bill (along with Edgar Bergen and Charlie McCarthy), took a proprietary liking to the band. According to Sager, Niesen "tried to talk us into giving the band to her and getting rid of Ada!" Some of the musicians were tempted to take Niesen up on the offer, but Sager, impressed with Leonard and infuriated with her fickle colleagues, "fought them like a tiger." Then, to add insult to injury, Leonard had a costume mishap with a metallic red skirt designed to elevate while she twirled, a sure audience pleaser. "We were playing a frantic chart of the 'Bugle Call Rag,' " recalled Sager, "and, as she was twirling, the snap at the top of her skirt broke, and the skirt almost came completely off! The pandemonium in the audience was almost to the point of riot. They were yelling 'Take it off, take it off!' *Oh, brother!*"

Such heckling dogged Ada Leonard's All-American Girls for years.

Ada Leonard and her "Girl Band Revue" advertised on State Lake Theater marquis, Chicago, 1941. *Courtesy Mary Demond.*

Theater window display advertising Ada Leonard and her All-American Girls' Band "featuring World's Greatest Girl Trumpeter Jane Sager" in the "Oomph Review of 1941." State Lake Theatre, Chicago, 1941. *Courtesy Mary Demond.*

As late as fall 1943, alto saxophonist Roz Cron would be stunned by the unexpected foot stomping and "bedlam" that greeted Leonard's entrance at the Oriental Theater in Chicago (Cron writes that this display gave her new admiration for Leonard's "guts to gamble to change her image").[13] Still, the band received rave notices, and the musicians did not mutiny. They played major ballrooms, including the Trianon and the Aragon in Chicago, neither of which were known to hire all-girl bands. The winning combination of the well-rehearsed, versatile assembly of experienced professional musicians — most of whom had previously played with the likes of Ina Ray Hutton, Rita Rio, and Phil Spitalny — and the provocative leader was a hit.

Down Beat heralded the band's success with the headline: "Strip-Tease Ada Leonard Fronts Ace Fem Outfit": "Ada Leonard, stately brunette crown princess of the strip-tease, lit out of here for Youngstown, Ohio to open a four week date at Hotel Ohio a week ago, fronting one of the best all-gal orks yet to be turned out." The enthusiastic reviewer went on to list the entire "ork" personnel, comment on individual talents, and focus on the musicality of the group (and briefly report on which band members were unmarried). *Down Beat* even made a point of qualifying the references to Leonard's past with the observations that she was "stately" and a "princess." And the magazine was soon referring to her burlesque career only obliquely, calling her "one of the more gifted theater artists."[14] The ability of Ada Leonard's all-girl band to recall burlesque without actually being burlesque, to play top-notch music while appearing single, wholesome, and glamorous all at once, was already part of its audience draw. This combination would become increasingly attractive as the United States entered the war.

The timing was right for Ada Leonard's All-American Girls. Not only was the orchestra ready, willing, and able to entertain the soldiers by 1941, but the field of glamorous white all-girl bands had lost two of its major contenders, Ina Ray Hutton's and Rita Rio's bands. Hutton dropped her popular all-girl band in the summer of 1939 in order to lead a men's band, explaining to *Down Beat* that she was "sick of glamour" (the disavowal was unconvincing given the cheesecake photograph on the cover).[15] By May 1940, the "blonde bombshell of swing" had become a brunette, prompting the photo caption "ex–glamour girl."[16] Hutton's hair color was still news in November, when *Down Beat* confirmed, "She's a blonde no longer — and she meant what she said when she told a *Down Beat* reporter six months ago that she was 'through with glamour.' "[17] The only other bandleader who could have given Leonard a run for her money in the glamour game was Rita Rio. But, by the summer of 1940, Rio had disbanded her group in order to concentrate her energy on a new career as a film actress (under a different, but still alliterative, name — Dona Drake).[18] When the USO was looking for acts to send out on the first Camp Show circuits, Ada Leonard's band was an obvious choice.

In November 1941, the "Ada Leonard Revue" became unit 9 of the USO–Camp Shows. Among the first acts sent out to entertain soldiers, unit 9 was one of ten units already performing by 7 December 1941, when Japan bombed Pearl Harbor. Recalled Leonard, "I was playing for the [Army] Air Force. And they blacked out the minute they heard about Pearl Harbor, and I fell over a radiator and badly burned myself. That's how I remember it. We played USO before we were in the war."

Not only had the USO been activated before the United States entered World War II, but the draft had been as well, thanks to the Selective Service and Training Act of 1940, which enabled the conscription of soldiers for a twelve-month (later eighteen-month) tour of duty, the first peacetime draft in U.S. history. New and expanded military camps were already changing the demographics of towns and cities across the country. As we have seen in the previous chapter, the USO was incorporated to deal with anxiety about soldiers on leave. In the words of Paul McNutt, federal security administrator, "What for example, can a village of, say two thousand do when 20,000 soldiers from a nearby camp come to town to spend their leave? Shall those men be left to loiter on street corners — or in other less savory surroundings where they are open to every kind of vicious exploitation?"[19] Soldiers had ample pocket money and, thus, the potential to fuel a boom in business for local pool halls, card rooms, bars, and brothels. Part of the USO's job was to provide activities that the public would find wholesome and servicemen appealing. A former burlesque queen leading all-American girls in a swing band might just work.

Another part of the USO's job early on in the war was radically to transform public opinion about soldiers on leave. On 29 September 1941, Lieutenant Colonel M. M. Montgomery, from the Morale Branch of the War Department, advised the participants at the Defense Recreation Conference in Baltimore that a major problem faced by the United States during its preparation for war was the hypocrisy of a public that glorified the soldier on the battlefield and loathed the soldier on leave. Such contradictory attitudes would not wash with GIs preparing to risk their lives in a not-yet-popular war, and they would not be good for morale, civilian or military. "One of our problems should be to see that this differentiation never becomes painfully apparent," argued Montgomery.[20] The emphasis on wholesome entertainment provided by the USO functioned as much to construct an attractive image of soldiers as "boys next door," even as "our boys" as it did to shelter civilians from GI leisure. Soldiers and sailors ogling an actual burlesque show would do little to transform public attitudes about military personnel. Soldiers and sailors going out to see all-American girls play in a band, however, contributed to the image of doughnut-chomping, mail-craving, homesick "boys" that inspired a public, once fearful of military strangers, to become such enthusiasts of boys in uniform that they would pick them up hitchhiking and take them home to their families.

Down Beat Christmas issues customarily ran pages of holiday wishes that doubled as promotions for the musicians and agents who bought them. On 1 December 1941, *Down Beat* announced Ada Leonard's presence on a sixteen-week USO tour of military camps.[21] In the very next issue appeared a three-inch-square "Season's Greetings" message from "Ada Leonard and her 16-piece All American Girl Orchestra." Beneath the sultry head shot of the leader were printed the names of all the musicians. Although no pictures accompanied the names, the ad acted as a Christmas card to "our boys" from sixteen representative all-American girls.[22]

In a letter, Sager explained the band's name: "All American Girls. W.W. II gave us that name. We wore red-and-white-striped blouses and deep blue skirts!! *'Oh Say Can You See?'* " This comment, and Sager's sense of humor about the patriotic extremes embodied by a band she had worked hard to help organize, raised questions about what it was like for women musicians to find themselves working as cheerleaders for soldiers during World War II. I wrote back, asking this and other questions about the USO. Sager responded with another letter, promising that someday she would fill me in. Then, on 30 July 1995, the phone rang, and Sager informed me that she had made some notes and was ready to tell the "true story of the USO." She told me to "roll the tape" and call her back.

We hung up. I scrambled to hook up my tape recorder and then dialed her number. I began to express my gratitude, but there was no time for preliminaries. "I've got some for you," she said. "Oh, brother. I mean, this is right out of the horse's mouth."

Sager began her USO history by telling me that her friend of fifty-two years, Mary Sawyer, was a dancer on the very first unit organized by the impresario Billy Rose. Sawyer had recently passed away, but Sager knew her friend's history well. For one thing, she knew that, eight to ten weeks prior to the November 1941 launching of the Ada Leonard Revue, Sawyer had danced in the inaugural USO–Camp Shows troop, which starred Gypsy Rose Lee. Sager related Sawyer's memories of the military camps in the months before the United States entered the war. "They were just starting to train," Sager explained. "And [Mary] said they'd go out there to entertain them in the field, and they would be training with broomsticks and making believe they were bayonets, and they would say, 'Hit the guy, and pull it up, and cut him right in two!' " Sager recalled her friend talking about how frightened the soldiers appeared, how she saw one young man vomit when ordered to draw and quarter a make-believe enemy with his broomstick. She also remembered that Sawyer spent the entire tour dancing on the tailgate of a truck and that she had nearly ruined her legs.

At the end of the run, Sawyer returned to New York, where she was once again courted by the USO. She was given a choice of three shows in which she could appear. Looking over the lists of acts, she asked, "Hey, what's this show with a girl band named Ada Leonard?" The agent replied, "Well, this is going to be the first big band we're going to put on the USO." "Mary said, 'I'd never worked with a girl band. I thought it'd be kind of fun.' So, wasn't that funny?" marveled Sager. "She picked that show over the other two?" For Sager, this juncture in the narrative marks the beginning of a friendship that would span half a century and include opening a trumpet studio in Hollywood together in the 1950s and organizing a successful music and comedy act called the Frivolous Five that would perform coast to coast, on national television, and would cut a record parodying Herb Alpert's Tijuana Brass.[23] And all because that day in the fall of 1941 Sawyer decided it would be fun to play with a girl band for a change.

Unit 9 proved to be extraordinarily popular with soldiers. "We were out for twenty-six weeks," said Sager, "because they kept holding us. Well, you can imagine, those poor fellas. We come out there all girls, a total girl show." Sager is a vivid and spontaneous storyteller, but she likes to make detailed notes ahead of time so as not to get stuck on names, dates, or places. She consulted her notes briefly, then continued: "Now, we opened in Watertown, New York, which was practically in

Canada, and we worked straight down the coast, all the way down into the South, all the way across the United States in the South, up through San Diego, on up north to Fort Lewis, Washington, and doubled back again across the country, and finally ended in that big camp in North Carolina. The names of the camps, some of them, are coming back to me. Honestly, that was something else. Of course, we were thrilled. We'd go by train. Of course, we ended up on a lot of buses. But the first big problem we had was that we had no days off at all because the day that we were supposed to take off they said, 'You've got to go do hospital shows.' Well, now, who's going to turn down a hospital show?"

During the war, musicians, and particularly girl musicians, were seen more as comforters of soldiers than as laborers. So, even though Ada Leonard's musicians were card-carrying members of the AFM, performing two shows a day, six days a week, and traveling colossal distances between gigs, the concept of "all-American girls" had no room for turning down hospital shows or workers who deserved a day off. Travel conditions were not as bad for USO bands as they were for most civilian bands since USO bands did not have to worry about gas coupons, tires, and chartering buses. Still, USO shows were not immune from having their coaches yanked off a train in the middle of nowhere to make room for cars full of priority military passengers. Sager spoke of running up and down the train tracks on winter nights trying to keep warm while waiting six or eight or twelve hours for the next train. She also noted that the USO had not yet figured out how to keep its entertainers from starving. On trains, military personnel were served first at the food concessions, which were monopolized by the Fred Harvey Company. The musicians learned to coax soldiers to bring them back something before the supplies ran out. Even then, recalled Sager, "those darn Fred Harvey sandwiches were the thinnest little piece of ham you ever saw in your life. You could see through it. And that rotten white bread. And they'd clamp it together, and that was a sandwich. But, I'll tell you, it would be like a turkey dinner. We'd give [soldiers] the money, and they'd go get us these terrible sandwiches, bring them back to us. And that's the only way we ate. I lived on those rotten sandwiches so much, I'm surprised I didn't get ulcers."

Under these conditions, it is not surprising that the performers began to wonder what happened to the day off that had been guaranteed by their contracts. It was not merely the prospect of recuperation or privacy or even sleep that made the issue of a day off crucial. Being denied a day off also made it difficult for the musicians to maintain their fresh, glamorous image. "We couldn't do our laundry!" exclaimed Sager, the exasperation of fifty years past discernible in her voice. "We were getting dirty! They didn't have laundromats in those days. So what we used to do when we'd get into a place, we would fill the bathtub up with laundry soap, and then we would jump up and down with our feet, hanging on to the shower curtains, and I would be singing the 'Anvil Chorus,' you know, 'Dum, dum, dum, da-dum, da-dum, da-dum, da-aaah-dum. . . .' And then we would always have a little bottle of Seagrams Five — we couldn't afford anything better, the government wouldn't give it to you, anyway. So we'd have this little bottle of Seagrams Five, and I got the brilliant idea of pouring it into the tub, so I poured the whole half pint down into the tub as we were doing our washing. I want to tell you, that washing turned out to be absolutely beautiful. It was the cleanest washing I've ever seen. From the Seagrams Five. That's all we could get hold of, and we had to have a few little nips, or we'd go crazy."

It may have been easy for the USO and the American public to forget that entertainers were workers, but there was little chance that Ada Leonard's experienced musicians would. The promised day off soon became the impetus for the first major conflict between the band and the USO: "It was over having a day off. The management said we couldn't have it. And Ada and all of us were just going crazy." A meeting was held between unit 9, the Chicago agent, Al Borde, and well-known Broadway producer Harry Delmar, who, according to Sager, "had all those big shows running. And he also had his fingers in the pot at the USO, and he was making a fortune. We were taking a 33⅓ percent cut from our regular salary. But they weren't."

"Anyway, Harry came down, and we had a meeting in some little auditorium there in one of the camps." Sager had been chosen ahead of time by the performers to be their spokesperson. "I guess I had a big mouth or something," she explained. Delmar looked around the room and asked, "Now, what is your beef?" Sager replied, " 'Well, this is it, Mr. Delmar. . . .' I laid the whole thing out, how we couldn't get any of our laundry done, we didn't have time to iron things, we were just absolutely a mess. So he looked at me, and I remember he had a very good-looking pipe, a real debonair type of guy. And he says 'Well, now, let's see.' So he looked at all the girls — there were about thirty-five of us. He pointed at each individual person, all the different acts and the band girls and all, and said, 'Do you want to do what she says? Are you with her?' " The suave producer's intimidation techniques served him well. She groaned. "They chickened out on me."

Still, after the meeting, the troop did receive an occasional night off, although not as often as their contracts promised. But the situation was not resolved, and dissatisfaction soon resurfaced—with a vengeance: "We had a manager named Brown. Mr. Brown, I'll never forget him. I think they handpicked managers to be real sardonic and mean and scare the hell out of you and everything. Well, he didn't scare me, but he did something that made Ada just wild. And Ada was, you know—Ada is very much of a lady. But something came off over this business of having another day off, a chance to clean up and all that, and he ratted on Ada." According to Sager, the manager reported to the USO office that Leonard was a complainer. "Well, I never saw anything like it. Ada looked at him, and she had very, very long legs. The longest legs I've ever seen. And she swung one of those legs and hit him right in the balls. I mean, she kicked him so hard, he turned about five colors. She about near killed him. And then she called him a son of a bitch, and she ran. Mary was dressing with her and also rooming with her, and the dressing room—you know how you have your lights down the side? The makeup lights? She broke every light; she broke every mirror. She threw things. Mary had to dodge. She threw their makeup all up against the walls. And then she took her gorgeous gowns and pulled them one after the other off the hangers, and Mary kept running and getting them and putting them back on the hangers so they wouldn't tear. But she just went out of her mind. Well, let me tell you, after that, they changed their tune."

Leonard had already given me her account of the battle, in which the issue was compounded by other practices she considered exploitative. "Unfortunately," Leonard said, "the USO was controlled by a bunch of agents, and a lot of hanky-panky went on in the financial area. It took me a long time to catch on because I had always worked as a lone person and I was not acquainted with the different things that they do." One complaint that she had was with the way in which the band members were hired. According to Leonard, by hiring her as an individual performer rather than as the bandleader, the agents were able to present the band as a package and sell it for much more than they were paying its members. Not being hired as the bandleader also meant that Leonard was not authorized to hire her own band manager but had to accept whomever the USO assigned to the job. It was more than the day off that pushed Leonard into the rage described by Sager, but the day off was the catalyst. To a typical request for a Sunday hospital show, Leonard reports that she had responded, " 'We will do it tomorrow, but not today. This is our day off.' The manager called the office and said that I refused to do a hospital show. No explanation. So when that got back to me, I grabbed him, and I said, 'Don't you ever, ever lie about me again,' and I kicked him up a flight of stairs. All these GIs were watching through the window, and they started applauding."

In Leonard's version of the story, the GIs cheered her efforts to advocate on behalf of her band members. As underlings in the military hierarchy, perhaps they felt solidarity with the performers in this rift between workers and management. One can also imagine that some GIs would not have sympathized with the musicians, but would have been dismayed at the hesitancy of any entertainer — man or woman — to play a hospital show. The applauding soldiers occupy an interesting place in Leonard's story. They represent a badly needed vote of confidence for a bandleader trying to balance the needs of her musicians with the needs of the GIs. Perhaps they offer a vision of solidarity that makes it possible to tell the story. And perhaps they were simply applauding her legs.

Not even the bombing of Pearl Harbor brought the musicians a night off. The night of 7 December 1941 December theaters across the country were dark. Even the Andrews Sisters, who had been playing to packed houses at the Schubert in Cincinnati, arrived at the theater that night to find the sidewalk outside empty.[24] To USO–Camp Shows, however, the bombing of Pearl Harbor brought chaos and confusion, but not a night off. That evening, the band traveled by bus from Virginia to play for officers stationed at Fort Belvoir near Washington, D.C. When the bus crossed the bridge over the Potomac, Sager was stunned to see "them putting World War I machine-gun nests. I said 'Look what they're doing. This war is going to be all cannons and modern, and here they are with these little, old-fashioned machine-gun nests." At the fort, the band was detained for five hours. "We waited and waited and waited, and the guy had to turn the motor off because you couldn't waste gas. We were freezing. Our feet were cold. By eleven o'clock at night they finally got themselves organized enough to realize that we weren't enemies. We were the USO show. So we went in and did our shows. I don't know what in the heck time we got through that night."

The details of how USO entertainers would be fed, housed, transported, and protected during their arduous camp-to-camp tours had not yet been ironed out, nor were such issues high on the priority list in the days immediately following U.S. entry into the war. With the bombing of Pearl Harbor, military and civilian minds alike were preoccupied with the possibility that an invasion by the Japanese or the Germans was imminent. Most all-woman bands that traveled with the USO were signed toward the end of the war, either to play for troops overseas waiting to be shipped home or to tour the United States on the stateside "Victory Circuit." In Sager's words, "That was the gravy train. This was number one. And this is the way it was."

Sager offered yet another example of the disorganization and chaos faced by early USO–Camp Shows performers: "We were in Norfolk, Virginia, and all of a sudden this big general came over, and he said, 'Stop!' We just quit playing right in the middle of what we were doing. 'Now, look,' he says, 'play something happy. Just play jazz and happy stuff. I've got to empty this whole auditorium out. They're all fliers. They fly the black widow fliers, and we've sighted. . . .' German subs were sighted right outside the Norfolk air base, the Norfolk navy base! And they had to empty the house out while we were playing. And I had one of those metal derbies that you played jazz with, you know, and I put it on my head! We put them on our heads in case they started to bomb us! Wasn't that dumb? But there I was, sitting in that derby hat, playing 'Happy Days Are Here Again' or something like that. All those fellows are all on their way up. You could hear them, the planes warming up. You could hear them zooming up overhead."

With the auditorium emptied, the musicians packed up their equipment and boarded the bus that would take them back to town. As was rapidly becoming common, a blackout had been imposed — even headlights. How we didn't get killed [driving back] I don't know. Well, we got out of the bus. I used to carry one of those little pen flashlights. The darn battery was out. And I was in total darkness. How I even got into the hotel, I don't know. I found the hotel, all of us together, and we remembered our room number, and we started up the halls, and the sailors were so drunk and scared and up in the air that they just started grabbing any woman they could and threw her down on the ground. I mean it, I mean on the floor. So we got to our room, and there was a sailor chasing after us. My roommate and I, we opened the door, and he fell in the room. I pushed him so he would sober up. And my roommate, who was a very feminine girl, she took her fist and hit him in the mouth and knocked him out on the floor. We thought we'd killed him. We slammed the door shut, and in total darkness we were thinking, Any minute they're going to come after us because we've committed a murder. We were shaking with fear. But that town of Norfolk, Virginia, that night, I tell you, there was a war on, and they were acting like fools, crazies. Well, I guess they thought, 'We're going to die, let's find a girl. Let's find a woman.' "

While the war years may have been a time when the definition of "all-American girl" was up for grabs — she could build airplanes, earn money of her own, flirt with men she'd never seen before and would never see again — this did not mean that all women always benefited from these relatively flexible parameters. As the (hetero)sexual possibilities of the "girl next door" increased, her right to say no became increasingly compromised, especially if the solicitor was a "boy in uniform." This is not to say that the good girl/bad girl dichotomy was a thing of the past. In an article in *Yank* magazine entitled "Gypsy Gyps Us," a soldier grappled with the 1942 marriage of Gypsy Rose Lee. His sensibilities were offended, it seems, not because he had hoped to marry her himself (which would have made her a "good girl") but because her appeal was grounded in his understanding of her as not marriageable. "For too long I and my colleagues of the second platoon have looked upon Gyp as our own," complained Private Al Hine. "It's a bitter thing to think of her as a spouse. Maybe marriage is all right for some people, but for Gypsy, no."[25]

"Good girls" and "bad girls" still existed in the minds of most Americans, but now that the country was at war, both were considered potential sexual partners for those "all-American boys" in uniform. As with other American women, Ada Leonard's All-American Girls encountered pressure to render sexual favors as a patriotic duty, only the pressure was intensified by a schedule that included performing for military audiences daily, attending after-show parties, and often sleeping in military camps. According to Sager, officers, especially, tended to expect the musicians to step off the stage and into their arms: "We'd play a show at 6:30. The show would go an hour and a half or two. Then they'd empty out the house. Then back-to-back we'd play another show for another gang because the camps were so big. They'd fill the theater, and then empty the theater, and then fill it again. Two shows a night. And, when we got through, we were dead. And do you know those officers thought that we were going to go out and entertain them after we got through playing? We said, 'Look, there's a musicians' union!' And I got mad at one of them, and I said, 'Look, I don't make my living on my back. If I did, I wouldn't be playing the trumpet.' I said, 'I see that bus over there.' Each camp brought in prostitutes. They were all tested so they weren't supposed to give them diseases, but they got diseases, don't worry. I know that, too. I said, 'You've got your whores out there. What do you think you can do? Turn *us* into something like that?' "

The war-time parameters of "good girl" were loosened enough to allow some permissible sex outside of marriage for single girls to "send soldiers off happy," but the category was still not all encompassing. New definitions of "woman" didn't radically alter public opinions about prostitutes, for instance. While prostitutes labored near most military camps, and were sometimes transported into bases in the buses mentioned by Sager, the general public considered them a necessary evil, at best. Soldiers who perceived themselves as "all-American boys" didn't necessarily want their final sexual experience before shipping out to be with a woman they saw as a "bad girl." They felt entitled to their counterparts, good "all-American girls," the women they were constantly told they were fighting to defend. American women could no longer claim a "good girl" persona as protection against unwanted advances, not that it had ever been a fool-proof method or even available to all women at all times. But during the war, turning down a dance or a kiss with a male soldier of the same race was tantamount to turning down a hospital show. And turning down the sexual advances of an "all-American boy" before he shipped off to combat and possibly death was no longer a clear case of common morality. While World War II certainly marked a time when American women enjoyed many new freedoms, it was also a time when many American women struggled in the gray areas of what exactly were their sexual obligations to "boys in uniform." Was it a smile, a dance, love letters (to all of them?), a spur-of-the-moment marriage, sex?

"We just instinctively knew what we were up against," said Sager. "We knew we were there to remind them of the girl next door. And we would try to play that role as far as we could." The complexities of the role hit home for Sager when the tour reconnected her with a soldier who was, literally, a boy from home: "He was a boy that I'd played in high school band with. We'd been very friendly, but not *that* friendly. And he discovered I was on one of the shows, and he worked in a hospital. So he asked me after the show, 'Janie, will you go out with me?' I said, 'Why sure I will.' So, egads, he took me to an off-limits place out of town, in a cab, and we went in there, and they were having fights, and I was hiding under the tables for fear I'd get hit. And then, coming home, we couldn't find a cab, and we were walking, and he tried to throw me down in the field. And I said, 'I can't do that.' And he said, 'Yeah, but you're a good, clean girl, and I'm going away.' And I said, 'I may be a good, clean girl, and you're going away, but I can't do it, Bob, I can't be a whore for you. In the first place, I don't love you.' He said, 'It isn't love.' I said, 'That's what I know, that's what I realize.' But he tried to throw me right down in the field. I said, 'Think of your mother, your sister.' And I put on an act like you never heard of. And I finally got him out of the mood. But he was going overseas very soon, and he thought he had somebody from home and this was going to be it. That's all that was on his mind. He played the third trumpet [in the high school band]. I was the first trumpet. And he said, 'I always admired your playing,' and I said, 'What's that got to do with going to lay me out here in the field?' And that's exactly what it was going to be. I got out of it, though. I'll admit I had a few bumps and bruises when I came in. My clothes were torn. And Ada and Mary said, 'What is this? You were all dressed so nice and everything.' He apologized, and we cried. He cried. He said, 'Jane, I'm so sorry.' I said, 'I understand.' "

What Sager understood was not that it was OK for men to force themselves on women but that soldiers' fears were all too often commensurate with their futures: "Some of them would come up and grab your hand, you know, and you'd hang on to them, and they'd say, 'I know I'm going out tonight, and I'm never going to come back,' and I always said the same thing: 'You are, too,' you know, 'Sure, you're coming back.' We were kind of goodwill ambassadors for those poor things. And sometimes they'd get drunk and try and get fresh. You couldn't get mean to them because, the poor things, their lives were just about through. And, of course, if somebody touched your heart enough, you'd give in to them, but I never had to do that. I think some of the kids did; they just couldn't stand it. These poor little guys. And you didn't dare develop a friendship while you were on a base or anything because you knew you were going to lose it anyway."

Sager had already lost a dear friend in the early days of the war. But nothing brought home the tragedy of war more than the hospital shows. "We were up at the Long Beach Naval Air Station," she said, "and that's where they brought in all the horribly injured men and what they called the *basket cases*." Basket cases were victims of such extensive injuries that they could not lie in a bed or on a stretcher but had to be accommodated literally in a basket. Sager continued, "Well, let me tell you, we were playing one of the hospitals, and a note was sent back to me." It seemed that one of the patients had heard of Sager, whose reputation as an outstanding trumpet soloist was growing (even *Down Beat* was prais-ing her "high-voiced Harry James style").[26] The nurse who delivered the note said that the patient was also a trumpet player (not her high school friend) and that he wished to hear Sager play Bunny Berigan's solo from "I Can't Get Started": "Well, of course, I loved that. And I was all ready to go, and she wheels him in. And he was a stump. He had no arms, no legs, just this face, and he stared at me, and I'll never forget those eyes. You talk about two burnt holes in a blanket. They were the most terrify-ing eyes yet, at the same time, so pitiful. And I had to look at those eyes, and you know, you can't blow a horn when you laugh or cry. But some-how I just said, 'Dear God, I've got to do this for this guy.' And I got the strength, and I played it, but I'll never forget the tears. The nurse had to wipe his eyes because the tears were pouring down. My eyes, the tears were running all down my face. It was the most terrible experience, and I remember I just said, 'Oh, God, I'll never be able to do this again.' Thank God I never had to. But, you know, the last day of my life, when I leave this world, I'm going to see that fellow's eyes, his face. I know it. It haunts me."

As Sager remembers it, a typical hour-and-a-half show of the Ada Leonard Revue of 1942 would kick off with an instrumental piece like "Bugle Call Rag." Then a singer would be featured. Perhaps tenor sax-ophonist Brownie Slade would do one of her vocal numbers, stirring up the crowd's emotions with a ballad popular during the war — "White Cliffs of Dover" or "Once in a While." Then Mary Sawyer would dance. Sager would follow with a trumpet solo, regaling the troops with her renowned rendition of Harry James's "Trumpet Concerto." Then she would go out in front of the stage and ask the soldiers what else they wanted to hear, or, as she put it, "give them something from home, pop songs of the day." "What's your favorite song?" she would ask them. And they would shout out song titles. Then, accompanied only by bass and piano, she would grant one of their requests. A comedy act would follow. At some point, Leonard would give them a torch song. And then the band would play another instrumental arrangement. It was a variety show built around the band as its feature attraction, and Sager was a featured attraction within the band.

On one occasion, as Sager stepped down to the front of the stage to perform her solo feature, a young voice called out a request for the Harry Barris melody "I Surrender, Dear." She could not see the soldier because of the carbon spotlights, but the request caught her ear. "Well, you know, that wasn't called out too much among those guys; they always wanted pretty corny stuff. So I said, 'Sure, I'll play it.' So I'm playing this solo, and I'm feeling it in my heart and soul and, oh, just really enjoying doing something I like. And I hear a lot of commotion down there. And I couldn't see, but stuff's going on like mad."

When the show was over, Sager went down to the area where the young man had been sitting and where a group of officers now stood. She demanded to know what had happened: "One says, 'Can you take it?' I said, 'I don't know what you mean.' He says, 'Come here.' So I did, and it was that thick with blood — all over the seat, my God. So, to make a long story short, they saved the kid's life. He had cut his wrists. That was his favorite song, and he didn't want to go the bullet way. He wanted to die that way. Well, they let me go to the infirmary the next morning, and I saw him with his arms bandaged, and I hugged him, and I said, 'Look, that's the wrong way to go. You may never get a bullet. I could get one before you, walking around. Who knows?' He said, 'Oh, thank you.' I said, 'Now you have somebody write for you, and you write your mother, and you just tell her, you know, this is all crap.' "

At the end of twenty-six weeks, Sager left the All-American Girls and the USO and moved to Los Angeles with the intention of becoming Rosie the Riveter: "I went out and took a test, and they called me. I had a degree, you see, and they thought they wanted me to push a couple of holes together, you know, pound something through a hole. And that very day I got a chance to play the horn again, and, boy, did I dump that in a hurry. That patriotic business went right out the window. But the shows I played, we were always doing camps anyway. My days off were always doing free shows for servicemen." In September 1942, she triumphed in an audition for a vacated trumpet chair in Johnny Richards's otherwise all-man band and stayed with the group until it went on the road. Having had enough of life on the road, she elected to remain in Los Angeles, taking advantage of opportunities virtually unheard of for a woman before the war. She played days in a CBS radio band, the all woman Victory Belles, led by tenor saxophonist Peggy Gilbert on the "Ona Munson Show," as well as the swing and night shifts in the (men's) house band at the Casino Gardens.

Leonard was able to keep the band going after Sager left, and the All-American Girls returned to theater and ballroom tours after their first stint with the USO. Because the group was now considered important enough to list in *Down Beat*'s "Where the Bands Are Playing" column, it is possible to track its movements week by week, to know, for instance, that it spent the latter half of 1942 playing such venues as the Trianon and the Oriental in Chicago, the Happy Hour in Minneapolis, and the Paramount Theater in Des Moines.

Musically, the band was entering a period of transition, as Leonard anticipated the sounds that audiences would find pleasing and acceptable coming from all-American girls in wartime. In December 1942, *Downbeat* quoted Leonard as saying, "People don't expect girls to play high-powered swing all night long. It looks out of place." Reporter Bob Fossum found the statement a generally accurate description of the program of pop tunes and standards that he heard, but he also noted that the band swung out occasionally on such numbers as "One O'Clock Jump" and "St. Louis Blues" and that drummer "Dez Thompson stole the show with her rock-bound beat and flashy solos."[27] In 1943, another reviewer described the music as "definitely on the jump side."[28]

By 1944, the band included a number of soloists who were able to take off on improvised solos. According to trumpet player Mary Demond, who had played with the original band and had friends in the later one, the orchestra transformed into "a jazz-swinging band. The first one they formed was, in my opinion, more of a commercial Phil Spitalny type."[29] Although the instrumentation still included three violins, the repertoire and style inspired a reviewer to expound, "When the band went through a jivey arrangement of 'Seven Nights in a Bastille,' they put up a strong argument against those who claim only male musicians can handle fast music."[30] Lionel Hampton took an interest in the band and, on one occasion, loaned Leonard the services of his arranger to help her rehearse the band's rendition of Count Basie's "One O'Clock Jump." Arranger Gene Gifford, of Casa Loma Orchestra fame, came on board, writing such exciting charts that reeds player Betty Rosner, whose goal in music was "to play with the best and be the best," turned down an offer with Claude Thornhill's famous band in order to work as Gifford's copyist and perform improvised sax solos in Leonard's band.[31] Ethel "Kirk" Kirkpatrick (Drehouse) was hired in 1944 specifically to handle the tenor takeoff solos.[32] Leonard must have changed her mind about girls playing hard swinging jazz; it had evidently become acceptable as long as a glamorous visual image was offered at the same time. After all, the U.S. public was willing to accept Rosie the Riveter performing men's work in wartime, as long as she maintained her femininity, her sex appeal, and her patriotism.

Ada Leonard's vast theatrical experience gave her, however, a practical approach to glamour. For her, the role of all-American girl was simply that — a role, one to be assumed on the job, not a lifestyle to be kept up twenty-four hours a day, and certainly not an advertisement of sexual availability. Her experience in burlesque in particular may be responsible for the infinitely sensible distinction that she drew between onstage fantasy and private reality. When Leonard was not performing, Sager recalled, she "basked in sloppiness." She traveled in "frumpy" clothes and wore no makeup. When her admirers asked where she was, band members were instructed to reply, "She'll be along soon. She'll be coming in a limousine." Gossip flew about the men that Leonard was supposedly dating, but, according to Sager, the "sultry siren of swing" most often spent her few free moments refilling her bath with hot water, over and over, and reading *Popeye* comic books. Glamour was a product to be sold during work hours only.

While Leonard expected her musicians to be visually appealing on-stage, she also believed that glamorous women are made and not born: "I don't care what you look like; if you are well groomed, you're attractive. If you know how to make up, you're attractive. I tried to instill that in them." I asked Leonard the extent to which glamour was a part of her job: "I certainly didn't sell them my talent. It was the way I looked. So I made the most of it. And you learn different things. There are tricks to every trade."

On 15 January 1943, *Down Beat* ran a sexy photograph of Leonard, skirt pulled up, leg extended, rolling down her stockings, with the explanation, "This is a patriotic strip tease, if you please — and you're bound to please, or at least be pleased by this shot of beauteous Ada Leonard stripping off her silk hosiery for the duration."[33] This scenario blending sex and patriotism was a familiar one during the war, performed many times by starlets who bared their legs while stockings and cameras rolled. Somehow, the silk stockings shed by attractive young women would wind up in the parachutes that saved servicemen's lives, an apt emblem of the sexual dimensions of U.S. women's patriotism. Leonard's surrender of stockings was doubly effective as both propaganda and an in-joke.

The same issue of *Down Beat* heralded Leonard's return to the USO, this time under the Frederick Brothers agency, the same company that booked Ina Ray Hutton's all-man band and would eventually book the International Sweethearts of Rhythm. The second time out on a USO tour, Leonard attempted to secure more control over the band's working conditions by bringing along her own manager. "They had a fit," she recalled. "They sent me another manager." In addition, there was a battle over who would be paid, Leonard or the booking agency. "So the result was, we quit. And we did a vaudeville tour." Even though Leonard's relationship with the USO remained troubled, she and her band spent the entire war bouncing back and forth between the USO and theater and ballroom tours.

As the band's *sound* swung harder, with jazzier arrangements, more up-tempo numbers, and more improvised solos, its *look* became softer, as if to ensure the band's overall reception as acceptably feminine. Leonard's own onstage wardrobe was consistently formfitting and slinky, but the outfits of the musicians behind her changed — from the flag-waving red, white, and blue skirts and blouses of the first tour to, first, more sedate black skirts and white blouses and, then, a series of florid gowns. In August 1943, *Down Beat* praised the musicians for their "tailored blouses and long skirts," along with their "serious music-making," and celebrated the absence of "the incongruous aspect of horns and cymbals rising awkwardly out of billowing frills and flounces."[34] Yet, by the fall of 1943, the "serious" costumes preferred by the *Down Beat* reviewer had given way to the "monstrous pink things" remembered by Roz Cron, who disliked the low-cut gowns worn by the band that season because they allowed her saxophone neck strap to bite into her unprotected skin and because it was so difficult to run — and catch trains! — in them.[35]

Betty Kidwell (Meriedeth), who joined the band as an alto player in September 1943 at the age of eighteen, recalled that the musicians wore black skirts at times and floral halter top gowns at others. She also remembered that the band was jumping in the years between 1943 and 1946, with outstanding Gene Gifford charts "that made our four saxes sound like five or six" and a number of soloists who could really "take off."[36] Drummer Fagel Liebman infused the band with a jazz beat. Other outstanding soloists included pianist Rita Kelly, saxophonist Betty Rosner, and trumpet player Frances Shirley.[37] Helen Day (Schuster), who joined Leonard's band on lead alto in late 1943, described her tenure as the "best musical experience" of her ten years in all-woman bands.[38]

Kidwell recalled that, during her four years with Leonard, the band alternated between USO tours and the Kemp Time, a circuit of small-time theaters and one-night dance hall bookings that was run by Stan Kemp, brother of bandleader Hal Kemp. Kemp Time kept the band working mostly in the South and East, with the schedule split between theaters on the weekend and one-nighters at military camps and dance halls weekdays. When Kidwell joined the band, Leonard's manager, Murray Rose, gave her a choice between making twelve dollars a day seven days a week or fourteen dollars each day she worked. She chose the seven-day guaranteed plan but said that the band worked so much that the two plans probably paid just about the same.[39]

Periodically, the band would get an offer to join an overseas USO tour. There would be a secret ballot, but the vote would have to be unanimous in order for the band to go. "I couldn't get the girls to go over to Europe," said Ada Leonard, wistfully. "They were afraid. Some would go, but some wouldn't. And then, at that time, they read about that singer that was in a plane crash in Europe and she was crippled." The singer was Jane Froman, and her dire injuries included a nearly severed leg. Only a fraction of her immense medical bill was picked up by the USO, the accident insurance policy covering a maximum of $1,000. There was indeed cause for alarm since most USO casualties resulted from plane crashes.[40] While Kidwell always voted yes — she had chosen her career in part because she was lured by the adventure of travel — there was always at least one no vote whenever the issue of overseas travel arose. Even so, Kidwell recollected that, between 1943 and 1946, Leonard's band worked two stateside USO tours, sometimes traveling by C-47 with young pilots who liked to give these particular passengers a thrill by tilting the wings and letting them look out the bombsights. She recalled no difficulties with days off, sexual harassment, or food shortages.[41] Ethel Kirkpatrick (Drehouse) also recalled that the later USO tours presented no food problems, "with one exception — [the military camps] always fed us steak, thinking these civilians needed a treat!"[42] (Not many people were then in a position to grow weary of steak.) All this suggests that, by the middle of the war, Leonard may have finally whipped the USO and the armed forces into shape.

During the summer of 1944, writer, promoter, and outspoken civil rights advocate John Hammond was serving in the army's Information and Education Division at Camp Plauché, Louisiana, near New Orleans. Thanks to family connections, Hammond's tour of duty involved arranging entertainment for the segregated and ill-treated black GIs at Plauché — nearly half the camp's population. Ada Leonard's All-American Girls was one of several bands that Hammond secured. In his autobiography, Hammond states, "I was fascinated to find a couple of

Negro girls in the band, passing as Orientals. Naturally, Ada's bunch was one of the biggest hits we ever had."[43]

This reference has been cited in Alan Pomerance's *Repeal of the Blues* as an example of racial mixing in jazz and swing bands. However, it is important to note that Hammond did not indicate how he was able to determine that there were "Negro girls . . . passing as Orientals," nor have I been able to verify this statement. The women with whom I spoke who played in the band at that time have unanimously told me that Hammond was mistaken. Certainly, in the 1930s and 1940s, many light-skinned people with black ancestry passed as white, and some passed "Hindu," "Oriental," or "Spanish." According to Jane Sager, band-leader Rita Rio's parents both had known black ancestry, yet Rio's "Spanish" persona enabled her to lead one of the most famous white all-girl bands of the 1930s and to be booked by the powerful CRA (Consolidated Radio Artists) agency on white entertainment circuits in both the North and the South. She achieved this new identity by changing her name (she had been born Una Westmorlanda), adopting a new wardrobe, using "La Cucaracha" as her theme song, and perhaps emphasizing select strands of her ethnic and cultural background that were a part of her identity as a multi-racial woman. Passing did have its obvious advantages, but it also had heartbreaking disadvantages. On at least one occasion, in order to enter the New York City hotel at which the band was staying, Rio's mother had to pass as her maid.

Another legally black woman who is known to have passed as white in order to play in white all-girl bands is trumpet player Leora Meoux, wife of Fletcher Henderson. But many people who passed for white found it necessary to pass so completely that they cut off ties to relatives and would probably not have disclosed this information to mere employers or coworkers. So it is possible that my informants either did not know that there were women with black ancestry in Leonard's band of 1944 or were still protecting friends' carefully held secrets. Black-to-white passing or "passing out of the race," as it has been called, historically carries the connotation "race traitor," does not fit as easily into a post–civil rights movement paradigm as does white-to-black passing, and is, therefore, not so readily disclosed to researchers today. It is of course *feasible* that black women passing for white would confide in Hammond, a well-known integrationist whose idea it had been for Benny Goodman to hire Teddy Wilson, Lionel Hampton, and Charlie Christian in his otherwise all-white swing band. But it is curious that the women with whom I spoke also denied that there were Asian women in the band, throwing doubt on Hammond's claim. Leonard's band had to be perceived as white in order to enjoy the high-profile exposure and major circuits it played, not to mention the active sponsorship of the USO and armed services, both segregated institutions during World War II. To have left room for even the slightest suspicion that the band was mixed would have been to risk losing these opportunities.

"There were never any black women in the band when I was in it," wrote Ethel "Kirk" Kirkpatrick (Drehouse), who played in the band from 1944 to 1945.[44] Betty Kidwell (Meriedeth), an Ada Leonard alumnus from the years 1943–46, concurred, adding that, while some white women played with black bands during that time period, black women did not play with white bands. Kidwell added that, after leaving Leonard's band, several white women passed as black in order to play with the International Sweethearts of Rhythm and that at least one of those white women had already played with the Sweethearts when Hammond brought Leonard's band to Camp Plauché. It is possible that Hammond, who surely would have seen the Sweethearts both before and after his tour of duty, was confused by these multiple passings. Since he does not reveal where he got his information, it is also possible that he was judging the already evasive concept of race by the same imperfect technology that white police employed in the South — his own eyes. When I asked Leonard if she knew of any leaders of white all-woman bands who hired black members, she proudly replied that *she* had — but in the 1950s.[45] In trying to make sense of Hammond's remark, Betty Kidwell (Meriedeth) noted that trumpet player Norma Carson "needed glasses and squinted a lot" and may have been taken as Asian if "the band was playing in the sun and [Hammond] was watching from far away."[46] Another band member, Delores Gomez, was of half Mexican, half German ancestry and could have stirred Hammond's integrationist sentiments given that Mexicans were subject to Jim Crow in some regions (Texas, e.g.), Mexican musicians sometimes played in black bands and sometimes in white bands, and some legally black musicians passed as Mexican to play in white bands. Yet Hammond makes no mention of a Mexican woman in the band, only of "Negro women . . . passing for Orientals."

Despite Hammond's perception of a mixed band, shaped, no doubt, by his sincere hopes for an end to segregation and racism, I think that it is probably more accurate to say that, even as personnel changed, the band's status as all white did not. What did change was that, as old members left and new ones were hired, the band as a whole was rapidly becoming younger. By 1944, Leonard found herself conducting an entirely different band than the one with which she had begun. Between the years 1943 and 1944 alone, there were approximately thirteen personnel changes in the sixteen-piece organization. Still, it was the band of 1944 that turned out to be Leonard's all-time favorite. "I have a big blowup picture of them in my living room," she said, proudly. "They were just wonderful. I had a great deal of pleasure with them because they were ambitious and they loved to play. They had not been through what the older band girls had been through." Veterans of the all-girl band business tended to be bitter, having been stranded and shortchanged far too many times.

Even though the band of 1944 was fresh, Leonard herself was wearing down. "I had burnout about three times," she said. "I quit. I just walked. I couldn't take it. And the best band that I had I disbanded because I couldn't do it anymore. I was on the verge of a breakdown. So I said, 'Who needs it.' "

After the war, Leonard led a smaller, society-type orchestra. But, with the return of servicemen who had been musicians before the war, jobs for all-girl bands were difficult to obtain. "To give you an example," said Leonard, "when I was out here [in Los Angeles], a big nightclub opened. And the house band was going on vacation. So this nightclub wanted to hire my band to fill in for two weeks. Well, the business manager from the musicians' union said that, if they hired another standby band, they could use us, but only if they hired another band." In other words, the club would have had to pay for two bands, Leonard's and a men's band. Naturally, the club chose the path of least expenditure. According to Leonard, this union decision, and others like it, was the AFM's way of saying, " 'The girls can't work; we've got to get work for the men.' So we lost the job. And that happens over and over." Although her band was used in movies, sometimes men musicians were brought in to dub in the sound: "For instance, I did a short for Universal. They used my music but not my girls. There was a violinist there who was excellent. . . . They recorded her, and, the minute she left, they got a man up there to record it. That's the way it goes." Leonard had a television show on KTTV, Channel 11, from 1952 to 1954, along the lines of the KTLA show featuring Ina Ray Hutton's band. The theme song was Duke Ellington's "Sophisticated Lady," a piece that fit Leonard's style and persona. "And our last sponsor — can you imagine this? Could you ever be glamorous in

Ada Leonard's "young" band of 1944–45. *Left to right:* Eunice "Johnny" Johnson (bass), Florence "Fagle" Liebman (drums), Norma Carson (trumpet), Betty "Roz" Rosner (tenor), Dolores Gomez (trumpet), Betty Kidwell (alto). *Top:* Pat Stullken (lead alto). *Courtesy Betty Kidwell Meriedeth.*

Ada Leonard leading her All-American Girls at the Golden State Theatre, San Francisco, March, 1944. *Left to right, top:* Virginia Wurst (trombone); Delores Gomez, Norma Carson, Fran Shirley (trumpets). *Left to right, bottom:* Betty Rosner, Betty Kidwell, Jenny Dudek (saxes); Rita Kelly (piano). *Courtesy Betty Kidwell Meriedeth.*

front of a big sign that said 'Gas'? The gas company sponsored us with this huge sign in back of us that said 'Gas.' I weathered that one."

In 1955, Ada Leonard finally got what she had set out to find in 1940, an all-man band. She explained to *Down Beat* that too few women musicians could "handle their parts in a band such as I have now" and that those who could "don't like to work in all-girl bands. They like to feel that they've been hired not because of their looks or sex appeal, but because they are good musicians."[47] In Leonard's own quest for that purely professional space, uncluttered by issues of sex and gender, she ran into additional forms of sex- and gender-related aggravation. "Unfortunately, it was the worst experience of my entire life," she said. "One of them said to me one day, 'If you'd like to fly, call me.' I said, 'If I want to fly, I'll take a plane.' Finally, I just threw up my hands and said, 'Go someplace else.'"

In 1992, musicians from her 1950s all-girl television band decided that Leonard deserved a surprise party honoring her years as a bandleader and thanking her for the breaks she had given women musicians. Peggy Gilbert, Kay Boley, and Evelyn Pennak tracked down musicians who had played with Ada Leonard's All-American Girls at any time in the band's history, not only on television, but from the very beginning. The enthusiastic response of those who wished to pay homage to Ada Leonard resulted in a cross section of party goers — women who had played in the rehearsal band that Leonard was hired to lead in 1940, who had traveled with her on the road, who had played her charts in ballrooms and theaters, who had played for the troops and fought labor battles with her on USO tours, who had appeared with her in motion pictures, who had played in her television band. From the guest list, published in the Los Angeles musicians' union newspaper, it appears that members of her all-man band were not invited.[48]

"I was completely caught by surprise." Leonard's voice carried an air of incredulity, as if she was still amazed that her musicians reunited after over forty years to give her a party. "I understand that Polly [Gan, Leonard's former secretary,] was taking me and Peggy and Kay out to lunch. And we were stopping to pick them up. So I was completely unaware. And I walk in and see all these kids. They aren't kids anymore. But to me they are. They're the closest thing to children that I ever had." As she walked into the room, the strains of her theme song, "Sophisticated Lady," accompanied her entrance, just as it had underscored so many of her entrances in years past. "I was so stunned. I came in out of the sun —

you know how you're blinded? And I see all these people, but I can't see them. And I stood there. And here is a girl that worked for me when she was seventeen — with gray hair." She chuckled as she let the picture sink in: the blinding light, the disorientation, the gray-haired "teenagers" slowly materializing before her eyes. Her well-timed pause, just long enough to set up the punch line, marks a life spent in show business. "And I said, 'Haven't you guys ever heard of Clairol?' "

Chapter 9

"And, Fellas, They're *American* Girls!"

On the Road with the Sharon Rogers

All-Girl Band

Looks like *Down Beat* will have to hire a couple of more office

boys to open the letters we've been receiving about Sharon Rogers

Overseas band. We've never heard Sharon ourselves but if her band

sends us as much as her picture does then she's our girl.

— "That's Our Girl"

They laughed together, cried together,

crashed and almost died together,

Listen to the rhythm, talk about your rhythm,

Sharon Rogers Band!

—Florence Shefte Kuhn, lyrics to "Sharon Rogers Band"

"USO Time" Radio Broadcast: Osaka, Japan, 1945

The thunderous crescendo and diminuendo of mass applause, a hush, then the reeds and brass sections of a twelve-piece dance band toll the opening notes to a popular Irving Berlin song: "A pret-ty giiiirl . . . is like a mel-o-dy. . . ." Dramatic pauses separate each set of harmonies, yet the 1919 tune is immediately recognizable to most Americans in the 1940s. This enduring anthem to the all-American girl next door had already been resurrected as the theme song for *The Great Ziegfeld* (1936) and recorded by many orchestras, including Artie Shaw's. Years later, in the 1960 film *The Rat Race,* the guileless Tony Curtis

The Sharon Rogers All Girl Orchestra performing at the Five O'Clock Club, Columbia, S.C., January 1945. This was an off-duty site favored by officers from nearby Fort Jackson army base. *Courtesy Sharon Rogers Wright.*

character betrays his lack of postwar cynicism with the confession, "I'm probably the last guy in New York who thinks a pretty girl is like a melody."

In the version at hand, more ponderous than Shaw's, the rhythm section joins the mix, infusing the "haunting refrain" with a slow dance pulse. The orchestration drops to *pianissimo.* A deep-voiced radio announcer intones: "Good afternoon everyone; it's USO time. And now, at 4:00 at WBTQ, it's special USO time, and, if you were here, you'd see exactly what I mean. For this afternoon it's Sharon Rogers and her orchestra. *All girls,* fellas, sixteen of them, and fresh from the States just three months ago. They've come from the Philippines, where they've been putting on their show for the past three months for every GI within a million miles. You'd love to see them. It's their first, men. Their first show in Japan."[1]

Presented as "pretty girls," the musicians who play "A Pretty Girl Is

Like a Melody" are simultaneously like a melody and producers of melodies as a twelve-piece orchestra in which pretty girls play the four saxophones, three trumpets, one trombone, piano, bass and drums (there is also a girl vocalist, but she is not featured on this tune). Part of their appeal appears to be that they are fresh from the States — untainted by contact with foreign lands? by too much time on the road? perhaps by sex-starved GIS? — a freshness that allows them to represent women back home, halos and pedestals intact. They represent what Gene Kelly's character meant in the film *Anchors Aweigh* (1945) when he described his sweetheart as "not a girl just for a leave" but "the kind you come home to." An editorialist for *Stars and Stripes* cautioned women entertainers: "Call it sentimental, but when the doughboy thinks of girls from home, he thinks of his mom, his sister, or his best girl. He's seen enough of the other girls. Girls from home have to be nice."[2]

As "nice girls" on their unsullied "first show in Japan," the Sharon Rogers All-Girl Band provided the troops with a combination of American popular music and idealized white American womanhood. In his study of wartime pinup posters, Robert Westbrook observed that Betty Grable's popularity was linked to her "obvious whiteness," giving her "an advantage over competitors such as [Rita] Hayworth (née Margarita Cansino) in the eyes of white soldiers waging a brutal struggle against a racial enemy in a setting in which, they often complained, white women — especially women as white as Grable — were in short supply."[3] The appearance of the twelve white American women of the Sharon Rogers band in occupied Japan coincided a period of low morale, when restless GIs were being urged to stop fraternizing with Japanese women devastated by the war and instead wait patiently for the Army to ship them home — no matter how many months it took. "The determination to 'get the job done' had been the glue that held the GI Army together," wrote Lee Kennett. "Now that the job was done, the glue was beginning to dissolve."[4] Like Grable's famous photograph and the Andrews Sisters' musical evocation of the faithful loved one sitting "under the apple tree," entertainment featuring American "pretty girls" fueled GI fantasies of someone nice waiting at home, someone who had been worth the fight. "And it doesn't matter much if they aren't there when you come back," wrote one soldier. "The important thing is to have this dream."[5]

The prolonged, grand arrangement rises in volume for the big finish. Although this version is instrumental, American audiences in 1945 do not need a vocalist to help them summon the lyrics to mind. After another wave of applause, the announcer returns. "I see the audience staring me down, so I'd better introduce Sharon Rogers without any further delay."

"Thanks a lot," calls the youthful female voice of the bass-playing leader. "And now, getting our program off to a jumping start with 'Volga Boatman. . . .'" Syncopated tom-toms kick off a jazzy rendition of a folk song of the Russian Allies popularized as a dance standard by Glenn Miller. It is a tight arrangement, with reeds and brass taking turns calling out and returning phrases and leading up to a featured improvised tenor saxophone solo by Laura Daniels, who remains, nevertheless, unnamed by the radio host.

More enthusiastic applause from the studio audience ensues. "Gee, girls, that was swell," chirps the announcer. "Think I'd better get me out of the way now and turn things over to a very lucky guy, the emcee of this USO unit, Jack Wilson."

"Thank you, Bernie, thank you," says a second male voice. "I *am* lucky. Fellas, it's too bad you can't be in the studio with the rest of the boys here and see a very lovely sight, twelve lovely looking girls sitting up there in the stand, and, fellas, they're *American* girls. But why say anything more about it? We have a very charming little vocalist, a very sweet girl who is going to do a sweet tune. She comes from a sweet city, Chicago. So here she is, Jackie Webber and 'Candy.' "

The program continues. The band plays syrupy ballads with lyrics often pertaining to romantic anxiety, humiliation, and abandonment (as in "It's the Talk of the Town") or offering reassurance of dandy, problem-free reunions (as in "Candy"). The band also plays hot dance numbers replete with tight section work and dazzling solos, despite the announcer's many diminutive and/or sexualized references to the "clever kids," "splendid little trumpet players," and "beautiful little lips" that produce the music.

Not Just a Pretty Tune

Although the members of the Sharon Rogers All-Girl Band were not among the many thousands of women who served in the U.S. military during World War II, as USO musicians they saw themselves very much as participants in the war effort. Like soldiers, USO entertainers received their orders in sealed envelopes. There was no room for griping, and plenty of possibility for danger.[6] During the Sharon Rogers tour of the Fox Hole Circuit (June 1945 to February 1946), they endured their share of discomfort and danger. They dodged enemy submarines while shipping out from San Francisco to Hawaii. Many places they stayed had no separate facilities for women. They often lived in bombed-out quarters, sharing bathrooms with servicemen. Guards would stand duty while they showered. And two months after the Osaka radio broadcast, the all-woman band, along with the entire USO unit of which they were a part, boarded a plane for Korea for a flight they would never forget.

Nation, Narration, and Aviation

YOKOHAMA, Japan, Jan. 22 (AP) — Sharon Rogers and her eleven-girl orchestra were rescued from the sea by Japanese fishermen today after a transport plane crashed off the southern tip of Kyushu Island while they were returning to Japan from Korea.

Everyone was saved, but an unnamed drummer suffered a fractured leg and the others were bruised. The plane struck the water about fifty feet from an ammunition barge and sank within twelve minutes.

It is eerie to review these words from the 23 January 1946 *New York Times* as my "gambler's special" wobbles through the turbulence over Lake Tahoe en route to the 1993 Sharon Rogers reunion in Las Vegas. Like any good researcher with a bad memory, I must endlessly review my files. The particular folder in front of me contains newspaper clippings such as the one above plus three years worth of correspondence with four members of the Sharon Rogers organization, the twelve-piece all-woman swing band from Chicago that entertained U.S. troops in the Philippines, Japan, and Korea with Unit 687 of the USO–Camp Shows.

Trumpet player Florence Shefte (Kuhn) — whom I will finally meet today after a lengthy correspondence — has even supplied me with a photocopy of the letter she wrote her mother after the crash, or, rather, "ditching," the deceptively casual lingo in aviation circles for the pilot, gravity, and the weather all working together to bring a mechanically disabled plane to what is hoped will be a safe "wheels-up" water landing. This letter, written the very day of the incident, provides a chilling

THE CRASH!!

Sheminoseki Bay off Moji, Japan

Pictures of our plane being salvaged after the crash

"The Crash!! Sheminoseki Bay off Moji, Japan. Pictures of our plane being salvaged after the crash." *Courtesy Florence Shefte Kuhn.*

account of the harrowing experience as well as insights into wartime U.S. nationalism. If nationalism is not the "awakening" but the "invention" of nations,[7] then Kuhn's letter provides insights into one particular nation that was being constructed at one particular time—a nation that officially narrated itself as waging a scrupulous war effort in the name of freedom, democracy, and equality, even as its own historic inequalities, although embattled, remained entrenched.

Informed both by the upbeat, heroic war narratives found in films, comics, ads, and news reports (made under the watchful eye of the Office of War Information) and by the flying lessons she had taken in 1944, Kuhn blends aeronautical know-how with cheerfully understated references to very real danger in much the same "reassuring, often light hearted narrative voice" as dominated such Hollywood war films as *Guadalcanal Diary* (1943).[8] Her letter provides clues as to how women USO musicians could be, simultaneously, traditional and nontraditional participants in a nationalist wartime discourse. It also reflects the ideology of the day, in which "routine use of racial slang in the media, [and] official memoranda," helped manifest a hegemonic patriotism dependent on the unconditional hatred of the Japanese people.[9] The letter gives us a decidedly American narrative of the war years; note the positive tone, the singing of a popular tune in the face of danger, the comforting recitation of technical knowledge, and the curious gap regarding the Japanese fishermen who approach the plane:

20 January 1946
Moyi, Kyushu, Japan
Dearest Mom,

I just decided to write all the details of today's trip, but I won't mail this home. You'll get to read it when I get there to explain anything and you can see for yourself that I'm all right.

We left Korea at 2:15 P.M. after three attempts to take off (the first two times we tried to take off, we couldn't get enough manifold pressure) in a C-47B #316243.

We headed straight for Japan. It was supposed to be a four- or five-hour trip in a C-47. When we were out about an hour and a half, we got into some pretty rough weather, and all of a sudden we hit a thunderhead, and the plane dropped 3,500 feet in a few seconds. We were all in the top of the plane, floating around. . . .

The next hour was a pretty bumpy ride. Bobbie, Wanda, Sylvia (she was as white as a ghost, with a greenish cast), and Julieanne were passing the bucket from one to the other, fast. I sat in my corner singing "Boogie Woogie Serenade," trying to keep my mind off of everything . . . especially my stomach, which was beginning to turn in circles. . . .

We looked for a landing field and couldn't find one big enough or one that wasn't full of bomb craters. We went down and buzzed several fields and one time almost crashed into a mountain. . . .

About 5:45 P.M. the navigator came back and told us to sit back to back and brace ourselves best we could because we were going to come down in a parking lot. We all sat real close — the landing bell rang, and down we went. The landing was smooth compared to what I thought it was going to be (!), but imagine my surprise when someone said we're in the water!! . . . Sylvia, Alice, Irene, Julieanne, Lois, Wanda, and Dottie got into two rafts, and then a Jap fishing boat came up and got the rest of us. . . . It was dark, and the life rafts had floated away . . . we couldn't even see them. Lucky one of the kids in the raft had a lighter, and we spotted them.[10]

The use of the derogatory term *Jap* is jarring, even in the context of the rescue, although Kuhn explained later that, at the time, she saw it as "merely a descriptive adjective." No insult was intended, she said, and, indeed, she was very happy to see the fishermen — and their boat.[11] The term's very normalcy during the war must be located in its historical context: the wartime nationalistic construct of the Japanese as subhuman. John Dower has observed that the implications of "perceiving the enemy as 'Nazis' on the one hand and 'Japs' on the other" left open the possibility of the " 'Good German' but scant comparable place for 'good Japanese.' "[12] So ingrained was this notion that it was not unusual for government propaganda to employ such slogans as "Have you killed a jap soldier today?" when urging citizens to buy war bonds.[13] The popular media demonized the Japanese as one woman recalled: "They were always evil in the movies, characters slinking around knifing people. You begin to think of them not as human beings but as little yellow things to be eradicated. They looked different from the Germans."[14]

In the United States, virulent racism against Asians — rife in "Yellow Peril" propaganda dating back to the late nineteenth century — had already resulted in restrictive immigration policies and quickly contributed to the massive national mobilization that followed the bombing of Pearl Harbor. This history of anti-Asian sentiment made possible the internment of 110,000 Japanese Americans (two-thirds of whom were U.S. citizens) even though there was no record that any of them had ever engaged in any subversive activity.[15] (German Americans were spared this treatment — despite the fact that the German-American Bund publicly supported Hitler.)[16] While the black press held a more critical stance against Japanese internment, the mainstream (white) press overwhelmingly supported it.[17] And the bombings of Hiroshima and Nagasaki — which had taken place mere months before the Sharon Rogers plane ditching and rescue — enjoyed widespread popular support in the United States.

The Sharon Rogers musicians were American war workers in the midst of an ideological, as well as brutally violent, physical war. Having spent three months in the Philippines in the summer of 1945, they had witnessed evidence of the atrocities of that February and March, when Japanese forces slaughtered 100,000 Filipinos in Manilla alone. They had no reason to doubt that such grisly war crimes revealed what Allied propaganda called the "unique and inherent savagery" of the Japanese people.[18] Perhaps this dissonance between ideology and event explains why the role of the Japanese fishermen in their rescue tends to blur and disappear in Kuhn's and other band members' accounts: "[Some of the others] were picked up by a small rowboat, and, finally, we (on the fishing boat) picked up both rafts and the rowboat."[19]

Why did Japanese fishermen rescue a planeload of Americans less than six months after the bombing of Hiroshima? What were the relationships during this scenario of danger and deliverance? Why is this part of the rescue so unclear? Perhaps the event lay so far outside a nationalist paradigm in which there was no such thing as "good Japanese" people that, by war's end, a patriotic white U.S. subject could not accommodate such a radical rupture in the unifying discourse as "Japanese heroism," even after being fished from death out of a heavily mined sea.

Later, tenor saxophonist Laura Daniels, who had been one of those rescued directly from the plane, would try to help me understand the ambivalence surrounding the rescue: "We didn't know if the approaching fishing boat would be helpful or try to harm us. But we knew we had to get off the wing of the plane as it was sinking. Nobody spoke Japanese, but I remember someone holding out cigarettes — which were happily accepted. The Japanese fishermen (I think there were just two or three) were very hesitant to come close to the plane."[20]

But come close to the sinking plane they did, close enough to rescue all the people (and the hand luggage) from the wing. Then they must also have picked up the women on the life rafts and deposited all of them safely on the shore. The fishermen's hesitation that Daniels recalls led me to reread the part of Kuhn's letter in which she adds that the body of water in which they landed was so dangerously mined that it was off limits to American vessels. Kuhn also pointed out that the fishermen may have been waiting to see if the ditched plane was going to explode, which sometimes happened even without the assistance of mines. Hesitation in approaching Americans would also make sense in the light of John Dower's observation that atrocities were committed by both sides during World War II. That both British and American forces shot and tortured prisoners, sank hospital ships, strafed lifeboats, and mutilated Japanese dead may have been as much on the minds of the Japanese fishermen as the atrocities in the Philippines were on the minds of the Americans. Owing to censorship in both the United States and Japan, "one's own side's atrocities appeared episodic while the other side's appeared systematic."[21] The entertainers and their rescuers were alike justifiably hesitant in approaching each other.

Kuhn has annotated the original missive to her mother. There is a sense of adventure in her handwritten addenda: "This was a letter to my Mom, and I didn't want to worry her by telling her there were only seven life preservers on the plane." Another note explains that they were all rushed to a hospital, which they later understood was under a smallpox quarantine. And, finally, she adds that the plane had only fifteen gallons of gas left, which, Kuhn explains, would have meant no more than five minutes of flying time.

No doubt, the impossible water landing in the heavily mined Shiminoseki Strait has something to do with the frequent reunions held by the Sharon Rogers band. This is the only all-girl band I know of that still gets together on a regular basis, forty-six years after it broke up. Another contributing factor is the length of time that the musicians have known each other. Originally called the Melody Maids, the group came out of Chicago's North and South Side high schools in 1940. Some of the members even went to grammar school together. Their parents knew each other. Like many all-girl bands of the day, the Sharon Rogers All-Girl Band was already a professional organization, enjoying excellent bookings and popularity, before the war broke out.[22] The core group played together for seven years, from 1940 to 1947. Several members continued on with a combo after that.

After the San Antonio reunion in 1991, Sharon Rogers (now Wright) had written me that she had shared my paper on all-girl bands and that it had brought back memories for everyone. My invitation to attend the 1993 reunion came from both Kuhn and Wright, and I look forward to interacting with a nearly intact group from the 1940s. What do they talk about? How do they make decisions? Is their group identity as a swing band still an important part of their group activities during these reunions? Do they still think about the war?

Reunion: Day One

My plane lands (smoothly), and soon a shuttle bus whizzes me through the desert and into the sprawling Nevada hub of Hollywood Orientalism. We pass a pyramid-shaped hotel with a Sphinx entrance and a green glass-covered hotel with a lion-head entrance and finally pull up to a hotel shaped like a Disneyland castle. Employees costumed like Robin Hood park cars and carry luggage. I have difficulty locating the check-in counter. The lobby is a casino the size and shape of a baseball diamond, yet it still manages to achieve a resolutely ahistorical feudal motif. There is even a nightly jousting tournament in the basement. Amid pseudo-medieval chaos and the constant, deafening crash of falling coins (real or piped in with the Muzak?), a desk clerk dressed like a Nottingham barmaid hands me a note from trombone player Lois Heise (Goleas). I am to meet the group at the "Café Caribe" in the "Hotel Mirage." Sphinxes, lions, mirages — five minutes in this town, and Euro-American fantasies/constructions of exotic otherness saturate the senses. Amid ubiquitous, spectacular references to histories of imperialism and conquest, titillated working- and middle-class Westerners exchange American dollars for American dreams.

The minute I step into my hotel room, the telephone rings. It is Wright, checking up on me like any good bandleader. Her voice is good-humored and gravelly, like Lucille Ball's. I hear myself promising to set out at once for Café Caribe.

Sand blowing into my eyes, I hurry windward down "the Strip," ignoring talking statues, opportunities to win millions of dollars, and numberless startling architectural juxtapositions. My only interest is in catching up with the Sharon Rogers All-Girl Band before they move on — my impression is that they are still very much an on-the-go kind of group. The Mirage sign looks as far away after thirty minutes as it did when I started out. It is difficult to judge distance in the desert. I am beginning to think that the Mirage will live up to its name when, finally, one hour from the moment I set foot on the street, I am standing on the crowded conveyor belt that will inch me forward, through a foyer full of live Siberian tigers (behind glass), and into the lobby. A sign for Café Caribe points cheerfully into a labyrinth of slot machines. I locate the café, and it, too, is world sized. I am inquiring at my fourth waitress station, displaying the group snapshot that Wright sent to help me in this very situation, when, suddenly, I notice a woman waving. She stands, and, even at this distance, I recognize the attractive, sixty-something brunette in the blue-and-white knit top as Sharon Rogers, waving me to the head of the table.

We embrace and hold hands. The bass-playing leader of the Sharon Rogers All-Girl Band has not given up on me. She has carefully guarded an extra seat and (I am touched) an empty coffee cup. Continuing to hold my hand, she introduces me around the table. I meet my prolific pen pal Florence Shefte (Kuhn), blonde and effervescent in a white pants outfit. I meet two other of my correspondents: alto sax player Dorothy Cygan (Wilmeth), who greets me across the long table with a warm smile, and trumpet soloist Sylvia Roth, wearing glasses and khaki shorts. Others present are Julieanne Holten (White), who was a USO dancer in the same show as the band; trumpet player Roberta "Bobbie" Taliaffero; Kuhn's husband, Jim Kuhn; Russ Foster, widower of saxophonist Mickey West (Foster), who has died since the last reunion; Merle, the new woman in Russ's life; Joe Zinno, the pilot whose "coolness saved us all from death" (as the 1946 Associated Press wire quotes Sharon as saying); his wife, Fran Zinno; trombonist Lois Heise (Goleas); and tenor saxophonist Laura Daniels. The band alumnae range in age from the mid-sixties to the early seventies. Everyone is casually and sensibly dressed for long walks up and down the Strip.

As I wolf down a salad, band members play musical chairs, checking me out, asking questions about my research. I remember Trinh Minh-ha's writings about power dynamics between interviewer and interviewee, recall her words, "There will be much less arrogance . . . if the making subject is always vulnerably exposed in his or her making process."[23] I find myself confessing that I am a flute player by default, that at age ten I did not have the courage to tell the band director that I wanted to play the saxophone or the trombone instead, believing, along with my peers, that those were "boy's instruments." (There is nodding all around. This is not a group that needs to be convinced that saxophones and trombones are more interesting than flutes.) I hear myself explaining that I would have leaped at the chance to join an all-girl band and travel the world. Wright interjects that it was no easy decision to join the USO to be sent to war zones unknown. Bits and pieces of history tumble toward me at once, mingled with dinner instructions and a democratic election led by "camp director" Daniels on whether we're doing Hoover Dam in the morning.

Sexual Expectations

One thing I notice immediately about the Sharon Rogers group is that their frequent reunions have kept their memories alive. So often the women I interviewed had not thought about their band years lately and were not in touch with others with whom they could collectively reconstruct events. This group is practiced at recalling the 1940s; it is one of their activities. It does not seem to bother them when their memories differ. They do not quibble over details. One version leads to another, and their collected stories are vivid and telling.

Part of their shared history is the battle, fought, it seems, on several fronts, to earn the right simply to play music and not have to succumb to the extramusical expectations of military officers. "Women in the USO had a bad reputation," explains Wright, with a weary smile. "Nothing could have been further from the truth for us. Maybe there were groups out there that were looser than we were, but I always had the theory that the 'bad reputation' was just wishful thinking."

When the smokers leave, Wright among them, Daniels and Kuhn relate a series of Phil Spitalny tales. Kuhn tells a story in which a young woman shows up for an audition and Spitalny answers the door in his underwear. Several more stories follow, all containing this gruff character pacing and swearing in his underwear while one serious young woman after another plays her most difficult piece. Another story has it that, when the "Hour of Charm" had an opportunity to appear in a movie, Spitalny tried to get the older musicians to quit so that he could hire younger ones. Some of these stories would later be contested or modified by "Hour of Charm" musicians, but these were the stories that the Sharon Rogers musicians knew and that they shared with me with great enthusiasm. Although the term *sexual harassment* was not used in the 1940s, the Sharon Rogers musicians have come to see themselves as women who experienced sexual harassment — and who fought it.

Wright returns from her cigarette break, grabs the check out of my hand, and announces with gusto, "From now on, you're on your own!" I feel spoiled and slightly foolish, a new member of the organization. As we float on the moving sidewalk in front of those live tigers, the bandleader proudly informs me of the later achievements of her musicians. Roth, who had taken flying lessons in 1944 with Kuhn, retired from a long and illustrious career as a pilot in 1988. In fact, she had been inducted into the South Carolina Aviation Hall of Fame just two days before — skipping the ceremony in order to attend the Las Vegas reunion. Roth's accomplishments include logging over 23,500 hours in the air and becoming, in 1968, the first woman ever appointed by the FAA as an airline transport pilot examiner. Daniels returned to college and studied chemistry. After many years, during which she worked her way through school, she earned a master's degree and became a high school chemistry teacher. She is also, currently, a serious advanced student of jazz saxophone. At this point, Wright runs across the street to catch a bus back to the Circus Circus RV park, where she is staying with her companion, Ed Hayes.

"I don't know if Sharon told you," mentions Daniels, on the walk back down the strip. "She's modest. But she really knew how to handle those men." Actually, I had gotten that impression from Wright's first letter to me, in which she described how the band was almost fired by the USO. While the band was staying in San Francisco, waiting to be shipped out, "our manager," wrote Wright,

> had made some promises on our behalf that we would show up for a "party" with some top-ranking officers. We went out to eat and sightsee a little but kept calling the manager's hotel looking for him and leaving word we called. He never got the messages. Bottom line, no "party" — we wouldn't have gone anyway. So, next day, a captain called me and said the whole group was being dismissed and returned to Chicago for disobeying orders. *But* he'd like to talk to me, and I should come to his hotel room. Suspicious? You bet! I had two of my gals come with me and wait on a bench on his floor at the elevators. I went down to his room, knocked, the door flew open, he grabbed me by the arm, pulled me into his room, and there he stood, naked and drunk. We fought; I got loose and out the door. Later, a full meeting of officers and our band was called for the next morning at the base at Treasure Island. Purpose, to dismiss us. When I got there in the morning, I let this capt. know that I would expose him, with the help of my witnesses, if he allowed this to happen. We stayed on.

Additional difficulties were encountered in Hawaii: "The general consensus of opinion among the officers (the enlisted men were great) was apparently we girls were supposed to be their playthings, and our manager, Al, gave them the impression that 'just tell him which gal they wanted and he'd take care of it.' "[24]

Despite the army's love of regulations and the fact that USO entertainers were forbidden by contract from "conduct[ing themselves] in a manner offensive to public decency or morality" — stage door Johnnies were strictly prohibited — many women USO entertainers ran afoul of officers' sexual expectations.[25] The material used to recruit officers exacerbated the problem by dangling the promise of willing women as bait, as in the U.S. Army Air Force film *Winning Your Wings,* in which Jimmy Stewart demonstrates how quickly a shapely blonde woman loses interest in her GI dance partner when an officer strolls into the room: "And you see the effect those shiny little wings have on a gal. It's phenomenal."[26]

The Sharon Rogers Band again found itself threatened with dismissal, this time in Manilla. Sharon Rogers herself, then twenty years old, appeared before a panel of five officers and pled her case. Not only did the officers believe her, but they "openly admitted that our whole file of complaints . . . was based on men expecting us to fraternize with the officers."[27] The panel fired Al the manager, put Rogers in charge, and asked her to put a show together.

Daniels is tall, white haired, a world traveler, and a good walker. She has a thoughtful way of reflecting before answering my questions. She is called the *camp director* by the group because of her talent for organizing bus tours and other outings. "Why did you join the USO?" I asked her. "Adventure," she replies. "We were young. Also, some of us had brothers or boyfriends overseas at that time, and we wanted to help out." Lois Heise (Goleas)'s brother was, in fact, missing in action at the time the Sharon Rogers group signed up.

Unfortunately, the musicians' notions of what was patriotic about young women playing big band music for the troops differed markedly from those of many servicemen. Officers, in particular, sometimes expected this patriotic entertainment to include sexual attentions of adoring American women. For the Sharon Rogers musicians, some of the attention lavished on them by servicemen was welcome and some was not, but their refusal of unwanted advances did not harm their images of themselves as patriots. Such refusals, in fact, were deeply connected to their identities as "nice" American girls, and were also part of their ongoing struggle for self-determination and better working conditions. These goals were important to the band members long before they joined the USO.

Originally a band led and managed by men, the musicians of the

Sharon Rogers band had worked hard to gain their autonomy. Things came to a head when one of their leaders, Carl Schreiber, insisted that the musicians quit any day jobs they might have, guaranteeing that they would make the same money playing the bookings he would get them. When he was unable to live up to his promise, the young women filed an official complaint with the union, and, on the basis of the verbal agreement, the union forced Schreiber to make up the musicians' lost wages. The band then decided to dump Schreiber, chose an agent, and appointed Rogers bandleader.

I ask several women why Rogers was chosen to lead them. I am told repeatedly that the decision was reached by the group as a whole, although the reasons given for that decision range from her figure and personality to the fact that, as the bass player, only she could be positioned onstage so that all the other musicians could see her and therefore take their cues from her. In any event, when the USO hired the twelve young women from Chicago, they got not just a swinging band that was easy on soldiers' eyes but a group of professionals experienced in recognizing and fighting unfair labor practices, that functioned as a collective, and that was represented by a leader of their own choosing.

Their vitality as a group is still admirable. While everyone else takes in a Las Vegas review, this decades-younger researcher drops, exhausted, into her bed.

Reunion 1993: Day Two

Definitely a get-up-and-go group, this. When I show up at the Sherwood Forest Café fifteen minutes early for our 7:00 A.M. breakfast, six other members of our group have already arrived. I am quickly told how the extravaganza last night unwittingly opened with the Sharon Rogers theme song, "A Pretty Girl Is Like a Melody," only, instead of an all-girl band sitting on the stage, there were nude women dancing across it. Rather than causing offense, this strikes the Sharon Rogers group as extremely humorous.

I sit with Kuhn and her husband, Jim. The trumpet player tells me about several of the other bands with which she played in the 1930s and 1940s, including Mary Marshall's Bachelorettes, the Chicago Women's Concert Band, and groups led by Count Berni Vici (whose real name, she tells me, was Harry Wolff), Betty McGuire, and Gloria Parker. We move on to discuss the business structure of the Sharon Rogers band, which was "unusual because it was a co-op." The musicians all chipped in to buy costumes and other necessities and then afterward split the proceeds. Kuhn also describes how she and some of the others would travel to New York City for music lessons during the wartime blackouts. In New York, they would get a room in a musicians' hotel where guests received free tickets to Glenn Miller's rehearsals. She describes the white swing bandleader's precision with nostalgia and great admiration. She tells me that the sound that the Sharon Rogers band aimed at was that of "a Glenn Miller or a Harry James."

The bus tour of the Hoover Dam gives me a taste of what it must have been like to go on the road with the Sharon Rogers band. The in-jokes and comfortable, across-the-aisle conversations betray a group that has lived this way together for long stretches at a time. They are patient travelers, obediently disembarking and waiting as we are ordered to switch buses for no apparent reason, appearing interested in facts about the Colorado River, chuckling politely in response to the numerous jocular directives to "enjoy the *dam* tour." It is easy to picture them, good sports, enduring the hardships associated with overseas USO tours, all the time observing army rules and regulations and USO directives to refrain from "griping." We are the only tourists who return to the bus before departure time. Others not in our group drag in, hot, late, and complaining, but we in the Sharon Rogers contingent remain cheerful, USO troopers.

On the return trip over the desert, Wright describes some of the horrors they saw in the Philippines. She reminds me that, when the USO approached them about joining, they were enjoying some success, playing Coney Island and resorts and even radio broadcasts. One of the band members was so upset at the others' willingness to abandon the success that they had found in New York that she quit the band. The war was already over in Europe; other groups were being sent to Germany to entertain the soldiers who were waiting to be shipped home, and that's where they thought they would be going. Instead, their first extended stop was in Manila, where the fighting continued. General MacArthur had already liberated the city, but the Japanese fought on elsewhere in the Philippines until the end of the war in the Pacific. Wright recalls that the smell of burning bodies was in the air and that body parts were being dug out of the ground near where they rehearsed. Wilmeth became ill and was hospitalized for a time — meeting her future husband, a fellow patient. Wright described the war's end just as she had written about it to me earlier. It ended when they were in Manila: "Guns blasted. Bedlam in the streets. What a happy, happy day. Not so for the many men we visited on a daily basis in the hospitals, some with arms or legs or both amputated. They were bitter — and rightfully so." [28]

The band was then sent to Japan with the first occupying forces. They were even taken to Hiroshima to see the destruction. As the bus rumbles through the dusty suburbs of Las Vegas, I ask Wright how this experience affected her feelings about World War II. Her silence tells me that this is probably not an easy thing for her to talk about. She looks out the window, waits for a while, then replies, "It made me realize that there must never, never be another war." Neither of us mentions the wars that came after. Later, I would learn that having visited Hiroshima was a factor contributing to Laura Daniels's subsequent antinuclear peace activism. [29]

At 4:00, we all meet in Daniels's room for a party that has been moved forward a day so that I can attend. Although many in the group have put down their instruments for good, there is to be a jam session for those who still play. Roth was the solo trumpet player in the 1940s, but, since pianist Shirley Moss passed away, she has taken up the electric keyboard. She balances her instrument on the arms of a hotel chair and sits on the bed. Daniels warms up on her tenor in the bathroom. It's going to be a duo today, as trumpet player "Bobbie" Taliaferro hasn't been feeling well. Earlier, she had broken the news that she can no longer play Clarence Williams's "Sugar Blues." Now the fact that she feels too ill even to pick up her trumpet sobers everyone. She sits with her cane on the other side of Daniels's bed while Roth and Daniels play a few tunes. Daniels keeps apologizing for her tone, explaining that, if she played full out, we'd all be kicked out. I don't know what she sounds like when she plays the way she likes to, but today her sound is supple and richly nuanced, and her solos show off her range and facility. She does not reserve her navigations of the changes for her solos only, embellishing the melodies of the heads with inventive harmonics and softly swinging rhythmic figures.

After a couple of instrumentals, song sheets are distributed that Kuhn has typed up. There are nearly twenty people jammed into the single hotel room. Vodka and chips circulate from the bureau. Roth and Daniels play an upbeat "Sweet Georgia Brown" while everyone sings, and Julie-anne Holten (White) is persuaded to re-create her dance number from the USO–Camp Show. When the duo launches into the band theme song,

Wright rises and waves her arms in firm, sweeping strokes like the bandleader she is. Roth and Daniels follow her cues precisely. Everyone else sings from the song sheets with solemn reverence. This is their anthem:

> A pretty girl, is like a melody,
> That haunts you night and day
> Just like the strain
> of a haunting refrain,
> She'll start upon a marathon
> and run around your brain,
> You can't escape
> she's in your memory
> By morning, night and noon
> She will leave you and then
> come back again
> A pretty girl is just
> like a pretty tune.[30]

What do these words mean to these women? What do they think when they sing this Irving Berlin song? Written for the Ziegfeld Follies of 1919 as entrance music "to accompany the sedate parade of 'long-stemmed American beauties,'" its original context was not that different from that in which it appeared in the Las Vegas review the group had seen the previous night (except the latter was probably not so "sedate").[31] What positive connection to either of these celebrations of femininity as spectacle can possibly be found by women who fought so long and so hard to be considered not mere spectacle but professional musicians worthy of serious consideration? And why on earth would they pick "A Pretty Girl Is Like a Melody" as their theme song?

It is easy to see how, for servicemen, the woman of the song who lingers like a "haunting refrain" might represent a real-life or fantasy girl back home, a mental picture of someone nice to help them through the horrors of war. And, of course, when the song was played by the Sharon Rogers Band, the orchestra would not only evoke memories about pretty girls back home but would physically represent them.

Perhaps in the minds of the musicians the song linked music making and all-American femininity in another way, as a bridge between identities as pretty girls and as musicians. Although the Sharon Rogers musicians rejected the stigma of "loose women" that hounded women in show business, an attractive feminine image was important to them. But what image? What models were available to them? They could hardly model themselves after domestic women waiting patiently at home for their men to return. They were musicians working on the road, playing two and three shows a night for audiences made up mostly of servicemen. A loose reputation came with the territory.

Before hitting the road, they held meetings among themselves and with their parents, discussing how best to construct and maintain an acceptable group identity. As Wright put it, they "believed that what each of us did reflected on the whole — and we wanted a clean reputation. We each had a roommate and stuck together on double dates etc."[32] Maintaining a good reputation was essential if they were to project the wholesome, girl-next-door image with which they identified — and that the soldiers would respect.

But *wholesome* did not necessarily imply *prudish*. During a snack break, Wilmeth gleefully recalled having "a boyfriend in every town." Back in 1945, Daniels had kept her parents constantly informed about the social whirl in which she found herself. In August, she marveled, "It's strange how popular a person can be when there's a shortage." By September, she was dating "five fellows" in Manila. And, in December, she found herself making a "rude but speedy exit" from an officers' party: "What a bunch of jerks. I couldn't get out of there fast enough."[33]

The dilemma, then, was to find a model for a type of woman who could enjoy herself as adventuresome and attractive on the road, who was available for some romantic encounters on her own terms, while resisting a "bad girl" reputation of guaranteed sexual availability that would make USO travel more difficult and dangerous than it already was. Berlin's song certainly seems to fit the bill. The woman in the song "haunts you," "run[s] around your brain," "leave[s] you and then/come[s] back again," but she is never forced to give up her respectability, her independence, or her sex appeal. She is an enigma, but an autonomous one.

After the first chorus, Wright motions for the nonplaying members to come to the front of the bed and dance. At first hesitant, former reeds player Wilmeth rises and soon becomes comfortable with flirtatious hip and arm gyrations to the music. "Next," calls the bandleader, motioning for more dancers. "No!" protests Wilmeth, hands caressing her rib cage to the gentle beat of Roth's programmed electronic rhythm. "Solo! Solo!"

The full attention of the group is on Wilmeth's dance, which is lovingly encouraged by cheers from the group. Later, I ask Wright whether the band had actually danced to their own theme song in the old days. "No," she replied, whispering. "This is a recent tradition that I started so that those who don't play their instruments any more won't feel left out when the rest of us play."

Next, Kuhn, who also no longer plays, leads the singing of the lyrics of "The Sharon Rogers Band" — which she herself wrote — to the tune of "Ragtime Cowboy Joe":

Spoken
Way back when in World War II
Entertainment to build the morale was the decent thing to do
There was the swingingest, youngest, gals by far, the
Sharon Rogers Band.

Sung
Oh, how they play, swingin' music to the GIs as they swayed
Way out in the South Pacific with a show
Spoken
A real fine show
Sung
A syncopated rhythm
Oh, there's such a catchy meter, and there's nothing any sweeter
How they play, when they hear the fellas clappin' 'cause the
USO folks know
They laughed together, cried together, crashed and almost died together
Listen to the rhythm, talk about your rhythm,
Sharon Rogers Band!

This song — not part of the band's wartime repertoire — reveals what at least one band member felt was important about playing in an all-girl band on a USO tour. Kuhn describes entertaining the troops as "the decent thing to do" and alludes to the group's youthfulness as one of its attractions. But the primary theme of Kuhn's song is clearly pride in the group's "swinging," "syncopated" style and of the danger the women risked to bring their music to GIs. She describes a group that "swayed" as it "played," but she does not describe the experience of being looked at nearly so vividly as she describes that of being listened to. The interaction that she depicts is one of a women's band building the morale of the men in the audience and of that band playing better and better ("how they play") "when they hear the fellas clappin' " to the "catchy meter."

Before the party breaks up, everyone makes plans to attend the implosion of the Dunes, an old casino that is being destroyed Las Vegas style to make way for a new one. This timid researcher cannot persuade herself to attend, even though she will be missing a media event complete with pirates, cannonballs, and the biggest fireworks display west of the Mississippi. Is it any wonder, then, that the Sharon Rogers women are the ones who toured the world at war in a swing band and I spend my free time looking at microfiche or that they are Las Vegas regulars and I've never been here before? Some of these women are twice my age, yet their appetite for adventure, sensation, performance, spectacle, far exceeds mine, and they rush from the party to secure pollen masks and front-row standing room. Even Taliaffero, who is too ill to play her trumpet, who can no longer play "Sugar Blues," will not miss the opportunity to stand in the middle of a crowd of thirty thousand to watch a live implosion. This researcher decides to write up her notes and watch the thing on television.

Reunion 1993: Day Three

On my last day with the indefatigable Sharon Rogers band, I am to meet the group at Treasure Island. The casino is enormous. We are there just days after the grand opening, and there must be thirty restaurants in the place, but I luck out and find the right one just as everyone is being seated for lunch.

I sit with Daniels and tell her how much I admire her sax playing. She tells me that, when she was with the band, she had neither the time nor the money to buy records and hear what was going on. Only in the last ten years has she had the opportunity to study jazz improvisation. She has even attended jazz camps where most everyone is in high school — "so it isn't very interesting, socially" — but where she has learned a great deal of jazz theory. She is in her sixties.

I tell her about the improvisation class I am currently taking with Dianthe Spencer, director of jazz/pop performance studies at San Francisco State. "Do you have your flute with you?" she asks. I still have the same flute I had in the fourth grade, a nickel-plated Bundy in a green case. I take it every place I go but rarely admit it. "Yes," I admit. After a quick planning session between Roth and Daniels, a party planned for later in the evening is moved up to 3:30, and I am invited to sit in. Word spreads from table to table. I am pointed to and waved at. It is too late to back out.

Entering the Research

Daniels and I walk back to the hotel, taking pictures of one another in front of casinos. By 3:30, I am seated on the hotel bed next to Roth, looking on at her ancient fake book, which is propped on the electric keyboard, trying not to knock over the oversized ceramic lamp with my flute.[34] Taliaffero has recovered enough to take her trumpet out of the case and warm up on a full chorus of a Liza Minelli show stopper. "Don't waste it, Bobbie!" someone says, and everyone laughs. Daniels is once again running arpeggios in the bathroom to warm up. She reappears, complaining that the desert air has split most of her reeds.

"This reminds me of all those cold theaters," says Julieanne, sitting on the bed and extending her legs in front of her. She wears a pink blouse with a dark sweater draped over her shoulders. "Remember how you had to warm up the horns over a charcoal pot?" Suddenly, everyone is remembering the freezing weather in Japan so soon after the hot weather in the Philippines. The intervening forty-seven years have disappeared, and all are suddenly reminiscing about playing two outdoor shows in their evening gowns in Osaka, snow covering the ground. Afterward, hundreds of soldiers were found to be lining up, and they agreed to do a third, unscheduled show. Nostalgia is as much a part of these parties as are the jam sessions. In fact, the two go together, memories spurring tunes, tunes spurring memories, collective improvisation taking place in both media.

This is how arrangements are made at a spontaneous jam session of the Sharon Rogers alumnae: "OK, everybody play the melody; then, Sherrie, you take the first part the second time around, do whatever you want; Bobbie, you take the bridge; Laura, take a solo; then we'll all come in on the melody, and let's play the last four bars three times at the end. OK, OK, one, two, one-two-three. . . ." I use one set of quotation marks, but this is a group quote. I couldn't keep track of who spoke during these whispered planning sessions.

We sounded good. They were better than I was, but I didn't mind. It was a pleasure to blend tones with an all-girl band after researching such

Florence Shefte (Kuhn), defrosting her trumpet valves over hot coals, Sharon Rogers All-Girl Orchestra USO tour. *Courtesy Florence Shefte Kuhn.*

groups — a rare, visceral research opportunity. We played "Call Me Irresponsible," Taliaffero donning a mute and Daniels all over the scale with swinging, improvised embellishments. Then we frolicked through Ellington's "Satin Doll," Roth's knee keeping time and the bed we are sitting on bouncing. Trumpet, sax, and keyboard rendered a gorgeous, introspective version of "Don't Take Your Love from Me." Then I picked up my flute again for a raucous "Basin Street Blues," in which Taliaffero's popular "dirty growls" brought squeals of delight from her peers. Finally, and most reverently, we closed with the Sharon Rogers theme song, "A Pretty Girl Is Like a Melody." For about thirty minutes there, in the surreal, faux medieval surroundings of a Las Vegas hotel room, this author died and joined the band.

Radio Broadcast of 1945

A month after I returned home and was pondering how I would ever translate my memories of the reunion into a meaningful history of the group, I received an unexpected package from Roth. It seems that, besides being a talented instrumentalist and celebrated pilot, she is also a skilled videotape editor and restorer of damaged audio recordings.

One item in the package was a souvenir videotape containing key moments from the Las Vegas reunion, complete with music of the original Sharon Rogers band dubbed into the background. Viewing it within moments of receiving it, I was overcome with joy to find and relive the jam session in which I had participated. Also included in the package was a cassette copy of an audiotape of a radio show broadcast from Osaka, Japan, in November 1945, two months prior to the plane crash. Roth's description of her restoration of the audio recording is harrowing:

> The broadcast was recorded on 10-inch recording discs (metal base with a vinyl tape coating) 78 RPM inside out on two machines that overlapped each other by maybe two minutes. Anyway, 35 years later, I found these gems mildewed, some with the recording material cracked and warped — some worse than others. I still had a 78 RPM hi-fi turntable at that time, so, with my trusty Sony portable cassette, I recorded and tried to match the overlap inside out 78 RPM discs as best I could (good thing I still remembered the arrangements) as the ol' Japanese records flaked and cracked away — gone forever! As bad as they are, they're great to have *48* years later!!![35]

In boogie tempo, Sharon Rogers's bass thump-walks eight beats to the bar, while the reeds and brass trade a rambunctious call and response. Then the instrumental phrases alternate with the instrumentalists yelling "Hey!" Section work, solos, and lots of swing — aside from the women's voices shouting in unison, there is nothing about the music that would signal the gender of the musicians. But, of course, the live audience is well aware of the presence of American girls, and the radio announcers remind us as often as possible.

"Well, fellas," calls the breathless emcee, "thanks for tuning us in. . . . For some splendid entertainment, watch the announcements for the Sharon Rogers All-Girl Band." As the "USO Time" announcer signs off, stately harmonies ring forth from the band. It is the final bars of the theme song, rising in volume for the big finish: "A pret-ty giiirl . . . is just like a pret-ty tuuuuune!"

The women hold their last notes. The audience goes wild. Meanings proliferate for spectators and players: "girls from home," potential dates, patriots, professional musicians, adventurers, independent women. In the postwar years, "pretty girls" playing "pretty tunes" would face even more changes.

Conclusion

Postwar Changes, Familiar Refrains

> Right now, [winning the war] is more important than anything
> else to Rosie the Riveter. But there'll come a day (after a certain boy
> with MacArthur comes flying triumphantly home to a big church
> wedding) when a lot of the good new things of peacetime will
> become important to Rosie the Housewife.
>
> — Monsanto Chemicals ad, *Newsweek,*
>
> 8 November 1943, back cover

> This guy wanted to marry me. He said, "It's me or the horn."
>
> I said, "Well, it ain't you, babe."
>
> — Martye Awkerman, *conversation with author*

Just as Rosie the Riveter, as the patriotic pinch hitter of the wartime workforce, did not mirror the experiences of most American women during World War II (women who had previously worked, e.g.), neither did the cheerful stay-at-home suburban "Rosie the Housewife" characterize most women's lives in the 1950s. Although visions of Donna Reed, Harriet Nelson, and June Cleaver remain indelibly imprinted on the national consciousness as archetypes of the 1950s, historians have pointed out that women's participation in the workforce grew, rather than decreased, after the war. William Chafe's observation that "the most striking feature of the 1950s was the degree to which women continued to enter the job market and expand their sphere" could easily be applied to the music industry.[1] Despite postwar AFM policies and broader social pressure for women to leave the bandstand, enough continued to work to inspire this headline from a story about women musicians in the *Chicago Defender* in September 1945: "War is over but Girls Still Rule on West Coast."[2]

That said, it is also true that radical changes confronted women, musicians and otherwise, who, by necessity or choice, continued to work after the war. The term *nuclear family,* coined in 1947, promoted the compact kinship unit of male breadwinner, female homemaker, and one or two children, all living the good life in the suburbs. As with other dominant and dominating images, this symbol of peacetime normalcy affected both those who lived it and those who did not. As the Truman administration strove to equate national security with America's ability to dominate the world both economically and militarily (a plan that included rebuilding imperialist nations and ensuring the economic dependency of decolonizing nations), Americans were urged to create domestic security through marriage, children, and the home. More than a lifestyle, the nuclear family expressed an ideology of cocoonlike conformity and was variously credited with protecting the American way of life against nuclear threat, Communist takeover, the plotting of subversives to undermine the U.S.-controlled international capitalist system, and a postwar reprise of the Great Depression.[3] While some women musicians hung up their horns, at least temporarily, to embrace (retooled) traditional gender roles, those who continued playing for a living encountered a public that felt quite differently about women in nontraditional jobs than it had during the war.

The nuclear family as a lived possibility excluded many of the people who had gained the most from the home-front wartime changes. Working-class people were no longer celebrated as heroic. Although the GI Bill and GI loans did indeed bring a college education and home ownership — and thus entry into the middle class — within the reach of many more people than before, Americans were also inundated with misleading messages that membership in a prosperous mainstream was universally available, and on a single income no less. African American men and women did not encounter a postwar democracy free from racist exclusions; in addition to job discrimination, unemployment, and segregated schools, housing covenants barred their entry into suburbia. African American women and men both suffered from defense plant industries' "last hired, first fired" lay-off patterns. *Music Dial,* anticipating these trends as early as 1943, advised black musicians who worked in defense plants to keep up their musical skills.[4] African American women who had moved out of domestic work during the war struggled to keep from slipping back in, as lay-offs and job discrimination threatened to leave them no option but to fill the "maid shortage."[5] Returning nonwhite servicemen — African American, Mexican American, Asian

American, and Native American — were subject to violent attack by white supremacists eager to "put them back in their place," a repeat of treatment received by black veterans of World War I.[6] At the same time, the national suppression of radical critiques and pressure to conform that were the outgrowths of the escalating cold war resulted in new civil rights strategies that largely abandoned earlier links to international anti-racist and anti-imperialist struggles.[7]

Working women, single women, women whose primary relationships were with other women, women who lived with friends or relatives, all of whom had enjoyed relative acceptance during the war, were also marginalized by the normalization of the nuclear family. Women who were "not June Cleaver," to borrow the title of a collection of essays on women of the 1950s, were swept aside into feminized, lower paid, "pink-collar" occupations.[8] For women musicians, this often meant once again scrambling to find viable niches on the margins of (or outside) the AFM's domain. These feminized and devalued musical spheres included teaching, accompanying, performing in novelty acts and in cocktail lounges, and working for churches. Women musicians often supplemented insufficient incomes with a variety of day jobs.

For all home-front civilian musicians, women and men, the return of GIs meant an influx of competition just as the swing industry faced a changing economy and social structure. Ballrooms were converted to bowling alleys as defense industry dollars dried up and reckless spending gave way to conservatism. People saved their money, stayed home, and turned on their new televisions. Door receipts no longer covered the expenses of most big bands. As the size of bands dropped, unemployment among musicians rose.

In July 1944, one-third of AFM members were still in the armed forces.[9] Puzzling over how to provide for them on their return, the AFM issued lapel labels for them to wear and instructed civilian members to watch for the emblem and remember

> that its wearer, in order to do this for you, has had to make grievous sacrifices. It means that he has had to relinquish for months, even for years, his right as a citizen to find and further himself in gainful employment. It means he has had to remain out of the running during the best days of his youth, the while others won public favor. It means he has come back after fighting your battles to see you holding the position he might have held and pocketing the money he might have earned.[10]

Women AFM members who had taken jobs in studios, orchestras, and major ballrooms for the first time during the war and with the nation's blessing traveled during gas and rubber rationing, entertained the troops, and provided the music for dances where hellos, good-byes, and other emotional surpluses were mediated by lush section work, soaring solos, and a swinging pulse now found that they were considered greedy opportunists. The implication of this view was that the least that they could do would be to bow out gracefully and let the returning GIs claim the jobs that were rightfully theirs.

"I was in the studios, CBS and everything," recalled trumpet player Jane Sager. "When the war was on, I got all these wonderful jobs. And, at the end of the war, the head of the music department said to me, 'Janie, I've got to let you go.' I said, 'Why?' He said, 'They're coming back from the service, and they've got families.' I said, 'Well, I've got a family, too, that I've got to take care of.' But that's what I had to take."[11] Sager's postwar career included working as a music therapist with hospitalized soldiers, playing with Ina Ray Hutton's 1950s all-girl band on her television show, and opening a trumpet studio in Hollywood, where she became a highly acclaimed high-note doctor and private teacher for professional trumpet players. Later, she had an all-woman comedy band called the Frivolous Five. Although the musicians in the band were all experienced players who had worked in earlier all-girl bands, their postwar popularity was achieved by playing badly on purpose: "We were so crummy and funny, and people would laugh. Listen, I made more money getting laughs. . . ."[12]

Although the AFM did not pass gender-specific rules, its emphasis on making way for returning GIs effectively put women out of the running for many desirable jobs. *International Musician* found it "heartening" that bandleaders were "sens[ing] their personal responsibility in reintroducing the service men to civilian life." Such values were consistent with postwar labor practices, intensified, perhaps, by the vagaries of the music world. As *International Musician* put it, "musical jobs have a way of evaporating overnight, of changing their locale, of altering their character."[13] Some women musicians spoke of losing work in the 1950s when — not as a rule, but on a case-by-case basis — AFM locals ordered that a standby men's band be hired in addition to an all-girl band when the job in question was particularly lucrative.

Some women musicians did leave their careers, at least temporarily, to marry and start a family. Though childcare had not been adequately

Frivolous Five comedy act. "Tearing it up." Rose Parenti (accordian), Pee Wee Preble (trombone), Jean Lutey (drums), Jane Sager (trumpet), Frances Rosu (clarinet). John Mahoney of the *Hollywood Reporter* was quoted on the combo's 1967 poster: "This Sun City contingent of dixieland dowagers are one of the wildest novelty attractions in the country." *Courtesy Jane Sager.*

provided to enable women to be both mothers and workers during the war, some childcare had been set up and the availability of such services was at least considered a worthwhile goal. In the postwar period, the provision of childcare for working mothers became a moot point. Mothers who worked were simply seen as irresponsible. But even those who did as the propaganda urged did not necessarily escape the disdain now accorded women whose musical careers had flourished during the war. One woman, who did the "right thing" by marrying her high school sweetheart, arrived home one day to find her husband in the backyard, burning her memorabilia. Also a musician, and jealous that his wife had occupied the bandstand while he was in combat, he destroyed the objects that would remind her of her career.

Some musicians, like Roz Cron, found themselves taking a break when the competition from returning GIs became too great. Having returned to Boston after her USO trip with the International Sweethearts of Rhythm, Cron attempted to keep working, but "by this time all the musicians were coming out of the Army Air Force bands and everyplace. And they all wanted work."[14] She married in 1948. The hiatus did not last forever, however. While working as a secretary in the 1970s, she and drummer Bonnie Janovsky cofounded the all-woman big band Maiden Voyage, which continues to flourish, now led by Ann Patterson. Over the years, Maiden Voyage has included many women musicians who played in earlier all-girl bands, including Betty O'Hara, an accomplished performer on several brass instruments, and trumpet player Martye Awkerman.

AFM president James C. Petrillo no doubt had men's jobs in mind when he fought the trend toward "canned" instead of live music, but at least one woman benefited from these measures. When Petrillo won an agreement with the networks that AFM members would be hired to play the records that were replacing live band broadcasts over the airwaves, trumpet player Florence Shefte (Kuhn) landed a job as a technician for WBBM, the CBS affiliate in Chicago.[15] The Sharon Rogers band had broken up, so AFM jurisdiction over radio technician jobs was welcome news for Kuhn, who had played in all-girl bands since the 1930s.

Many women musicians who played in the 1940s were able to maintain their careers throughout the 1950s and 1960s — in combos, as singles, on television, in cocktail lounges, as music teachers, as church musicians — whether they married and had babies or not. Clora Bryant toured the Western states with the Queens of Swing after she married in 1948 and continued to work even after her children were born: "I played up until eight months. And then I'd go back to work after I'd had my six-week check-up."[16] Her first two children traveled on the road with the Queens of Swing as babies. By the time her daughter April was born in 1951, the combo was not traveling as much but playing Los Angeles clubs, the Last Word and the Down Beat. Bryant played in an all-girl combo with jazz violinist Ginger Smock on a television variety show in 1951, but "The Chicks and the Fiddle" lasted on CBS for only six weeks. Advertisers were simply too cautious to sponsor a television show featuring African Americans. Even Nat "King" Cole could not get a sponsor in the 1950s.

Some white women were able to get jobs in television, however. Trombone and trumpet player Lois Cronen (Magee) remembered the 1950s as a time of great opportunity, having worked in both Ina Ray Hutton's and Ada Leonard's television bands and having also led an all-

The Sepia Tones worked steadily at the Last Word, Los Angeles, from 1943 to 1945. *Left to right:* Mata Roy (piano), Ginger Smock (violin), Nina Russell (Hammond organ). After the war, some women musicians from all-girl bands found work in combos, and some found more opportunities on piano and Hammond organ than on band instruments when men returned from the war. *Courtesy the late Ginger Smock Shipp.*

girl combo called Lois and Her Rhythm Queens that included the great drummer Jean Lutey. Cronen also worked in combos with men in the 1950s, although she was usually the only woman.

Putting together a single act and getting booked into nightclubs was one strategy employed by many women adjusting to postwar life. Clora Bryant's transformation from band soloist to solo entertainer made her a hit in nightclubs around the United States and Canada. Traveling with her trumpet and her charts, she could be booked into any club with any band. She perfected her respectful impersonation of Louis Armstrong's trumpet playing and singing to the point that bandleaders who hired her in later years, including Billy Williams and Johnny Otis, would feature her doing "Louis" at some point in their shows. When Armstrong learned of her tribute to him in Las Vegas in the 1960s, he showed his appreciation when he marched his entire band "out of the big room in the casino, into the lounge, up on the stage with me and played. Now you know that was a thrill. Sang with me, and played with me"[17] Viola Smith worked as a single in nightclubs, booked as Viola and Her Seventeen Drums. Other women worked in duos, an alternative that clubs also found economical. Drummer Helen Cole, of the Prairie View Co-Eds and Tiny Davis' Hell Divers, and pianist Maurine Smith worked as a duo until Smith's death in 1971. Drummer Gloria Simpson, who had played in numerous 1940s all-girl bands, including the Rhythm Rockets and Nita King and the Queens of Rhythm, was still playing in a duo with pianist Helen Kissinger when I contacted her in 1991.

Some women found the social and economic climate conducive to putting down their band instruments for good and taking up in their place the piano or Hammond organ. Many musicians from all-girl bands had started out on piano, so the adjustment was not necessarily difficult, and, of course, each band on the road in the 1940s had a pianist in the rhythm section whose skills were at peak level by the end of the war. Many of these women became private piano teachers or found work in dance studios. Yet others worked piano bars or switched to Hammond organ (which was becoming increasingly popular in the 1950s) and got steady jobs in hotels and nightclubs. Sarah McLawler recalled that switching from leading all-girl combos as a pianist to working as a single on the Hammond organ (later as a duo with her husband, violinist Richard Otto) brought more work her way but also antagonism from some men in the AFM. The first Hammond organist to play the entire show at the Apollo Theatre, McLawler remembered that musicians (men) approached her afterward, saying, "You're knocking the bands out of work." "I ain't knocking nobody," she replied. "Get the hell out of here. You know if I asked you guys for a job you all would look dumb, deaf, and blind as if I didn't even exist."[18] The AFM's discomfort with the Hammond organ had led to many rules aimed at discouraging clubs from hiring organists as opposed to bands since its invention in 1935. Women's relative acceptance on the organ in the 1950s meant that the labor of many women musicians once again existed on the fringes of the music scene.

Many all-girl big bands from the 1940s contained core groups of musicians who did not want to quit playing. Many excellent combos were formed as a result. From Virgil Whyte's band emerged the Vadel Quintet; from the Darlings of Rhythm came the bass, drums, and sax for the Syncoettes. From the Prairie View Co-Eds, Darlings of Rhythm, and International Sweethearts of Rhythm sprang Tiny Davis' Hell Divers, from Ada Leonard's ranks the Debutones. The Sharon Rogers band produced a combo. Vi Burnside and Myrtle Young both led all-woman

Clora Bryant, publicity photo, ca. 1960. Some women musicians created solo acts after the war. *Courtesy Clora Bryant.*

combos made up of former members of the International Sweethearts of Rhythm and its spin-off groups. Betty McGuire, former leader of the Sub-Debs, led a quartet in 1953 called the Belle-Tones.

The turn to combos was a welcome change for some. After spending many years in the third and fourth trumpet chairs of big bands, trumpet player Thelma Lewis enjoyed being able to "really play" in quartets and quintets. She continued to play in small groups throughout the 1950s, 1960s, and 1970s, enthusiastically making the transition from jazz to rock and roll and eventually picking up a Fender electric guitar. Vi Wilson continued her music career as she began working for the U.S. Postal Service, adding an electric bass to suit the range of popular material covered by such combos as the Kristells. Some coed and interracial combos flourished in the postwar period. Gurthalee Clark, technical sergeant and musician in the segregated WAC of the war years, started an integrated all-woman combo in Los Angeles. Trumpet player Maxine Fields married white trombonist Jimmy Knepper, and the couple formed an interracial and coed combo that included, at various times, International Sweethearts of Rhythm bassist and vocalist Margaret "Trump Margo" Gibson and bassist Vivian Garry.[19]

Although the USO–Camp Shows had originally not been meant to outlast World War II, the organization flourished in the postwar years,

Vi Wilson was a bass player with many all-girl bands of the 1940s, including the Darlings of Rhythm. Los Angeles, 12 June 1994.

entertaining soldiers stationed around the world. Many of the women who traveled in all-girl bands with the USO in the 1940s entertained troops during the Korean War, only this time in combos. Toby Butler switched from trumpet to bass in the 1950s and joined combos for several USO tours. Drummer Marjorie Kiewitt toured Japan, China, and Korea with a later version of D'Artega's band and returned to Asia again with a combo in a USO tour that took her to Japan, Korea, and the Philippines.

One unusual employer of many white women musicians in the 1950s was the Hormel Meat Company, whose chairman of the board, Jay C. Hormel, felt that "everyone was concerned with GI Joe and nothing was done for the returning GI Jane."[20] In a most unusual promotional campaign, ex-servicewomen were hired to travel cross-country, caravan style, in thirty-five white Chevy coupes with cows, chickens, and pigs painted on the sides. On Mondays and Tuesdays, the musicians visited grocery stores, selling meat products such as Spam and handing out concert tickets. Wednesday was rehearsal day. Every Thursday night, the band performed an elaborate stage show for the grocers they had visited. These performances were recorded and broadcast over network radio every weekend on ABC and NBC. When the "Hormel Girls" — an orchestra of six violins, five saxophones, four trombones, five trumpets, one harp, one marimba-vibes, and a four-piece rhythm section — ran out of women veterans, the band opened its ranks to civilian women musicians.

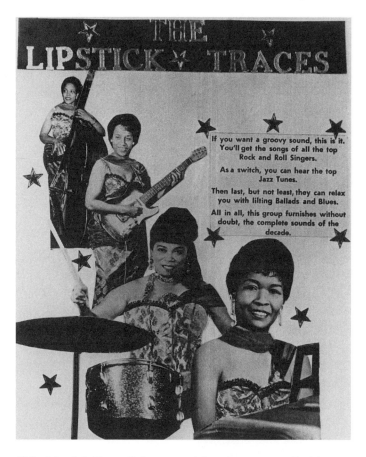

The Lipstick Traces

If you want a groovy sound, this is it. You'll get the songs of all the top Rock and Roll Singers.

As a switch, you can hear the top Jazz Tunes.

Then last, but not least, they can relax you with lilting Ballads and Blues.

All in all, this group furnishes without doubt, the complete sounds of the decade.

"The Lipstick Traces." Some musicians in postwar all-girl combos welcomed the change from big band to small group format. Trumpet player Thelma Lewis picked up the Fender guitar and enjoyed playing rock. *Left to right:* Vi Wilson (bass), Thelma Lewis (electric guitar), Frances Grey (drums), unknown (piano). *Courtesy Vi Wilson.*

Many former members of the civilian all-girl bands of the 1940s joined the Hormel Girls, including drummer Marjorie Kiewitt from D'Artega's band; Laverne Wollerman, trumpet player from the bands of Dave Schooler, Ruth Gehlert, Freddie Shafer, and Virgil Whyte; tenor player Alice Hinton from Freddie Shafer; Mary Demond and Virginia Wurst from Ada Leonard; and Gloria Ryan, who, along with Wurst, had played in a combo called the Debutones. Martye Awkerman, a trumpet soloist for the WAF (Women's Air Force) band in the early 1950s, recalled her

The Hormel Girls caravan was a unique source of employment for white women musicians in the 1950s. Musicians traveled caravan style across the country, selling meat products, and performing weekly concerts aired on network radio. *Courtesy Gloria Ryan.*

experiences with the Hormel Girls as "a great job, fun, a lot of lifetime friends made."[21] Although the AFM gave the Hormel Girls caravan an enthusiastic report in a cover story in *International Musician* in November 1951, it is difficult to imagine men in the 1950s agreeing to AFM members' double duty as traveling sales people.[22]

Many women musicians turned to careers in music education after the war, among them Bettye Bradley (Kimbrough), Margaret Bradshaw, and

The Hormel Girls caravan, ca. 1950s. *Courtesy Gloria Ryan.*

Argie Mae Edwards of the Prairie View Co-Eds, Toby Butler from the International Sweethearts of Rhythm, Eddie Durham's All-Stars, and the Darlings of Rhythm, and "Hour of Charm" violinist Jean Phillips (Soroka). Some taught privately; some taught in schools for decades. Many shared their teaching methods during our interviews. Rhoda Rabin, who had played bass in Bonnie Downs' All-Girl Orchestra in the 1940s (made up of students from the Eastman School of Music), developed her own method of teaching improvisation to children, which she was preparing to publish when we spoke in 1994.[23] In addition to leading professional combos in the Denver area, Joy Cayler became a jazz educator and organized a number of student jazz bands. In 1974, she started a non-profit jazz education program for young people. When we spoke in 1995, she was still giving private lessons, teaching fifty to sixty students a week. Some women musicians who had performed in the 1940s became high school band directors, including former Prairie View Co-Ed Melvia Wrenn, "Hour of Charm" trumpet soloist Phyllis Clendening, and bassist Laura Bohle (Sias) from the bands of Al D'Artega and Ada Leonard. One woman, who preferred not to be named, taught and led a high school band for decades without ever telling her students that she had been a professional bandleader during World War II. She kept her experience secret for fear that public knowledge of it would damage her reputation as a respectable woman fit to teach.

An entire book could (and should) be devoted to the ways in which women musicians negotiated the postwar changes, but I hope that, by ending on this note, or cluster of notes, the reader is left with an impression of a complex, and largely unrecorded, cultural and labor history. Despite being relegated to devalued and feminized subcategories many women musicians continued to *play the changes* after the war. Granted, they often did so less visibly than during the war, making it possible for women's bands such as Sisters in Jazz and Maiden Voyage to seem like the heralds of a brand-new phenomenon when they appeared on the scene in the 1970s. The perpetual phenomena phenomenon.

During our interviews, I was continually inspired by women who, in their sixties, seventies, eighties, and nineties, were still finding ways to incorporate music into their lives. Poor health forced Clora Bryant to put down the trumpet in the 1990s, but, as she approached seventy, she continued to stay busy in the Los Angeles jazz scene as a lecturer (on the history of Central Avenue), a vocalist, a concert producer, a writer, an educator, and a mentor to young musicians. At their 1999 San Diego reunion, the Sharon Rogers musicians, now all in their seventies, created a USO show for a public audience. In 1998, at age eighty-eight, former trombonist Velzoe Brown could still be found taking her multigenerational combo to play for dancers at senior centers several times a month. With the onset of the swing revival (evidence recent Gap commercials), young people began following the band. When the new dancers made the centers nervous, Brown met with center managers to fight for the right to hold "junior/senior" dances. Saxophonist Peggy Gilbert was still playing professionally in her early nineties, making television and live appearances with her popular Dixie Belles. Tenor saxophonist Edna Lewis,

Clora Bryant and Jane Sager, two trumpet giants from the all-girl bands of the 1940s, both of whom maintained careers in music into the 1990s. Los Angeles, 10 June 1994.

who had led a number of all-girl combos during World War II, played steadily until at age eighty-eight she found out that she was dying, at which point she hired a new band to replace hers at the Salinas Senior Center, broke in the new musicians, and checked into the hospital.

Many women with whom I spoke were members of community or nostalgia bands that played music from the Swing Era. Trombonist Alice Jacoby was playing in a fifteen-piece group called the Golden Era when I heard from her in 1992. Elise Blye (Henderson) grew old with her fans, spending thirty-seven years in the Hamiltones big band in Portland, Oregon. Helen Day (Schuster), who had played with Ada Leonard, sent me contemporary reviews of the Starliters big band in Galesburg, Illinois, with which she had played lead alto since 1979. Many women from the 1940s bands were devoted members of church bands and choirs, whose congregations may not have known of their earlier careers.

That we know so little about these ongoing histories should be no surprise. It certainly does not surprise the women whom I interviewed.

Conclusion 331

"Among my peers I was known as a lead trumpet. Nobody else knew my name," wrote Laverne Wollerman.[24] In the words of Lillian Carter (Wilson), "We took off. We took solos. We did it all. I'll tell you something about being female. We were never taken seriously."[25] To repeat a familiar refrain, without a place in the discourse, one is silenced. Contemporary women drummers, brass players, and saxophonists are still treated as novelties, sexualized, as glamour girls, desexualized as deviant, and they continue to find themselves traveling different career tracks than their male peers. Wrote contemporary saxophonist Leigh Pilzer, "I wonder if it would surprise the women in your study to hear that, some fifty to sixty years after their days as young female players facing stereotypes and ignorance, I still hear that I'm the first woman saxophonist someone has ever seen. I still encounter bandleaders who won't hire me. I still encounter contractors who will hire me only when they've been asked to supply an all-female ensemble."[26] The press still writes about all-women bands as though jazz has been discovered on other planets. And patterns one might think long outdated continue to plague all-woman bands, women-in-jazz panels, and women's music festivals.

A contemporary drummer complains that I am asking too many questions about gender in our interview. She likens the experience to being placed in all-woman pickup bands at women's jazz festivals. Too often, she laments, the only thing the musicians have in common is gender. I hear the same thing from other women musicians. It finally hits home when, one day, I receive a frantic call from someone who knows nothing about my work, asking me to be on a women-in-jazz panel. My presence is urgently needed, I am told, because the organizers have just realized that there are all men on the panel, which will look bad.

At a women's jazz festival in the 1990s, a young woman asks me what I play. I tell her I'm writing a book about all-girl bands of the 1940s. "Oh, that's wonderful," she exclaims. "I understand that the women's bands were more integrated back then." I start to correct her, to tell her that, in the 1940s, Jim Crow laws actually prevented blacks and whites from working and traveling together. Then I think about the bands we are seeing this weekend. The only big band appears to be all white. I think of the contemporary all-girl bands I know and realize that I have no educative rejoinder. What if she's *right*? What does that *mean*?

What it means *to me* is that the situation today can no more be reduced to a case of talented women simply needing to prove that they can play in order to be accepted and treated fairly than it could in the 1940s. It is still about powerful stories that get told all around us and through us, about gender, race, class, and other areas where inherent ability is ranked and structured. And these stories, of course, are not just about jazz. Though we've been focusing on all-girl bands of the 1940s, the insidious operations of past and present inequities that plagued women musicians resonate beyond the bandstand. Similarly, learning the histories of all-girl bands may render counter-narratives that also have far reaching effects.

A young African American woman jazz drummer hesitates when I ask her if she has been inspired by the history of women in jazz. She tells me that she has been more inspired by the history of women in the civil rights movement. She is resisting the gender isolation of second wave music discourse — insisting on the inextricability of gender and race, on the continued importance of the struggle for civil rights, and on the interrelatedness of music and politics.[27]

A women-in-jazz symposium opens with three white women and one white man playing a musical interlude and a panel of six African American women analyzing the situation of women in jazz. My gut reaction is, Why is this band all white? Why is there a man in the band? Why are the black and white women separated? Then I realize that, although the configuration appears segregated, it questions stereotypes about who is creative and who intellectual, who is gendered and who normal. How often have white people comprised the panel of experts while black people played the tunes without such divisions of labor being questioned? How often have audiences stared at the one woman in a men's band and wondered what she was doing there?[28]

Four African American women in their sixties take the stage. Two wear gowns, two tuxedos. At first just the vocalist sings, accompanied by the rhythm section, but soon the drummer, bassist, and pianist all sing too, scatting back and forth, trading distinctive solos. Sight and sound challenge audience expectations: What is a combo? What do older black women look/sound like? What is the gender organization of instrumentalists and singers? What is the age/race of these women bending gender norms? What kinds of counterdiscourses are possible when women play jazz?[29]

When crafting counternarratives, it is helpful to know what came before. Which counternarratives were most effective? What were the pitfalls? Standard histories will not yield this information — the types of jazz and swing in which women were accepted are not recognized by the historians. This was true in the postwar years, the war years, and no doubt in other specific times and places that warrant further study. Challenging this "disappearing woman" routine requires looking at the feminized areas of jazz as parts of history, rather than parts outside of history, and analyzing how ideas about gender, race, class, sexuality, and nation shaped how jazz has been defined, practiced, and remembered at particular times and places. Feminist theory, cultural studies, oral history, ethnomusicology, and jazz studies all offer theories and methods that could be usefully employed toward this end.

The narrators who know best how to tell jazz histories that include both women and men are the very women who played the changes of jazz and swing history. It behooves us to listen to them while we can, to learn new frameworks for thinking about jazz and swing history that include *their* stories, *their* strategies, the spheres in which *they* labored, the music that *they* played.

This is urgent, not only for the past, but for the future. As Vi Wilson put it, "We really don't want to see the women musicians die out. We've got young ones coming up. They should come forth, and it should be known that we had some in those days but we never got the recognition. *They never gave us the recognition.*"[30]

It may not be possible to drown out the dominant discourse, but it is certainly possible, and necessary, to learn the alternatives and bear witness to their silence. To crank up the volume, listen closely, and say, Yes, these are the comfortable beats that repeat certain stories and suppress others. To listen for dissonances, patterns, breaks. Between familiar grooves, although nearly inaudible and excluded for historically telling reasons, may travel hundreds of all-girl bands.

Introduction

"It Don't Mean a Thing If It Ain't in the History Books"

1 For critical reevaluations of second wave feminist oral history practices, see Gluck and Patai, eds., *Women's Words;* and also Visweswaran,
"Betrayal."

2 Antonio Gramsci used the term *hegemony* to refer to the complex of
factors, including the cultural, that contribute to the creation of something
that can be perceived as *common sense.* There is nothing natural about
common sense in this formulation; rather, it is a key battleground that
determines who rules, who benefits, who belongs (see Williams, *Marxism
and Literature,* 108–14).

3 I am grateful to the authors of the growing library of books that attempt
to forge new ways of framing jazz and swing histories, ways in which
women's bands are not simply mentioned as gimmicks but contextualized
historically. Books on women in jazz include Dahl, *Stormy Weather;*
Handy, *Black Women in American Bands and Orchestras,* and *The International Sweethearts of Rhythm;* and Placksin, *American Women in Jazz.*
Some new books on jazz and swing allude to women's participation.
Among these are recent works that attend to swing in the World War II
years, including Erenberg, *Swinging the Dream;* Peretti, *Jazz in American
Culture;* and Stowe, *Swing Changes.*

4 The most vitriolic of these is George T. Simon, whose dismissals of all-
girl bands simultaneously ridiculed the musicianship and womanhood of
the instrumentalists and sexualized and delegitimated women bandleaders. Typical is his rejection of Rita Rio's band as "a bunch of rather
unattractive girls who looked as stiff in their imitation tuxedos as their
music sounded, thereby setting off Miss Rio's undulating torso all the
more dramatically" (Simon, *The Big Bands,* 510). A respectful nod to all-
girl bands, uncharacteristic of these kinds of texts, comes from Leo
Walker — possibly because he includes the 1940s in his viewfinder. Although Walker refrains from going into detail in his otherwise painstaking
history of the big bands, he does at least mention the names of two all-girl
bands in *The Wonderful Era of the Great Dance Bands* and remarks on "a
substantial number of all-girl orchestras enjoying the success of the war
years" (p. 101).

5 See the Lou Schurrer cartoons that appeared in *Down Beat,* 15 August
1943, 15 March, 1 July 1944. In the former, two women and a man are
seen exiting a stage, arm in arm, as spectators wonder, "Are they his third

or fourth wives, or two new members of the brass section?" The March 1944 cartoon is a classic derogatory depiction of a girl singer. The July 1944 cartoon features a woman nonmusician unhappily sitting in the saxophone section of a men's band. Why? Her musician boyfriend can't afford to buy her a ticket. These are just some examples of the ways women's bodies were summoned by *Down Beat* to define women on the bandstand as not real musicians and thus mark the boundaries of authentic jazz.

6   The black press tended to treat chorines more respectfully than the white trades or newspapers did. Sympathetic coverage, e.g., of chorines' demands for higher pay and shorter hours at the Apollo Theater appeared in the *Chicago Defender* (e.g., " 'American Guild of Variety Artists' Takes Over"), which also covered the formation of a social organization for chorines in Harlem ("Chorines of Harlem Organize").

7   "They Have a Gene Krupa in Girls' Clothes!" "Anne Wallace Weds, Quits."

8   Allen, *A Horrible Prettiness,* 234.

9   Alto saxophonist Rosalind Cron recalled her father taking her to see a variety act in which Siamese twins, joined at the back, played saxophones while roller-skating. Her father thought she would enjoy them since the girls were about her age and played her instrument. The impact on Cron was quite the opposite; the act haunted her. Years later, she saw an obituary for these women in a magazine. They had spent their whole lives playing their saxophones, one skating backward, one skating forward (Rosalind Cron, conversation with author, 7 March 1996).

10   See Scott, *Gender and the Politics of History,* 42–43.

11   Short, *Black and White Baby,* 97. I heard this rumor both affirmed and contested many times during the course of my research.

12   The one-drop rule (according to which any known African American ancestry defines a person as black) and its variations were entrenched throughout the United States by 1915. For more on the one-drop rule, see Davis, *Who Is Black?* and Omi and Winant, *Racial Formation in the United States.*

13   Collins, *Black Feminist Thought,* 67.

14   Evelyn Brooks Higginbotham writes, "For African-Americans, race signified a cultural identity that defined and connected them as a people, even as a nation. To be called a 'race leader,' 'race man,' or 'race woman' by the black community was not a sign of insult or disapproval, nor did such titles refer to any and every black person" ("African-American Women's History," 267).

15   Statistics on black newspapers are from William O'Neill's fascinating study of contradictions in U.S. wartime democracy (*A Democracy at War,* 240).

16   Higginbotham, "African-American Women's History," 266. See also Hine, "Black Migration to the Urban Midwest"; and Davis, *Women, Race, and Class.*

17 Carby, "It Jus Be's Dat Way Sometime," 332–33. For Carby's analysis of how African American women novelists deconstructed and reconstructed black womanhood through depictions of race women, see *Reconstructing Womanhood.* For a fascinating analysis of how the works of Ma Rainey and Bessie Smith and other blueswomen provided a site for performers and audiences to construct a model for working-class black womanhood, see Davis, *Blues Legacies and Black Feminism.*

18 Placksin, *American Women in Jazz,* 142.

19 Evelyn McGee Stone, telephone interview with author, 30 November 1996.

20 The Darlings are sometimes mentioned in discussions of bandleader Clarence Love's career, but even these references betray a sense of the band not being "real." Albert McCarthy (*Big Band Jazz*) offers complete listings of Love's men's territory bands over two decades. However, when it comes to the all-girl band that Love led between 1944 and 1946, McCarthy simply states that Love spent a couple of years "controlling an all-female band called the Darlings of Rhythm" (p. 143). The personnel are not listed, although that information was readily available in issues of the *Chicago Defender,* the *Pittsburgh Courier,* and *International Musician* of the 1940s.

21 Jackson, *The World of Big Bands,* 78.

22 Peggy Gilbert, letter to author, 14 November 1990.

23 Simon, *The Big Bands,* 261.

24 Kenney, "Historical Context and the Definition of Jazz," 101. Counternarratives that challenge the Eurocentrism of conventional texts include Amiri Baraka (then LeRoi Jones), *Blues People* and *Black Music;* A. B. Spellman, *Four Lives in the Bebop Business,* and Albert Murray, *Stomping the Blues.* Compensatory women-in-jazz histories include Dahl, *Stormy Weather;* and Placksin, *American Women in Jazz.* D. Antoinette Handy's *Black Women in American Bands and Orchestras* and *The International Sweethearts of Rhythm* adopt both approaches. New works in jazz studies include Gabbard, ed., *Jazz among the Discourses,* and *Representing Jazz.*

25 Sarkissian, "Gender and Music," 338–39.

26 For example, McClary (*Feminine Endings*) demonstrates that the sonata form's embedded narrative of a briefly destabilized protagonist subduing and subsuming an exotic "Other" reflects and contributes to its historical contexts of European colonization projects and women's rights struggles.

27 Simon, *The Big Bands,* 24.

28 Baraka, *Blues People,* 186.

29 Goodman and Kolodin, *The Kingdom of Swing,* 171.

30 Holiday, *Lady Sings the Blues,* 97.

31 Schuller, *The Swing Era,* 9. At least Schuller puts the *king* in *king of swing* in quotation marks.

32 Tanner, Megill, and Gerow, *Jazz,* 94.

33 Firestone, *Swing, Swing, Swing,* 315.

34 This theory would seem to be confirmed by the increased mentions of women in recent jazz history texts that include the World War II years (see Stowe, *Swing Changes;* and Erenberg, *Swinging the Dream*).

35 Baraka, *Blues People,* 143. On the Swing Era as the invention of the white-owned music business, see ibid., 142–65.

36 Reed, *The Black Music History of Los Angeles,* 16–45. Typically, the first books on jazz in Los Angeles focused on white artists in the 1950s. Lately, several excellent accounts of the African American jazz scene on Central Avenue have appeared. In addition to Reed, see Porter, *There and Back;* and Bryant et al., ed., *Central Avenue Sounds.*

37 Meltzer, *Reading Jazz,* 143.

38 Tucker, "The Politics of Impermanence," 12.

39 Carby, *Reconstructing Womanhood,* 23–24.

40 An example is the Monsanto Chemicals ad that ran on the back cover of *Newsweek* on 8 November 1943. As a muscular Rosie in lipstick rivets away, the copy reads: "When Rosie the Riveter becomes Rosie the Housewife, what will Santocel be doing then?" Why, building refrigerators, of course, as well as "dozens of new comforts and conveniences for Rosie and her sisters, new jobs and greater opportunities for those fighting menfolk that they're backing now with their love, their work, their War Bond buying."

41 In a 25 June 1945 "Mopsy" comic strip, Gladys Parker depicted her title character in full Rosie the Riveter regalia—including jump suit, lunch pail, and snood—entering a beauty parlor and requesting "a complete reconversion job. I especially want to lose the muscles I developed on my war job!" (Robbins, *A Century of Women Cartoonists,* 84).

42 Davis, *Women, Race, and Class,* 98.

43 Simon, *The Big Bands,* 511.

44 Eric Lott has argued that blackface minstrelsy was only the first cultural product in an enduring history of "white obsession with black male bodies" (*Love and Theft,* 3). Ingrid Monson argues that the concept *hipness,* so persistently associated with jazz and jazz musicians, was patterned on "a style of black masculinity that held, and continues to hold, great appeal for white audiences and musicians" ("The Problem with White Hipness," 402).

45 I certainly do not mean to say that this is the only way to talk about sexuality when narrating histories of all-girl bands. I do feel that a historically specific approach is crucial, but I also hope that this does not preclude the development of historical narratives that tell us more about nontraditional sexualities. See the discussion in chap. 5 below of Andrea Weiss and Greta Schiller's documentary about "Tiny" Davis and Ruby Lucas. Ronni Sanlo is currently working on a history of women-identified women in all-girl bands of the 1930s.

46 An incomplete list of the diverse literature that I am calling *new works in*

jazz studies includes Gabbard, ed., *Jazz among the Discourses,* and *Representing Jazz;* Ogren, *The Jazz Revolution;* Stowe, *Swing Changes;* Berliner, *Thinking in Jazz;* and DeVeaux, *The Birth of Bebop.*

47 See Kenney, "Historical Context and the Definition of Jazz"; and Rasula, "The Media of Memory."

48 See, e.g., Elworth's gender analysis of Frank Sinatra as "boy singer" ("Jazz in Crisis," 61–62). For other gender analyses of masculinity in jazz studies, see also Monson, "The Problem with White Hipness"; Ake, "Re-Masculating Jazz"; and Gabbard, *Jammin' at the Margins.* While I would agree with Gabbard that jazz has historically offered an intriguing "number of alternatives" to "conventional notions of masculinity and male sexuality" (p. 7), I would also add that a complex variety of notions about race-specific femininities and female sexualities have flourished in jazz contexts, that ideas about femininity have also been historically embedded in discourses about jazz authenticity, boundaries, performance elements, and genres, and that analyses of both women's and men's jazz practices will benefit from explorations of historical struggles over competing and related ideas about masculinity and femininity.

49 Dance, *The World of Swing,* 32.

50 Handy, *Black Women in American Bands and Orchestras,* 37.

51 Dance, *The World of Swing,* 167.

52 Ibid., 404. For the list itself, compiled by Walter C. Allen and Jerry Valburn, see pp. 404–16.

53 See Ogren, " 'Jazz Isn't Just Me' "; and Peretti, "Oral Histories of Jazz Musicians."

54 I have written on this at length in my "Telling Performances."

55 Clifford, "Traveling Cultures," 105.

1. Working the Swing Shift:
Effects of World War II on All-Girl Bands

1 "Femme Crew for Jiggs."

2 Ina Ray Hutton led an all-man band throughout the war, returning to an all-woman format in the 1950s. Rita Rio was featured in several "Soundies" shot during the war, but she no longer traveled on the road with her all-girl band as she had done in the 1930s. (See chap. 5 on Soundies.)

3 For more information on the prewar all-girl bands and the continuum of women musicians throughout the history of jazz, see Dahl, *Stormy Weather;* Handy, *Black Women in American Bands and Orchestras;* and Placksin, *American Women in Jazz.*

4 See any number of propaganda films aimed at recruiting women war workers. For a stunning array of clips, see Lucy Massie Phenix and Connie Field's documentary *The Life and Times of Rosie the Riveter* (1980).

5 Ernestine May, telephone interview with author, 5 January 1997.

6 Perri Lee Poston, interview with author, Oakland, Calif., 13 April 1994.

7 Reverend Frances Scher N.S.T., telephone interview with author, 28 August 1990.

8 "Rosie the Riveter," words and music by Redd Evans and John Jacob Loeb, 1942, popularized by the Four Vagabonds, also performed by the Sportsmen Quartet.

9 Rowe, "Arranger Eddie Durham Embarks on New Venture."

10 Deloros Conlee Goodspeed, letter to author, 23 September 1991.

11 I thank Steven Feld for the insight that, during World War II, the job of musician was feminized, even when men held the position. Feld, whose father worked with army bands throughout the war, informs me that men military musicians were often perceived (sometimes correctly) as willfully avoiding combat, that sometimes they were thought to be homosexual, and that one of their primary duties was to comfort soldiers (playing in hospitals, e.g.). Additional evidence that wartime musicianship was feminized is that the Women's Army Corps (WAC) had five bands during the war, all of which were deactivated at the war's end. Army band membership was once again exclusively a man's job until 1947, when the Fourteenth Army Band WAC — the one official WAC band in existence in the 1990s — was activated at Fort Meade, Md. The existence of five WAC bands was a World War II phenomenon.

12 Antrim, "Should Music Be War-Conscripted?"

13 "Essential (Unpaid) Industry."

14 Petrillo, "Members to Play 'Star Spangled Banner.' " For more on the AFM and army band controversy, see "Army Bands."

15 Laverne Wollerman, letter to author, 10 February 1992.

16 Peri, "Who Said Girl Musicians Could Play?" Hudee, "If a Chick Has Talent, Why Not Make Use of It?"

17 Dynamite, "And on the Contrary." Banana, "Girls Are too Hep!"

18 Gibson, "Give Youth a Chance!" Toney, "That Fem Question, Again!"

19 "Top-Flight Bands," March 1942.

20 Cons, "The Effect War Is Having on Music World"; "New Laws and Changes."

21 For more on the role of the representation of the "all-American girl" in mobilizing soldiers for war, see Westbrook, " 'I Want a Girl . . .' "; and also Costello, *Virtue under Fire.* For the role of swing music in mobilization, see Stowe, *Swing Changes,* 141–79.

22 Peggy Gilbert, letter to author, 14 November 1990.

23 Jane Sager, telephone interview with author, 30 July 1995.

24 Ada Leonard Bernstein, telephone interview with author, 5 July 1994.

25 Roz Cron, telephone interview with author, 13 August 1990.

26 Dance, *The World of Count Basie,* 69. For an excellent account of the history of Durham's band, see Placksin, *American Women in Jazz,* 149–51.

27 Columnist Ted Yates gave jazz and gender discourse a different twist when he wrote, "Although not one of the fairer sex 'Lips' is quite a sender with the skins" ("I've Been Around," 11 December 1943; see also Yates, "I've Been Around," 18 December 1943, and "Keed Lips Hackette." George Yoshida notes that trombonist Paul Higaki briefly played in Allen Reed's all-girl band (*Reminiscing in Swingtime,* 214).

28 Kovan, "Sharps and Flats," 3.

29 Jane Sager, telephone interview with author, 31 July 1995.

30 Lillian Carter Wilson, telephone interview with author, 24 August 1991.

31 I have referred to this story in an earlier publication ("And Fellas, They're American Girls"), indicating that the bands involved were the Sharon Rogers All-Girl Band and the International Sweethearts of Rhythm. Subsequently, Kuhn recalled that it was not the Sharon Rogers musicians who had this experience with the International Sweethearts of Rhythm but members of Betty McGuire's Sub-Debs. Several Sharon Rogers alumnae also played with Betty McGuire, and both groups played the same club in Flint, Mich., at one time or another (Florence Shefte Kuhn, letters to author, 24 November 1992 and 17 November 1996).

32 Thelma Lewis, telephone interview with author, 12 June 1994.

33 Norma Teagarden, telephone interview with author, 20 July 1992.

34 Velzoe Brown, interview with author, 29–30 August 1995. Elise Blye Henderson, telephone interview with author, 21 September 1990. Clora Bryant, interview with Sally Placksin, 26–28 March 1993.

35 Betty Kidwell Meriedeth, questionnaire, March 1992 (Meriedeth reported that she spent eleven years on the road, never working in one place longer than six weeks). Lillian Carter Wilson, telephone interview with author, 24 August 1991. Laverne Wollerman, letter to author, 10 February 1992.

36 Handy, *The International Sweethearts of Rhythm,* 27. The only time the original members of the Sweethearts made union scale was when they traveled overseas on USO tours.

37 Lillian Carter Wilson, telephone interview with author, 24 August 1991.

38 Violet Wilson, telephone interview with author, 9 November 1993.

39 Stewart, "All-Female Band Diva Breaking Stereotypes."

40 Fraser, *Unruly Practices,* 124.

41 A notable exception is Angela Davis's brilliant analysis of the social implications of Holiday's reworkings of Tin Pan Alley love songs as well as the significant place in her repertoire of "Strange Fruit" (*Blues Legacies and Black Feminism,* 161–80, 181–97).

42 O'Day, *High Times, Hard Times,* 102.

43 Joy Cayler, letter to author, 21 July 1995.

44 Clora Bryant, telephone interview with author, 5 August 1993.

45 Doris Jarrett Meilleur, telephone interview with author, 22 June 1994.

46 Cron, "My Road to Zanzibar," 45. Roberta Morrison, telephone interview with author, 23 September 1996.

47 Handy, *The International Sweethearts of Rhythm*, 178.
48 Roberta Lee Ellis Brower, questionnaire, 26 November 1992.
49 Florence Shefte Kuhn, letter to author, 17 September 1996.
50 Thelma Dwyer, telephone interview with author, 18 August 1990. Lee Ann Savage, letter to Virgil Whyte, 12 November 1945.
51 Ada Leonard Bernstein, telephone interview with author, 5 July 1994.
52 Ernest May Crafton Miller, telephone interview with author, 16 October 1993.
53 Laura Bohle Sias, telephone interview with author, 2 July 1994. Toby Butler, letter to author, 6 August 1997. Ada Leonard Bernstein, telephone interview, 5 July 1994. (At the annual AFM conference in 1941, the mileage limit for musicians traveling by privately owned automobiles or buses was set at four hundred miles within twenty-four hours. The next year, the bylaw was changed to three hundred miles in twenty-four hours ["Important Changes in Federation Laws," August 1941, July 1942].) Doris Jarrett Meilleur, telephone interview with author, 22 June 1994. Clora Bryant, telephone interview with author, 7 October 1990.
54 Betty Knudsen, interview with Florice Whyte Kovan, from Kovan's video series, *Virgil Whyte's 'All-Girl' Bands*, vol. 3, *Betty Knudsen: "To Instill the Joy of the Love of Music"* (1991).
55 Clarence Love, interview with Nathan Pearson and Howard Litwak, 13 April 1977.
56 Joy Cayler, telephone interview with author, 28 May 1995.
57 For more on shortages, rationing, and wartime conversion, see Kennett, *For the Duration*. See also the fascinating essays on the U.S. home front in O'Brien and Parsons, eds., *The Home-Front War*.
58 Kovan, "Sharps and Flats," 3.
59 Joy Cayler, telephone interview with author, 28 May 1995.
60 Ibid.
61 Doris Jarrett Meilleur, telephone interview with author, 22 June 1994. Willie Mae Wong Scott, telephone interview with author, 3 December 1996.
62 Helen Jones Woods, telephone interview with author, 20 February 1995. Laura Bohle Sias, telephone interview with author, 2 July 1994. Violet Wilson, interview with author, 12 June 1994.

2. "Hours of Charm" with Phil Spitalny

1 All radio excerpts in this chapter are from "The Hour of Charm," 1 October 1944.
2 Evelyn McGee Stone, telephone interview with author, 30 November 1996.
3 *International Musician*, October 1938, 8; August 1941, 8.
4 One example of how Spitalny worked the talent search into his stage

routine is described in a story about the orchestra's appearance in San Antonio, Tex., on 15 April 1941: "In conjunction with the appearance here this week of Phil Spitalny and his 'Hour of Charm' all gal orchestra at the Majestic theatre here, a contest is being held to select a girl vocalist or instrumentalist in the area." The report goes on to explain that, "each morning Monday through Thursday, entrants are being auditioned by Spitalny. On Friday the finalists selected will be presented as part of stage show. At the concluding performance Friday evening the audience will be asked to select three winners. Each prize winner will be awarded $65, second place will be $25 and third place winner will receive $10. Only rule is that the girl must be over 16 years of age" ("Spitalny's Theatre Stunt").

5 These and subsequent quotations are from Viola Smith, interview with author, New York, 17 October 1996.

6 Handy, "Conversation with Lucille Dixon," 307. Bass player Lucille Dixon, who had studied with Fred Zimmerman of the New York Philharmonic, was one of two African American members of the National Youth Administration Orchestra in 1941. When she contacted Spitalny's organization in 1942, she learned that being talented, classically trained, and a woman were not the only requirements for the job. Whiteness was also prerequisite.

7 This and subsequent quotations are from Phyllis Clendening, telephone interview with author, 13 March 1994.

8 Martye Awkerman, letter to author, 21 July 1995.

9 "Majestic, San Antonio."

10 "Top Flight Bands," March 1943; "News from the Home Front."

11 "Why Not Draft Spitalny's Girl Band into the Army?"

12 "Gal Tooters Not Rushing to Join the WAAC Bands."

13 "Spitalny Loses Tuba to Navy."

14 "Waves Try Out."

15 "Top Flight Bands," March 1943.

16 Phil Spitalny quoted in Heylbut, " 'The Hour of Charm,' " 40.

17 See Chafe, *The American Woman,* 12–15.

18 Jean (Jeanne Phillips) Soroka, telephone interview with author, 2 April 1994. Robin Vernell Wells, telephone interview with author, 6 April 1994. Viola Smith, interview with author, 17 October 1996.

19 All program quotations are from "Presenting the General Electric Hour of Charm."

20 Hartmann, *The Home Front and Beyond,* 194–95.

21 Robin Vernell Wells, telephone interview with author, 6 April 1994.

22 "Are Girl Musicians Superior?"

23 Robin Vernell Wells, telephone interview with author, 6 April 1994.

24 Phyllis Clendening, telephone interview with author, 13 March 1994.

25 The Spitalny image was apparently not vulnerable to the stigma of the unpatriotic waste of fabric. The acceptability of the Spitalny gowns con-

stitutes one more good argument that the 1943 Zoot Suit Riots, in which white male sailors attacked mostly Mexican American wearers of zoot suits in Los Angeles, were not so much a case of patriotic fervor against excess fabric as they were a case of racist violence.

26 Jean Soroka, telephone interview with author, 2 April 1994.
27 Kellogg, *Ladies Guide in Health and Disease,* 185.
28 Davis, *Women, Race, and Class,* 228–29.
29 Carby, *Reconstructing Womanhood,* 23–25.
30 Allen, *A Horrible Prettiness,* 84–87.
31 Loesser, *Men, Women, and Pianos,* 65, 267–68.
32 Jean Soroka, telephone interview with author, 2 April 1994.
33 Bruun, "The World Loved Spitalny's Hour of Charm."
34 "Are Girl Musicians Superior?" 27.

3. Extracurricular Activities with the Prairie View Co-Eds

1 Heintze, *Private Black Colleges in Texas,* 17–19, 45.
2 Davis, *Women, Race, and Class,* 105.
3 The Freedman's Bureau was a federal office erected after the Civil War and charged with setting up services for newly freed slaves.
4 Roebuck and Murty, *Historically Black Colleges and Universities,* 28; Hill, *The Traditionally Black Institutions of Higher Education,* 11.
5 Hartmann, *The Home Front and Beyond,* 107–15.
6 Heintz, *Private Black Colleges in Texas,* 80.
7 Other choral groups based at black colleges included the Hampton Institute Choir, the Tuskegee Institute Choir, the Morehouse College Quartet (which performed for both Franklin D. Roosevelt and Herbert Hoover), the Wilberforce College Octette (composed of four women and four men), and the Howard University Glee Club (Hare, *Negro Musicians and Their Music,* 55–57, 248–52).
8 For an excellent overview and personal memoir of black dance bands in the 1920s and 1930s, see Morris, "The Wiley Collegians." See also Porter, *There and Back.*
9 Handy, *Black Women in American Bands and Orchestras,* 134–36.
10 "Texas Collegians Entertain Soldiers."
11 This and the following quotations are from Margaret Grigsby M.D., interview with author, 30 October 1997.
12 Hill, *The Traditionally Black Institutions of Higher Education,* 11–12.
13 Hartmann, *The Home Front and Beyond,* 103–15. One report set the ratio of women to men at black colleges in 1944 at five to one (Kittrell, "Current Problems and Programs in the Higher Education of Negro Women," 13–15).
14 Bettye Bradley Kimbrough, telephone interview with author, 21 September 1997.

15 Argie Mae Edwards Medearis, telephone interview with author, 11 November 1997. Margaret Bradshaw, telephone interview with author, 1 December 1997.

16 Bettye Bradley Kimbrough, telephone interview with author, 21 September 1997. Argie Mae Edwards Medearis, telephone interview with author, 11 November 1997.

17 Apollo Theater ad, *New York Age,* 19 September 1942, 10; "Durham Band to Gale"; Gale Agency ad, *Pittsburgh Courier,* 12 December 1942, 21. *Down Beat* attributed Gale's signing of Eddie Durham's All-Stars to the agent's concern about draft boards ("Moe Gale Adds Cocktail Dept.").

18 Yates, "Greatest Aggregation of Girl Stars Have Plenty of Zing When It Comes to Swing."

19 In addition to my own interviews with Clora Bryant on 7 October 1990 and 5 August 1993, I am informed by Bryant's "Trumpetistically Speaking" and by two interviews/oral histories of Bryant conducted by other interviewers: Sally Placksin, 26–28 March 1993; and Steven Isoardi, 29 March, 4, 18 April 1990. Portions of the UCLA oral history project conducted by Isoardi are reprinted in Bryant et al., eds., *Central Avenue Sounds,* 342–68.

20 Clora Bryant, telephone interview with author, 7 October 1990.

21 For more on cultural meanings for both black and white audiences of African American musicians and composers in traditions of European classical music, see Spencer, *The New Negroes and Their Music.*

22 Elizabeth Thomas Smith, telephone interview with author, 25 November 1997.

23 These and subsequent quotations are from Helen Cole, telephone interview with author, 21 November 1997.

24 *Bulletin of Prairie View State Normal and Industrial College* 35, no. 6 (May 1944): 5.

25 Ernest Mae Crafton Miller, telephone interview with author, 16 October 1993, and questionnaire, 20 September 1993.

26 Player, "The Negro College and Women's Education," 364–65.

27 Margaret Bradshaw, telephone interview with author, 1 December 1997.

28 Bettye Bradley Kimbrough, telephone interview with author, 21 September 1997. Margaret Bradshaw, telephone interview with author, 1 December 1997.

29 "Prairie View Girls' Band Scores Triumph."

30 Margaret Bradshaw, telephone interview with author, 1 December 1997.

31 Margaret Grigsby M.D., interview with author, 30 October 1997. Thelma Lewis, telephone interview with author, 12 June 1994.

32 Clora Bryant, telephone interview with author, 7 October 1990.

33 Argie Mae Edwards Medearis, telephone interview with author, 11 November 1997.

34 Elizabeth Thomas Smith, telephone interview with author, 25 November 1997.

35 Margaret Grigsby M.D., interview with author, 30 October 1997. Argie Mae Edwards Medearis, telephone interview with author, 11 November 1997. Clora Bryant, telephone interview with author, 10 January 1998.

36 "Co-Ed Trumpeter."

37 *Bulletin of Prairie View State Normal and Industrial College* 35, no. 6 (May 1944): 5.

38 "Prairie View Co-Eds to Play at Apollo." A photograph of the Co-Eds in the archives at the John B. Coleman Library at Prairie View A&M University has the handwritten caption "Apollo Theater 1943 NY," but my research suggests that the inscriber was mistaken about the year. Most of the women I interviewed felt positive that the first trip to the Apollo was in the summer of 1944, and the newspapers called the 1944 appearance their "debut."

39 Zolotow, "Harlem's Great White Father," quoted in Stowe, *Swing Changes,* 103.

40 Bettye Bradley Kimbrough, telephone interview with author, 21 September 1997.

41 Bettye Bradley Kimbrough, telephone interview with author, 21 September 1997. Margaret Grigsby M.D., interview with author, 30 October 1997. Clora Bryant, interview with Steven Isoardi, 29 March, 4, 18 April 1990.

42 Prairie View State College Co-Ed All Girl Orchestra Press Book.

43 Debate over the effects of World War II on U.S. women's labor generally divide into two camps: the watershed theory, represented by William Chafe (*The American Woman*), who concludes that World War II transformed women's options and laid the groundwork for the second wave feminist movement, and the continuity theory, represented by, among others, Leila Rupp (*Mobilizing Women for War*), Karen Anderson (*Wartime Women* and "Last Hired, First Fired"), Susan Hartmann (*The Home Front and Beyond*), and D'Ann Campbell (*Women at War with America*), who are more skeptical about the degree to which postwar perceptions of women differed from those of the prewar period. But even historians in the continuity camp pause when regarding the situation of African American women. Sherna Gluck (who has argued for less emphasis on the degree of change and more on the process of change and on consciousness as a key site for change) has pointed out that, although Anderson argues that "continuity rather than change characterized women's lives after the war," her evidence on black women's lives "suggests net gains" (*Rosie the Riveter Revisited,* 259, 273–74). Hartmann lists African American women's move from domestic or fieldwork to factory work as one of the "momentous changes" in "individual women's" lives (*The Home Front and Beyond,* 214).

44 Margaret Grigsby M.D., letter to author, 14 November 1997.

45 Clora Bryant, telephone conversation with author, 10 January 1998. Argie Mae Edwards Medearis, telephone interview with author, 11 No-

vember 1997. Bettye Bradley Kimbrough, telephone interview with author, 21 September 1997.

46 Clora Bryant, telephone interview with author, 7 October 1990. Elizabeth Thomas Smith, telephone interview with author, 25 November 1997.

47 McKissack and McKissack, *Red-Tail Angels;* Jakeman, *The Divided Skies.*

48 Bettye Bradley Kimbrough, telephone interview with author, 21 September 1997. Clora Bryant, *Trumpetistically Speaking.* Margaret Grigsby M.D., interview with author, 30 October 1997. Elizabeth Thomas Smith, telephone interview with author, 25 November 1997.

49 Margaret Grigsby M.D., interview with author, 30 October 1997.

50 See Maureen Honey's discussion of heterosexual bonding in home-front and battlefield imagery (in "Remembering Rosie").

51 In 1941, Franklin D. Roosevelt named the Four Freedoms as freedom of speech, freedom of worship, freedom from want, and freedom from fear.

52 Argie Mae Edwards Medearis, telephone interview with author, 11 November 1997. Clora Bryant, telephone interview with author, 5 August 1993.

53 Argie Mae Edwards Medearis, telephone interview with author, 11 November 1997. Bettye Bradley Kimbrough, telephone interview with author, 21 September 1997.

54 Bettye Bradley Kimbrough, telephone interview with author, 21 September 1997.

55 Margaret Grigsby M.D., interview with author, 30 October 1997.

56 Argie Mae Edwards Medearis, telephone interview with author, 11 November 1997.

57 Argie Mae Edwards Medearis, telephone interview with author, 11 November 1997.

58 Cooper, *Amateur Night at the Apollo,* 155.

59 Yates, "I've Been Around," 15 July 1944.

60 Clora Bryant, telephone interview with author, 30 October 1997. Argie Mae Edwards Medearis, telephone interview with author, 11 November 1997.

61 Margaret Grigsby M.D., interview with author, 30 October 1997. Helen Cole, telephone interview with author, 21 November 1997.

62 Apollo Theater ad, *New York Age,* 28 July 1945, 10.

63 Margaret Grigsby M.D., interview with author, 30 October 1997.

64 "For Girls Only — Prairie View Offers Music Scholarships."

65 "Scholarships for Girls."

66 "Co-Eds Seek Girl Musicians," 14 July 1945.

67 "Co-Eds Seek Girl Musicians," 20 April 1946.

68 Helen Cole, telephone interview with author, 21 November 1997.

69 As Tiny Davis and Her Orchestra, the sextet recorded six sides in October 1949: "Race Horse," "How about That Jive," "Draggin' My Heart Around," "I Never Get Tired of Doin' It," "Bug Juice," and "Laura."

70 Stowe (*Swing Changes*) attributes the demise of swing to such things as high overhead, declining demand, the desire of postwar audiences to stay home or partake of passive consumption (movies) rather than go out dancing, and ideological changes reflected in the shift from an interest in the collective (the band) to the individual (the star vocalist).

4. Surveillance and Survival in the Jim Crow South

1 Lester Young's punishment at the hands of military officers included not being allowed to play in the band on the base where he was stationed and being incarcerated for ten months in army detention barracks for possessing drugs. Historian Douglas Henry Daniels ("History, Racism, and Jazz," p. 95) mentions that a white army officer searched Young's possessions and came across a photograph of Young's "white (or white-looking) wife or girlfriend," which also may have contributed to the army's motivation to punish the tenor saxophonist. My definition of *policing* includes such things as the lack of access to medical treatment for Bessie Smith, who died en route to a distant black hospital because nearer facilities were for whites only.

2 For accounts of all these forms of harassment, see Holiday, *Lady Sings the Blues;* Gillespie, *To Be or Not to Bop;* Bernhardt, *I Remember . . . ;* Wells, *The Night People;* and Calloway, *Of Minnie the Moocher and Me,* to list only a few sources.

3 Clora Bryant, "Trumpetistically Speaking." Doris Jarrett Meilleur, telephone interview with author, 22 June 1994.

4 Van Starrex, "Earl Hines," 6.

5 Calloway, *Of Minnie the Moocher and Me,* 140.

6 Wells, *The Night People,* 50.

7 Calloway used the black press to call for a boycott of Shell after the incident and reported the incident (which received sympathetic coverage in *Down Beat* ["Blanche Calloway Jailed and Fined in Mississippi"]) to the NAACP.

8 Most black bands were "relegated to the road upwards to seven months a year with the South being their most important bread basket" (Rowe, "Buses Gone").

9 "Hammond, Delany Named by ODT."

10 "Sweethearts War-Proof Orchestra."

11 Helen Jones Woods, telephone interview with author, 20 February 1995.

12 Roz Cron, telephone interview with author, 13 August 1990.

13 Evelyn McGee Stone, telephone interview with author, 30 November 1996. Willie Mae Wong Scott, telephone interview with author, 3 December 1996. Ernestine May, telephone interview with author, 5 January 1997.

14 Willie Mae Wong Scott, telephone interview with author, 3 December

1996. Evelyn McGee Stone, telephone interview with author, 30 November 1996. Maxine Fields Knepper, telephone interview with author, 17 November 1996.

15 Davis, *Who Is Black?* 63.

16 Davis, "Race and Criminalization."

17 For more on the relation between the fallen woman and the criminalization of women, see Freedman, *Their Sisters' Keepers,* 18–19; and Fletcher, Shaver, and Moon, *Women Prisoners,* 136–44. So long as middle- and upper-class white women stayed within the boundaries of the domestic sphere, they were considered morally superior beings. However, once they transgressed those boundaries — or "fell" — they were considered vile and in need of punishment. Having no pedestal from which to fall, black women were considered lower than the white prostitute (see "A Negro Woman Speaks," in which an African American woman describes her experience of attending a meeting for people concerned with helping fallen women in 1902 and being told to sit in a separate area while the white prostitutes were allowed to sit with the white society women).

18 The Hayes-Tilden deal, which secured the presidency for Rutherford B. Hayes, hinged on the removal of federal troops from Southern states, a move that returned power over the future of the South to former Confederates. State by state, African Americans were stripped of the right to vote, segregated from all forms of close personal contact with whites, and thus systematically relegated to lower citizenship status. In 1883, the Supreme Court declared the Civil Rights Act of 1875 unconstitutional, resting on the argument that discrimination had nothing to do with slavery. The *Plessy v. Fergusson* ruling of 1896 protected white supremacists' right to segregate. The discrimination allowed by this decision was justified by the argument that *separate* could also be *equal.* But, of course, separate did not translate into equal in a system in which former slaveholders and their descendants continued to benefit from the subjugation of African Americans. By 1910, writes James Davis, "restoration of Southern Blacks to an inferior legal status was complete" (*Who Is Black?* 52–60).

19 Ibid., 79.

20 White racial superiority was supported by nineteenth-century scientists, including criminologists, who held "the view that criminals formed a separate biological class that had to be controlled" and that class could be detected by physical appearance (Freedman, *Their Sisters' Keepers,* 111). Born criminals were said to be a type "resembling the Mongolian, or sometimes the Negroid" (Havelock Ellis quoting Cesare Lombroso, cited in Dobash, Dobash, and Gutteridge, *The Imprisonment of Women,* 115). Such claims conveniently bolstered the criminalization, harassment, and incarceration of African Americans.

21 For more on the struggles that predate the 1950s and 1960s civil rights

movement, see Korstad and Lichtenstein, "Opportunities Found and Lost." Korstad and Lichtenstein argue that the 1940s civil rights movement actually addressed labor and economic issues in ways that were not possible in the postwar period. For war-era civil rights struggles over public transportation, see Kelley, *Race Rebels,* 55–75; and Barnes, *Journey from Jim Crow.*

22 Baldwin, *The Fire Next Time,* 135.

23 Charlie Rouse, quoted in Gitler, *Swing to Bop,* 16.

24 Jane Sager, interview with author, 10 June 1994.

25 Davis, *Women, Race, and Class,* 172–201.

26 Davis, *Who Is Black?* 59.

27 Helen Jones Woods, telephone interview with author, 20 February 1995.

28 Violet Wilson, interview with author, 12 June 1994.

29 Roberta Morrison, telephone interview with author, 23 September 1996.

30 Violet Wilson, interview with author, 12 June 1994.

31 Violet Wilson, interview with author, 12 June 1994.

32 David Stowe (*Swing Changes*) argues that, in the 1930s, swing did inspire ideology of racial equality, while Burton Peretti (*The Creation of Jazz*) is more critical of the intentions and desires of the white musicians who played with African Americans (see also each author's review of the other's book). Examples of stories in the black press celebrating mixed bands include Robinson, "Artie Shaw Likely to Have Mixed Band"; and "Mixed Band at Cafe Society Proves a Hit." Another interesting place in which to explore the complexities of integration politics in jazz is musicians' narratives about AFM mergers, which frequently did not result in the end of Jim Crowism in the AFM. See, e.g., the variety of viewpoints and experiences expressed by African American musicians about the merger of Los Angeles locals 767 (black) and 47 (white) in Bryant et al., eds., *Central Avenue Sounds.*

33 "Earl 'Father' Hines and Band to Appear at Apollo This Week." See also Apollo Theater ad, *New York Age,* 18 September 1943, 10.

34 "South Keeps up Ban on Fletcher's Mixed Band."

35 "Lionel Stars White Sax Ace on All Dates."

36 Evelyn McGee Stone, telephone interview with author, 30 November 1996.

37 Willie Mae Wong Scott, telephone interview with author, 3 December 1996. Helen Jones Woods, telephone interview with author, 20 February 1995.

38 Toby Butler, letter to the author, 22 July 1996, and telephone interview with author, 11 May 1996. Original Sweetheart Helen Jones Woods vividly recalled Butler's enthusiasm: "She heard us play in Virginia. And I think she wanted to join us because Toby didn't have such a stable home life. She had learned to play a trumpet, so she kept following us. Every time we'd play there, she'd come to see us, and finally she joined the band" (telephone interview with author, 20 February 1995).

39 Toby Butler, telephone interview with author, 11 May 1996.

40 Helen Jones Woods, telephone interview with author, 20 February 1995.

41 Roz Cron, telephone interview with author, 13 August 1990.

42 Roz Cron, "Jim Who?" 47–50.

43 Maxine Fields Knepper, telephone interview with author, 17 November 1996.

44 I am familiar with Frederick Douglass's response to blackface minstrelsy from Eric Lott's masterful *Love and Theft.*

45 "South Keeps up Ban on Fletcher's Mixed Band."

46 Hampton, *Hamp,* 90.

47 Violet Wilson, interview with author, 12 June 1994.

48 Lott, *Love and Theft,* 26–27.

49 "Sweethearts."

50 Horne, *Lena,* 10.

51 Maxine Fields Knepper, telephone interview with author, 17 November 1996.

52 Doris Jarrett Meilleur, telephone interview with author, 22 June 1994.

53 This and the following quotation are from Ruth Raymer, telephone interview with author, 12 June 1994.

54 Helen Jones Woods, telephone interview with author, 20 February 1995. Evelyn McGee Stone, telephone interview with author, 30 November 1996.

55 Roz Cron, telephone interview with author, 13 August 1990.

56 Maxine Fields Knepper, telephone interview with author, 17 November 1996.

57 Roberta Morrison, telephone interview with author, 23 September 1996.

58 Ernestine May, telephone interview with author, 5 January 1997.

59 Ernestine May, telephone interview with author, 5 January 1997.

60 See Shapiro, *White Violence and Black Response,* 344–48.

61 See, e.g., Werner, *Playing the Changes,* 212–40; as well as the indispensable James Baldwin text that Werner discusses, *The Fire Next Time.*

62 Rivera, "Sweethearts Defy Threats."

5. Internationalism and the Sweethearts of Rhythm

1 Women's music, also known as *womyn's music* or *women-identified music,* emerged in the United States in the early 1970s and has been defined as "music that had as its self-conscious textual content the expression of women's oppression by men, the celebration of the beauty of women in their struggle to overcome this oppression, and the beauty of women loving women in a sexual relationship" (Petersen, "Women-Identified Music in the United States," 206).

2 Evelyn McGee Stone, telephone interview with author, 30 November 1996. Toby Butler, telephone interview with author, 11 May 1996.

3 I am grateful to jazz film archivist Mark Cantor for providing the following information on the Sweethearts' Soundies. In 1946 and 1947, the Sweethearts made three ten-minute shorts for Associated Artists Productions and/or William Alexander Productions: *The International Sweethearts of Rhythm, featuring Anna Mae Winburn, How 'Bout That Jive,* and *Harlem Jam Session*. All three films were produced by William Alexander, an African American entrepreneur and founder of Associated Producers of Negro Motion Pictures. Each short included three musical performances by the band. Soundies Corporation of America acquired the first of the three shorts and released the musical numbers as three Soundies: "Jump Children" (August 26, 1946), "That Man of Mine" (September 23, 1946), and "She's Crazy with the Heat" (November 3, 1946). The song "Jump Children," credited to Maurice King and the International Sweethearts of Rhythm, is a modified version of an earlier song, "Do You Wanna Jump, Children?" by Al Donohue, Jimmy Van Heusen, Willie Bryant, and Victor Selsman. The "Jump Children" Soundie, on which Anna Mae Winburn is the featured vocalist, may be seen on the Reitz's video *Jazz Women*. The Sweethearts also recorded a version featuring Ernestine "Tiny" Davis singing the vocal, which may be heard on *International Sweethearts of Rhythm* and *Forty Years of Women in Jazz*.

4 Schiller and Weiss, *International Sweethearts of Rhythm*.

5 Considered a visual rather than auditory attraction, all-girl bands were rarely recorded, but they were sometimes featured on Soundies. While Soundies are highly mediated sources of information on all-girl bands, they can at least let us hear and see such bands and speculate on what live performances may have been like. Researchers need to be aware that some bands so recorded are pickup bands. Still, Soundies provide information on lucrative representations of women musicians and on one type of employment available to women musicians between 1940 and 1947.

6 According to jazz film archivist Mark Cantor, the Sweethearts' Soundies were never included in the regular weekly reels distributed to Panoram operators; they were instead special-order items from the "M" series of extra Negro subjects. I am assuming that, because the Sweethearts were well known among black audiences and virtually unknown among white audiences, black establishments were more likely to order these films.

7 Rich, *Blood, Bread, and Poetry*, 217.

8 Carby, "In Body and Spirit," 178.

9 While in her "Whiteness as Property" critical race theorist Cheryl Harris refers to black-to-white passing, it seems to me that white-to-black passing in black all-girl bands also threatened to "undermine property interest in whiteness" itself. When the police patrolled the color line, they protected whiteness as a kind of property that brought its owners privilege in a segregated society.

10 Lillian Carter Wilson, telephone interview with author, 24 August 1991.

11 Gilroy, *"There Ain't No Black in the Union Jack."*

12 Schiller and Weiss, *International Sweethearts of Rhythm.*

13 I am grateful to Andrea Weiss for her candid remarks about the controversy surrounding the making and reception of the documentary *Tiny and Ruby.* According to Weiss, many Sweethearts alumnae objected to the making of the film. In addition, despite the filmmakers' sensitivity in not using terms to describe the relationship that Tiny and Ruby did not themselves use (they did not use the word *lesbian,* e.g.) and in letting Tiny and Ruby define their own relationship on the screen, enthusiastic critics nevertheless hailed the documentary as a lesbian film. While the film was overwhelmingly well received by critics and audiences, the women in the film were not always happy with the terms of reception.

14 Handy, *The International Sweethearts of Rhythm,* 27.

15 Pipik, "Woman-Identified Music," 89.

16 *Women in Jazz: All-Woman Groups* and *Women in Jazz: Swingtime to Modern.* Judging from the radio stations where I have worked, these usually got filed among the novelty anthologies, such as compilations of songs about marijuana.

17 Armstrong, "The Great White Folk Music Myth," 22.

18 Gossett, "Jazzwomen," 68.

19 Combahee River Collective, "The Combahee River Collective Statement," 281. I am grateful to Maylei Blackwell for pointing out that what is often seen as a 1980s intervention by women of color was actually in full swing in the 1970s. Although my citation source is an anthology published in 1983, "The Combahee River Collective Statement" was written in 1977. The collective itself was founded in 1974, but even this was, by no means, the first black feminist organization. As demonstrated by Springer, Harris, and Roth, black feminist organizations began in the 1960s, the same time as white feminist organizations, but historians of the second wave have tended to mark the white organizations (which black feminists did not necessarily join) as "authentic," with black feminists being seen either as absent or as "intervening" in the 1980s.

20 Reagon, "Coalition Politics," 360.

21 Feminist art historian Whitney Chadwick characterizes early second wave feminist investigations of women's creativity as dominated by a "belief in a female nature or feminine essence, which could be revealed by stripping away layers of patriarchal culture and conditioning" (*Women, Art, and Society,* 9–10). In women's music discourse, such assumptions thrived in theories about women's collective musical unconscious and the possibility of distinctly female rhythms, modes (the mixolydian mode was supposedly "woman identified" since it was invented by Sappho), and compositional forms (because women are "naturally cyclical beings," they write in circular forms) (see Petersen, "Women-Identified Music in the United States," 205; and Kay Gardner, quoted in Scovill, "Women's Music," 158).

22 Dahl, *Stormy Weather,* 53.

23 Stone, "Jamming with the Gals."

24 Evelyn McGee Stone, telephone interview with author, 30 November 1996.

25 Handy, *The International Sweethearts of Rhythm,* 199–200.

26 The slogan is taken from Morgan, *Sisterhood Is Global.*

27 "Florida Dance Lovers Swing with 'Sweethearts.' " "Sweethearts of Rhythm."

28 "This Girl Band Is Much Too Much with Swing and Jitter."

29 Willie Mae Wong Scott, telephone interview with author, 3 December 1996.

30 "Dorothy Donegan and Those Sweethearts at Regal Next."

31 "Those 'Sweethearts of Rhythm' All-Nations."

32 "Sweethearts of Rhythm Get Welcome in Dallas."

33 Lipsitz, *Dangerous Crossroads,* 31.

34 Penny Von Eschen (*Race against Empire*) notes that the "Double V" campaign may well have been called "Triple V," so centrally did decolonization struggles around the world figure in the political concerns of African Americans in the war years (see also Plummer, *Rising Wind*). For more on African American internationalism and pan-Africanism before and during the 1940s, see the essays in Lemelle and Kelley, eds., *Imagining Home;* the many volumes that C. L. R. James devoted to the topic, especially "*My Friends*"; and the essays in Stanton, ed., *Fighting Racism in World War II.*

35 A powerful example of how the major black newspapers' concerns regarding imperialism and racism supported differently figured international alliances than the mainstream (white) U.S. newspapers is the coverage of the events surrounding the imprisonment by the British of Gandhi and other members of the All-India Congress on 9 August 1942. While the mainstream U.S. press sympathized with Britain's refusal to grant India independence during the war crisis, the *Pittsburgh Courier* interpreted the situation through a lens of anti-imperialism and black and brown race solidarity (see, e.g., "Gandhi Tells Churchill"). While mainstream British and U.S. news reports portrayed Gandhi as an unrealistically pacifistic wild card who could, if unchecked, intentionally or accidentally play into the hands of the Japanese, the black press was more sympathetic, devoting a great deal of space to African American leaders who favored support of the "Quit India" campaign. A. Philip Randolph, president of the March on Washington Movement, argued that "Negro people of America, the West Indies and Africa should support this grim, determined and courageous battle for freedom of the Indian people under the gallant, wise and dauntless leadership of Mohandas K. Ghandi [*sic*] for they constitute one of the great oppressed and exploited sections of the darker races of the world" ("Negroes Should Back India Says Randolph"). A readers poll in the *Pittsburgh Courier* showed that 87.8 per-

cent of a sample of ten thousand African Americans — consisting equally of women and men — supported India's fight for national independence ("India Justified in Freedom Fight, Readers Declare").

36 Madam Chiang Kai-shek made front-page news in the black press when she assured 13 million black Americans that her opposition to segregation was so great that she had no "special" message for them because, "when I speak to America, I feel that the Negroes are a vital segment of the country, not to be differentiated from any other America" (Brooks, "Mme. Chiang Sees Race Vital in U.S. Democracy"). In 1945, Vijaya Lakshmi Pandit, Jawaharlal Nehru's sister and a formerly incarcerated All-India National Congress leader herself, refused to speak at Baltimore's Lyric Theater unless African Americans were allowed to attend, explaining, "We Indians are opposed to all forms of oppression. . . . I feel very close to the Negroes in America; in fact I feel like one of them, and I am certainly in sympathy with their struggle for full citizenship rights" ("Madame Pandit Wins over Maryland Theater Barrier").

37 On the Jamaican farmworkers, see McAlpin, "U.S. Jails 600 Jamaicans in Florida." On the Mexican consul's protest, see "Mexican Consul Raps Bias as Citizenship Damper." On the Chinese ambassador's protest, see "Mississippi Is Now Jim Crowing Chinese."

38 "An Example for 'Democratic' America to Follow."

39 Helen Jones Woods, telephone interview with author, 20 February 1995.

40 Willie Mae Wong Scott, telephone interview with author, 3 December 1996.

41 Evelyn McGee Stone, telephone interview with author, 30 November 1996.

42 Helen Jones Woods, telephone interview with author, 20 February 1995.

43 Frann Gaddison, telephone interview with author, 7 July 1994.

44 "Sweethearts of Rhythm"; "Sweethearts of Rhythm Clicks in South and West."

45 Albertson, *Bessie,* 27.

46 Handy, *The International Sweethearts of Rhythm.*

47 Harrison, *Piney Woods School,* 116.

48 Willie Mae Wong Scott, telephone interview with author, 3 December 1996.

49 Loewen, *The Mississippi Chinese;* Davis, *Who Is Black?* 114–16.

50 Willie Mae Wong Scott, telephone interview with author, 3 December 1996.

51 Evelyn McGee Stone, telephone interview with author, 30 November 1996.

52 God had delivered the children of Israel from slavery, and he would liberate black people, too, because they were his children. James Cone writes that the term *God's children* affirmed slaves' "somebodiness" (*The Spirituals and the Blues,* 34–35). John Lovell notes additional meanings, including Africans' belief in themselves as children of the

gods and the importance of kinship terminology in forming strong communities under slavery (*Black Song,* 31, 274–81).

53 Rust, *Jazz Records,* vols. 1–2. Within a three-month period in 1938, "Do You Wanna Jump, Children" was recorded by bands led by Erskine Hawkins, Cab Calloway, Charlie Barnet, Count Basie, and Gene Krupa. The bridge and title from this novelty tune became the basis for the Sweethearts' version.

54 Major, *Juba to Jive,* 265.

6. The Darlings of Rhythm:
On the Road and Ready to Run

1 Frann Gaddison, telephone interview with author, 7–8 July 1994.

2 Frann Gaddison, telephone interview with author, 7–8 July 1994.

3 Davis, *Blues Legacies and Black Feminism,* 102.

4 Wells, *The Night People,* 68. Many jazz musicians have described this distinction. See bassist John Brown on the liability of tight arrangements: "Basie's was a looser type of thing, and Lunceford's swing wasn't as relaxed because the arrangements were more complicated" (Dance, *The World of Swing,* 23). Even Duke Ellington, whose writing was a primary factor in his orchestra's sound, instructed his soloists to "keep some dirt in there, somewhere" (O'Meally, "Improvisation," 43).

5 Sarah McLawler, telephone interview with author, 12 July 1994.

6 Doc Cheatham, quoted in Dance, *The World of Swing,* 307–9.

7 Clora Bryant, telephone interview with author, 7 October 1990.

8 The Sweethearts' humble background and ultimate fame was often framed in the black press as a rags-to-riches narrative (see "Why Girl Bands Don't Click"). This framework is somewhat misleading, for the original Sweethearts were grossly exploited.

9 Thelma Lewis, telephone interview with author, 26 March 1998.

10 I thank Kyra Gaunt for encouraging me to think about the effects of colorism on second wave consumption of the Sweethearts.

11 Although the Sweethearts' shorts were produced by William Alexander, an African American, a bias for light-skinned black women existed in black entertainment circuits. Colorism may certainly have influenced the white-owned Soundies Corporation of America to acquire Alexander's Sweethearts footage. I am grateful to Mark Cantor for information regarding the Sweethearts' Soundies.

12 Most of the women who played with the Darlings were older than the women who played with the Sweethearts, so fewer of them remain alive today.

13 Portions of Brown's questionnaire are reprinted in Handy, *The International Sweethearts of Rhythm,* 191.

14 Ibid.

15 Ibid.

16 Ad, "Merry Xmas and Happy New Year, Clarence Love and His Orchestra," *Down Beat,* 15 December 1941, 22.

17 McCarthy, *Big Band Jazz,* 41–47.

18 Clarence Love, interview with Nathan Pearson and Howard Litwak, 13 April 1977.

19 Press clipping, 22 January 1998, source unknown.

20 Rowe, "Billy Rowe's Note Book," 29 January 1944.

21 "Darlings of Rhythm Newest 'Find.' "

22 "Swing's Newest Rave Sensations Capture Nation."

23 "All-Girl Crew Set to Reopen Grand Terrace."

24 "Darlings Build Business."

25 I am grateful to Mark Miller and Ron Sweetman for alerting me to Howard Rye's "What the Papers Said" (a study of the "Traveling Musicians" listings in local AFM reports in *International Musician*), from which most of the information on 1930s personnel in this chapter is drawn. I have also studied the listings from the 1940s issues of *International Musician* in my attempts to track the movement of personnel between the Darlings of Rhythm, Eddie Durham's All-Star Girl Orchestra, and the International Sweethearts of Rhythm.

26 "Margaret Backstrom Joins Darlings' Reed Section."

27 "Who's Best Sax — Backstrom or Vi?"

28 Violet Wilson, interview with author, 12 June 1994.

29 Thelma Lewis, telephone conversation with author, 26 March 1998.

30 Sarah McLawler, telephone interview with author, 12 July 1994. Lillian Carter Wilson, telephone interview with author, 24 August 1991.

31 Frann Gaddison, telephone interview with author, 7–8 July 1994.

32 Thelma Lewis, telephone interview with author, 12 June 1994.

33 Violet Wilson, interview with author, 12 June 1994.

34 "Swing's Newest Rave Sensations Capture Nation."

35 "All-Girl Crew Set to Reopen Grand Terrace." "Darlings of Rhythm Score."

36 "Helen Taborn Scores."

37 Driggs quoted in Rye, "What the Papers Said," 176. Handy, *Black Women in American Bands and Orchestras,* 45.

38 Fox's firing of Holiday is described in most Holiday biographies (Holiday, *Lady Sings the Blues,* 63; Chilton, *Billie's Blues,* 35–37; Nicholson, *Billie Holiday,* 76). Interestingly, although the newspapers reviewed her Grand Terrace return and appearance with the Darlings in 1944, I have yet to find a Holiday biography that mentions the all-girl band. Two posters advertising the event are reprinted, however, in Vail, *Lady Day's Diary,* 71–72.

39 "Grand Terrace, Chicago, Preps Colored Show."

40 Handy, *The International Sweethearts of Rhythm,* 163.

41 Evelyn McGee Stone, telephone interview with author, 30 November 1996.

42 Nicholson, *Billie Holiday,* 134–35. Holiday's Met appearance predates Marian Anderson's 1955 appearance by over a decade. Anderson, who is often credited with being the first black person to sing at the Met, was indeed the first African American to sing a role with the Metropolitan Opera Company (Spencer, *The New Negroes and Their Music,* 105).

43 "Darlings Score for Camp Hill."

44 Frann Gaddison, telephone interview with author, 7–8 July 1994.

45 I am grateful to Angela Davis for sharing insights about Billie Holiday's transformative contributions that inform how I am reading this clash with the Darlings.

46 Jones, *Talking Jazz,* 249.

47 Lester Young, interview with Chris Albertson, 1958.

48 Chilton, *Billie's Blues,* 42. Sexual overtones abound in labored textual explanations of what Stuart Nicholson called Holiday and Young's "deep, platonic love affair" (Nicholson, *Billie Holiday,* 51). The tendency in the jazz literature either to present Young as a feminine man or to present the Holiday/Young collaboration/friendship as sexually over-determined warrants further scholarly jazz/race/gender analysis. James Lincoln Collier refers to their musical collaboration as a "marriage" and includes Young in a list of Holiday's lovers: "She had had her affairs in the past, one with Basie's guitarist, Freddie Greene; another with sometimes accompanist Bobby Henderson. And she had had some sort of platonic friendship with Lester Young" (Collier, *The Making of Jazz,* 309).

49 Clora Bryant told interviewer Steve Isoardi that her "main purpose" in dressing in irrefutably feminine clothes was to avoid the stigma of lesbianism, the assumption being that, if a woman played trumpet, she "had to be a man" (Bryant et al., eds., *Central Avenue Sounds,* 356).

50 This story appears in most biographical material on Lester Young. Young told it to François Postif in a 1959 interview (in Porter, ed., *The Lester Young Reader,* 191).

51 Whiteman and McBride, *Jazz,* 210.

52 Antrim, ed., *Secrets of Dance Band Success,* 61.

53 Susan Cook ("Billie Holiday and the Performance of Race and Gender") has spoken eloquently on this subject.

54 Davis, *Blues Legacies and Black Feminism,* 165.

55 *Trav'lin' Light,* Paul Whiteman and His Orchestra, with Billie Holiday, was recorded for Capital Records on 12 June 1943 (CAP-30-A).

56 Frann Gaddison, telephone interview with author, 7–8 July 1994.

57 " 'Darlings of Rhythm' Hit Peak at Terrace."

58 Monroe, "Swinging the News," 22 July 1944.

59 "Darlings of Rhythm Take to Road."

60 "Lady with a Horn."

61 "Darlings Feature Pat Lamarr, Helen Taborn."
62 "Darlings of Rhythm Set for Twelve Mo Ball."
63 Monroe, "Swinging the News," 14 April 1945.
64 "B-29 Drops 'Darlings' in Los Angeles."
65 " 'Darlings of Rhythm' to Play Coast's Plantation."
66 "All Girls' Band Scores."
67 Violet Wilson, interview with author, 12 June 1994.
68 Price, "Fifty Years of Memories."
69 Violet Wilson, interview with author, 12 June 1994.
70 Violet Wilson, interview with author, 12 June 1994.
71 Violet Wilson, interview with author, 12 June 1994.
72 Violet Wilson, interview with author, 12 June 1994.
73 "Out of Tune!"
74 "Jim Crow Stuff Still Spreading!" See also "Jail Girl Musician."
75 "Out of Tune!"
76 Violet Wilson, interview with author, 12 June 1994.
77 Violet Wilson, interview with author, 12 June 1994.
78 Violet Wilson, interview with author, 12 June 1994.
79 This precise quote appeared in both "Jail Girl Musician" and "Jim Crow Stuff Still Spreading!" A paraphrase appeared in "Out of Tune!"
80 "Negro and White Band Folds."

7. Female Big Bands, Male Mass Audiences:
Gendered Performances in a Theater of War

1 Carson, *Home away from Home,* 112.
2 Marjorie Kiewitt, telephone interview with author, 1 April 1997.
3 Excerpted from Rutherford, "Our Cook's Tour."
4 Andrews and Gilbert, *Over Here, over There,* 230.
5 Laura Bohle Sias, telephone interview with author, 2 July 1994.
6 It would be incorrect to assume that USO performances were segregated simply because there was no precedent for doing things differently. Although separate white and black units of the WPA Federal Theater Project (FTP) existed in the mid-1930s, this federally supported organization mandated that there would be no segregated seating in any FTP theater and that FTP acting companies would not have to endure segregated travel accommodations (Haskins, *Black Theater in America,* 92).
7 Potter, Miles, and Rosenblum, *Liberators,* 107.
8 Dick Campbell, interview with Jean Hudson, 5 May 1982.
9 The posters for "Dixie Jubilee" and "Harlem on Parade," e.g., depict dolls and actors in blackface (Camp Shows Publicity Records 8MWEZ, box 29.044, folder 11, Billy Rose Theater Collection, New York Public Library for the Performing Arts, Lincoln Center).
10 For a useful application of Antonio Gramsci's notion of the "national-

popular" in popular music studies, see Grossberg, *We Gotta Get out of This Place,* 255–56.

11 Rowe, "Billy Rowe's Note Book," 21 July 1945. See also Southern, *The Music of Black Americans,* 458–61; Stowe, *Swing Changes,* 156–57.

12 On the Double Victory campaign and the black press, see Senna, *The Black Press and the Struggle for Civil Rights,* 118–24. A. Philip Randolph's proposed March on Washington was canceled after the threat of such an enormous protest secured Roosevelt's signature on Executive Order 8802 (25 June 1941), which aimed to curtail discrimination in the defense industries. Because that order fell short in so many ways — including its failure to address integration of the armed forces (a central demand of Randolph and his marchers) — the March on Washington Movement remained vital (see Randolph, "Why Should We March?" 418–21).

13 "Chicago Women Afraid to Comment on Conscription."

14 Cooper, "Woman Sheds Bitter Sidelight on U.S. and War."

15 Goss, "A Negro Mother Looks at War."

16 See, e.g., "36,000 Race Men Face Draft as FDR signs Bill."

17 Although Truman's 1948 Executive Order 9981 called for "equality of treatment and opportunity" for all members of the armed forces "without regard to race, color, religion, or national origin," only a few U.S. troops were integrated during the Korean War. After *Brown v. Board of Education* (1954), it became more difficult to argue that separate was equal. And, in 1963, the Kennedy administration issued a directive forbidding the segregation of military personnel. Blacks were at long last free to fight and die alongside whites — an ironic victory. (For more detail on the struggle to integrate the armed forces, see Potter, Miles, and Rosenblum, *Liberators,* 273–75; Nalty, *Strength for the Fight;* and Dalfiume, *Desegregation of the U.S. Armed Forces.*)

18 Not all African Americans supported the Double Victory campaign. Some black soldiers felt that it set out "to buy first-class citizenship with the blood of the Negro soldier" (Nelson Peery, quoted in Muwakkil, "Patriotism and Prejudice," 17). For another perspective that explores the government's perception of Double Victory as a threat to national security, see Washburn, *A Question of Sedition.*

19 "Snub Moseley's Crew Is First Sepia Ork to Go Overseas."

20 "USO Troupe Thrills Doughboys in Persia."

21 Duckett, "Assignment in New York."

22 Southern, *The Music of Black Americans,* 458–61; Stowe, *Swing Changes,* 156–57; Helen Jones Woods, telephone interview with author, 20 February 1995; " 'Sweethearts' Get Groovy in Paris."

23 Poster depicted in liner notes to Reitz's video *The International Sweethearts of Rhythm.*

24 Willie Mae Wong Scott, telephone interview with author, 3 December 1996.

25 Evelyn McGee Stone, telephone interview with author, 30 November 1996.

26 Adler, "Thanks for the Memories."

27 In the words of Clayton Hamilton, they had "anathematized every theatrical exhibition of normal human levity as mechanization of the devil" (" 'Keep 'Em Laughing' ").

28 Hamilton, outline for " 'Keep 'Em Laughing.' "

29 Ely, *Stars and Stripes.*

30 See Anderson, *Imagined Communities,* 141–45.

31 Westbrook, " 'I Want a Girl . . . ,' " 588.

32 Laura Bohle Sias, telephone interview with author, 2 July 1994.

33 D'Emilio and Freedman, *Intimate Matters,* 274.

34 "Army Bars Mixed Marriages, Sanctions Illegitimate Babies!"

35 Potter, Miles, and Rosenblum, *Liberators,* 257–61.

36 Robinson, "Post-War Europe and the Negro Entertainer."

37 This theory is not without precedent. Although WAC leaders fought the stereotype of camp followers throughout the war, WACs were often perceived by the army as a means for controlling men's sexuality. According to Leisa Meyer (*Creating GI Jane,* 48), stationing African American WACs near black soldiers was the army's idea of how to uphold prohibitions on interracial relationships between black soldiers and white civilian women. Black WACs were often caught in the cross fire between army plans to provide black female companionship for black soldiers and the counterstrategies of WAC leaders to assert to the army and the general public that servicewomen of all races were serious patriots, not members of the comfort industry. Doris Stevens Richardson recalls that WAC regulations controlled the social lives of black servicewomen so stringently at Fort Benning, Ga., that she had to obtain a special pass to date her own husband (Doris Stevens Richardson, [interviewer unknown,] 6–10 October 1988).

38 "*Courier* 'Double V' Girl of the Week."

39 "Letters to the Editor," *Music Dial,* December–January 1944–45, 4.

40 This feature can be found in many issues of *Downbeat* from the mid-1940s. Kay Starr's "Kiss Autograph" appeared in *Downbeat,* 1 August 1944, 2.

41 Rowe, "Billy Rowe's Note Book," 2 December 1944.

42 Westbrook, "I Want a Girl . . . ," 605. It is also interesting to note that, like Harry James, Ozzie Nelson was a popular white bandleader during the war and that Ozzie and Harriet Hilliard, his wife and vocalist, were the darlings of *Downbeat* before becoming radio and television symbols of white suburban postwar domesticity ("Music and Marriage Will Mix").

43 A typical example of Horne's celebration in the black press is this excerpt from George Brown's "Lena Defies Washington, D.C. 'Jim Crow' Policy": "Miss Lena Horne . . . requested that she be booked into the Howard theater in Washington in direct defiance of the Capital City's segregation

policy. She would not play one of the downtown houses because she knew that her people would be barred from seeing her."

44 Horne, *Lena,* 132–35.

45 "Battery 600 Selects Hazel Scott as Pin-Up."

46 Stowe, *Swing Changes,* 149.

47 Joy Cayler, telephone interview with author, 28 May 1995.

48 Stowe, *Swing Changes,* 156.

49 Dower, *War without Mercy,* 4–5.

50 Shaw writes explicitly of this function of musical style in his identity: "It was a zigzag path indeed, the various interacting processes that brought about the curious metamorphosis of a shy, introspective little Jewish kid named Arthur Arshawsky into a sort of weird, jazz-band-leading, clarinet-tooting, jitterbug-surrounded Symbol of American Youth during an entertainment era characterized by the term 'Swing' " (Shaw, *The Trouble with Cinderella,* 37). While Goodman's autobiography (*The Kingdom of Swing*) is not crafted as a self-conscious analysis of identity, it is similarly constructed as a journey from ethnic to mainstream whiteness.

51 Stowe, *Swing Changes,* 157.

52 Recollection of E. G. McConnell as reported in Kindall, "Black Vets Recall Battle of the Bulge."

53 Schuller, *The Swing Era,* 390–91.

54 Baraka, *Black Music,* 15–16.

55 Wynn, *The Afro-American and the Second World War,* 88–89.

56 Musicians' narratives indicate that, while these musical descriptions referred to cultural traditions, they could also be applied cross-culturally to refer to style. For example, Andy Kirk, leader of the famous African American band the Twelve Clouds of Joy, described the stylistic differences between his group and Jack Teagarden's white band as, "We played more white than Jack's band" (as told to Amy Lee in *Twenty Years on Wheels,* 57).

57 Ruth Raymer, telephone interview with author, 12 June 1994.

58 Schiller and Weiss, *International Sweethearts of Rhythm.*

59 For a discussion of the constructed category *classical music,* see Walser, *Running with the Devil,* 60. See also Levine, *Highbrow/Lowbrow.*

60 I am loosely paraphrasing Bhabha, *The Location of Culture,* 147.

61 Ogren, *The Jazz Revolution,* 156.

62 For more on this white jazz subculture, see Peretti, *The Creation of Jazz;* and Meltzer, *Reading Jazz.*

63 Schuller, *The Swing Era,* 148. For more on the obstacles facing African Americans who produced music that incorporated the theories and techniques of European classical music, see Spencer, *The New Negroes and Their Music.*

64 Sharon Rogers Wright, letter to author, 12 August 1990.

65 On boosting morale, see Hartmann, *The Home Front and Beyond,* 198–99.

66 Delie Hahn, cited in Terkel, *"The Good War,"* 114.

67 Sharon Rogers Wright, letter to author, 12 August 1990.

68 Peggy Gilbert, interview with author, 22, 23 September 1998.

69 Andrews and Gilbert, *Over Here, over There,* 240.

70 Quotes and information from Doris Kahl Nilo are cited from Florice Whyte Kovan's video *Virgil Whyte's All-Girl Bands,* vol. 4.

71 Dotty Cygan Wilmeth, conversation with author, 11 April 1999.

72 Joy Cayler, telephone interview with author, 28 May 1995.

73 Evelyn McGee Stone, telephone interview with author, 30 November 1996.

74 Willie Mae Wong Scott, telephone interview with author, 3 December 1996.

75 Roz Cron, letter to author, 31 January 1995.

76 Willie Mae Wong Scott, telephone interview with author, 3 December 1996.

77 Jones, *Liberating Voices,* 91.

78 Schuller, *The Swing Era,* 391. The "Salt Peanuts" riff is an example of what Paul Gilroy calls the "premium placed on history" in jazz and other black musical forms, in which "the past is literally audible in the present" (*"There Ain't No Black in the Union Jack,"* 209). See also George Lewis's comparison of what he calls the *Afrological* and *Eurological* aesthetics of improvised music. Although he compares African American musical traditions with European traditions that distance themselves from jazz, the distinctions that he highlights may also be applied to jazz and swing approaches associated with black and white styles. He notes, e.g., that, while the Eurological approach to improvisation values "the elimination of memory and history from music," the Afrological approach "cannot countenance the erasure of history" and includes the "background, history, and culture of one's music" as part of the artist's discipline ("Improvised Music after 1950," 109).

79 Krupnick, "18-Gal Combo Jumpin' for 7th Army Hepcats."

80 "Robeson in Mixed Unit for Overseas Tour."

81 D. Antoinette Handy (telephone conversation with author, 6 February 1997) confirms that Johnny Mae Rice also recalled performing in WAC officers' uniforms.

82 I am grateful to Catherine Parsons Smith for this suggestion, offered in response to my "Female Big Bands, Mass Male Audiences."

83 Alberta Hunter, interview with Chris Albertson, 17 December 1976.

84 Meyer, "Creating GI Jane," 581.

85 Leisa Meyer writes that it was "no coincidence that the whispering campaign against the women's corps gained momentum at the precise moment that the WAAC was trading its marginal status for full membership in the Army" (*Creating GI Jane,* 38). (The word *Auxiliary* was struck as WAAC became WAC in 1943.)

86 Mattie Treadwell argues that USO and canteen inhospitality toward servicewomen stemmed from confusion over which rules should apply to

women in uniform: rules that applied to the hostesses or rules that applied to servicemen. Protocol broke down when servicewomen "[went] outdoors with men between dances, which hostesses could not do" (*The Women's Army Corps,* 198). For more on discrimination against servicewomen at the Hollywood Canteen, see Soderbergh, *Women Marines,* 79–80.

87 Treadwell, *The Women's Army Corps,* 554.

88 Laura Bohle Sias, telephone interview with author, 2 July 1994. On a different note, Virgil Whyte's all-girl band was graciously received by the Marine Corps Women's Reserve Band at Camp LeJeune, N.C., an event that was recalled by women musicians of both bands at the "Women of World War II Conference" organized by Florice Whyte Kovan and sponsored by the Naval Historical Center, Public and Private Research, and the Johnson Foundation, 18 October 1991.

89 The sentencing and eventual acquittal of the four court-martialed WACs was a major story in the *Pittsburgh Courier* in March–April 1945. The 6888th is the subject of Brenda Moore's *To Serve My Country, to Serve My Race.* Examples of WAC beatings in the South may also be found there (see p. 77).

90 Gurthalee Clark, interview with Eunice M. Wright, 12 May 1988.

91 A transcript of Clementine McConico Skinner's oral history can be found in Sims-Wood, "We Served America Too!" 216–17.

92 For accounts of the black WAC band, see Moore, *To Serve My Country, to Serve My Race,* 75–76; Putney, *When the Nation Was in Need,* 56–60; Sims-Wood, "We Served America Too!" 194–238; and Meyer, *Creating GI Jane,* 96.

93 Helen Jones Woods, telephone interview with author, 20 February 1995.

94 Marjorie Kiewitt, telephone interview with author, 1 April 1997.

95 Ibid.

8. Battles of a "Sophisticated Lady": Ada Leonard and the USO

1 Patrick Devaney, letter to author, 5 September 1990.

2 The most famous stage door canteen was in New York, but canteens where servicepeople could drop in to dance and be entertained could be found throughout the country. The canteen in *Two Girls and a Sailor,* however, is a privately run center that for the first half of the movie is located in the patriotic sisters' apartment.

3 Hanifin, "A Night at the Moulin Rouge Is Staged at Curran Theater."

4 " 'Night at Moulin Rouge' Is Glittering Fantasy."

5 Throughout this chapter, quotations from Ada Leonard Bernstein are taken from her 5 July 1994 telephone interview with the author.

6 "Strip-Tease Ada Leonard Fronts Ace Fem Outfit."

7 Throughout this chapter, quotations from Jane Sager are taken from ei-

ther her 10 June 1994 interview with, her 29 January 1994 letter to, or 11 March 1995 telephone conversation with the author.

8 Ad, *Chicago Tribune,* 19 December 1940, 24.

9 Ad, *Chicago Tribune,* 20 December 1940, 27.

10 "Vaudeville."

11 Ad, *Chicago Tribune,* 15 May 1941, 20.

12 "State-Lake, Chi."

13 Cron, "My Road to Zanzibar," 46.

14 *Down Beat,* 1 August 1941, 1, photo caption.

15 *Down Beat,* 15 April 1940, caption to cover photo.

16 *Down Beat,* 1 May 1940, 2.

17 "Ina Ray Knocks out a Biscuit."

18 "Judy Ellington Fronting New All-Girl Band."

19 *Defense Morale,* 10.

20 *Defense Recreation Conference,* 25.

21 "Ada Leonard Ork Will Tour Camps." At the end of this tour, Leonard's USO contract was extended ten more weeks.

22 "Season's Greetings."

23 Alpert was a trumpet student of Sager's. The album was a parody of the Tijuana Brass's *Whipped Cream and Other Delights,* entitled *Sour Cream and Other Delights.*

24 Andrews and Gilbert, *Over Here, over There,* 5.

25 Hine, "Gypsy Gyps Us."

26 "Ada Leonard Band Clicks in Army Camps."

27 Fossum, "Girls Shouldn't Play Too Much Jazz, Says Ada."

28 "Ada Leonard (Reviewed at Loew's State, New York)."

29 Mary Demond, interview with author, 27 July 1996.

30 Kissel, "Ada Leonard, Variety Makes Good Stage Show at Palace."

31 Betty Rosner, questionnaire, October 1992, and letter to author, 29 December 1994.

32 Ethel C. Kirkpatrick Drehouse, questionnaire, 30 November 1992.

33 "Take 'Em off, Take, Etc.!"

34 "Ada Leonard (Reviewed at Loew's State, New York)."

35 Cron, "My Road to Zanzibar," 45–46.

36 Betty Kidwell Meriedeth, telephone conversation with author, 6 July 1997.

37 Shirley left the band to play with Charlie Barnet's famous band, later returning to Leonard's after having been, in Betty Rosner's words, "completely demoralized" (letter to author, 29 December 1994). According to Leonard, whenever anyone in Barnet's brass section played a wrong note, the entire band would turn — onstage — and glare at Shirley, making the audience think that *she* was the weak link.

The problem was not isolated. Jane Sager recalled Johnny Richards asking her whether her playing deteriorated during her period. "I play twice as good when that happens," she replied. Melba Liston alluded to more serious difficulties when she told interviewer Steve Isoardi that her problems as the only women traveling with all-man bands meant "rapes and everything" (Melba Liston, interview with Steven Isoardi, 12 September 1992). The experiences of women who played in otherwise all-man bands clearly warrant further research.

38 Helen Day Schuster, letter to author, November 1992.
39 Betty Kidwell Meriedeth, telephone interview with author, 6 July 1997.
40 As Bob Hope once quipped about air travel with the USO, "I knew the plane was old when I saw the pilot sitting behind me wearing goggles and a scarf" (Bob Hope, foreword to Coffey, *Always Home,* ix).
41 Betty Kidwell Meriedeth, telephone conversation with author, 6 July 1997.
42 Ethel C. Kirkpatrick Drehouse, letter to author, 5 July 1997.
43 Hammond, *John Hammond on Record,* 255.
44 Ethel C. Kirkpatrick Drehouse, letter to author, 5 July 1997.
45 Leonard had hired Clora Bryant for her KTTV television band. Bryant confirms this — adding that complaints from racist viewers alarmed the show's sponsors and led to her firing (Clora Bryant, interview with Steven Isoardi, 4 April 1990).
46 Betty Kidwell Meriedeth, telephone conversation with author, 6 July 1997.
47 Holly, "Why Ada Selected Men to Replace Girls in Band."
48 Gilbert, "Ada Leonard Honored at Reunion."

9. "And, Fellas, They're *American* Girls":
On the Road with the Sharon Rogers All-Girl Band

1 This and further quotations from the radio show are from a WBTQ radio broadcast, November 1945, Osaka, Japan, provided by Sylvia Roth.
2 Andrews and Gilbert, *Over Here, over There,* 232. *Stars and Stripes* was a periodical for service personnel.
3 " 'I Want a Girl . . . ,' " 599.
4 Kennett, *G.I.,* 224.
5 Costello, *Virtue under Fire,* 91.
6 In fact, twenty-eight USO entertainers were killed in the line of duty during World War II, mostly in airplane crashes (Andrews and Gilbert, *Over Here, over There,* 122).
7 Brennan, "The National Longing for Form," 49. Brennan defines nations as "imaginary constructs that depend" on "cultural fictions."
8 Roeder, *The Censored War,* 22.
9 Dower, *War without Mercy,* 81.
10 Florence Shefte Kuhn, letter to her mother, 20 January 1946. I am grateful to Florence Shefte Khun for sharing this letter.
11 Florence Shefte Kuhn, letter to author, 17 November 1996.

12 Dower, *War without Mercy,* 78–79.

13 Roeder, *The Censored War,* 61.

14 Terkel, *"The Good War,"* 521.

15 Hartmann, *The Home Front and Beyond,* 4.

16 Dower, *War without Mercy,* 79.

17 See, e.g., the editorial "Their Problem One of Color Too." Surprisingly, American-style swing bands were a staple of camp life (see the discussion of internment camp swing bands in Yoshida, *Reminiscing in Swingtime*).

18 Dower, *War without Mercy,* 66.

19 Florence Shefte Kuhn, letter to her mother, 20 January 1946.

20 Laura Daniels, letter to author, 25 June 1994.

21 Dower, *War without Mercy,* 61–66.

22 See Tucker, "The Politics of Impermanence," 12.

23 Trinh, *Framer Framed,* 184.

24 Sharon Rogers Wright, letter to author, 12 August 1990.

25 USO Camp Shows, Inc., standard contract (dated 30 September 1944), courtesy Laura Bohle Sias, bassist with D'Artega's All-Girl Orchestra.

26 Ely, *Stars and Stripes.*

27 Sharon Rogers Wright, letter to author, 12 August 1990.

28 Ibid.

29 Laura Daniels, letter to author, 27 May 1996.

30 Lyrics from Irving Berlin's "A Pretty Girl Is Like a Melody" (1919) as they appear in the song sheet compiled by Florence Shefte Kuhn.

31 Wilk, *They're Playing Our Song,* 277.

32 Sharon Rogers Wright, letter to author, 12 August 1990.

33 Laura Daniels, letters to her parents, 14 August, 6 September, 9 December 1945. I am grateful to Laura Daniels for sharing these letters with me.

34 Fake books are compilations of lead sheets — melody lines and chord changes — rather than the entire scores. Illegal (because of copyright infringement) and difficult to obtain in the 1930s and 1940s, legally compiled versions are now easily available in music stores.

35 Sylvia Roth, letter to author, 1 December 1993.

Conclusion: Postwar Changes, Familiar Refrains

1 Chafe, *The American Woman,* 218. Chafe points out that, in 1960, twice as many women worked for wages as did in 1940.

2 This article on the continued presence of women on the Los Angeles jazz scene featured the rave notices given to trumpet player Valaida Snow and the all-female sextet led by Edna Williams.

3 For a historical analysis of Truman administration efforts to construct U.S. world domination as "natural and right," see Leffler, *A Preponderance of Power.* For a fascinating analysis of how postwar normative gender roles symbolized and supported U.S. cold war foreign policy, see

May, *Homeward Bound.* See also the essays in Meyerowitz, ed., *Not June Cleaver.*

4 "Post War Planning and the Musician."

5 Wrote *Pittsburgh Courier* columnist Marjorie McKenzie, "The most disgruntled group of victory workers of the entire war effort, the ladies who unwillingly got acquainted with the decor of their own kitchens, are making some quiet peace plans of their own. They have their sights well aimed on the thousands of Negro women who are currently unemployed as a result of munitions cutbacks." Arguing for black women's employment at the "highest levels of skill and at wages which preserve their ability to buy the goods they need for a decent standard of living," she urged that it should not be necessary to "sacrifice Negro women workers to the maintenance of American homes" ("Pursuit of Democracy").

6 One of the most brutal cases was that of twenty-seven-year-old army veteran Isaac Woodard, who was "mercilessly beaten and permanently blinded" by Georgia police less than four hours after he was honorably discharged ("Veteran's Eyes Gouged out by Hate-Crazed Dixie Police").

7 Von Eschen, *Race against Empire,* 96–121; Plummer, *Rising Wind,* 167–216.

8 Meyerowitz, ed., *Not June Cleaver.*

9 "New Laws and Changes."

10 "A.F. of M. Urges Consideration for Returned Service Men."

11 Jane Sager, telephone interview with author, 2 April 1994.

12 Jane Sager, interview with author, 10 June 1994.

13 "The Musicians' Post-War World."

14 Rosalind Cron, telephone interview with author, 13 August 1990.

15 Petrillo, "New Agreement for Turn-Table Operators (Pancake Turners) in Radio Stations."

16 Clora Bryant, telephone interview with author, 5 August 1993.

17 Ibid.

18 Sarah McLawler, telephone interview with author, 12 July 1994.

19 This is a very incomplete list of postwar combos. For more information, see Dahl, *Stormy Weather;* Handy, *Black Women in American Bands and Orchestras;* and Placksin, *American Women in Jazz.*

20 Laverne Wollerman, letter to author, 12 October 1996.

21 Martye Awkerman, letter to author, 12 February 1992.

22 "Music in Business."

23 See Rabin, *At the Beginning.*

24 Laverne Wollerman, questionnaire, 10 February 1992.

25 Lillian Carter Wilson, telephone interview with author, 24 August 1991.

26 Leigh Pilzer, letter to author, 16 March 1999.

27 Terri Lyne Carrington, interview with author, 11–12 July 1996.

28 I refer here to the first day of "Sung and Unsung Jazzwomen," presented by the Smithsonian Institution and 651, An Arts Center, Brooklyn, 19 October 1996. This remarkable symposium was directed by Janice McNeil.

29 The band is called Jazzberry Jam! and represents a collaboration among pianist Bertha Hope, bassist Carline Ray, vocalist Pat Spann, and percussionist Paula Hampton. The description is of their set at the symposium "Sung and Unsung Jazzwomen" (see n. 28 above).

30 Violet Wilson, telephone interview with author, 9 November 1993.

Bibliography

Secondary Sources

"Ada Leonard Band Clicks in Army Camps." *Down Beat,* 15 February 1942, 19.

"Ada Leonard Ork Will Tour Camps." *Down Beat,* 1 December 1941, 20.

"Ada Leonard (Reviewed at Loew's State, New York)." *Down Beat,* 1 August 1943, 20.

Adler, Amy E. "Thanks for the Memories: The USO at Fifty." *USA Today Magazine,* November 1991, 87–88, 92–95.

"A.F. of M. Urges Consideration for Returned Service Men; Many Locals Already Making Special Concessions for Honorably Discharged Members." *International Musician,* August 1945, 1, 9.

Ake, David. "Re-Masculating Jazz: Ornette Coleman, 'Lonely Woman,' and the New York Jazz Scene in the Late 1950s." *American Music* 16, no. 1 (spring 1998): 25–44.

Albertson, Chris. *Bessie.* New York: Stein and Day, 1982.

Allen, Robert C. *A Horrible Prettiness: Burlesque and American Culture.* Chapel Hill: University of North Carolina Press, 1991.

"All Girls' Band Scores." *Chicago Defender,* 11 August 1945, 14.

"All-Girl Crew Set to Reopen Grand Terrace." *Pittsburgh Courier,* 18 March 1944, 13.

" 'American Guild of Variety Artists' Takes Over. *Chicago Defender,* 20 March 1940, 20.

Amott, Teresa L., and Julie A. Matthaei. *Race, Gender, and Work.* Boston: South End, 1991.

Anderson, Benedict. *Imagined Communities: Reflections on the Origin and Spread of Nationalism.* London: Verso, 1983.

Anderson, Karen. *Wartime Women: Sex Roles, Family Relations, and the Status of Women during World War II.* Westport, Conn.: Greenwood, 1981.

———. "Last Hired, First Fired: Black Women Workers during World War II." *Journal of American History* 69 (1982): 82–97.

Andrews, Maxene, and Bill Gilbert. *Over Here, over There: The Andrews Sisters and the USO Stars in World War II.* New York: Zebra, 1993.

"Anne Wallace Weds, Quits." *Down Beat,* 1 September 1940, 8.

Antrim, Doron K., ed. *Secrets of Dance Band Success.* New York: Famous Stars Publishing Co., 1936.

———. "Should Music Be War-Conscripted?" *International Musician,* December 1940, 1, 15.

Aptheker, Herbert, ed. *A Documentary History of the Negro People in the United States: From Colonial Times to the Founding of the NAACP in 1910.* New York: Citadel, 1961.

——, ed. *A Documentary History of the Negro People in the United States: From the New Deal to the End of World War II.* New York: Citadel, 1992.

"Are Girl Musicians Superior? Yes! Says a Famous Orchestra Leader." *Up Beat,* January 1939, 5, 8, 27.

Armstrong, Toni L. "The Great White Folk Music Myth." *Hot Wire: Journal of Women's Music and Culture* 4, no. 3 (July 1988): 22.

"Army Bands." *International Musician,* June 1941, 23–24.

"Army Bars Mixed Marriages, Sanctions Illegitimate Babies!" *Chicago Defender,* 5 May 1945, 1.

Baldwin, James. *The Fire Next Time.* New York: Dell, 1963.

Banana, Joe. "Girls Are Too Hep!" *Down Beat,* 1 May 1942, 10.

Baraka, Amiri [LeRoi Jones]. *Blues People: The Negro Experience in White America and the Music That Developed from It.* New York: William Morrow, 1963.

——. *Black Music.* New York: William Morrow, 1970.

Barnes, Catherine A. *Journey from Jim Crow: The Desegregation of Southern Transit.* New York: Columbia University Press, 1983.

"Battery 600 Selects Hazel Scott as Pin-Up." *Pittsburgh Courier,* 6 January 1945, 13.

Berliner, Paul. *Thinking in Jazz: The Infinite Art of Improvisation.* Chicago: University of Chicago Press, 1994.

Bernhardt, Clyde E. B., with Sheldon Harris. *I Remember . . . Eighty Years of Black Entertainment, Big Bands, and the Blues.* Philadelphia: University of Pennsylvania Press, 1986.

Berube, A. *Coming Out under Fire: The History of Gay Men and Women in World War II.* New York: Free Press, 1990.

Bhabha, Homi K., ed. *Nation and Narration.* New York: Routledge, 1991.

——. *The Location of Culture.* New York: Routledge, 1994.

"Blanche Calloway Jailed and Fined in Mississippi." *Down Beat,* August 1937, 2.

Bogle, Donald. *Brown Sugar: Eighty Years of America's Black Female Superstars.* New York: Da Capo, 1980.

Brennan, Timothy. "The National Longing for Form." In *Nation and Narration,* ed. Homi K. Bhabha. New York: Routledge, 1991.

Brooks, Deton J., Jr. "Mme. Chiang Sees Race Vital in U.S. Democracy." *Chicago Defender,* 27 March 1943, 1.

Brown, George F. "Lena Defies Washington, D.C. 'Jim Crow' Policy; to Play Howard Theater Instead." *Pittsburgh Courier,* 21 October 1944, 13.

Bruun, Paul M. "The World Loved Spitalny's Hour of Charm." [1970?] Source unknown.

Bryant, Clora. "Trumpetistically Speaking, Love, Cora Bryant." Typescript.

Bryant, Clora, et al., eds. *Central Avenue Sounds: Jazz in Los Angeles.* Berkeley and Los Angeles: University of California Press, 1998.

"B-29 Drops 'Darlings' in Los Angeles." *Pittsburgh Courier,* 23 June 1945, 13.

Buckner, Reginald T., and Steven Weiland, eds. *Jazz in Mind: Essays on the History and Meanings of Jazz.* Detroit: Wayne State University, 1991.

Calloway, Cab, and Bryant Rollins. *Of Minnie the Moocher and Me.* New York: Thomas Y. Crowell, 1976.

Campbell, D'Ann. Women at War with America: Private Lives in a Patriotic Era. Cambridge, Mass.: Harvard University Press, 1984.

Carby, Hazel V. "In Body and Spirit: Representing Black Women Musicians." *Black Music Research Journal* 11, no. 2 (fall 1998): 177–92.

———. "It Jus Be's Dat Way Sometime: The Sexual Politics of Women's Blues. In *Unequal Sisters: A Multi-Cultural Reader in U.S. Women's History* (2d ed.) ed. Vicki L. Ruis and Ellen Carol DuBois. New York: Routledge, 1994.

———. *Reconstructing Womanhood: The Emergence of the Afro-American Woman Novelist.* New York: Oxford University Press, 1987.

Carson, Julia M. H. *Home Away from Home: The Story of the USO.* New York: Harper Bros., 1946.

Chadwick, Whitney. *Women, Art, and Society.* London: Thames and Hudson, 1990.

Chafe, William. *The American Woman: Her Changing Social, Economic, and Political Roles, 1920–1970.* New York: Oxford University Press, 1972.

Chevigny, Paul. *Gigs: Jazz and the Cabaret Laws in New York City.* New York: Routledge, 1991.

"Chicago Women Afraid to Comment on Conscription." *Chicago Defender,* 21 September 1940, 1.

Chilton, John. *Billie's Blues: The Billie Holiday Story, 1933–1939.* New York: Da Capo, 1975.

"Chorines of Harlem Organize." *Chicago Defender,* 27 July 1940, 20.

Clifford, James. "Traveling Cultures." In *Cultural Studies,* ed. Lawrence Grossberg, Cary Nelson, and Paula Treichler. New York: Routledge, 1992.

"Co-Ed Trumpeter." *Chicago Defender,* 4 March 1944, 8.

"Co-Eds Seek Girl Musicians." *Pittsburgh Courier,* 14 July 1945, 13; 20 April 1946, 18.

Coffey, Frank. *Always Home: Fifty Years of the USO.* Washington, D.C.: Brassey's, 1991.

Collier, James Lincoln. *The Making of Jazz: A Comprehensive History.* New York: Dell, 1978.

Collins, Patricia Hill. *Black Feminist Thought: Knowledge, Consciousness, and the Politics of Empowerment.* New York: Routledge, 1990.

Combahee River Collective. "The Combahee River Collective Statement."
 In *Home-Girls: A Black Feminist Anthology,* ed. Barbara Smith. New
 York: Kitchen Table, 1983.

Cone, James H. *The Spirituals and the Blues.* New York: Seabury, 1972.

Cons, Carl. "The Effect War Is Having on Music World." *Down Beat,*
 1 January 1942, 1, 22.

Cook, Susan. "Billie Holiday and the Performance of Race and Gender."
 Paper presented at the Conference "Feminist Theory and Music II," Eastman School of Music, 19 June 1993.

Cooper, Esther V. "Woman Sheds Bitter Sidelight on U.S. and War; Recalls
 Slur on Husband; a Soldier in '19; Alabama Whites Ripped Buttons off
 Uniform of World War I Vet." *Chicago Defender,* 31 August 1940, 12.

Cooper, Ralph, with Steve Dougherty. *Amateur Night at the Apollo: Ralph
 Cooper Presents Five Decades of Great Entertainment.* New York: Har-
 perCollins, 1990.

Costello, John. *Virtue under Fire: How World War II Changed Our Social
 and Sexual Attitudes.* Boston: Little, Brown, 1985.

"Courier 'Double V' Girl of the Week." *Pittsburgh Courier,* 27 June 1942,
 13.

Cron, Rosalind. "Jim Who?" and "My Road to Zanzibar." In *A Class Act:
 Scaling the Chords and Discords of Life,* ed. Bernard Selling. Hollywood,
 Calif.: A Class Act, 1996.

Dahl, Linda. *Stormy Weather: The Music and Lives of a Century of Jazzwomen.* New York: Limelight, 1989.

Dalfiume, Richard M. *Desegregation of the U.S. Armed Forces: Fighting on
 Two Fronts, 1939–1953.* Columbia: University of Missouri Press, 1969.

Damousi, Joy, and Marilyn Lake, eds. *Gender and War: Australians at War
 in the Twentieth Century.* Cambridge: Cambridge University Press, 1995.

Dance, Stanley. *The World of Swing.* New York: Da Capo, 1974.

———. *The World of Earl Hines.* New York: Da Capo, 1977.

———. *The World of Count Basie.* New York: Charles Scribner's Sons.

Daniels, Douglas Henry. "History, Racism, and Jazz: The Case of Lester
 Young," *Jazzforschung/Jazz Research* 16 (1984): 87–103.

———. "Oral History, Masks, and Protocol in the Jazz Community." *Oral
 History Review* 15 (Spring 1987): 143–64.

"Darlings Build Business." *Chicago Defender,* 10 June 1944, 8.

"Darlings Feature Pat Lamarr, Helen Taborn." *Pittsburgh Courier,*
 25 November 1944, 13.

" 'Darlings of Rhythm' Hit Peak at Terrace." *Chicago Defender,* 8 July
 1944, 8.

"Darlings of Rhythm Newest 'Find': The Darlings of Rhythm Are the Current Darlings of Orchestra Whirl." *Pittsburgh Courier,* 18 March 1944, 13.

"Darlings of Rhythm Score." *Chicago Defender,* 22 April 1944, 8.

"Darlings of Rhythm Set for Twelve Mo Ball." *Music Dial,* March–April
 1945, 10.

"Darlings of Rhythm Take to Road." *Chicago Defender,* 22 July 1944, 6.

" 'Darlings of Rhythm' to Play Coast's Plantation." *Chicago Defender,* 23 June 1945, 10.

"Darlings Score for Camp Hill." *Chicago Defender,* 8 May 1944, 8.

Davis, Angela Y. *Women, Race, and Class.* New York: Random House, 1983.

———. "Race and Criminalization: Black Americans and the Punishment Industry." Paper presented at the conference "Race Matters: Black Americans, U.S. Terrain," Princeton University, 30 April, 1994.

———. *Blues Legacies and Black Feminism: Gertrude "Ma" Rainey, Bessie Smith, and Billie Holiday.* New York: Pantheon, 1998.

Davis, F. James. *Who Is Black? One Nation's Definition.* University Park: Pennsylvania State University Press, 1991.

D'Emilio, John, and Estelle Freedman. *Intimate Matters: A History of Sexuality.* New York: Harper & Row, 1988.

Defense Morale: A Transcript of the Proceedings of the Defense Morale Conference of United Service Organizations for National Defense, Inc., at Washington, D.C., April 17, 1941. New York: United Service Organizations for National Defense, 1941.

Defense Recreation Conference: Proceedings of the Defense Recreation Conference, September 29, 1941. New York: National Recreation Association, 1941.

De Veaux, Scott. "Constructing the Jazz Tradition: Jazz Historiography." *Black America.*

———. *The Birth of Bebop: A Social and Musical History.* Berkeley and Los Angeles: University of California Press, 1997.

"Discrimination Crumbles as War Hysteria Mounts." *Chicago Defender,* 7 September 1940, 1.

Dobash, Russell, Rebecca Dobash, and Sue Gutteridge. *The Imprisonment of Women.* Oxford: Basil Blackwell, 1986.

Doherty, Thomas. *Projections of War: Hollywood, American Culture, and World War II.* New York: Columbia University Press, 1993.

"Dorothy Donegan and Those Sweethearts at Regal Next." *Chicago Defender,* 17 July 1943, 10.

" 'Double V' Band a Hit." *Pittsburgh Courier,* 1 August 1942, 15.

Doukoullos, Ellen Stone, and Bonnie Smallwood Medin. *Musical Women Marines: The Marine Corps Women's Reserve Band in World War Two.* n.p. Ellen Stone Doukoullos and Bonnie Smallwood Medin, 1981.

Dower, John. *War without Mercy: Race and Power in the Pacific War.* New York: Pantheon, 1986.

Driggs, Franklin S. "Kansas City and the Southwest." In *Jazz,* ed. Nat Hentoff and Albert J. McCarthy. London: Cassell, 1959.

Duckett, Alfred A. "Assignment in New York." *New York Age,* 22 May 1943, 10.

"Durham Band to Gale." *Metronome,* November 1942, 33.

Dynamite. "And on the Contrary." *Down Beat,* 15 April 1942, 11.

"Earl 'Father' Hines and Band to Appear at Apollo This Week." *New York Age,* 18 September 1943, 10.

Earley, Charity Adams. *One Woman's Army: A Black Officer Remembers the WAC.* College Station: Texas A&M University Press, 1989.

Elworth, Steven B. "Jazz in Crisis, 1948–1958." In Jazz among the Discourses, ed. Krin Gabbard. Durham, N.C.: Duke University Press, 1995.

Erenberg, Lewis A. *Swinging the Dream: Big Band Jazz and the Rebirth of American Culture.* Chicago: University of Chicago Press, 1998.

"Essential (Unpaid) Industry." *International Musician,* June 1943, 12.

"Ex-Glamor Gal." *Down Beat,* 1 May 1940, 2.

"An Example for 'Democratic' America to Follow: No Racial Discrimination in British A.T.S.; Colored West Indian Girls Enjoy State of Absolute Equality." *Pittsburgh Courier,* 5 February 1944, 20.

"Femme Crew for Jiggs." *Metronome,* May 1942, 9.

Firestone, Ross. *Swing, Swing, Swing.* New York: Norton, 1993.

Fletcher, Beverly R., Lynda Dixon Shaver, and Dreama G. Moon. *Women Prisoners: A Forgotten Population.* Westport, Conn.: Praeger, 1993.

"Florida Dance Lovers Swing with 'Sweethearts.' " *Chicago Defender,* 20 April 1940, 20.

For Girls Only — Prairie View Offers Music Scholarships." *Pittsburgh Courier,* 27 January 1945, 13.

Fossum, Bob. "Girls Shouldn't Play Too Much Jazz, Says Ada." *Down Beat,* 1 December 1942, 14.

Foucault, Michel. *Discipline and Punish: The Birth of the Prison.* New York: Vintage, 1979.

Frankenberg, Ruth. *White Women, Race Matters: The Social Construction of Whiteness.* Minneapolis: University of Minnesota Press, 1993.

Fraser, Nancy. *Unruly Practices: Power, Discourse, and Gender in Contemporary Social Theory.* Minneapolis: University of Minnesota Press, 1989.

Freedman, Estelle B. *Their Sisters' Keepers: Women's Prison Reform in America, 1830–1930.* Ann Arbor: University of Michigan Press, 1984.

Frisch, Michael. *A Shared Authority: Essays on the Craft and Meaning of Oral and Public History.* New York: SUNY Press, 1990.

Frith, Simon. *Sound Effects: Youth, Leisure, and the Politics of Rock 'n' Roll.* New York: Pantheon, 1981.

———. *Performance Rites: On the Value of Popular Music.* Cambridge, Mass.: Harvard University Press, 1996.

Gabbard, Krin, ed. *Jazz among the Discourses.* Durham, N.C.: Duke University Press, 1995.

———, ed. *Representing Jazz.* Durham: Duke University Press, 1995.

———. *Jammin' at the Margins: Jazz and the American Cinema.* Chicago: University of Chicago Press, 1996.

"Gal Tooters Not Rushing to Join the WAAC Bands." *Down Beat,* 1 December 1942, 2.

"Gandhi Tells Churchill: Free India and Africa and the Colored Races Will Help the United Nations Turn Japan Out of the Countries She Has Conquered." *Pittsburgh Courier,* 8 August 1942, 20.

Gibson, Ellis. "Give Youth a Chance!" *Down Beat,* 15 March 1942, 10.

Giddings, Paula. When and Where I Enter: The Impact of Black Women on Race and Sex in America. New York: William Morris, 1984.

Gilbert, Peggy. "Ada Leonard Honored at Reunion." *Overture,* April 1992, 15.

Gillespie, Dizzy, with Al Fraser. *To Be or Not to Bop.* New York: Da Capo, 1979.

Gilroy, Paul. *"There Ain't No Black in the Union Jack": The Cultural Politics of Race and Nation.* Chicago: University of Chicago Press, 1987.

Gitler, Ira. *Swing to Bop: An Oral History of the Transition in Jazz in the 1940s.* Oxford: Oxford University Press, 1985.

Gluck, Sherna Berger. *Rosie the Riveter Revisited.* New York: Meridian, 1987.

Gluck, Sherna Berger, and Daphne Patai, eds. *Women's Words: The Feminist Practice of Oral History.* New York and London: Routledge, 1991.

Goldberg, David Theo. *Racist Culture: Philosophy and the Politics of Meaning.* Oxford: Blackwell, 1993.

Goodman, Benny, and Irving Kolodin. *The Kingdom of Swing.* 1939. Reprint, New York: Frederick Ungar, 1961.

Gray, Herman. *Watching Race: Television and the Struggle for "Blackness."* Minneapolis: University of Minnesota Press, 1995.

Grewal, Inderpal, and Caren Kaplan, eds. *Scattered Hegemonies: Postmodernity and Transnational Feminist Practices.* Minneapolis: University of Minnesota Press, 1994.

Grossberg, Lawrence. *We Gotta Get out of This Place: Popular Conservatism and Postmodern Culture.* London: Routledge, 1992.

Goss, Margaret Taylor. "A Negro Mother Looks at War." *Chicago Defender,* 31 August 1940, 13.

Gossett, Hattie, with Carolyn Johnson. "Jazzwomen: They're Mostly Singers and Piano Players Only a Horn Player or Two Hardly Any Drummers." *Heresies* 3, no. 2, issue no. 10 (1980): 65–69.

"Grand Terrace, Chicago, Preps Colored Show." *Variety,* 24 June 1944, 45.

Hall, Stuart. "The Problem of Ideology — Marxism without Guarantees." In *Marx 100 Years On,* ed. Betty Matthews. London: Lawrence & Wishart, 1983.

——. "Gramsci's Relevance for the Study of Race and Ethnicity," *Journal of Communication Inquiry* 10, no. 22 (summer 1986): 5–27.

——. "New Ethnicities." In *Black Film, British Cinema,* ed. Kobena Mercer. London: Institute of Contemporary Arts, 1988.

——. "What Is This 'Black' in Black Popular Culture?" In *Black Popular Culture,* ed. Michele Wallace and Gina Dent. Seattle: Bay, 1992.

Hamilton, Clayton. " 'Keep 'Em Laughing': A Commentary on the Contributions of USO-Camp Shows, Inc. to the Winning of the War." 15 September 1945. Camp Shows Publicity Records, 8MWEZ, box 29042, file 1, Billy Rose Theatre Collection, New York Library for the Performing Arts, Lincoln Center.

———. Outline for " 'Keep 'Em Laughing': A Commentary on the Contributions of USO-Camp Shows, Inc. to the Winning of the War." 15 September 1945. Camp Shows Publicity Records, 8MWEZ, box 29042, file 1, Billy Rose Theatre Collection, New York Library for the Performing Arts, Lincoln Center.

Hammond, Delany Named by ODT." *Pittsburgh Courier,* 5 September 1942, 21.

Hammond, John, with Irving Townsend. *John Hammond on Record: An Autobiography.* Middlesex: Penguin Books, 1977.

Hampton, Lionel, with James Haskins. *Hamp: An Autobiography.* New York: Warner, 1989.

Handy, D. Antoinette. "Conversation with Lucille Dixon," *The Black Perspective in Music* 3, no. 3 (fall 1975): 299–311.

———. *Black Women in American Bands and Orchestras.* Metuchen, N.J.: Scarecrow Press, 1981.

———. *The International Sweethearts of Rhythm.* Metuchen, N.J.: Scarecrow, 1983.

Hanifin, Ada. "A Night at the Moulin Rouge Is Staged at Curran Theater." n.d. Courtesy Shirley Stearns. Clipping from an unknown San Francisco newspaper.

Hare, Maud Cuney. *Negro Musicians and Their Music.* 1936. Reprint, New York: Simon and Schuster, 1996.

Harris, Cheryl. "Whiteness as Property." *Harvard Law Review* 106 (1993): 1709–91.

Harris, Duchess. "From Kennedy to Combahee: Black Feminist Organizing, 1960–1980." Paper presented at the conference panel "Black Women's Cultural and Political Production in the 1970s," chaired by Adrienne Dale Davis, American Studies Association, Seattle, 20 November 1998.

Harrison, Alferdteen B. *Piney Woods School: An Oral History.* Jackson: University Press of Mississippi, 1982.

Hartmann, Susan M. *The Home Front and Beyond: American Women in the 1940s.* Boston: Twayne, 1982.

Haskins, James. *Black Theater in America.* New York: Thomas Y. Crowell, 1982.

Heintze, Michael R. *Private Black Colleges in Texas, 1865–1954.* College Station: Texas A & M University Press, 1985.

"Helen Taborn Scores." *Chicago Defender,* 3 June 1944, 8.

"Help Wanted." *Down Beat,* 1 April 1941, 23; 15 June 1941, 23.

Heylbut, Rose. " 'The Hour of Charm,' the Most Unusual Girls Orchestra of the Times, from a Conference with Its Director Phil Spitalny Secured Expressly for The Etude Music Magazine." *Etude* 56 (October 1938): 639–40.

Higginbotham, Evelyn Brooks. "African-American Women's History and the Metalanguage of Race." *Signs* 17, no. 2 (winter 1992): 251–74.

Hill, Susan T. *The Traditionally Black Institutions of Higher Education, 1860–1982.* Washington, D.C.: National Center for Education Statistics, 1985.

Hine, Al, Pvt. "Gypsy Gyps Us." *Yank,* 16 September 1942, 15.

Hine, Darlene Clark. "Black Migration to the Urban Midwest: The Gender Dimension, 1915–1945." In *The Great Migration in Historical Perspective: New Dimensions of Race, Class, and Gender,* ed. Joseph Trotter. Bloomington: Indiana University Press, 1991.

Holiday, Billie, with William Dufty. *Lady Sings the Blues.* New York: Avon, 1956.

Holly, Hal. "Why Ada Selected Men to Replace Girls in Band." *Down Beat,* 23 February 1955, 5.

Holm, Jeanne. *Women in the Military: An Unfinished Revolution.* Novato, Calif.: Presidio, 1982.

Honey, Maureen. *Creating Rosie the Riveter: Class, Gender, and Propaganda during World War II.* Amherst: University of Massachusetts Press, 1984.

———. "Remembering Rosie: Advertising Images of Women in World War II." In *The Home-Front War: World War II and American Society,* ed. Kenneth Paul O'Brien and Lynn Hudson Parsons. Westport, Conn.: Greenwood, 1995.

Horne, Lena. *Lena.* New York: Signet, 1965.

Hudee, Anne. "If a Chick Has Talent, Why Not Make Use of It?" *Down Beat,* 1 April 1942, 10.

Ihle, Elizabeth L., ed. *Black Women in Higher Education: An Anthology of Essays, Studies, and Documents.* New York: Garland, 1992.

"Important Changes in Federation Laws." *International Musician,* August 1941, 1; July 1942, 16.

"Ina Ray Knocks out a Biscuit." *Down Beat,* 15 November 1940, 1.

"India Justified in Freedom Fight, Readers Declare." *Pittsburgh Courier,* 10 October 1942, 1.

Jackson, Arthur. *The World of Big Bands.* New York: Arco, 1977.

Jakeman, Robert J. *The Divided Skies: Establishing Segregated Flight Training at Tuskegee, Alabama, 1934–1942.* Tuscaloosa: University of Alabama Press, 1992.

James, C. L. R. *"My Friends": A Fireside Chat on the War.* Published under the pseudonym "Native Son." New York: Workers Party, June 1940.

"Jail Girl Musician; 'Too Light' for All Negro Orchestra." *Chicago Defender,* 13 July 1946, 16.

Jones, Gayl. *Liberating Voices: Oral Tradition in African American Literature.* Cambridge, Mass.: Harvard University Press, 1991.

"Jim Crow Stuff Still Spreading! Girl Trumpeter Tastes Southern Chivalry and Color Ousts Mab's Men." *Down Beat,* 29 July 1946, 1.

Jones, Max. *Talking Jazz.* New York: Norton, 1987.

"Judy Ellington Fronting New All-Girl Band." *Variety,* 11 December 1940, 41.

"Keed Lips Hackette." *Music Dial,* November 1943, 7.

Keil, Charles, and Steven Feld. *Music Grooves.* Chicago: University of Chicago Press, 1994.

Kelley, Robin D. G. *Race Rebels: Culture, Politics, and the Black Working Class.* New York: Free Press, 1994.

Kellogg, J. H. *Ladies Guide in Health and Disease: Girlhood, Maidenhood, Wifehood, Motherhood.* Des Moines, Iowa: W. D. Condit, 1884.

Kelly, Joan. *Women, History, and Theory.* Chicago: University of Chicago Press, 1984.

Kennedy, Stetson. *Jim Crow Guide to the U.S.A.: The Laws, Customs, and Etiquette Governing the Conduct of Nonwhites and Other Minorities as Second-Class Citizens.* London: Lawrence and Wishart, 1959.

Kennett, Lee. *For the Duration: The United States Goes to War.* New York: Charles Scribner's Sons, 1985.

——. *G.I.: The American Soldier in World War II.* New York: Charles Scribner's Sons, 1987.

Kenney, William. "Historical Context and the Definition of Jazz." In *Jazz among the Discourses,* ed. Krin Gabbard. Durham, N.C.: Duke University Press, 1995.

Kessler-Harris, Alice. *Out to Work: A History of Wage-Earning Women in the United States.* Oxford: Oxford University Press, 1982.

Kindall, James. "Black Vets Recall Battle of the Bulge." *San Francisco Chronicle,* 19 December 1994, A3.

Kirk, Andy, as told to Amy Lee. *Twenty Years on Wheels.* Ann Arbor: University of Michigan Press, 1989.

Kissel, Bud. "Ada Leonard, Variety Makes Good Stage Show at Palace." *Columbus Citizen,* Wednesday, 2 August 1944, 12.

Kittrell, F. P. "Current Problems and Programs in the Higher Education of Negro Women." *Quarterly Review of Higher Education* 12 (January 1944): 13–15. Reprinted in *Black Women in Higher Education: An Anthology of Essays, Studies, and Documents,* ed. Elizabeth L. Ihle (New York: Garland, 1992).

Korstad, Robert, and Nelson Lichtenstein, "Opportunities Found and Lost: Labor, Radicals, and the Early Civil Rights Movement," *Journal of American History* 75 (December 1988): 786–811.

Koskoff, Ellen, ed. *Women and Music in Cross-Cultural Perspective.* Urbana: University of Illinois Press, 1989.

Kovan, Florice Whyte. "Sharps and Flats: A Diary of the Roadlife of America's Musical Sweethearts," *Image File: A Journal from the Curt Teich Postcard Archives* 8, no. 3 (1995): 3–6.

Krupnick, Jerry. "18-Gal Combo Jumpin' for 7th Army Hepcats." *Special Service Spotlight* (Seventh Army Headquarters, APO 758), 22 September 1945.

Kuhn, Florence Shefte. "The Sharon Rogers Band." Lyric sheet passed out at the 1993 reunion of the Sharon Rogers Band in Las Vegas.

"Lady with a Horn." *Pittsburgh Courier,* 26 August 1944, 13.

Lee, Amy. *Twenty Years on Wheels.* Ann Arbor: University of Michigan Press, 1989.

Leffler, Melvyn P. *A Preponderance of Power.* Stanford, Calif.: Stanford University Press, 1992.

Lemelle, Sidney J., and Robin D. G. Kelley, eds. *Imagining Home: Class, Culture, and Nationalism in the African Diaspora.* London: Verso, 1994.

Lerner, Gerda, ed. *Black Women in White America: A Documentary History.* New York: Random House, 1973.

Levine, Lawrence W. *Highbrow/Lowbrow: The Emergence of Cultural Hierarchy in America.* Cambridge, Mass.: Harvard University Press, 1988.

Lewis, George. "Improvised Music after 1950: Afrological and Eurological Perspectives." *Black Music Research Journal* 16, no. 1 (spring 1996): 91–122.

"Lionel Stars White Sax Ace on All Dates." *Pittsburgh Courier,* 24 March 1945, 13.

Lipsitz, George. *Dangerous Crossroads: Popular Music, Postmodernism, and the Poetics of Place.* London: Verso, 1994.

Litoff, Judy Barrett, and David C. Smith. *We're in This War, Too: World War II Letters from American Women in Uniform.* New York: Oxford University Press, 1994.

Loesser, Arthur. *Men, Women, and Pianos: A Social History.* New York: Simon and Schuster, 1954.

Loetz, Rainer E., and Ulrich Neuert. *The AFRS "Jubilee" Transcription Programs: An Exploratory Discography.* Vol. 1. Frankfurt: Norbert Ruecker, 1985.

Loewen, James W. *The Mississippi Chinese: Between Black and White.* Cambridge, Mass.: Harvard University Press, 1971.

Lott, Eric. *Love and Theft: Blackface Minstrelsy and the American Working Class.* New York: Oxford University Press, 1993.

Love, Preston. *A Thousand Honey Creeks Later.* Hanover, N.H.: Wesleyan University Press, 1997.

Lovell, John, Jr. *Black Song: The Forge and the Flame: The Story of How the Afro-American Spiritual Was Hammered Out.* New York: Macmillan/Collier-Macmillan, 1972.

"Madame Pandit Wins over Maryland Theater Barrier." *Pittsburgh Courier,* 14 April 1945, 1.

"Majestic, San Antonio (Review)." *Variety,* 16 April 1941, 47.

Major, Clarence. *Juba to Jive: A Dictionary of African-American Slang.* New York: Penguin, 1994.

"Margaret Backstrom Joins Darlings' Reed Section." *Music Dial,* November 1944, 15.

May, Elaine Tyler. *Homeward Bound: American Families in the Cold War Era.* New York: Basic, 1988.

McAlpin, Harry. "U.S. Jails 600 Jamaicans in Florida: Farm Laborers Protest New Discriminatory Contracts." *Chicago Defender,* 30 October 1943, 1.

McCarthy, Albert. *Big Band Jazz.* New York: Exeter, 1974.

McClary, Susan. *Feminine Endings: Music, Gender, and Sexuality.* Minnesota: University of Minnesota Press, 1991.

McGuire, Phillip. *Taps for a Jim Crow Army: Letters from Black Soldiers in World War II.* Santa Barbara, Calif.: ABC-Clio, 1983.

McKenzie, Marjorie. "Pursuit of Democracy: Women Who Got Acquainted with Own Kitchens Eager to 'Reconvert' to New Domestics." *Pittsburgh Courier,* 8 September 1945, 7.

McKissack, Patricia, and Fredrick McKissack. *Red-Tail Angels: The Story of the Tuskegee Airmen of World War II.* New York: Walker, 1995.

McPartland, Marian. "The Untold Story of the International Sweethearts of Rhythm." In *All in Good Time.* New York: Oxford University Press, 1987.

McRobbie, Angela. *Postmodernism and Popular Culture.* New York: Routledge, 1994.

Meltzer, David. *Reading Jazz.* San Francisco: Mercury, 1993.

"Mexican Consul Raps Bias as Citizenship Damper." *Chicago Defender,* 10 July 1943, 2.

Meyer, Leisa D. "Creating GI Jane: The Regulation of Sexuality and Sexual Behavior in the Women's Army Corps During World War II." *Feminist Studies* 18, no. 3 (fall 1992): 581–601.

——. *Creating GI Jane: Sexuality and Power in the Women's Army Corps During World War II.* New York: Columbia University Press, 1996.

Meyerowitz, Joanne, ed. *Not June Cleaver: Women and Gender in Postwar America, 1945–1960.* Philadelphia: Temple University Press, 1994.

"Mississippi Is Now Jim Crowing Chinese." *Pittsburgh Courier,* 6 May 1944, 5.

"Mixed Band at Cafe Society Proves a Hit." *Chicago Defender,* 30 December 1939, 17.

"Moe Gale Adds Cocktail Dept." *Down Beat,* 15 November 1942, 3.

Monroe, Al. "Swinging the News." *Chicago Defender,* 22 July 1944, 6; 14 April 1945, 17.

Monson, Ingrid. "Forced Migration, Asymmetrical Power Relations, and African-American Music: Reformulation of Cultural Meaning and Musical Form." *World of Music* 32, no. 3 (1990): 22–45.

——. "Doubleness and Jazz Improvisation: Irony, Parody, and Ethnomusicology." *Critical Inquiry* 20, no. 2 (winter 1994): 283–313.

——. "The Problem with White Hipness: Race, Gender, and Cultural Conceptions in Jazz Historical Discourse." *Journal of the American Musicological Society* 48 (fall 1995): 396–422.

Moore, Brenda. *To Serve My Country, to Serve My Race: The Story of the Only African American Wacs Stationed Overseas during World War II.* New York: New York University Press, 1996.

Morgan, Robin, ed. *Sisterhood Is Global: The International Women's Movement.* Garden City, N.Y.: Anchor, 1984.

Morris, Kelso B. "The Wiley Collegians: Reminiscences of a Black College Bandleader, 1925–35." *Annual Review of Jazz Studies* 1 (1982): 7–20.

Muwakkil, Salim. "Patriotism and Prejudice." *In These Times,* August 7, 1995, 17–19.

Murray, Albert. *Stomping the Blues.* New York: McGraw-Hill, 1976.

"Music and Marriage Will Mix: Nelsons Blend Domestic Life with Careers." *Down Beat,* 1 May 1943, 12.

"Music in Business: The Hormel Girls Caravan Orchestra." *International Musician,* November 1951, 16.

"The Musicians' Post-War World." *International Musician,* January 1944, 12.

Nalty, Bernard C. *Strength for the Fight: A History of Black Americans in the Military.* New York: Free Press, 1986.

"Negro and White Band Folds." *Down Beat,* December 1937, 12.

"A Negro Woman Speaks." In *A Documentary History of the Negro People in the United States: From the New Deal to the End of World War II,* ed. Herbert Aptheker. New York: Citadel, 1992.

"Negroes Should Back India Says Randolph." *Pittsburgh Courier,* 22 August 1942, 2.

"New Laws and Changes." *International Musician,* July 1944, 12, 14.

"News from the Home Front." *International Musician,* February 1944, 8.

Nicholson, Stuart. *Billie Holiday.* Boston: Northeastern University Press, 1995.

"Night at Moulin Rouge Is Glittering Fantasy." n.d. [1939]. Courtesy Shirley Stearns. Clipping from an unknown Denver, Colo., newspaper.

O'Brien, Kenneth Paul, and Lynn Hudson Parsons, eds. *The Home-Front War: World War II and American Society.* Westport, Conn.: Greenwood, 1995.

O'Day, Anita, with George Eells. *High Times, Hard Times.* New York: Limelight, 1981.

Ogren, Kathy. *The Jazz Revolution: Twenties America and the Meaning of Jazz.* New York: Oxford University Press, 1989.

——. " 'Jazz Isn't Just Me': Jazz Autobiographies as Performances." In *Jazz in Mind: Essays on the History and Meanings of Jazz,* ed. Reginald T. Buckner and Steven Weiland. Detroit: Wayne State University Press, 1991.

O'Meally, Robert. "Improvisation." In *Seeing Jazz: Artists and Writers on Jazz,* ed. Elizabeth Goldson. San Francisco: Chronicle, 1997.

Omi, Michael, and Howard Winant. *Racial Formation in the United States: From the 1960s to the 1990s.* 2d ed. New York: Routledge, 1994.

O'Neill, William L. *A Democracy at War: America's Fight at Home and Abroad in World War II.* New York: Free Press, 1993.

Operation USO, Report of the President, February 4, 1941–January 9, 1948. New York: United Service Organizations for National Defense, 1948.

Otis, Johnny. *Upside Your Head! Rhythm and Blues on Central Avenue.* Hanover, N.H.: Wesleyan University Press, 1993.

"Out of Tune! White Girl in Mixed Orchestra Arrested by Georgia Police." *Pittsburgh Courier,* 13 July 1946, 1.

Peretti, Burton W. *The Creation of Jazz: Music, Race, and Culture in Urban America.* Urbana: University of Illinois Press, 1992.

———. "Oral Histories of Jazz Musicians." In *Jazz among the Discourses,* ed. Krin Gabbard. Durham, N.C.: Duke University Press, 1995.

———. Review of David W. Stowe, *Swing Changes. Notes* 52, no. 3 (March 1996): 825.

———. *Jazz in American Culture.* Chicago: Ivan R. Dee, 1997.

Peri, William. "Who Said Girl Musicians Could Play?" *Down Beat,* 1 March 1942, letters to the editor, 11.

Petersen, Karen E. "Women-Identified Music in the United States." In *Women and Music in Cross-Cultural Perspective,* ed. Ellen Koskoff. Urbana: University of Illinois Press, 1989.

Petrillo, James C. "Members to Play 'Star Spangled Banner'; Compliance by Federation Members Pleases President Roosevelt." *International Musician,* August 1941, 1.

———. "New Agreement for Turn-Table Operators (Pancake Turners) in Radio Stations." *International Musician,* April 1944, 1.

Piper, Adrian. "Passing for White, Passing for Black." In *New Feminist Criticism,* ed. Joanna Frueh, Cassandra Langer, and Arlene Raven. New York: Icon, 1994.

Pipik, Jane E. "Woman-Identified Music: Moving On." *Heresies* 3, no. 2, issue 10 (1980): 88–90.

Placksin, Sally. *American Women in Jazz: 1900 to the Present.* New York: Wideview, 1982.

Player, Willa B. "The Negro College and Women's Education." *Association of American Colleges Bulletin* 33, no. 2 (May 1948): 364–65. Reprinted in *Black Women in Higher Education: An Anthology of Essays, Studies, and Documents,* ed. Elizabeth L. Ihle (New York: Garland, 1992).

Plummer, Brenda Gayle. *Rising Wind: Black Americans and U.S. Foreign Affairs, 1935–1960.* Chapel Hill: University of North Carolina Press, 1996.

Pomerance, Alan. *Repeal of the Blues: How Black Entertainers Influenced Civil Rights.* Secaucus, N.J.: Citadel, 1988.

Porter, Lewis. *Lester Young.* Boston: Twayne, 1985.

———, ed. *A Lester Young Reader.* Washington, D.C.: Smithsonian Institution Press, 1991.

Porter, Roy, with David Keller. *There and Back.* Baton Rouge: Louisiana State University Press, 1991.

"Post War Planning and the Musician." *Music Dial,* June 1943, 6.

Potter, Lou, William Miles, and Nina Rosenblum. *Liberators: Fighting on Two Fronts in World War II.* New York: Harcourt Brace Jovanovich, 1992.

"Prairie View Co-Eds to Play at Apollo." *Pittsburgh Courier,* 24 June 1944, 13.

"Prairie View Girls' Band Scores Triumph." *Chicago Defender,* 30 October 1943, 10.

Prairie View State College Co-Ed All Girl Orchestra Press Book. John B. Coleman Library, Prairie View A&M University.

"Presenting the General Electric Hour of Charm." Concert programs, 1940s. Courtesy Vernell Wells and Phyllis Clendening.

Price, Madalin O. "Fifty Years of Memories: The Radio Program 'Wings over Jordan.' " Paper presented at the conference of the Oral History Association, New Orleans, 25 September 1997.

Putney, Martha. *When the Nation Was In Need.* Metuchen, N.J.: Scarecrow, 1992.

"PV [Prairie View] Co-Eds Keep Music Alive While Boys Battle Axis." *Pittsburgh Courier,* 11 March 1944, 14.

Rabin, Rhoda. *At the Beginning: Teaching Piano to the Very Young Child.* New York: Schirmer/Simon and Schuster, 1996.

Randolph, A. Philip. "Why Should We March?" In *A Documentary History of the Negro People in the United States: From the New Deal to the End of World War II,* ed. Herbert Aptheker. New York: Citadel, 1992.

Rasula, Jed. "The Media of Memory: The Seductive Menace of Records in Jazz History." In *Jazz among the Discourses,* ed. Krin Gabbard. Durham, N.C.: Duke University Press, 1995.

Reagon, Bernice Johnson. "Coalition Politics: Turning the Century." In *Home-Girls: A Black Feminist Anthology,* ed. Barbara Smith. New York: Kitchen Table, 1983.

Reed, Tom. *The Black Music History of Los Angeles: A Classical Pictorial History of Black Music in Los Angeles from the 1920s to 1970.* Los Angeles: Black Accent on LA, 1992.

Rich, Adrienne. *Blood, Bread, and Poetry: Selected Prose, 1979–1985.* New York: Norton, 1986.

Rivera, A. M., Jr. "Sweethearts Defy Threats; Play Festival." *Pittsburgh Courier,* 29 June 1946, 20.

Robbins, Trina. *A Century of Women Cartoonists.* Northampton, Mass.: Kitchen Sink, 1993.

"Robeson in Mixed Unit for Overseas Tour." *Chicago Defender,* 28 July 1945, 14.

Robinson, Major. "Artie Shaw Likely to Have Mixed Band." *Chicago Defender,* 2 December 1939, 20.

Robinson, Robert. "Post-War Europe and the Negro Entertainer." *Music Dial,* July 1944, 28.

Roebuck, Julian B., and Komanduri S. Murty. *Historically Black Colleges and Universities: Their Place in American Higher Education.* Westport, Conn.: Praeger, 1993.

Roeder, George H., Jr. *The Censored War: American Visual Experience During World War Two.* New Haven, Conn.: Yale University Press, 1993.

Rogin, Michael. *Blackface, White Noise: Jewish Immigrants in the Hollywood Melting Pot.* Berkeley and Los Angeles: University of California Press, 1996.

Rose, Tricia. *Black Noise: Rap Music and Black Culture in Contemporary America.* Hanover, N.H.: Wesleyan University Press, 1994.

Roth, Benita. "A Couple of Things: The Emergence of Black Feminism in the Second Wave." Paper presented at the conference panel "Black Women's Cultural and Political Production in the 1970s," chaired by Adrienne Dale Davis, American Studies Association, Seattle, 20 November 1998.

Rowe, Billy. "Buses Gone; Bands Face Tough Days." *Pittsburgh Courier,* 27 June 1942, 1, 21.

——. "Arranger Eddie Durham Embarks on New Venture: Musical Man behind Many Famous Orchestras Heads All-Star Girl Unit." *Pittsburgh Courier,* 12 December 1942, 20.

——. "Billy Rowe's Note Book." *Pittsburgh Courier,* 29 January 1944, 15; 2 December 1944, 13; 21 July 1945, 13.

Rupp, Leila J. *Mobilizing Women for War: German and American Propaganda, 1939–1945.* Princeton, New Jersey: Princeton University Press, 1978.

Russell, Ross. *Jazz Style in Kansas City and the Southwest.* Berkeley: University of California Press, 1971.

Rust, Brian. *Jazz Records, 1897–1942.* 5th ed. Essex: Storyville, 1982.

Rutherford, Zoe. "Our Cook's Tour." 1945. Manuscript poem written while touring in Europe during 1945. Courtesy Laura Bohle Sias.

Rye, Howard. "What the Papers Said: The Harlem Play-Girls and Dixie Rhythm Girls (and Dixie Sweethearts)." In *Storyville,* ed. Laurie Wright. Chigwell, Eng., 1996–97.

Sarkissian, Margaret. "Gender and Music." In *Ethnomusicology: An Introduction,* ed. Helen Myers. New York and London: W.W. Norton, 1992.

"Scholarships for Girls." *Chicago Defender,* 20 January 1945, 13.

Schuller, Gunther. *The Swing Era: The Development of Jazz, 1930–1945.* New York: Oxford University Press, 1989.

Scott, Joan. *Gender and the Politics of History.* New York: Columbia University Press, 1988.

Scovill, Ruth. "Women's Music." In *Women's Culture: The Women's Re-*

naissance of the Seventies, ed. Gayle Kimball. Metuchen, N.J.: Scarecrow, 1981.

Sears, Richard S. *V-Disks: A History and Discography.* Westport, Conn.: Greenwood, 1980.

"Season's Greetings." *Down Beat,* 15 December 1941, 29.

Senna, Carl. *The Black Press and the Struggle for Civil Rights.* New York: Franklin Watts, 1993.

Shapiro, Herbert. *White Violence and Black Response: From Reconstruction to Montgomery.* Amherst: University of Massachusetts Press, 1988.

Shaw, Artie. *The Trouble with Cinderella: An Outline of Identity.* New York: Da Capo, 1979.

Short, Bobby. *Black and White Baby.* New York: Dodd, Mead, 1971.

Simon, George T. *The Big Bands.* London: Macmillan, 1967.

Sims-Wood, Janet Louise. " 'We Served America Too!' " Personal Recollections of African Americans in the Women's Army Corps during World War II." Ph.D. diss., Union Institute, 1994.

Smith, Barbara. *Home Girls: A Black Feminist Anthology.* New York: Kitchen Table, 1983.

Smith, Viola. "Give Girl Musicians a Break! — Idea: Some 'Hep Girls' Can Outshine Male Stars, Says Viola Smith." *Down Beat,* 1 February 1942, 8.

"Snub Moseley's Crew Is First Sepia Ork to Go Overseas." *Pittsburgh Courier,* 6 January 1945, 13.

Soderbergh, Peter A. *Women Marines: The World War II Era.* Westport, Conn.: Praeger, 1992.

Solie, Ruth A., ed. *Musicology and Difference: Gender and Sexuality in Music Scholarship.* Berkeley and Los Angeles: University of California Press, 1993.

"South Keeps Up Ban on Fletcher's Mixed Band." *Chicago Defender,* 25 December 1943, 12.

"South Likes Them Plenty." *Chicago Defender,* 17 April 1943, 18.

Southern, Eileen. *The Music of Black Americans.* New York: Norton, 1983.

Spellman, A. B. *Four Lives in the Bebop Business.* New York: Schocken, 1966.

Spencer, Jon Michael. *The New Negroes and Their Music: The Success of the Harlem Renaissance.* Knoxville: University of Tennessee Press, 1997.

"Spitalny Loses Tuba to Navy." *Down Beat,* 1 October 1942, 7.

"Spitalny's Theatre Stunt," *Variety,* 16 April 1941, 39.

Spivak, Gayatri Chakravorty. *The Post-Colonial Critic.* New York: Routledge, 1990.

Springer, Kim. "Cleopatra Jones vs. the Second Wave Feminist Empire: Black Feminist Organizations of the 1970s." Paper presented at the conference panel "Black Women's Cultural and Political Production in the 1970s," chaired by Adrienne Dale Davis, American Studies Association, Seattle, 20 November 1998.

Stanton, Fred, ed. *Fighting Racism in World War II.* New York: Monad, 1980.

"State-Lake, Chi." *Variety,* 25 December 1940, 47.

Stewart, Zan. "All-Female Band Diva Breaking Stereotypes." *Los Angeles Times,* Friday, 16 June 1995, F12.

Stone, Laurie. "Jamming with the Gals." *Ms.,* December 1986, 21.

Stowe, David W. Review of Burton W. Peretti, *The Creation of Jazz. Journal of American Ethnic History* 13, no. 4 (summer 1994): 70.

———. *Swing Changes: Big Band Jazz in New Deal America.* Cambridge, Mass.: Harvard University Press, 1994.

"Strip-Tease Ada Leonard Fronts Ace Fem Outfit." *Down Beat,* 15 June 1941, 6.

"Sweethearts." *Chicago Defender,* 14 December 1940, 20.

" 'Sweethearts' Get Groovy in Paris." *Chicago Defender,* 25 August 1945, 14.

"Sweethearts of Rhythm." *Chicago Defender,* 22 June 1940, 20.

"Sweethearts of Rhythm Clicks in South and West." *Chicago Defender,* 20 January 1940, 20.

"Sweethearts of Rhythm Get Welcome in Dallas." *Chicago Defender,* 27 January 1940, 20.

"Sweethearts War-Proof Orchestra." *Pittsburgh Courier,* 20 June 1942, 21.

"Swing's Newest Rave Sensations Capture Nation." *Chicago Defender,* 18 March 1944, 8.

"Take 'Em off, Take, Etc.!" *Down Beat,* 15 January 1943, 2.

Tanner, Paul O. W., David W. Megill, and Maurice Gerow. *Jazz.* 7th ed. Dubuque, Iowa: Wm. C. Brown, 1992.

Taylor, Frank C., with Gerald Cook. *Alberta Hunter: A Celebration in Blues.* New York: McGraw-Hill, 1987.

Terenzio, Maurice, Scott MacGillivray, and Ted Okuda. *The Soundies Distributing Corporation of America: A History and Filmography.* Jefferson, N.C.: McFarland, 1991.

Terkel, Studs. *"The Good War": An Oral History of World War Two.* New York: Ballantine, 1984.

"Texas Collegians Entertain Soldiers." *Chicago Defender,* 2 January 1943, 9.

"Texas Gals Step out in Music." *Chicago Defender,* 5 June 1943, 17.

"That's Our Girl." *Down Beat,* 28 January 1946, 1.

"Their Problem One of Color Too; 'Japanese-Americans' Fate Tied Up with That of Other Minorities,' Editor Writes." *Pittsburgh Courier,* 1 January 1944, 2.

"They Have a Gene Krupa in Girls' Clothes!" *Down Beat,* April 1937, 21.

"36,000 Race Men Face Draft as FDR Signs Bill; Provisions of Act Wipe Out Discrimination." *Chicago Defender,* 21 September 1940, 1.

"This Girl Band Is Much Too Much with Swing and Jitter." *Chicago Defender,* 15 June 1940, 20.

"Those 'Sweethearts of Rhythm' All-Nations." *Chicago Defender,* 30 November 1940, 20.

Toney, Robert. "That Fem Question, Again!" *Down Beat,* 1 May 1942, 10.

"Top Flight Bands." *International Musician,* March 1942; 8; March 1943, 10.

Treadwell, Mattie E. *United States Army in World War II: Special Studies: The Women's Army Corps.* Washington, D.C.: Office of the Chief of Military History, Department of the Army, 1954.

Trinh T. Minh-ha. *Framer Framed.* New York: Routledge, 1992.

Tsing, Anna Lowenhaupt. *In the Realm of the Diamond Queen: Marginality in an Out-of-the-Way Place.* Princeton, N.J.: Princeton University Press, 1993.

Tucker, Sherrie. "The Politics of Impermanence: World War II and the All-Woman Bands." *Hot Wire: Journal of Women's Music and Culture* 9, no. 2 (May 1993): 12–13, 59–60.

——. " 'And Fellas, They're *American* Girls!' On the Road with the Sharon Rogers All-Girl Band." *Frontiers: Journal of Women's Studies* 16, nos. 2/3 (spring 1996): 128–60.

——. "Female Big Bands, Male Mass Audiences: Gender, Race, Class, Nation on the 'Fox Hole Circuit.' " Paper presented to the conference of the Sonneck Society for American Music, Washington, D.C., 24 March 1996.

——. "Telling Performances: Jazz History Remembered and Remade by the Women in the Band." In booklet for the Smithsonian Institution symposium "Sung/Unsung Jazzwomen," 19–20 October 1996. Reprinted in *Women in Music: Journal of Gender and Culture* 1 (1997): 12–23; and *Oral History Review* 26, no. 1 (winter/spring 1999): 67–84.

USO: Five Years of Service: Report of the President, February 4, 1946. New York: United Service Organizations, 1946.

"USO Troupe Thrills Doughboys in Persia." *Pittsburgh Courier,* 13 January 1945, 13.

Vail, Ken. *Lady Day's Diary: The Life of Billie Holiday, 1937–1959.* Surrey: Castle, 1996.

Van Starrez, Al. "Earl Hines, A Date with Fatha." *Coda Magazine* 258 (November/December, 1994): 4–7.

"Vaudeville." *Chicago Tribune,* 22 December 1940, sec. 6, p. 2.

"Veteran's Eyes Gouged out by Hate-Crazed Dixie Police; Atrocity Called Dixie's Worst in NAACP Probe." *Chicago Defender,* 20 July 1946, 1.

Visweswaran, Kamala. "Betrayal: An Analysis in Three Acts." In *Scattered Hegemonies: Postmodernity and Transnational Feminist Practices,* ed. Inderpal Grewal and Caren Kaplan. Minneapolis: University of Minnesota Press, 1994.

——. *Fictions of Feminist Ethnography.* Minneapolis: University of Minnesota Press, 1994.

Von Eschen, Penny M. *Race Against Empire: Black Americans and Anticolonialism, 1937–1957.* Ithaca: Cornell University Press, 1997.

WAC Musicians — The 14th Army Band (WAC). Fact Sheet no. 53. Fort McClellan, Ala.: WAC Museum.

Walker, Leo. *The Wonderful Era of the Great Dance Bands.* Garden City, N.Y.: Doubleday, 1972.

Wallace, Michele. *Invisibility Blues.* New York: Verso, 1990.

Walser, Robert. *Running with the Devil: Power, Gender, and Madness in Heavy Metal Music.* Hanover, N.H.: Wesleyan University Press, 1993.

"War Is Over but Girls Still Rule on West Coast." *Chicago Defender,* 1 September 1945, 14.

Washburn, Patrick S. *A Question of Sedition: The Federal Government's Investigation of the Black Press during World War II.* New York: Oxford University Press, 1986.

"Waves Try Out." *Down Beat,* 15 February 1943, 17.

Wells, Dicky, as told to Stanley Dance. *The Night People: The Jazz Life of Dicky Wells.* Washington, D.C.: Smithsonian Institution Press, 1991.

Werner, Craig Hansen. *Playing the Changes: From Afro-Modernism to the Jazz Impulse.* Urbana: University of Illinois Press, 1994.

Westbrook, Robert B. " 'I Want a Girl, Just Like the Girl That Married Harry James': American Women and the Problem of Political Obligation in World War II." *American Quarterly* 42, no. 4 (December 1990): 587–614.

Whiteman, Paul, and Mary Margaret McBride. *Jazz.* New York: J. H. Sears, 1926.

"Who's Best Sax — Backstrom or Vi?" *Pittsburgh Courier,* 16 June 1945, 13.

"Why Girl Bands Don't Click." *Jet,* 11 February 1954, 60–62.

"Why Not Draft Spitalny's Girl Band into the Army?" *Yank,* 5 August 1942, 18.

Wilk, Max. *They're Playing Our Song.* Mount Kisco, N.Y.: Moyer Bell, 1991.

Williams, Raymond. *Marxism and Literature.* Oxford: Oxford University Press, 1977.

Women's Army Corps Bands, 1942–1976: Music Dedication, and Pride. Fort McClellan, Ala.: WAC Museum. Pamphlet.

"The World Famous Prairie View Co-Eds." Purple and Gold. Prairie View A&M University annual, 1946. John B. Coleman Library, Prairie View A&M University.

Wynn, Neil A. *The Afro-American and the Second World War.* New York: Holmes and Meier, 1993.

Yates, Ted. "Greatest Aggregation of Girl Stars Have Plenty of Zing When It Comes to Swing." *New York Age,* 4 December 1943, 10.

———. "I've Been Around." *New York Age,* 11 December 1943, 11; 18 December 1943, 11; 15 July 1944, 11.

Yoshida, George. *Reminiscing in Swingtime: Japanese Americans in American Popular Music, 1925–1960.* San Francisco: National Japanese American Historical Society, 1997.

Zolotow, Maurice. "Harlem's Great White Father." *Saturday Evening Post,* 27 September 1941, 37.

Interviews and Oral Histories

(Unless otherwise stated, all interviews and oral histories were conducted by the author)

Awkerman, Martye. Conversation. Alameda, Calif., July 20, 1994.

Bernstein, Ada Leonard. Telephone interview, July 5, 1994.

Bradshaw, Margaret. Telephone interview, December 1, 1997.

Brown, Velzoe. Interviewed by author, August 29 and 30, 1995. Jazz Oral History Program, Smithsonian Institution, National Museum of American History.

Bryant, Clora. Telephone interview, October 7, 1990.

——. Telephone interview, August 5, 1993.

——. Interviewed by Steven Isoardi, Los Angeles, California, March 29, April 4, and April 18, 1990. Central Avenue Sounds Oral History Project, Oral History Program, University of California, Los Angeles, California.

——. Interviewed by Sally Placksin, Washington, D.C., 1993. Jazz Oral History Program, Smithsonian Institution, National Museum of American History.

——. Telephone conversation, January 10, 1998.

Butler, Toby. Telephone interview, May 11, 1996.

Campbell, Dick. Interviewed by Jean Hudson, Videotape. May 5, 1982. Moving Image and Recorded Sound Division, Schomburg Center for Research in Black Culture, New York.

Carrington, Terri Lyne. Interview with author. Los Angeles, 11–12 July 1996. Jazz Oral History Program, Smithsonian Institution, National Museum of American History, and Sung and Unsung Jazzwomen, Smithsonian Institution Traveling Exhibitions Service.

Cayler, Joy. Telephone interview, May 28, 1995.

Clark, Gurthalee. Interviewed by Eunice M. Wright, May 12, 1988. Videotape. WAC Foundation Oral History Program, WAC Museum, Fort McClellan, Alabama.

Clendening, Phyllis. Telephone interview, March 13, 1994.

Cole, Helen. Telephone interview, November 21, 1997.

Cron, Roz (Rosalind). Telephone interview, August 13, 1990.

——. Conversation. Los Angeles, 7 March 1996.

Demond, Mary. Interview, Pebble Beach, California, July 27, 1996.

Durham, Eddie. Interviewed by Stanley Dance, Washington, D.C., August, 1978. Transcript, Institute for Jazz Studies, Rutgers, Newark, New Jersey.

Dwyer, Thelma "Tommie." Telephone interview, August 18, 1990.

Emich, Janice. Telephone interview, November 3, 1990.

Flemming, Bertha. Telephone interview, September 14, 1990.

Gaddison, Frann. Telephone interview, June 25, 7–8 July, 1994.

Gilbert, Peggy. Interviewed by author, September 22 and 23, 1998. Jazz Oral History Program, Smithsonian Institution, National Museum of American History.

Greenstein, Sylvia Price. Interviewer unknown, May 16, 1996. Video, WAC Foundation Oral History Program, WAC Museum, Fort McClellan, Alabama.

Grigsby, M.D., Margaret. Interview, Washington, D.C., October 30, 1997.

Hall, Audrey. Telephone interview, October 10, 1994.

Handy, D. Antoinette. Telephone conversation. February 6, 1997.

Hanson, Yolanda Lewis. Telephone interview, August 10, 1990.

Henderson, Elise Blye. Telephone interview, September 21, 1990.

Hunter, Alberta. Interviewed by Chris Albertson, Washington, D.C., December 17, 1976. Transcript, Institute for Jazz Studies, Rutgers, Newark, New Jersey.

Kiewitt, Marjorie. Telephone interview, April 1, 1997.

Kimbrough, Bettye Bradley. Telephone interview, September 21, 1997.

Knepper, Maxine Fields. Telephone interview, November 17, 1996.

Lewis, Edna. Interviewed by author, November 6 and 7, 1995. Jazz Oral History Program, Smithsonian Institution, National Museum of American History.

Lewis, Thelma. Telephone interview, June 12, 1994.

———. Telephone conversation, March 26, 1998.

Liston, Melba. Interviewed by Steven Isoardi, September 12, 1992. Transcript, Central Avenue Sounds Oral History Program, University of California, Los Angeles.

Love, Clarence. Interviewed by Nathan Pearson and Howard Litwak, April 13, 1977, Kansas City, Missouri. Transcript, Western Historical Manuscript Collection, Kansas City, Missouri.

Magee, Lois, Cronen. Telephone interview, January 17, 1995.

May, Ernestine. Telephone interview, January 5, 1997.

McLawler, Sarah. Telephone interview, July 12, 1994.

Medearis, Argie Mae Edwards. Telephone interview, November 11, 1997.

Meilleur, Doris Jarrett. Telephone interview, June 22, 1994.

Meriedeth, Betty Kidwell. Telephone conversation, July 6, 1997.

Merle, Marilyn. Telephone interview, August 28, 1990.

Miller, Ernest Mae Crafton. Telephone interview, October 16, 1993.

Morrison, Roberta "Bobbie." Telephone interview, September 23, 1996.

Nilo, Doris Kahl. Interview, Racine, Wisconsin, October 19, 1991.

O'Hara, Betty. Telephone interview, April 24, 1996.

Pfeil, Bill. Telephone interview, August 1, 1990.

Phelan, Ruby. Telephone interview, September 28, 1996.

Polivka, Rosemary. Telephone interview, August 12, 1990.

Poston, Perri Lee. Interview, Oakland, California, April 13, 1994.

Rabin, Rhoda. Telephone interview, January 10, 1994.

Ray, Carline. Interviewed by Sally Placksin. New York, October 14 and 19, 1992. Jazz Oral History Program, Smithsonian Institution, National Museum of American History.

Raymer, Ruth. Telephone interview, June 12, 1994.

Richardson, Doris Stevens. [Interviewer unknown.] Videotape. Sixth Black WAC Reunion, New York, 6–10 October 1988. WAC Museum, Fort McClellan, Alabama.

Sager, Jane. Telephone interview, April 2, 1994.

——. Interview, Hollywood, California, June 10, 1994.

——. Telephone conversation, March 11, 1995.

——. Telephone interview, July 30, 1995.

——. Interviewed by author, December 11 and 12, 1996. Jazz Oral History Program, Smithsonian Institution, National Museum of American History.

Scher, Rev. Frances, N.S.T. Telephone interview, August 28, 1990.

Scott, Willie Mae Wong. Telephone interview, December 3, 1996.

Sias, Laura Bohle. Telephone interview, July 2, 1994.

Smith, Elizabeth Thomas. Telephone interview, November 25, 1997.

Smith, Viola. Interview, New York, October 17, 1996.

Smock, Ginger. Interview, Las Vegas, Nevada, October 28, 1993.

Soroka, Jean (Jeanne) Phillips. Telephone interview, April 2, 1994.

Stearns, Shirley Sydney. Telephone interview, July 10, 1991.

Stone, Evelyn McGee. Telephone interview, November 30, 1996.

Stone, Jesse. Interviewed by Chris Goddard. March 2, 1981. Transcript, Institute for Jazz Studies, Rutgers, Newark, New Jersey.

Teagarden, Norma. Telephone interview, July 20, 1992.

——. Interviewed by Weslia Whitfield, February 19 and 22, 1993, San Francisco. Jazz Oral History Program, Smithsonian Institution, National Museum of American History.

Wells, Robin Vernell. Telephone interview, April 6, 1994.

Wilmeth, Dotty Cygan. Conversation, Ramona, Calif., April 11, 1999.

Wilson, Lillian Carter. Telephone interview, August 24, 1991.

Wilson, Violet. Telephone interview, November 9, 1993.

——. Interview. Los Angeles, California, June 12, 1994.

Woods, Helen Jones. Telephone interview, February 20, 1995.

Young, Lester. Interview with Chris Albertson. 1958. In *A Lester Young Reader,* ed. Lewis Porter. Washington, D.C.: Smithsonian Institution Press, 1991.

Personal Correspondence and Questionnaires

Awkerman, Martye. Letters to author, January 8, 1992, February 12, 1992, March 9, 1992, June 8, 1992, February 22, 1993, March 7, 1993, April 12,

1993, September 15, 1993, July 27, 1993, September 1, 1993, November 6, 1993, February 14, 1994, June 18, 1994, August 2, 1994, August 31, 1994, October 26, 1994, November 6, 1994, January 6, 1995, February 28, 1995, March 10, 1995, April 20, 1995, July 21, 1995, October 1, 1995, April 21, 1996, October 11, 1996, August 20, 1996, August 29, 1996, December 29, 1996.

Ball, Deedie. Letters to author, October 14, 1994, July 16, 1995.

Beyer, Pat. Questionnaire. September 1, 1991.

Braun, Betty Tagatz. Questionnaire, November 8, 1992.

Brower, Roberta Lee Ellis. Questionnaire, November 26, 1992.

Bryant, Clora. Letters to author, February 8, 1993, May 10, 1993.

Butler, Toby. Questionnaire, November, 1992.

——. Letters to author, July 22, 1996, August 6, 1997.

Carlson, Kay. Questionnaire, October 17, 1994.

Cayler, Joy. Letters to author, July 21, 1995, September 19, 1995.

Clendening, Phyllis. Questionnaire, January 1994.

——. Letters to author September 19, 1994, November 19, 1996.

Cron, Roz. Letters to author, September 11, 1992, January 31, 1995, February 14, 1995, March 10, 1995, December 30, 1995, April 12, 1996, June 10, 1996, October 8, 1996, November 11, 1996.

Danca, Dorothy. Questionnaire, November 1992.

Daniels, Laura. Letters to her parents. August 14, 1945, September 6, 1945, December 9, 1945.

——. Questionnaire and letter to author, December 4, 1993.

——. Letters to author, March 2, 1994, June 25, 1994, May 21, 1995, January 5, 1996, May 27, 1996, July 30, 1996, August 6, 1996.

——. Diary excerpt from January 20, 1946.

Day, Betty "Jill." Letter to author, December 4, 1996.

Demond, Mary. Letters to author, December 1, 1996, January 1, 1997.

Devaney, Patrick. Letter to author, September 5, 1990.

Doulton, Beverly. Letter to author, October 12, 1990.

Drehouse, Ethel C. Kirkpatrick. Questionnaire, December 1992.

——. Letters to author, September 12, 1996, July 5, 1997.

Dwyer, Thelma "Tommie." Letters to author, September 3, 1990, July 15, 1993.

Eilbeck, Donna Lewis. Questionnaire, October 20, 1991.

Gilbert, Peggy. Letters to author, August 26, 1990, November 14, 1990, January 15, 1991, October 5, 1991, August 24, 1993.

Goleas, Lois Heise. Questionnaire, October 1993.

——. Letter to author, November 14, 1996.

Goodspeed, Deloros Conlee. Questionnaire, September 23, 1991.

——. Letters to author, September 23, 1991, November 16, 1991, December 14, 1991, July 16, 1993.

Grigsby, Margaret. Letter to author, November 14, 1997.

Hayward, Barbara Carmichael. Questionnaire, April, 1994.

Huson, Avon J. Letter to author, August 22, 1990.

Jacoby, Alice M. Questionnaire, November 3, 1992.

Kiewitt, Marjorie. Questionnaire, February 15, 1997.

Kuhn, Florence Shefte. Questionnaire and letter to author, November 24, 1992.

———. Letter to her mother, January 20, 1946.

———. Letters to author, June 15, 1993, August 7, 1993, November 22, 1993, October 17, 1994, May 8, 1995, March 20, 1996, September 17, 1996, November 17, 1996.

Leubkeman, Jean Getchell. Questionnaire, November 17, 1994.

Magee, Lois Cronen. Letter to author, November 27, 1994.

Meriedeth, Betty Kidwell. Questionnaire, March 1992.

Miller, Ernest Mae Crafton. Questionnaire, September 20, 1993.

———. Letter to author, October 16, 1996.

Mooney, Patricia. Letter to the author, August 17, 1990.

Murphy, Georgia Stieler. Questionnaire, February 12, 1994.

Nagel, Dorothy Sackett. Questionnaire, July, 1991.

Nelson, Claudia. Letter to author, March 18, 1991.

Newcomb, Eleanor Cotton. Questionnaire, February, 1992.

Nilo, Doris Kahl. Letters to author, November 5, 1991, February 15, 1992, March 4, 1992.

O'Hara, Betty. Letter to author, July 5, 1996.

Osseck, Elaine Evans. Questionnaire, March 12, 1994.

Pilzer, Leigh. Letter to author, March 16, 1999.

Polivka, Rosemary. Letter to author, August 6, 1990.

Prior, Margaret M. Letter to author, August 1, 1990.

Reichel, Betty. Questionnaire, November 9, 1992.

Reitz, Rosetta. Letter to author, May 28, 1990.

Roach, Lynne Corrinne. Questionnaire, September, 1991.

Rosner, Betty. Questionnaire, October, 1992.

———. Letter to author, December 29, 1994.

Roth, Sylvia. Questionnaire and letter to author, November 30, 1992.

———. Letter to author, December 1, 1993.

Ryan, Gloria. Questionnaire, February, 1992.

———. Letters to author, August 25, 1992, April 13, 1993, January 10, 1995, September 3, 1995.

Sager, Jane. Letters to author, June 22, 1994, September 14, 1994, September 21, 1994, October 26, 1994, January 29, 1995, February 26, 1995, March 21, 1995, June 11, 1995, April 16, 1996, August 10, 1996, September 12, 1996, November 24, 1996, December 2, 1996.

Savage, Lee Ann. Letter to Virgil Whyte. 12 November 1945. Virgil Whyte Collection, Archives Center, Smithsonian Museum of American History.

Scher, Rev. Frances, N.S.T. Letters to author, August 11, 1990, September 12, 1990.

Scholtz, Dorothy Coffman. Questionnaire, September 4, 1993.

Schuster, Helen Day. Questionnaire, November, 1992.
———. Letters to author, November 1992, January 8, 1995.
Shipp, Ginger Smock. Letter to author, August 3, 1994.
Sias, Laura Bohle. Questionnaire, April 1994.
———. Letter to author, July 4, 1995.
Simon, Grace Brueseke. Questionnaire, September 27, 1991.
———. Letter to author, September 27, 1991.
Simpson, Gloria. Letters to author, December 14, 1990, January 28, 1991,
    July 23, 1991, June 16, 1995.
Soroka, Jean Phillips. Questionnaire, January 15, 1994.
Stearns, Shirley Sydney. Letters to author, May 30, 1991, August 27, 1991.
Stullken, Pat. Questionnaire, December, 1992.
Teagarden, Norma. Letter to author, August 3, 1991.
Vossmeyer, Cecilia Czarnecki. Questionnaire, July, 1991.
Wells, Vernell Robin. Questionnaire, January 22, 1994.
———. Letters to author, April 26, 1994, May 17, 1994.
Wilmeth, Dorothy. Letter to author, September 10, 1990.
Wilson, Lillian Carter. Letters to author, May 20, 1991, June 18, 1991,
    July 20, 1991, January 6, 1992.
Wilson, Violet. Questionnaire, September 3, 1993.
Wollerman, Laverne. Questionnaire, February 10, 1992.
———. Letters to author, February 10, 1992, October 12, 1996.
Woods, Helen Jones. Letter to author, April 10, 1996.
Wright, Sharon Rogers. Letters to author, August 12, 1990, May 28, 1991,
    July 23, 1993, October 18, 1993, March 31, 1994.
Zieger, Geraldine Joan. Questionnaire, July 20, 1991.
———. Letter to author, July 20, 1991.

Discography

Forty Years of Women in Jazz. CD, Stash Records, Jass CD-9/10, 1989.
Frivolous Five. *Sour Cream and Other Delights.* LP, RCA LPM-3663, 1966.
"The Hour of Charm." Armed Forces Radio (AFR) broadcasts, Decem-
    ber 7, 1941 (Red network); October 1, 1944 (originated with NBC; re-
    broadcast by AFR); April 15, 1945 (NBC); April 29, 1945 (originated
    with NBC; rebroadcast by AFR). Cassettes 47509, 44551, 21621, 21622.
    Sandy Hook, Conn.: Radio Yesteryear.
International Sweethearts of Rhythm. LP. Rosetta Records, RR-1312, 1984.
Joy Cayler Orchestra. Radio recording from Jantzen Beach Park, 1945. In
    the possession of Joy Cayler.
Rhythm Rockets. Private recording in the possession of Gloria Simpson.
Tiny Davis and Her Orchestra: "Draggin' My Heart Around" and "I Never
    Get Tired of Doin' It." 45 RPM, Decca 48122. Recorded October 24 and
    27, 1949.

————. "Race Horse" and "Bug Juice." 45 RPM, Decca 48220. Recorded October 24 and 27, 1949.

————. "How About That Jive" and "Laura." 45 RPM, Decca 48246. Recorded October 24 and 27, 1949.

USO Time. Recording of WBTQ radio broadcast, November 1945, Osaka, Japan. In the possession of Sylvia Roth.

Virgil Whyte and His "All-Girl" Band. "America's Musical Sweethearts." Cassette, Florice Whyte Kovan, Public and Private Research, Washington, D.C.

Women in Jazz: All-Woman Groups. LP. Stash Records, ST-111, 1978.

Women in Jazz: Swingtime to Modern. LP. Stash Records, ST-113, 1978.

Film/Videography

Borzage, Frank. *Stage Door Canteen.* United Artists, 1943.

Capra, Frank. *The Negro Soldier.* War Department, Special Services, 1944.

Curtiz, Michael. *My Dream Is Yours.* MGM, 1949.

Ely, Marcia. *Stars and Stripes: Hollywood and World War II.* Television special. Film and Television Archive, University of California, Los Angeles.

Hawks, Howard. *I Was A Male War Bride.* Twentieth Century Fox, 1949.

Humberstone, Bruce. *Pin Up Girl.* Twentieth Century Fox, 1944.

Kovan, Florice Whyte. Virgil Whyte's All-Girl Bands: USO Tours, 1944–1946. Vols. 1–4, 1993. Privately produced.

Newman, Joseph M. *Love Nest.* Twentieth Century Fox, 1951.

Phenix, Lucy, and Connie Field. *The Life and Times of Rosie the Riveter.* Franklin Lakes, N.J.: Clarity Educational Productions, 1980.

Reitz, Rosetta. *Jazz Women.* Rosetta Records RRV-1320, 1990. Videocassette.

Schiller, Greta, and Andrea Weiss. *International Sweethearts of Rhythm.* Jezebel Productions, 1986.

————. *Tiny and Ruby: Hell-Divin' Women.* Jezebel Productions, 1988.

Selznick, David O. *Since You Went Away.* United Artists, 1944.

6th Black WAC Reunion 1988. WAC Museum, Fort McClellan, Alabama.

Thorpe, Richard. *Two Girls and A Sailor.* MGM, 1944.

Women in Defense. Office of Emergency Management, 1941.

Yarborough, Jean. *Here Come the Co-Eds.* Universal, 1945.

Index

Sherrie Tucker is Assistant Professor of Women's Studies at Hobart and William Smith Colleges in Geneva, New York. Her recent and forthcoming publications on women and jazz include articles in the *New Grove Dictionary of Jazz, Unequal Sisters: a Multicultural Reader in U.S. Women's History, Sung and Unsung Jazzwomen, American Music, The Black Music Research Journal, Frontiers: A Journal of Women's Studies, Hot Wire: A Journal of Women's Music and Culture, Jazz Now Magazine, Labor's Heritage, Oral History Review, The Pacific Review of Ethnomusicology,* and *Women and Music: A Journal of Gender and Culture.* She has conducted interviews for the Smithsonian Jazz Oral History Program, and is a former jazz radio programmer on KJAZ in the San Francisco Bay Area.

Library of Congress Cataloging-in-Publication Data

Tucker, Sherrie.
Swing shift : "all-girl" bands of the 1940s / Sherrie Tucker.
p. cm.
Includes bibliographical references (p.) and index.
ISBN 0-8223-2485-7 (cloth : alk. paper)
1. Women jazz musicians — United States. 2. Jazz — 1941–
1950 — History and criticism. I. Title.
ML82.T83 2000
784.4'81654'082 — dc21   99-046015